Secession, History and the So

Bruno Coppieters and Michel Huysseune (eds)

Secession, History and the Social Sciences

VUB BRUSSELS
UNIVERSITY PRESS

Cover illustration: © Koninklijke Bibliotheek, Brussel, Afdeling Kostbare Werken. 'Attaque des hollandais par le peuple sur la place de Meir', in: 'Les événements de Bruxelles, Anvers etc …', Bruxelles, Dewasme-Pletinck/Jobard, 1830.
Cover: Danny Somers
Layout: Boudewijn Bardyn

© Copyright 2002 VUBPRESS – VUB Brussels University Press
Waversesteenweg 1077 – B 1160 Brussels – Belgium
Fax + 32 2 629 26 94
e-mail: vubpress@vub.ac.be
www.vubpress.org

ISBN 90 5487 312 4   NUR 754
D / 2002 / 1885 / 009

Contents

Bruno Coppieters and Michel Huysseune

Preface

The term 'secession' has a strong emotional connotation. Secessionist crises are highly dramatic events in a state's history, entailing as they do the risk of a total disruption of the existing political and social order. Unilateral declarations of secession are often accompanied by the use of military force, but even a peaceful referendum on sovereignty puts a heavy strain on social cohesion. A secessionist process has particular consequences for the practice of history and the social sciences. The dramatic nature of secession challenges the virtues traditionally expected of scholars, once they are actively involved in a public debate on its legitimacy: when they analyse the issues at stake, scientists' traditional perception of themselves as being rational, dispassionate and unprejudiced is called into question. This self-image of the scholar has already been challenged by the generally accepted fact that the nation, as an imagined community, is largely a product of the social activities of intellectuals. It has been well established that intellectuals play a decisive role in the elaboration of national identities and the creation of national 'myths'. Historical research on the development of national movements has also revealed the political role of intellectuals in paving the way for effective political mobilization. Generally speaking, historians and social scientists seem to be more deeply involved than most other citizens in political disputes on the future of their nation. Imagining the nation, working out its identity and creating fertile ground for nationalist mobilization are activities that do not conform to the traditional view of scientific rationality. Despite all the knowledge at our disposal on the role of intellectuals in shaping the nation, however, there is still good reason to believe that the prescription that quality research should mean a dispassionate attitude towards the object of enquiry does in fact also apply to the study of nations and secession.

The following volume purports to analyse, on a comparative basis, the complex relations between scientific knowledge and political action in secessionist processes. This analysis is not confined to the intellectual passions aroused by the national question, nor to the specific meaning that objectivity may have in studies on the nation. It compares the multiple relations that exist between the political discourses to be found in particular countries among movements for and against secession with discourses in history and the social sciences. Secessionist crises, in which opposing concepts of nation-building and divergent interpretations of society and history clash with one another, reveal the significance of the idea of a nation for intellectuals. In addition, they show the importance scholars attach to ideals such as objectivity, truthfulness and moral responsibility. From these various perspectives, the contributions to this volume analyse the intellectual responses given to the question of secession in different national contexts.

The introduction outlines the key questions on which this volume will focus. The first field of enquiry concerns the relation between scholars and political practitioners. The institutional setting in which scientific research is carried out may either force researchers to depend on the state or favour their autonomy. Dependence may lead to an instrumental relationship between the political objectives of the state and academic activities. Alternatively, scholars may play an important political role through their contribution to the construction of oppositional identities. Both of these types of involvement may be decisive for the development of secessionist movements and for the outcome of secessionist crises. The second field of enquiry concerns the respective contributions of various scientific disciplines to debates on secession: scientific knowledge may highlight identities rooted in the past, support present grievances or develop blueprints for the future. The third question has to do with the criteria of scientific objectivity and truthfulness as used in discourses for, against and on secession. The way in which historians and social scientists deal with the 'myth-making' aspect – characteristic of nation-building processes – is highly relevant in this context.

Half of the case-studies in this volume concern processes of secession in former communist countries. Four of them are located in the former Soviet Union. Ivan Myhul presents a broad historical overview of the contribution made by Ukrainian intellectuals in producing social knowledge about their nation, and discusses the position of the social sciences in Ukraine during the tsarist and Soviet regimes and after independence. Moshe Gammer studies the role of Chechen historiography in re-moulding the Chechen national identity, and analyses how their historical narratives are related to the present struggle for independence. Alexei Zverev gives an overview of the role of Tatar intellectuals in the three periods of the Tatar national revival in the last century, and discusses the shifting attitudes of Tatar intellectuals towards Tatarstan's place in Russia. Bruno Coppieters discusses the role of intellectuals in exacerbating the conflict between the Georgian and Abkhaz communities, which led to the 1992-93 war and to the secession of Abkhazia from Georgia. In his analysis of the disintegration of the Yugoslav scientific community, Robert Stallaerts connects the emergence of nationalism among intellectuals with the institutional context of scientific research in Yugoslavia, especially its organization at the level of the republics.

The cases from outside the former communist bloc exemplify the wide variety of secessionist processes, and their context-bound political and intellectual agendas. Ronald Rudin parallels the emergence of the Parti Québécois and its struggle for the sovereignty of Quebec with the evolution of history-writing in Quebec. Louis Vos describes how the construction of a Belgian national identity through historiography has been challenged by the emergence of Flemish nationalism and its alternative interpretations of the past. Michel Huysseune describes how the creation of an 'imagined Padanian community' by the secessionist movement Lega Nord can be related to interpretations of the Italian North-South divide by historians and social scientists. In her analysis of the Taiwan independence movement, Xiaokun Song discusses the place of history, international law and the social sciences in its intellectual discourse. She retraces the role of intellectuals in creating a new national identity for Taiwan, and analyses the shifting meanings ascribed to that identity. Raphael Njoku describes how public debates in Nigeria remain marked by the trauma of the Biafran civil war. He highlights how, in the context of a central state as yet lacking full legitimacy, Nigerian intellectuals are deeply concerned to find peaceful alternatives to secessionist threats. Finally, the conclusion by the editors outlines, from a comparative perspective, how the cases presented in the book offer answers to the three research questions raised in the introduction.

The contributions to this volume were first discussed at a conference which took place in Brussels on 27 and 28 November 1998. The conference was organized by the Department of Political Science of the Vrije Universiteit Brussel in co-operation with the Institute for European Policy of the Katholieke Universiteit Leuven. We would like to thank the Flemish Community, which has given financial support for a research programme on secession, history and the social sciences. The publication of this book is one of the results of this project. Additional financial resources have been provided by the Vrije Universiteit Brussel. Our personal gratitude also goes to Frank Delmartino from the Katholieke Universiteit Leuven, who co-organized the Brussels conference, and to Veronica Kelly for her meticulous language correction of the texts. Finally, we would like to thank Kris van Scharen of VUB Brussels University Press and the two anonymous readers who looked upon our volume with favour.

Bruno Coppieters, Ivan M. Myhul and Michel Huysseune

Introduction

A large number of scientific disciplines have dealt with the break-up of states. Secession studies include disciplinary approaches such as philosophy, political science, law and history, and particular fields of research, like nationalism and federalism. Generally speaking, research has been conducted at the margins of a more all-encompassing endeavour. Secession has never constituted a central theme in the history of political philosophy or in such disciplines as international relations and constitutional law. Secession is likewise present in, but not central to, political science, where it is situated at the crossroads where domestic policies meet international relations,[1] without deriving much benefit for systematic purposes from this location in a frontier zone. The focal points in discussions on international relations theory have no bearing on the analysis of the origins of secession. Neo-liberal and neo-realist theories differ in their appreciation of the nature of state anarchy, the likelihood of international co-operation and the significance of the increasing number of international institutions.[2] Such debates have no relevance when it comes to providing principles of analysis to explain the emergence of a secessionist movement on the domestic scene, even though they may be very relevant in explaining the success or failure of secessionist movements on the international scene. Ethnic and federal studies, on the other hand, are capable of exploring the roots of secessionist conflict, and possible remedies, but lack the geopolitical perspective necessary for predicting the possible outcomes of such conflicts.

There is thus a lack of integration among the various disciplinary approaches to secession. There is an even deeper divide between the general cognitive frameworks or structures within which social scientists and political philosophers operate. Secession studies are characterized by the traditional opposition between normative and empiricist perspectives, and those working in this field generally subscribe to either one or the other. Each of these two major epistemic communities, which involve scholars from various disciplines, has its own group-specific criteria and its own 'consensual knowledge', accepted as valid within the parameters of its given perspective. The normative approach is concerned primarily with values and norms. Values for this approach refer to a desired state, a purpose, or a telos. They indicate what is deemed worthy. Norms pertain to blueprints for guiding action. Being deeply preoccupied with what ought to be, the normative approach is also concerned with what should happen, and how to achieve it. This essentially deductive, evaluative and prescriptive approach puts forth claims as to the nature of government, the relation between authority and the individual, political obligation, distributive justice, and the like. The normative perspective is preoccupied with such phenomena as freedom, justice and equity, but especially with rights. It lends itself readily to a moral and intellectual commitment to individual, but also collective, rights. Examples of this perspective in secession studies are the debates on the plausibility of a theory of secession focusing on the right to national self-determination, the value of appeals to minority group rights, or arguments concerning the discriminatory redistribution of economic resources. Depending on their choice of principles and selection of arguments from their chosen perspective, scholars may render a positive verdict on the legitimacy of secession in some cases, but not in others.[3]

In the empiricist approach, knowledge is considered to be scientific if it is primarily empirically based, objective, disinterested and value-free. Observation, the generation of testable hypotheses, verification and, if possible, experimentation are assumed to be indispensable methodological features. This explanatory approach is inductive and analytical. Social scientists should therefore not advocate any political cause – such as separatism, for example. Yet it is not easy for the social scientists who subscribe to this approach to filter out their values, opinions and concerns. This perspective, therefore, is neither as value-free nor as disinterested as it would at first sight appear. Ideological colourings, values, norms and opinions may be discerned beneath the veneer of social scientism. In the realm of politics, for example, scholarship adopting this orientation may assign positive valence to notions of efficiency, equilibrium and order, and the maintenance and stability of existing political systems and state formations. Such a built-in pro-status quo bias tends to interpret secession as a negative phenomenon.[4] Empirical research may, however, also bring a positive verdict on secession when focusing on concrete cases of economic discrimination or political oppression.

A closer look at both traditions reveals that there is little empirical or normative research on secession with the explicit aim of producing an overall conceptual framework whose systematic and encompassing character would be sufficiently developed for it to be generally accepted as constituting a theory, in the strong meaning of this word.[5] A demanding empirical concept of theory encompasses explanatory principles, which are capable of generating a set of verifiable hypotheses. The capacity to predict by constructing specific scenarios is essential in order for a theory to qualify as such. But it is surely also possible to understand political theory in a weaker sense. Theory – in both the empirical and normative traditions – may also be understood as something which gives a certain structure to a field of research, which systematizes the research questions and includes a coherent set of concepts.[6] In normative discussions, a 'thin theory' offers 'the bare framework for conceptualizing choice and agency but [leaves] the specific content of choices to be filled in by individuals'.[7]

Most empirical and normative literature on secession seems to be based on the presupposition that a more modest ambition is quite adequate to the present state of the art. In the field of empirical research on secession, in a comparative volume on secessionist movements, published in 1990, Ralph R. Premdas pointed out that attempts to explain secession by modernization theory, internal colonialism or political economy have at the very best been only partially successful.[8] The book *Theories of Secession*, edited in 1998 by Percy Lehning, discusses the main positions in the debates taking place in both normative and empirical research on secession.[9] Theory is here understood quite modestly as a way of exploring what is morally at stake when dealing with secession or when analysing the factors explaining secession as a political phenomenon. A similar use of the term 'theory' is also to be found in the various contributions to the book edited by Margaret Moore, *National Self-Determination and Secession*, which was also published in 1998.[10] In his contribution to that volume, Rogers Brubaker argues that the search for 'a' or 'the' theory of nationalism is misguided. In his view, 'the theoretical problems associated with nationhood and nationalism, like the practical political problems, are multiform and varied, and not susceptible of resolution through a single theoretical (or practical) approach'.[11]

The extensively inter-disciplinary nature of secession studies makes it difficult to produce very systematic theories, but it also gives these studies a particular flavour. The wide range of disciplines dealing with secession studies and, in turn, the profusion of issues addressed within this field, make it particularly attractive for scholars who like to work in the frontier zone of their own discipline. This volume aims to add one more theme to this already broad field of research, namely, the interaction between social cognition and political action. More specifically, this is a study of the relationship between the ideas advanced by intellectuals and scholars, especially social scientists, and the politics of secession. In a way, this study deals with the general problem of the role, influence and power of ideas in politics. The chosen approach is empirical. The authors do not have a primary interest in a normative analysis of the various principles to be found in debates on secession. They focus rather on the use made of normative principles by secession movements and on the involvement of intellectuals in political debates with normative content. The primary focus is on the role of intellectuals in these movements and on the relationship between their scientific and political discourses. The scientific arguments used by movements for and against secession pertain to various disciplines. The contributions to this volume explore the reasons why, in debates on secession, some disciplines are more prominent than others. They also reflect on the question of the truthfulness and objectivity of scientific approaches and on the question of moral responsibility when scholars willingly involve themselves in political disputes.

Contemporary controversies over secessionist claims take place in a context where standards of scientific objectivity have been questioned. Philosophers of science have a tradition of dealing with the socially embedded nature of the knowledge produced by the exact sciences.[12] Post-modern scholarship has likewise focused on the discursive nature of the social knowledge produced by the humanities and the social sciences. It interprets it as a meaning-making activity, based on interpretations of processes of social change. It has highlighted how the production of social knowledge is embedded in value-laden ideological discourses articulating visions of the direction social change should take.[13] This awareness of the discursive and ideological nature of the humanities and the social sciences and of their relative truth-value does not, however, necessarily make it impossible to assess scholarship or to exercise criticism. Moments of crisis or transition (such as secessionist crises) are in fact particularly appropriate for the critical assessment of scholarship, since the political polemics and confrontation they spark off between different schools of interpretation make it easier to uncover the ideological unconscious of these various schools of thought.[14] At the same time, an understanding of the discursive nature of scholarship in the humanities and the social sciences makes it possible to relate it to nation-building narratives.[15]

This post-modern outlook allows an analysis of social knowledge using an approach that acknowledges its relativity but nevertheless ascribes to it an important meaning-giving role within society. It thus follows a tradition previously articulated by sociologists of knowledge such as Karl Mannheim. Mannheim argued that the social sciences are in all circumstances an interpretative form of knowledge, and are hence ideological.[16] His vision of ideologies does not denounce their 'falseness' when set against the standard of an objective truth. His sociology of knowledge is rather concerned with 'the relationship of all partial knowledge and its component elements to the larger body of meaning, and ultimately to the structure of historical reality'.[17] He argues that the intelligentsia, since it is relatively unattached to class interests, not only produces ideologies but is also able to achieve a synthesis of the ideologies present in a specific social context.[18]

Contemporary scholars tend to be more critical than Mannheim of the role of the intelligentsia, its own group interests and its capacity for unmasking the 'ideological unconscious' – the interests behind political and scholarly discourses.

Pierre Bourdieu thus draws attention to how the institutional context in which scholars operate conditions their scholarly production.[19] Zygmunt Bauman depicts the role of intellectuals within a specific social and national context, which implies the 'relativity of knowledge (that is, its "embeddedness" in its own communally supported tradition)'.[20] In this context, the role of intellectuals is to facilitate communication between different traditions of knowledge, since the procedural rules of the intellectual professions enable them to go beyond particular interests and viewpoints and to act as critics of beliefs held in society.[21] Bourdieu likewise highlights how the social sciences may transcend their social conditioning, by arming themselves with 'a scientific knowledge of their social determination'.[22]

The role of intellectuals in secessionist movements and the function of scientific knowledge in nationalist discourses are prominent subjects in literature on nationalism. One of the classics in the analysis of the contribution of intellectuals to the process of nationalist mobilization is Miroslav Hroch's 'Social Preconditions of National Revival in Europe'.[23] This book by the Czech historian develops an evolutionary scheme in which scholarly interest in nationalism gradually leads, in a second stage, to patriotic agitation which, if successful, is followed in a third stage by mass support. The contribution of intellectuals to such processes of mobilization is closely linked to their elaboration of national identities. Intellectuals translate their scientific knowledge into a public discourse that proposes a vision of their nation; they evoke and reconstruct its past to root it in historic tradition, but at the same time such 'imagined communities' include a programme for the nation's future.[24]

In his description of the emergence and development of cultural nationalism in Ireland during the nineteenth century, John Hutchinson gives an example of how scientific knowledge and the construction of national identities may interact. He highlights how the political quest for autonomy stimulated scholars to rediscover their nation's past, and particularly its Gaelic roots, which thus became a central feature of Irish identity. Since the scholars involved in this process were also concerned about international scholarly recognition, their reconstruction of the Gaelic past met the then internationally accepted scientific standards.[25] The present contributions concur with this type of research endeavour.

As will be explored in the various contributions, scientific objectivity and moral responsibility acquire a particular meaning in each culture. The contributions to this volume offer a comparison between very different scientific traditions. They analyse the multiple, often country-specific factors that affect the involvement of the social sciences. The presence or absence of 'strong' or 'weak' state traditions, as well as the level of development of civil society, may account for the way in which the social sciences advance. The ubiquity of nation-specific institutional models; the extent of 'acceptable' involvement in academia by the polity; the degree of 'opportune' closeness between public intellectuals and the political elite, are examples of factors that have an impact on the constitution of the social sciences. Nor should the impact of established national intellectual legacies be forgotten. For instance, intellectual traditions that focus on collective entities such as states and nations rather than individuals have contributed to the emergence of social sciences that differ in focus and emphasis from those that emphasize the individual. Cultural heritages that stress agency leave a different imprint on the social sciences from those that underline structure. Inveterate normative traditions have contributed to different kinds of social science from those coloured by empiricism. The degree and emphasis of the instrumentalist features of the social sciences are conditioned, among other things, by political, cultural and ideological factors.[26]

To sum up, even though some traits are common to all of the social sciences, there are nevertheless country-distinct features. The closeness of the social sciences to the humanities, the ways of acquiring social knowledge and the character of social knowledge itself are rooted in country-specific conditions. These national traditions presuppose what ideas, beliefs, values and norms are to be taken for granted. Cultural cognizance thus acts as the foundation for what, in a given society, constitutes 'uncontested' or 'true' social-scientific insight and understanding. The culture-specific definitions ascribed to the social sciences contribute to the relativity of the concept of objectivity in evaluating social knowledge.

What exactly is the aim of this book? The relationship between social knowledge and secession has been studied for specific cases or in particular disciplines (especially the writing of national histories), but has not been assessed from a comparative, interdisciplinary perspective. Taking such a perspective, the case-studies in the present volume attempt to answer the following questions, which refer to strongly interrelated themes: (1) is there a kind of instrumental relationship between scholars and political leaders in public discussions on secession, and an institutional setting which favours closeness between these two groups? (2) what kinds of scientific disciplines are prominent in debates on secession, and what kinds of normative arguments can they support? (3) what are the particular criteria for scientific objectivity and truthfulness used in discourses for, against and about secession, and how do scholars involved in such debates reflect on these criteria – on both the epistemological and deontological levels? The theme will be examined from a comparative perspective, but the comparison itself will be presented only in the conclusions. This comparative analysis is not meant as a contribution to a future grand theory on secession, which would be rather difficult for the reasons mentioned above. Instead, the book is based on a more modest concept of theory, which aims to systematize the field of reseach through a coherent set of concepts and research questions, and to draw certain conclusions from it.

The book aims to reinterpret – and to a certain extent broaden – the scope of the problems with which research on secession has been confronted.

Some Questions of Terminology

These three questions addressed to the authors of this volume, and the title we have chosen for the book itself, involve a number of terminological problems which require clarification. The use of distinctions such as between the humanities and the social sciences, or the meaning of terms such as 'intellectuals' and 'secession', are linked to specific cultural traditions, which makes their use in a comparative perspective rather problematic. Both the social sciences and the humanities are domains of knowledge that are concerned with humankind and society. The distinction between the two is therefore not obvious. Some claim that the humanities constitute an over-arching discipline, subsuming the social sciences. Others recognize the two domains as separate fields of cognizance, but claim that the boundary between them is unclear. Still others attempt to classify the various branches of knowledge under one category or the other. If the humanities are said to include art, archaeology, education, history, literature, music, philosophy and philology, then anthropology, economics, geography, political science, public administration, psychology, social psychology and sociology are relegated to the social sciences. Branches of knowledge such as, for example, ethnography, ethnology and linguistics are left in limbo. Finally, the field of history may be seen either as overlapping the two domains, or as a component part of each. The broad distinction between diachronic and synchronic fields of study does not fully resolve the problem of what constitutes the humanities and what is social science.

In the final analysis, the classification of the various fields of knowledge is very much country– and culture-specific.[27] The Marxist-Leninist tradition to be found in the Soviet Union, for instance, blurred the distinction between humanities and social sciences, exalting history as the only truly scientific approach for analysing social change, and relegating disciplines such as political science to the dustbin of 'bourgeois' sciences. It would not make much sense to draw a strong dividing-line between the humanities and social sciences in the post-Soviet world, even though sociology and political science have been rehabilitated and historical materialism has been scrapped from the curricula of universities and scientific institutions. For all these reasons, several contributions to this volume and the comparative analysis in the conclusions will be based on a broad concept of the social sciences, which includes history and law.

'Intellectual' is another term whose meaning has to be located in a particular culture and a particular time. Both the boundaries and the internal stratification of the category are nation-specific. The use of the term 'intellectual' may be quite normal in one cultural context, whereas it would be altogether inappropriate in another, where terms such as 'scholar' or 'academic' would be used. It may have a particular meaning in a specific political context, as when referring to French scholars supporting or opposing the Algerian war of independence in the 1950s, but this meaning would not have been shared outside France, or even outside Paris. The term also has different political associations for the French public of the 1950s and for the same public half a century later. For the purpose of our comparison, we will set aside these specific connotations where the choice of such a term is concerned, and use 'intellectual' interchangeably with 'scholar' or 'social scientist'.

The term 'secession' is, politically, highly problematic. Most debates on secession are actually based on a vocabulary from which the word 'secession' has been expunged. The Soviet experience is illustrative in this respect. The right to secession was codified in the Soviet constitution for all Union republics. In Ukraine, secession has been a constant, but not tolerated, topic of discussion. The signature of the Belovezhskaya Agreement between the presidents of Russia, Ukraine and Belarus in December 1991 is generally not regarded as an act of secession. It is presented in the media and scientific literature alike as an act of dissolution, even though the act of secession from the Soviet Union and the constitution of independent states are both described in the agreement as constituent parts of this process of dissolution.[28] The terms 'secession' and 'secessionist' are also seldom used in Belgium. Some of those who consider that the right to self-determination of the Flemish people cannot be exercised within the framework of a Belgian federation use the concept of a 'confederation' to point to the positive content of their programme, whereas their adversaries would rather describe these contents in purely negative terms, such as 'separatism'. In Quebec, the term 'sovereignty' is propagated by those who strive for independent statehood, whereas their opponents describe themselves in equally positive terms as 'federalists'. The fact that those who claim the right to secession of a particular people or state are usually reluctant to describe themselves as 'secessionists' can also be explained by the fact that secessionist movements generally reject an unrestricted application of this right. In Quebec, before the 1995 referendum about 50 municipalities – representing one Quebecois citizen in twelve – voted that in the event of secession they would rather stay Canadian than remain part of Quebec.[29] This was unacceptable to the nationalist Parti Québécois. The secessionist leadership of Abkhazia has been refusing to discuss the option of allowing the region of Gali – where more than 90% of the local population is Georgian – to be separated from Abkhazia in exchange for Georgian concessions such as the lifting of the Georgian blockade of the secessionist region: they consider that this land is historically Abkhazian, and that most of its population were originally ethnic Abkhazians who were forcibly assimilated by Georgian colonization.[30]

'Autonomy' is another term whose meaning is strongly coloured by past experiences. It has a positive meaning for the Flemish and other West European national movements, but no positive connotations whatsoever for those movements in the post-Soviet world that are striving for independence or for greater powers within a federal framework. In the Soviet tradition, where a complex federal system involving various forms of autonomy was combined with a highly centralized leadership under the Communist Party, autonomy has been understood as a method of dissociating the formal from the real exercise of political power. Autonomy had a similar connotation in Yugoslavia. For this reason, it has been replaced by the term 'self-government' in the draft agreement designed to solve the Kosovo problem, prepared in February 1999 at Rambouillet. The draft would otherwise have been unacceptable to the delegation representing the Albanian population of the region. When used in the context of Corsica or Brittany, on the contrary, 'autonomy' has quite a radical programmatic content, coming close to what is described in other countries as 'secession'. For the sake of a comparative analysis, we will have to define the terms 'secessionist movement' and 'secessionist process' in such a way that they may describe even those processes where the concept of secession is absent from political debates or is replaced by terms such as 'autonomy'.

The terms 'secession', 'secessionist movements' and 'secessionist processes' refer in scientific literature to acts of withdrawal from the authority of the central government. The most radical form of withdrawal is the creation of a sovereign and independent state, which is what is generally meant when the term 'secession' is used. The terms 'secessionist movement' and 'secessionist process', however, mean more than movements or processes leading to full independence. It is generally accepted among authors writing on this subject that the forms of withdrawal from the authority of a central government may differ widely. The policies of secessionist movements may result not only in independence, but also in the constitution of an autonomous political unit within a federal state based on the principles of self-rule and shared sovereignty, or in the constitution of a sovereign state within a confederal union of states. Groups may seek either full sovereignty or, simply, greater political autonomy.[31] Seen from this perspective, secessionist movements or secessionist processes may lead to independence, but this is not necessarily the case. It only makes sense to use these two terms, however, in a context where the break-up of the existing state and the creation of a new, independent state may be regarded as a real possibility. Not all federalist movements are secessionist. Nor should all processes of federalization, regionalization or increased autonomy at a sub-national level be regarded as secessionist. The transformation of federated states into independent ones, for instance, is an option in the Belgian federalization process but not in the Federal Republic of Germany. The political dynamics of these processes have to be taken into account in order to classify them.

This broad conception of secessionist movements and processes, in which they lead to a new (independent) state unit on the international scene or to a new (federated) state unit on the domestic scene, may contrast with the commonly accepted meanings of these terms. Representatives of political movements who intend to withdraw their community from the authority of the state may deny that they are secessionists when, for instance, they are striving for the right to national self-determination within the framework of a federal state. They may regard membership of a federal state as more appropriate than independence for attaining such a right, taking their particular political circumstances into account. It does not make sense, however, to use these movements' own defini-tion of themselves. Not the rhetoric or declared intentions of political move-ments, based on their own perspectives, but rather the consequences of their actions, or the objective process of which their actions are part, should be assessed. Even in those federations in which the right to secession is not constitu-tionally enshrined, the choice of secession – understood as a withdrawal from the authority of the central government – remains a possibility which federal struc-tures cannot preclude. This is particularly true for ethno-federal constructions. Ethno-federations, which are based on the principle of self-government for eth-nic communities and on the principle of shared sovereignty between them, have to be regarded as open systems. Ever-increasing powers in a constitutional trans-formation process may culminate in full state sovereignty for the federated states and the dissolution of the federation. In this volume, no fewer than seven contri-butions on ethno-federal experiments have been included. The cases of Yugoslavia, Quebec, Flanders, Ukraine, Tatarstan, Chechnya and Abkhazia clearly demonstrate that the capacity of federal arrangements to contain seces-sionist movements may vary significantly.

The Institutional Context and Instrumentality of Scientific Knowledge

The first question formulated above - on the kind of relationship that exists between scholars and political leaders - refers to the institutional context of scholarship on secession. It may be useful, as a way of introducing the different case-studies, to reflect on some more general characteristics of the politicization of modern social sciences. In most countries it is the academic world that has become responsible for determining the boundaries of the social science profes-sion, the nature and identity of the discipline, its principles, and its scope and methods of enquiry. In some situations, not only social scientists but also publicists, politicians and administrators actively participate in the development of specific areas of scholarship. In such circumstances, academia may not be the exclusive determinant of its fields of knowledge. The form of such external interference differs according to discipline. Archaeologists, for instance, need substantial state support in order to carry out their primary research, which makes them particularly vulnerable to questions about their loyalty to the state or government.[32] Similar examples can be given for other scientific disciplines. This is a problem both of moral integrity and of methodology.

Normally, academia, research institutes and the professional associations of social scientists hold a near-monopoly over definitions of what constitutes scientific knowledge and how it is to be attained. This situation gives the social scientists not only a privileged position of authority, but also power. They regard themselves, and are perceived by others, as experts, possessing a certain 'cultural capital' which is sought out by political and social agents, as well as by the public at large. By assigning meaning to political dynamics, and by formulating beliefs, myths and symbols that are put into action in politics, social scientists also exert an overall influence on political debates. Often, the general public is aware only of the simplified or popularized versions of social knowledge. Such restrained and 'made simple' forms of information may be conveyed by the social scientists, in conjunction with the media. Popular knowledge may influence the public in numerous ways. It may contribute to the process of forming national identity, as well as to the public's political activity. There is always a possibility that this audience will regard this simplified social cognizance, with its components such as myths, as actually constituting received wisdom.[33]

Instrumentalism is a phenomenon intrinsic to the social sciences. After all, modern social sciences came into existence not only to give theoretical accounts of society, but also to provide answers to social problems. Even though, over time, in social science the notions of the 'betterment', 'amelioration' and 'social engineering' of society have become somewhat attenuated, they still persist. It is precisely the notion of instrumentalism that links social science cognitive structures, social knowledge and political action. Requests to the social sciences to exercise their instrumental, problem-solving potential may come from society or from the discipline itself. The public at large may demand that the often government-funded social sciences should be 'concerned' with 'real-life' issues, and should offer knowledge that will be useful for solving social problems. Public authorities may channel funding towards applied types of social scientific research, which they see as being 'concerned' with 'real-life' problems. This may cause fundamental social science research to be under-funded. After all, political players are primarily interested in knowledge that advances their agendas. Finally, the demand for instrumental knowledge may actually come from the social scientists themselves. They may promote their 'cultural capital' as consisting of a theoretically driven analysis of 'real' social problems, and as public-policy oriented social cognizance deemed indispensable for political decisions and public policy analysis.[34]

Most social scientists do not consider themselves to be neatly quarantined from the 'real world'. This means that they regard themselves as ultimately confronting 'real-life' issues. Thus 'concerned' status is inevitably bestowed on their social scholarship and knowledge. The issue of separatism or secession may serve to illustrate this situation. Some social scientists may put their opinions on the subject and their social scientific endeavours into different mental compartments. Others may avoid explicit references to separatism, while actually allowing their preoccupation with secession to colour their scholarship. There may be social scientists who actually indulge in a straightforward advocacy of autonomy or independence, while maintaining their academic rigour. Real-life political issues, such as the question of secession, may impact in a subconscious way on social scientific scholarship. The tendency to apply the label of 'concerned' scholarship only to works advocating secession may therefore be inappropriate. After all, social science scholarship that stands for the status quo may be equally 'concerned'. The same applies to such identifiers as 'tendentious', 'propagandistic' and 'nationalistic'. Often, these terms are used in a derogatory and dismissive way, to deride pro-secessionist learning, as if pro-status quo scholarship cannot possibly exhibit these traits. 'Concern' with the maintenance of existing polities, or with secession, does not necessarily mean the automatic enlistment of the social scientists in activist partisan causes. 'Concerned' scholarship and cognition do not necessarily have immediate political usefulness.[35]

The political constellation and the academic and intellectual traditions of a country determine how scholarly and political concerns will interact, and to what extent and in what forms the social sciences may be instrumentalized. Western countries generally have a solid and long-standing tradition of academic freedom. The emergence of a public sphere, access to the publishing market and the possibility of moving from universities to public life or other professions gave scholars significantly increased intellectual liberties.[36] Such liberties did not exclude the involvement of intellectuals in the process of constructing a national identity. A well-known example of ideological involvement is the English Whig interpretation of history, with its emphasis on the particularity of England's parliamentary tradition and liberty, which easily became a discourse on national exceptionalism, a complacent account of success, whereby England's providential history could serve as a legitimization for a sense of national mission and a justification for empire-building.[37] In the contemporary context, Hans Morgenthau considers that the choices open to academics in the West – they can serve, confront or ignore government – are all necessary roles. But he also stresses the necessity for academics to retain a certain immunity from outside pressure through job security, in particular through tenure.[38] He warns of the existence of an 'academic-political complex in which the interests of the government are inextricably intertwined with the interests of large groups of academics. These ties are both formal and informal, and the latter are the more dangerous to intellectual freedom, as they consist in the intellectuals' unconscious adaptation to imperceptible social and political pressures'.[39]

In this volume, two particular forms of interaction between social scientists and policy makers are analysed. In both cases, the state takes a far more active role in shaping scientific production than is generally the case in the Western scientific tradition. The first type of instrumental relationship between power and knowledge is found in communist regimes, and the second in the so-called 'late nations', which are defined by their relatively recent attainment of statehood. Late nations have not necessarily acquired independent statehood. Federated states such as Quebec or Flanders may also be regarded as late nations. Within the Soviet federal framework, a certain form of statehood was granted to Union republics such as Ukraine and to autonomous republics such as Tatarstan, Chechnya and Abkhazia. In the case of Chechnya and Abkhazia, the concept of 'late nation' refers to states that are currently striving for international recognition of their de facto independence. The following distinction between the main characteristics of the type of interaction between scholars and political leadership existing in communist regimes on the one hand, and late nations on the other, is not to imply that these types of interaction are mutually exclusive. Some of the studies on the post-Soviet world presented in this volume clearly demonstrate that, in concrete cases, characteristics of both types may be present simultaneously. These contributions deal with the development of social knowledge in late nations that were governed according to communist principles.

The instrumentality of the social sciences in the Soviet Union demonstrated a particular configuration. The institutional arrangements of this polity were designed to ensure closeness between social scientists and public authorities. In addition, there tended to be a lack of distinction between the public and private spheres, which favoured interventionist involvement by politicians and administrators in the academic realm. Not only did the authorities identify the spokesperson for the discipline, but they also determined the general political and ideological principles that the social sciences were expected to follow. The principles served as the taken-for-granted basis for what were claimed to be social-scientific mental frameworks and social knowledge. The task of social scientists was limited to the 'fine tuning' of uncontested, top-down induced frameworks, and to reproduce social knowledge with a 'within system' bias. The peculiarity of the frameworks used for cognizance and of the social knowledge itself was that both were highly prescriptive, laudatory and apologetic. In addition, the rhetoric of the social sciences tended to be replete with myths. Finally, the scholarship itself utilized a hegemonic and officialese *langue de bois*. Even though the social sciences tended to be perceived as assisting in the implementation of political agendas, in reality their instrumentality was limited to the legitimization of the regime. Otherwise, this form of social knowledge offered little usefulness to the public authorities for tackling 'real-life' social problems, or for establishing public policies. Yet there tended to be an aura around this highly ideologized, 'bureaucratic scholarship', as if it actually constituted applied research.[40]

The knowledge systems of late nations tend to exhibit a peculiar form of instrumentalism. Their knowledge systems and social cognizance are often produced in situations where there is little distance between public intellectuals in general and those involved in learned enterprises. In addition, there is a blurring of the distinction between the humanities and the social sciences. The public intellectuals concerned with such matters repeatedly find themselves outside official academic structures. Late-nation scholarship becomes institutionalized in civic associations, provided it is allowed by the state. The instrumentality of 'late-nation' scholarship resides in an attempt to grasp 'the national problem' theoretically, and to offer a 'concerned' way of overcoming it. Such social science is assumed to lend support to the process of nation– and possibly state-building endeavours. The myths generated by late-nation scholarship are intended to challenge the myths propagated by the dominant scholarly projects of the country of which a late nation is a component entity. In addition, the myths are instrumental in moulding a late nation's identity. Nevertheless, it would be a mistake to assume that this essentially normative, evaluative and prescriptive scholarship is devoted solely to myth-building. Much of this scholarship is just as sound as that of 'established' nations.[41]

The notion of culture tends to receive a good deal of attention in late nations. In such circumstances, culture does not refer simply to ideational aspects of behaviour, such as beliefs, myths, historical ideas and their related values, as well as knowledge. Culture, in fact, acts as a surrogate for politics. Public intellectuals – social scientists included – generate '*discours nationalitaires*' or 'nationalizing discourses'. Although consciously produced, these discourses are also determined by cultural knowledge. 'Nationalizing discourses' are intent on generating social knowledge inspired by insights drawn from the cultural environment, heritage and traditions of 'late nations'. Otherwise, this discourse would be artificial and would not find a receptive audience. Various solidarity myths, such as those pertaining to a common national ancestry, language, history, and so on, constitute important elements of any such discourse. 'Nationalizing discourses' help to forge a collective 'sharedness' and 'togetherness', or an 'imagined' national community.[42]

Clearly, the elaboration by the social sciences of such sensitive issues as nationhood and statehood is not confined to the case of late nations. Governments or political movements in any context may be preoccupied with such questions and may elicit social science-expertise in these domains. In some instances, 'national' or 'state problems' may focus on how to maintain existing political arrangements, as well as state boundaries. In other instances, 'state' or 'national problems' may refer to desired changes in existing polities, border shifts or secession. Both public authorities and political movements may value and give a high priority to social science scholarship that expounds the notion of communality. Political agents with secessionist agendas may require social scientists to help develop the notion of this communality, with their own future national-statehood in mind. Governments intent on halting separatism may value scholarship that emphasizes the idea of a civic understanding of nationhood or of multiculturalism. Social knowledge that predicts a collective solidarity web is of interest to all political players.[43]

Choosing between Disciplines

The second question addressed in the various case-studies in this volume concerns the kinds of scientific discipline that are prominent in debates on secession and the kinds of normative argument they are able to support. In nation-building discourses, history looms large. History is traditionally close to public discourse. Nicola Gallerano explains this phenomenon by the fact that the 'political function of historiography is to regulate memory and oblivion in order to shape the characteristics and the collective identity of a community and to distinguish it from others; and to construct, thanks to the past, a project and a prophesy for the future'.[44] History is, moreover, 'a scientific activity *sui generis*, whose cognitive dimension touches and mingles with the affective dimension, which is steeped in values, predilections, and non-scientific or pre-scientific discourse',[45] and as such it is easily amenable to transformation into a vulgarized public discourse. History as a scientific discipline is itself closely linked with the development of national identity. The transformation of history into a professional practice based on scientific rules in fact paralleled the construction of national histories. European historians of the nineteenth and early twentieth centuries were deeply involved in the writing of histories with a markedly teleological point of view. For them, the construction of a national state was the ultimate goal of national history. They shared a conception of the past as a country which was seen as an adumbration of the present. In this respect, present-day historians who espouse a secessionist cause are often repeating a traditional pattern in writing national histories. This pattern remains highly influential, despite the fact that recent generations of historians have severely criticized the teleological features of such historiography and its projection of present-day values onto the past.

While history offers the narrative of a nation's development and destiny, the social sciences contribute to the formulation of nationalist claims and self-affirmations. Sociology plays a role because of its interest in the social cohesion of a nation: 'Only through a sociological understanding can the fraternity of a nation be grasped; and so, in turn, it is hardly surprising if one of the central preoccupations of sociology has been with social cohesion and types of community, and the ways in which social change, particularly modernization, has undermined or facilitated new kinds of community'.[46] This concern with social cohesion was articulated for example by the French intellectuals who launched a revival of republican nationalism in the late 1980s. Following Durkheim, they emphasized the importance of the national bond for social integration.[47] Such visions can, however, also be deployed by secessionists, contrasting their 'real' national community with the 'artificial' one of the state.

In many contemporary secessionist crises, the economy plays an important role, particularly in political discussions on discriminatory redistribution to certain nationalities. Theories explaining uneven development among regions are a fruitful terrain in the search for legitimation for secession. The theory of internal colonialism, for instance, which highlights the role of governments in reproducing uneven development and discriminating against minorities, has had a strong impact on the political discourses of national minorities in Western Europe, particularly in the 1970s.[48] The popularity of the theory of internal colonialism among intellectuals active in national minority groups was due largely to the universal relevance of its vocabulary of exploitation and colonialism. As international law justifies secession by colonies from the colonizing country, the theory of internal colonialism made it possible to extend this form of legitimacy to some developed countries where the situation of minorities could be described in these terms. A further ground for the wide acceptance of this theory among secessionist groups was its historical dimension, highlighting the continuity of colonialism across the ages. Such a type of narrative could easily be linked to a teleological discourse on nation-building, where national emancipation would appear to be the inevitable outcome of political struggle.

Truthfulness and Moral Responsibility

The third and final topic addressed in the various contributions to this volume has to do with the criteria for scientific objectivity and truthfulness in discourses for, against and about secession, and how scholars involved in such debates reflect on these criteria and on their moral responsibility as scholars. The social sciences have developed heuristic devices for making sense of the social world. The various cognitive structures, frameworks, approaches, and the like, are supposed to render genuine and true accounts of social reality. Acting as frames of reference, they establish the criteria for truthfulness and channel enquiry and meaning in one direction, to the exclusion of others. Even though the frames of reference are the products of conscious and cognizant players, they are contextually conditioned. Their assumptions about reality are based on culturally acknowledged truth criteria. Over time, these reference frameworks, as systems of internalized acquired learning, take on an almost independent existence, and become a *habitus* for those who subscribe to them. Consequently, social scientists may become imprisoned by such a *habitus*, which was essentially of their own making in the first place.[49]

The various case-studies in this book analyse how such systems of acquired learning react and are being transformed during debates on secession crises. It may be assumed not only that the institutional setting in which scientific research takes place is of great importance in establishing the criteria for truthfulness, but also that the crisis which has affected scientific institutions – as it has, for instance, in Eastern Europe since *perestroika* and *glasnost* – may lead to a profound transformation of the guiding principles on which scientific production is based. It may further be assumed that the types of discussion on objectivity and truthfulness will not be the same in all the social science disciplines involved in discussing secession, and that the types of reflection on their involvement also differ widely. A third assumption concerns the specific nature of the social sciences and the humanities, as compared with the natural sciences, when confronted with their moral and political responsibility for the possible use and abuse made of their knowledge. The involvement of natural scientists in the peace movement during the Cold War was related to the moral dimension of their scientific activities. It had nothing to do with the methodological rules to be followed by scientific research. Social science dealing with research on nationalities after the Cold War has been affected in a different way by deontological considerations. Contrary to the reaction of natural scientists during the Cold War – who founded associations or scientific journals such as *The Bulletin of Atomic Scientists* to discuss the application of scientific knowledge by the military-industrial complex – historians and other social scientists have directed their criticism of the abuse of knowledge directly against their peers. The self-critique of the social sciences has taken the form of traditional scientific polemics on methods and ideas.

Historiography is a good example of this type of critical reflection. In the 1990s, historiography became the focus of moral reprimand when it was perceived as being responsible for the strengthening of nationalist currents in Eastern and Central Europe. This critique primarily took the form of a self-critique. Eric Hobsbawm, for example, reflected on the disruptive power of knowledge in the following terms: 'For historians are to nationalism what poppygrowers in

Pakistan are to heroin addicts; we supply the essential raw material for the market'.[50] Many similar statements are to be found in the literature on recent ethnic conflicts. The use and abuse of history in the Yugoslav wars, for instance, is a widely publicized topic, which confronts us with the fact that knowledge means power and that power may be used to various ends. By editing (together with Terence Ranger) the volume *Invented Traditions*, Eric Hobsbawm has himself made a prominent contribution to this critique of nationalist instrumentalization, by highlighting how many venerable and allegedly age-old 'national' traditions are in fact quite recent inventions (e.g. the Scottish kilt), often the conscious creations of governments and/or nationalist militants.[51] Another prominent scholar of nationalism, Ernest Gellner, has argued that nationalist historical narratives suffer from a pervasive false consciousness. Of nationalism, he wrote: 'Its myths invert reality: it claims to defend folk culture while in fact it is forging a high culture; it claims to protect an old folk society while in fact helping to build up an anonymous mass society.'[52] For Gellner, nationalism – the tendency whereby 'societies worship themselves brazenly and openly'[53] – is an ideology of self-interest.

While agreeing that national identities are cultural constructs, other scholars of nationalism such as Benedict Anderson and Anthony Smith have critiqued this merely instrumentalist vision of nationalism. Rather than interpreting 'invention' as 'fabrication' and 'falsity', they propose to understand it as 'imagining' and 'creation'.[54] Anthony Smith thus focuses on how national imaginings sustain national cohesion by presenting 'a vision of ethnic fraternity of elites and masses through a historical drama' which evokes 'deeper meanings of collective destiny and community in the face of the dangerous fragmentation and alienation that modern industrialism and science unfold'.[55] This process actively involves intellectuals, since they act both as producers of scientific knowledge and as myth-transmitters.[56] Scientific disciplines 'translate the idealised images of the ethnic past into tactile realities, according to modern canons of knowledge'.[57] Nations and their traditions may be inventions, but they are seldom mere fabrications,[58] since myths are themselves constrained by the language of science. At the same time, the disciplines in the social sciences are themselves involved in constructing a vision of a national community (sociology) and in rooting national identities in the past (history and archaeology).[59]

At the methodological level, historians have reacted by criticizing primordialist assumptions in defining ethnic and national identities (which locate the birth of an ethnic group at the beginning of recorded history), and by refuting claims about the immutability of national groups and their identification with a particular territory. Similar reflections on methodological fallacies resulting from an attempt to define timeless and unchanging boundaries in national identities can be found in other disciplines. Archaeologists have highlighted the importance of cultural diffusion and the concomitant porosity of ethnic boundaries. Anthropologists have documented the emergence of ethnic identities in Third World countries as a (not always intended) consequence of colonial policies. By affirming that 'a language is a dialect which has an army and a navy', linguists have likewise debunked claims about the primordial status of language.[60] Scholars who, with such criticism, highlight the shifting and often contingent nature of ethnic and national identities, are nevertheless aware of their continued political relevance.

Mythological Knowledge

One of the key terms to be found in scholarship on nationalism and its political impact is 'myth'. The term itself, as explained by Joanna Overing, goes back to the distinction made in Greek philosophy, in the fifth century BC, between 'logos' and 'muthos', which became a constituent of the Western conception of scientific thought. In the tradition of the Enlightenment, myth was understood as a still uncivilized mode of thought, opposed to logos or reason itself. In the twentieth century, it gradually lost its exclusively negative connotation. Even if mythological knowledge does not necessarily have anything to say about the 'real world' (knowledge of which remained reserved for scientific discourse), and is therefore irrational and false, it still gives an outsider access to the worldview of a particular culture.[61] Myths are a favourite subject of anthropological research. In 1997, Geoffrey Hosking and George Schöpflin edited the collective volume *Myths and Nationhood* in which, together with scholars such as Anthony Smith and Andrew Wilson, they applied this concept to particular traditions in historiography.[62] Myths are analysed on the basis of their contribution to the social cohesion of a community by, for instance, legitimizing the social order, upholding particular identities or enabling identity transfers.[63]

With the creation of myths, identities can shift more easily, or a new identity can be superimposed on an older one, during radical transformation processes. In the creation of the post-Soviet states, for instance, there was a need to create new identities which had to replace or be superimposed on the old Soviet identity. The simplification of reality as a precondition for facilitating communication within a political community, and for enabling the community to respond in a coherent way to radical challenges, is central to such an analysis. Myths are not seen as being congruent with reality in the sense of a scientific truth, but as expressing a community's postulates about reality. These postulates are of both a moral and a cognitive nature.[64] Myths are not freely invented or imagined. In order to be adopted by those who control and direct public communication, they have to be acceptable to public opinion at large. They have to have a certain relationship with the memory of the community, in order to elicit its consent, and for this purpose falsified or invented materials are quite inappropriate.[65]

This conception of myths is particularly important for the analysis of scientific production in late nations. Myths are constructed, but at the same time they are grounded in common cultural experiences and socially shared beliefs. Myths capture national cultural values, organize a multitude of social beliefs, and blur the line dividing past from present. Clusters of myths offer nation-specific schemata, and contribute towards nationally peculiar structures of cultural knowledge. Myths assure nations of a 'worthwhile distinctiveness', hence their particular importance for 'late nations', as these communities may be lacking in indubitable collective memory. Myths extend them instant gratification, by offering a respectable national past, which is recalibrated if necessary. Myths that attribute antique origins to national identities root them in sentiments of eternity and destiny that parallel the religious imagining.[66] Ancestry, founding and other myths sustaining 'late nations' dispute the long-standing myths of established nations. This being so, the public intellectuals and social scientists of a 'late nation' and those belonging to the states of which a 'late nation' is a part may deride each other's scholarship as being untrue, unrealistic, artificial, and riddled with myths, in the negative sense of the word. Conversely, the social-scientific formulations of one's own national community are depicted as being true, authentic, realistic, and devoid of myths.[67]

Myths appeal to the legitimate moral claims of particular communities and have to be congruent with their perception of reality. But what, then, is the difference between the truth of mythical knowledge and the truth of scientific knowledge? What is the difference between the normative meaning of a myth and the normative discourse of political theory? The difficulty in answering this question indicates that the traditional distinction between logos and muthos has only limited value for analysing the characteristics of secessionist discourses and their use of scientific disciplines. Several arguments can be given to support this thesis. First, mythical and scientific discourses share the characteristic of being ineffective when they are manipulated, created or imagined at will. They each have to rely on collective memories or historical facts, which remain external to their discourses. In this respect, the 'true' content of mythical knowledge and its moral message cannot be dismissed as being in opposition to an enlightened logos.

Second, neither can it be stated that the transformation of existing scientific approaches on the basis of ideological needs (the creation of new 'myths') necessarily has negative consequences for what is traditionally described as one of the main features of scientific progress, namely, methodological precision in assessing reality. Ethnically inspired archaeology may, as stated by Philip Kohl and Clare Fawcett, help to 'build justifiable pride in a specific cultural tradition' and simultaneously stimulate 'research into the past development of that tradition'.[68] Nationalism, for instance, had a decisive influence on archaeology, causing the original focus on evolution to be shifted over to the record of particular peoples. This had a positive effect on methodology, as it stressed the importance of a systematic description of spatial variations.[69]

Third, what is even more important in this context is the fact that too strong a focus on the dichotomy between mythological and scientific discourses may distract attention from the problem of objectivity in scientific research itself. Myths are described as being reductive in creating a particular coherent apprehension of reality, and as being inward-oriented in creating legitimacy for the moral claims of a particular community. The ascription of such characteristics to the world of myths does not solve the problem of their presence in standard scientific research. Normative and cognitive elements are intermingled in 'myths of territory' and 'myths of oppression'. They are likewise intermingled in any scientific analysis of migration processes in history and in the economic analysis of discriminatory redistribution. When we ascribe everything we consider irrational or illegitimate in scientific discourse to the world of myths, the question of objectivity in social science and the problem of formulating rules for scientific research remain unresolved.

The relativization of the distinction between scientific and mythological knowledge should not necessarily lead to the abandonment of this distinction or to epistemological relativism and moral scepticism. On the contrary, the presence of opposing national narratives – characteristic of secessionist crises – confronts scholars with the question of how to evaluate such narratives, and thus requires reflection on the scientific standards for choosing between alternative narratives and explanations of events. Almost inevitably, however, such reflection also includes a normative dimension – a judgement on the impact of such narratives on political events, and thus on the moral responsibility of historians and social scientists. The cases put forward in this book offer material for such reflection. They discuss a wide variety of political situations, and of political involvement by historians and social scientists, but they all concur in observing a particular relation between scholarly and political concerns. By comparing the problems raised by such a relation, we aim to give structure to this field of research, to systematize the research questions involved, and thus to make a contribution towards a better understanding of secession.

Notes

[1] Donald L. Horowitz, *Ethnic Groups in Conflict*, Berkeley/Los Angeles/London, University of California Press, 1985, p. 230.

2   See the overview of the main issues in the debate on international relations theory: Charles W. Kegley Jr, 'The Foundations of International Relations Theory and the Resurrection of the Realist-Liberal Debate', in Charles W. Kegley Jr (ed.), *Controversies in International Relations Theory. Realism and the Neoliberal Challenge*, New York, St Martin's Press, 1995, p. 32.

3   Giovanni Sartori, 'Philosophy, Theory and the Science of Politics', *Political Theory*, Vol. 2, May 1974, pp. 133-162. Allen Buchanan, *Secession: The Morality of Political Divorce from Fort Sumter to Lithuania and Quebec*, Boulder, Westview Press, 1991.

4   Ronald H. Chilcote, *Theories of Comparative Politics*, Boulder, Westview Press, 1981, pp. 62-67, 156, 179-180. Barry Clark, *Political Economy*, Westport, Praeger, 1991, pp. x-xii. Oskar Lange, 'Note sur l'idéologie et les tendances dans la recherche en sciences économiques', *Revue internationale des sciences sociales*, Vol. 16, No. 4, 1964, pp. 567-573.

5   A good overview of the different empirical approaches to secession is to be found in Ralph R. Premdas, 'Secessionist Movements in Comparative Perspective', in Ralph R. Premdas, S.W.R. de A. Samarasinghe and Alan B. Anderson (eds), *Secessionist Movements in Comparative Perspective*, London, Pinter, 1990, pp. 12-29.

6   According to Barry Buzan and Ole Waever, in international relations theory the first meaning is generally to be found in Europe, whereas Americans would use a more demanding concept of theory. Cf. Barry Buzan and Ole Waever, 'Security Complexes: A Theory of Regional Security', paper presented to the conference 'Central Asia in a New Security Context', organized by the Swedish Institute of International Affairs in Stockholm on 2-3 September 1999.

7   Jeremy Waldron, 'Minority Cultures and the Cosmopolitan Alternative', in Will Kymlicka (ed.), *The Rights of Minority Cultures*, Oxford, Oxford University Press, 1996, p. 98.

8   Premdas, 'Secessionist Movements in Comparative Perspective', *op. cit.*, pp. 17-24.

9   Percy B. Lehning (ed.), *Theories of Secession*, London/New York, Routledge, 1998. See also Michel Huysseune, *An Analysis of the Relation Between Research in the Social Sciences and Nation-Building Discourses: the Case of the Lega Nord in Italy*, doctoral dissertation, Vrije Universiteit Brussel, 2001, p. 22.

10 Margaret Moore (ed.), *National Self-Determination and Secession*, Oxford, Oxford University Press, 1998.

11 Rogers Brubaker, 'Myths and Misconceptions in the Study of Nationalism', in *ibid.*, p. 260.

12 Thomas Kuhn, *The Structure of Scientific Revolutions*, Chicago, University of Chicago Press, 1970; Bruno Latour, *Science in Action. How to Follow Scientists and Engineers Through Society*, Cambridge, Mass., Harvard University Press, 1987.

13 See e.g. Jeffrey Alexander, who argues that there is 'always an eschatology, not merely an epistemology', in theorizing about social change'. Cf. Jeffrey A. Alexander, 'Modern, Anti, Post, and Neo: How Social Theories Have Tried to Understand the "New World" of "Our Time"', *Zeitschrift für Soziologie*, Vol. 23, No. 3, 1994, pp. 165-197. Quotation p. 167.

14 Karl Mannheim, *Ideology and Utopia. An Introduction to the Sociology of Knowledge*, London, Routledge & Kegan Paul, 1949 (originally published as *Ideologie und Utopie*, Bonn, F. Cohen, 1929), p. 75.

15 See e.g. Hayden White, *The Content of the Form. Narrative Discourses and Historical Representations*, Baltimore/London, The Johns Hopkins University Press, 1987.

16 Mannheim, *op. cit.*, p. 91.

17 *Ibid.*, p. 77.

18 *Ibid.*, pp. 136-146.

19 Pierre Bourdieu, *Homo academicus*, Paris, Les Editions de Minuit, 1984, pp. 11-52.

20 Zygmunt Bauman, *Legislators and Interpreters. On Modernity, Post-modernity and Intellectuals*, Cambridge, Polity Press, 1987, p. 4.

21 *Ibid.*

22 Bourdieu, *op. cit.*, p. 47.

23 It was first published in German in 1968 but became popular in its English translation in 1985. On Hroch see Louis Vos, 'Nationalisme: Reflecties van een Historicus', *Cahiers d'histoire du temps présent*, No. 3, 1997, pp. 291-320.

24 Quoted in John Hutchinson and Anthony Smith, *Nationalism*, Oxford, Oxford University Press, 1994, p. 130.

25 John Hutchinson, *The Dynamics of Cultural Nationalism. The Gaelic Revival and the Creation of the Irish Nation-State*, London, Allen & Unwin, 1987.

26 Bruno Jobert and Pierre Muller, *L'Etat en action*, Paris, PUF, 1987, pp. 67-70; Luk Van Langenhove, 'Rethinking the Social Sciences? A Point of View', in *The Social Sciences at a Turning Point*, Paris, OECD, 1999, pp. 45-47.

27 Burton R. Clark and Guy R. Neave (eds), *The Encyclopaedia of Higher Education*, Oxford, Oxford University Press, Vol. 4, 1992, pp. 1981-1989 and 2071-2080.

28 On 8 December 1991, the presidents of Russia, Ukraine and Belarus signed a Joint Declaration, establishing a Commonwealth of Independent States and stating that 'the objective process of secession by republics from the USSR and the formation of independent states have become a reality' (Abram Chayes *et al.*, 'The Development of US Policy Toward the Former Soviet Union', in Alexei Arbatov *et al.*, *Managing Conflict in the Former Soviet Union*, Cambridge, Mass., MIT Press, 1997, p. 493). The term *vykhod* (literally meaning 'exit'), used in the original Russian text, may indeed be loosely translated as secession. The exact Russian term for secession, however, would be *otdelenie*. The term *vykhod* was also used in the paragraph of the various Soviet constitutions giving the right of secession to the Union republics.

29 *The Economist*, 19 December 1998.

30 See the interview with the Abkhaz president Vladislav Ardzinba in *Moscow News*, No. 39, 8-14 October 1998, p. 5.

31 Cf. Allen Buchanan, 'Secession and Nationalism', in Robert E. Goodin and Philip Petit (eds), *A Companion to Contemporary Political Philosophy*, Oxford/Cambridge, Mass., Basil Blackwell, 1993, p. 587; see also Horowitz, *op. cit.*, pp. 231-232. S.W.R. de A. Samarasinghe makes a distinction between separatism, defined as 'an attempt that seeks some degree of self-government short of total independence for a minority in conflict with the existing state' and secession, conceived as 'an attempt to establish a separate sovereign state', Introduction to Premdas, de A. Samarasinghe and Anderson, *op. cit.*, p. 2. In our opinion, it makes more sense to view secession as a gradual process which may be used as a synonym for separatism, rather than to make a clear-cut distinction between separatism, conceived as a search for autonomy, and secession, defined as a search for sovereignty.

32 Philip L. Kohl and Clare Fawcett, 'Archaeology in the Service of the State: Theoretical Considerations', in Philip L. Kohl and Clare Fawcett (eds), *Nationalism, Politics, and the Practice of Archaeology*, Cambridge, Cambridge University Press, 1995, p. 8.

33 Bjorn Wittrock and Peter Wagner, 'Social Science and the Building of the Early Welfare State: Towards a Comparison of Statist and Non-Statist Western Societies', in Dietrich Rueschemeyer and Theda Skocpol (eds), *States, Social Knowledge, and the Origin of Modern Social Policies*, Princeton. Princeton University Press, 1996, pp. 90-113.

34 J. Michael Brittain, 'Les frontières culturelles des sciences sociales dans les années 1990', *Revue internationale des sciences sociales*, Vol. 39, No. 119, 1989, pp. 111-122.

35 Richard P. Nathan, *Social Sciences in Government*, New York, Basic Books, 1988, pp. 31-56; *Sciences sociales et décisions*, Paris, OECD, 1979, pp. 30-35.

36 Stefan Berger, Mark Donovan and Kevin Passmore, 'Apologias for the Nation-state in Western Europe since 1800', in Stefan Berger, Mark Donovan and Kevin Passmore (eds), *Writing National Histories. Western Europe Since 1800*, London, Routledge, 1999, pp. 3-14.

37 Benedict Stuchtey, 'Literature, Liberty and Life of the Nation. British Historiography from Macaulay to Trevelyan', in Stefan Berger, Mark Donovan and Kevin Passmore (eds), *Writing National Histories. Western Europe Since 1800*, London, Routledge, 1999, pp. 30-46.

38 See the Preface to Christopher Hill and Pamela Beshoff (eds), *Two Worlds of International Relations*, London/New York, Routledge, 1994, pp. vi-vii.

39 Hans J. Morgenthau, *Truth and Power: Essays of a Decade. 1960-70*, London, Pall Mall Press, 1970. See also the Preface to Hill and Beshoff, *op. cit.*, p. vii.

40 Kenneth Dyson, *The State Tradition in Western Europe*, Oxford, Martin Robertson, 1980, pp. 81-110. Rainer Lepsius, 'Sociology in Germany and Austria 1919-1954', *EUI Working Papers*, No. 104, 1984, pp. 60-71. Françoise Thom, *La Langue de bois*, Paris, Julliard, 1987, pp. 63-107.

41 Bernard Giesen, *Intellectuals and the Nation*, Cambridge, Cambridge University Press, 1998, pp. 22-40. Brian Jenkins and Spyros A. Sofos, 'Nation and Nationalism in Contemporary Europe', in Brian Jenkins and Spyros A. Sofos (eds), *Nation and Identity in Contemporary Europe*, London, Routledge, 1996, pp. 9-37.

42 Anouar Abdel Malek, *L'Egypte: société militaire*, Paris, Seuil, 1962. The author probably originated the concept '*discours nationalitaire*'. Rogers Brubaker, 'National Minorities, Nationalising States, and External Homelands in the New Europe', *Daedalus*, Vol. 124, No. 2, 1995, pp. 107-132. Brubaker's more recent usage rests on a slightly different conceptualization.

43 Françoise Lorcerie, 'Les sciences sociales au service de l'identité nationale', in Denis-Constant Martin (ed.), *Cartes d'identité: Comment dit-on 'nous' en politique?*, Paris, Presses de la Fondation nationale des sciences politiques, 1994, pp. 245-281.

44 Nicola Gallerano, 'History and the Public Use of History', in François Bédarida (ed.), *The Social Responsibility of the Historian*, Providence/Oxford, Berghahn Books, 1994, p. 90.

45 *Ibid.*, p. 91.

46 Anthony D. Smith, *The Ethnic Origins of Nations*, Oxford, Blackwell, 1986, p. 172.

47 Lorcerie, *op.cit.*, especially p. 252.

48 The main theoretician of internal colonialism was Michael Hechter. In his historical overview of uneven development in Great Britain, he argued that the Celtic fringe of the United Kingdom had systematically been discriminated against and kept in a state of dependence by British governments, to the advantage of the English part of the country. See Michael Hechter, *Internal Colonialism. The Celtic Fringe in British National Development, 1536-1966*, London, Routledge & Kegan Paul, 1975.

49 Johann Mouton, 'The Structuration of Social Knowledge', in Jana Gosporikova *et al.* (eds), *Methodological Challenges of Interdisciplinary Research in the Social Sciences*, Pretoria, HSRC Publishers, 1996, pp. 31-50. Bruno Maggi, 'Les conceptions de la formation', *Economies et sociétés*, Vol. 30, Nos 11-12, 1996, pp. 151-177. Yves Surel, 'The Role of Cognitive and Normative Frames in Policy-Making', *EUI Working Paper*, RSC 98/45, 1998.

50 Quoted in Kohl and Fawcett, *op. cit.*, p. 13.

51 Eric J. Hobsbawm and Terence Ranger (eds), *The Invention of Tradition*, Cambridge, Cambridge University Press, 1983 (especially Eric J. Hobsbawm, 'Mass-Producing Traditions: Europe, 1870-1914', pp. 263-307).

52 Ernest Gellner, *Nations and Nationalism*, Oxford, Blackwell, 1983, p. 124.

53 *Ibid.*, p. 56.

[54] Benedict Anderson, *Imagined Communities: Reflections on the Origin and Spread of Nationalism*, London, Verso, 1983, p. 15.

[55] Smith, *op.cit.*, p. 173.

[56] *Ibid.*, p. 215.

[57] *Ibid.*, p. 180.

[58] *Ibid.*, pp. 177-178.

[59] *Ibid.*, p. 172.

[60] Anna Laura Lepschy, Giulio Lepschy and Miriam Voghera, 'Linguistic Variety in Italy', in Carl Levy (ed.), *Italian Regionalism, History, Identity and Politics*, Oxford/Washington, D.C., Berg, 1996, p. 70.

[61] Joanna Overing, 'The Role of Myth: An Anthropological Perspective, Or: The Reality of the Really Made-Up', in Geoffrey Hosking and George Schöpflin (eds), *Myths and Nationhood*, London, Hurst & Company, 1997, pp. 1-18.

[62] *Ibid.*

[63] George Schöpflin, 'The Functions of Myths and a Taxonomy of Myths', in *ibid.*, pp. 19-35.

[64] Overing, *op. cit.*, p. 12.

[65] Schöpflin, *op. cit.*, p. 26, Andrew Wilson, 'Myths of National Identity in Belarus and Ukraine', in Kohl and Fawcett (eds), *op. cit.*, p. 182.

[66] Anderson, *Imagined Communities, op.cit.*, pp. 17-20.

[67] Anthony Smith, *National Identity*, London, Penguin Books, 1999, pp. 22-23 and pp. 65-68.

[68] Kohl and Fawcett, *op. cit.*, p. 5.

[69] See Bruce G. Trigger, 'Romanticism, Nationalism, and Archaeology', in Kohl and Fawcett (eds), *op. cit.*, p. 269.

Ivan M. Myhul

1. Ukrainian Social Knowledge and Secession

Introduction

Social knowledge is a mode of diagnosis and cognizance of the *problématique* of the social world. When 'social world' and 'things social' are taken in the broad sense of the term, they encompass not only civil society, but also the historical, political and economic realms. This distinct mode of knowing about the social world developed in the nineteenth century into specific disciplines. The distinction between the social sciences and the humanities then as now, remains, however, problematical and is very much country-specific. The quest for knowledge of 'things social' evolved in a variety of ways. Early social-knowledge-generating cognoscenti were diverse in terms of training and focus. Some were scholars and academics, while others were amateurs and even dilettantes. There has not always been a clear demarcation, either in the past or today, between the tasks of a rational apprehension of social knowledge, the diagnosis of 'things social', and the effort of 'advocating', 'teaching' and 'ameliorating' societies and nations. These social-knowledge-generating cognoscenti were to be found in numerous sites. They operated within and through civic organizations, the civil service and educational-academic institutions. Some of the specifically knowledge-generating academic-educational institutional arrangements were in the public sphere, while others were found in civil society.

Whatever the case, the individuals involved were the formulators, explainers and transmitters of discourses about the issues of the social world. They were the makers of knowledge and the manipulators of meanings. It was they who determined the nature of social knowledge, in terms of what it was about and what it was for. In some cases social knowledge contributed towards the legitimization of the existing set-ups, while in other situations it was conducive towards alterations and changes. Since these individuals put forth experiential knowledge pertaining to how social, political, economic and national affairs were to be made sense of, they were the shapers of the consciousness of the population at large and, to some extent, of public affairs. These cognoscenti acted as 'public intellectuals' and their knowledge-bearing communities occupied a privileged space in their societies. Despite the fact that the knowledge produced was the task of individuals, it was also contingent on the society-specific intellectual traditions and the configuration of knowledge-formulating and -bearing institutions. The nature of the political regime and the political-bureaucratic arrangements also impacted on the construction and the nature of social knowledge. In most societies today, social knowledge is primarily constructed by academia-based social scientists, and the instrumental aspect of the social sciences has become somewhat attenuated, but it has not disappeared.[1]

The Emergence of Ukrainian Social Knowledge

Ukrainian social science offers an apt illustration of the above-stated generalizations. It emerged in very specific circumstances: those characterized by the 'statelessness' of the Ukrainian nation. This arduous condition derived from the fact that the territory that comprises contemporary Ukraine was divided for centuries among the contiguous states – although, by the nineteenth century, Ukrainian lands were found principally within the Tsarist and Austro-Hungarian empires. Nineteenth-century Ukrainians interested in forging knowledge were found in both the public and the private spheres. These public intellectuals were not only the makers of social knowledge, they were also the 'teachers of the nation', and as such concerned by various 'things social' of the Ukrainian community. They were advocators of causes, including that of the altering of the existing political and cultural situation. These public intellectuals made sense of public affairs, and as such acted as moulders of consciousness of the population at large.

Several Ukrainian 'national revivals' (*natsional'ne vidrodzhennya*) emerged and suffered a demise in the Tsarist Empire during the so-called 'long' nineteenth century (1780s-1918). Such revivals were more sustained in the Austro-Hungarian empire. All of the revivals were the work of public intellectuals. Each renewal was accompanied by the development of Ukrainian scholarship, an enterprise involving scholars and at times amateurs in the field. 'Ukrainian studies' (*ukrainoznastvo* or *ukrainistyka*), an early manifestation of studentship, were marked by an exclusive concern with the acquisition of social knowledge about things Ukrainian. Even though *ukrainistyka* dealt with many fields of knowledge, historical studies, philology and literature constituted the de facto quintessence of this field of reflection. While *ukrainoznavstvo* started off primarily from a humanities perspective, the social science dimension was layered on when the social sciences began to develop in Europe in the nineteenth century. Ukrainian studies were therefore a hybrid, 'socio-humanities' domain of knowledge. They were based on an ill articulated, but often taken-for-granted undercurrent which adumbrated that knowledge about things Ukrainian was grounded on culture. Thus, *ukrainoznavstvo* qualified as knowledge, because it was insinuated that it was founded on a Ukrainian cultural knowledge. The idea of cultural knowledge, though also not well articulated, was inferred to be true and was uncontested precisely because it was based on the assumption that it was shared collectively by the national community.

Notwithstanding this condition, Ukrainian studies were far from being a holistic field of knowledge devoid of internal differentiation. Various approaches were present. An ideographic or figurative representation of ideas was intertwined with an attempt to find general stipulations as to Ukrainian development. This nomothetic reasonableness spilled over into a diachronic basis of argumentation that focused on historical development in time. There was also, however, an approach featuring a synchronic focus on descriptions that underlined specific eras, past or present. Even though these socio-humanities were replete with references to meaningful sequences in Ukrainian history, attributed to agents or structures, narratives concerning national origin were also present. Open or latent interpretations of historical sequences and narrative scripts were interspersed with generalizations concerning national character. *Ukrainoznavstvo* often tended to focus on nation and society – collective entities – rather than on individuals. However, the strong concern with social processes and social change, evident in Ukrainian studies, contributed towards the nation- and society-building projects of the Ukrainian public intellectuals. Ukrainian studies were therefore unquestionably instrumental in precipitating the catch-up course of nineteenth-century Ukrainian nation-building.

Informed by social knowledge, the national project of the public intellectuals was oriented towards the construction of a Ukrainian 'imagined community'. This building process operated via self-definition as well as a through a mode of positing Ukrainian national identity and character in contradistinction to those of the neighbouring nations. Generally speaking, Ukrainian studies offered normative-explanatory cognitive schemes and generated a social knowledge that was in the rationalist intellectual tradition of reasoning. Finally, there was a 'concerned' dimension to some of *ukrainoznasvstvo*. The *engagé* and advocative characteristics of the discourse of this learning resided in the concern to 'enlighten' and educate Ukrainian society or the national community. This trait was very much in keeping with the instrumentalist tradition of nineteenth-century social sciences. It exalted the thought of the 'betterment' and 'amelioration' of the Ukrainian society and nation. This cognitive assessment on the part of public intellectuals of the Ukrainian 'national question', in the Tsarist and eventually the Austro-Hungarian empires, was entwined with an instrumentalist 'solution'.

This made the public intellectuals something akin to 'policy intellectuals' – as was evident in the built-in assumption found in the socio-humanities of the *ukrainoznavstvo* variety, of a 'nation to state' path of Ukrainian development. In this respect, the 'concerned' feature of Ukrainian studies contributed towards the formation of a Ukrainian independence movement, and may be considered to have been a distant cause of early twentieth-century Ukrainian political independence itself.[2]

The national revival at the end of the eighteenth and early nineteenth centuries, and their accompanying learning, manifested a primary concern with the task of a scholarly legitimization of the Ukrainian Cossack polity of the recent past. Both the Cossack Hetmanate and the Zaporizhs'ka Sich were glorified, and the liquidation of both by the tsarist regime in the seventeenth and eighteenth centuries was decried. The subsequent national renewal that followed was deeply concerned with popular culture and everything Ukrainian that was 'folk' (*narodne*). By the mid-nineteenth century and in the 1870s, the revival exhibited a preoccupation with Ukrainian political history, past political institutions and the elaboration of projects for national development. In the time span preceding the first world war and during the era of the establishment of the Ukrainian statehood of 1917-20, stress was placed on combating rampant Russification in the Tsarist Empire, as well as Russian-centred scholarship. There is evidence of a romantic idealization at that time of the Ukrainian 'people', its customs and traditions, popular peasant culture, Cossack heritage, Ukrainian language, and so on, while de-emphasizing the institutional political agents of the Ukrainian past. Even though an ebb followed each revival, the overall process was a cumulative one. Scholarship and activism led to a step-by-step enhancement of national consciousness. The study of things Ukrainian emerged as a form of social knowledge that was in itself an important factor at the close of World War I, helping Ukrainians to divest themselves of the notion of Ukrainian 'statelessness' as something that could not be altered. In the process, social knowledge contributed towards Ukrainian *indépendantiste* thought and the eventual statehood of the 1917-20 period.[3]

The process of institutionalizing Ukrainian studies was a complex one. There were some within-system elements as well as those that operated exclusively within Ukrainian civil society. Attempts to institutionalize this scholarship in the public sphere may be traced back to the newly established Kharkiv and Kyiv universities, in the early nineteenth century. However, it is the Kyiv Archeographic (Arkheograficheskaya) Commission of 1843 that had an extremely important positive impact. This state-affiliated institution was set up with the explicit aim of deriding Ukrainian studies. In the process, the task of the Commission was to justify tsarist Russificatory policies by documenting the supposed 'Russianness' of the Ukrainians – an idea propagated at that time not only by the public authorities but also by the official, Russocentric tsarist scholarship.

Paradoxically, the results were contrary to those anticipated. The Kyiv Archeographic Commission, staffed to some degree by Ukrainian public intellectuals, actually documented the opposite. The idea of the distinctness of the Ukrainians bolstered Ukrainian studies. However, since by mid-nineteenth century the regime intensified its Russification policy, Ukrainian public intellectuals resorted to establishing Ukrainian social learning outside of the official channels. Operating on the periphery of the highly statist Tsarist Empire, the public intellectuals set up a loose network of clandestine educational-academic associations (*hromady*) within civil society. They remained as such until 1905. The aim of these organizations was to strengthen both the academic and the 'concerned' aspects of scholarship. However, the regime quickly reacted to this form of national revival, often called the 'Ukrainophile' movement (*ukrainofil'stvo*). The activities of the *hromady* were perceived by the public authorities as fomenting Ukrainian political separatism. Since the regime had already qualified the findings of the Archeographic Commission as politically unacceptable, it also clamped down on the *hromady* by the early 1860s. The secret Valuev circular of 1863 actually banned these and other Ukrainian educational-academic enterprises. Furthermore, the Valuev circular also severely restricted Ukrainian-language publications, thereby contributing towards the curtailment of Ukrainian scholarship and social knowledge.[4]

Despite these disconcerting and off-putting measures aimed at Ukrainian knowledge-generating institutions and individuals on the part of the absolutist-bureaucratic political system, the clandestine Ukrainian civil society academic-educational institutional arrangements were again reactivated by the mid 1860s and early 1870s. Continuing to operate on the periphery of the sanctioned state-bureaucratic ones, the society-based associations impacted on those of the public sphere. The most important of the civil society institutions, the Kyiv Hromada, actually contributed to setting up the South-Western Branch of the Imperial Russian Geographic Society. During the short existence (1873-76) of this independent academic institution, there was an enhancement of the socio-humanities in Ukraine, and an expansion of Ukrainian social knowledge. The Historical Society of Nestor the Chronicler (1873) was another Kyiv-based knowledge-generating organization which also enhanced Ukrainian scholarship. But again, the national revival and the accompanying Ukrainian scholarship were singled out by the tsarist government. The authorities accused the Kyiv and other *hromady* of propagating Ukrainophile ideas, which were again identified with Ukrainian separatism. The secret Ems Ukase of 1876 and other subsequent tsarist edicts reinforced the restrictions on Ukrainian studies. This led to the closing down of the South-Western Branch. Ukrainian-language publications were further curtailed.[5]

By the 1880s there was another rebirth of Ukrainian knowledge-producing institutional arrangements, and of scholarship. The Kyiv Hromada established the *Kievskaya starina* in 1887. This unofficial and privately financed *hromada* mouthpiece was published in Russian from 1887 to 1906, and afterwards in Ukrainian, as *Ukraina*. For over a quarter of a century this periodical publication acted in tsarist Ukraine as an unofficial Ukrainian learned society. However, given the repeated governmental restrictions placed on Ukrainian scholarship in the tsarist part of Ukraine, the Ukrainian public intellectuals in Austria-Hungary established a comparable knowledge-generating institution. The legally constituted Shevchenko Scientific Society was set up in L'viv in 1873. It would function until the 1920s, as the de facto Ukrainian Academy of Sciences for all of the Ukrainian territories. Divided into sections, this association allowed for the development of the humanities and the emerging social sciences within both the Economics and the Historical-Philosophical Sections. When in 1905 the political climate improved in the tsarist part of Ukraine, a new learned institution was set up there in 1907. Called the Ukrainian Scientific Society, it duplicated not only the organizational arrangements of the Shevchenko Scientific Society, but also its academic activities. Social science-oriented activities were located in the Economic History, History, Law and Ethnography Sections. All of these scholarly associations continued throughout the first world war. It is in the context of this series of national revivals and institution-building attempts that nineteenth-century Ukrainian historiography emerged. What is referred to as a nineteenth-century phenomenon really spans a longer period, until 1918. If historical studies constituted one of the core elements of the socio-humanities-bearing *ukrainoznavstvo*, historiography was something of a keystone in this edifice.[6]

Ukrainian Historiography as Social Knowledge: the Early Stages

Ukrainian historiography, like any national historiography, acted as a vehicle for the formulation, invention, recovery or rediscovery of the Ukrainian historical past and the institutionalization of collective memory. It evolved epistemic for-mulations, which acted as *référentiels* for the acquisition of Ukrainian social knowledge about the Ukrainian past. Using representations, narrative scripts and myths, the historiography made sense of the past and institutionalized a col-lective national memory. Since the myths as markers, signs and symbols put forth by Ukrainian historiography were socially embedded in national cultural knowledge, they were readily acceptable to the historiographers' audience. Con-sequently, the historiographical narratives were perceived as true and valid. In addition, it must be remembered that Ukrainian historiography was not an exclusively academic endeavour. It was also linked to politics, representing at least a symbolic form of public intellectual resistance to the politics of the states comprising Ukrainian territories. Ukrainian social knowledge reprehended the situation in which the Ukrainian national community found itself. In order to remedy this situation, it promoted the ideas of national freedom and national self-determination. The innate elements of 'advocacy' found in Ukrainian historiography made it a malleable national symbol. It is in this capacity that historiography as social knowledge contributed not only to the institutionalization of a collective national memory, but also to the forging of the Ukrainian 'imagined community.' In the final analysis, historiography also helped in the making of a politicized national identity, in the form of patriotism or nationalism.[7]

Ukrainian historiography established itself partially in contraposition to the official Russian historiography of the tsarist part of Ukraine. The tsarist authorities and official state scholarship viewed this development with alarm, because of its perceived latent regime-disruptive potential. Not only did the new historiography put an effective end to the idea propagated by regime-authoritative erudition – that Ukraine was 'without history' – but it also connoted that its audience, the Ukrainian population, was to unlearn the official state version. Ukrainian historiography demonstrated that a distinct Ukrainian history was a social fact. This evidence became an undisputed assumption and a reference point for all future Ukrainian historiographical developments in the following century. Compared to tsarist historiography, this new-fashioned one produced fundamental research that diverged in assumptions, hypotheses, schemata, scripts and myths.

A cognitive-normative dissonance developed between the tsarist and Ukrainian versions of social knowledge. This was due primarily to the fact that the prevalent tsarist historiography was based on an assumption and a myth of an alleged 'Russian unity' bolstered by the 'Russian idea', as well as the Russian state. A supposed 'all-Russian' (*obshcherusskaya*) community was claimed to exist. It encompassed not only the Russians, but also the Ukrainians and the Belorussians. For this tsarist-supported historiography, Kyivan Rus' was the first Russian state and the Tsarist Empire was a linear, dynastic and national continuation of it. Consequently, the very idea of the separation of any components of this *obshcherusskaya* community was incompatible with this political myth. When, at various points in history, portions of this alleged community assumed a separate existence (as was the case with Ukraine), the official historiography disavowed it. Such outcomes were not only professed to be temporary aberrations, but were abjured as being artificial, undesirable and lacking in legitimacy. There was no room in the dominant tsarist historiography for any notion of a distinct Ukrainian people or nation, and even less for a separate Ukrainian polity. The inhabitants of Ukraine were basically assumed to be Russians with 'borderland peculiarities'. Consequently, Ukrainian social scientists who rejected the notion of a 'one and indivisible' Russia were accused by the official historiography of tendentiousness and nationalism. The very fact of raising the 'Ukrainian question', even at an academic level, was considered to be an act of perfidy, treachery and disloyalty, if not treason itself. Scholarly and publicist tsarist publications disavowing alleged Ukrainian 'separatism' attest to this.[8]

The crux of Ukrainian historiography was its assertion that the Ukrainians were a distinct and singular people, a nation with its own culture, history, collective memory and myths, in addition to historical knowledge. This Ukrainian-centred notion became a founding assumption as well as a social fact. Since this notion could not possibly fit into the officially advocated myths, it was derided by the regime's scholarship as constituting a 'myth' in the negative sense of the word, that is, a form of falsehood. The 'statist' (*derzhavnyts'ka*) emphasis or orientation in Ukrainian historiography underlined the thesis of a continuing Ukrainian statehood throughout national history, despite interruptions, from Kyivan Rus' to the seventeenth- and eighteenth-century Cossack Hetmanate polity and the Zaporizhs'ka Sich. It stressed the role of institutional structures and political agents. The 'populist' (*narodnyts'ka*) version of historiography focused on the myth of the historical continuity of a Ukrainian people (*narod*) that was a holistic and almost undifferentiated entity with a similarly constituted adjunct culture. The Ukrainian *narod* was claimed to be distinct from its neighbours in origin, values and character. This *narod* was considered to be the very foundation of the nation and a leitmotif of Ukrainian historical development. Meaningful attributions of agency to such a collective entity as a 'people' de-emphasized the notion of the individual as a historical agent, including the role of statesmen and politicians.

Ukrainian historiography, therefore, endorsed a 'nationalizing discourse' that was replete with schemata, scripts and narratives, together with myths that created an image of a people, its national culture and values, as well as its institutions and expectations, that had been effectively thwarted by an enemy tsarist and Russian colonialism. This alternative to the official scholarship inherently denounced the abuse of tsarist power and domination, implying a diffuse notion of resistance. The problematic notion of being a colonized and stateless entity, with an underdeveloped national identity and consciousness, when tied to the salutary idea of undoing this state of affairs, meant a problem-/solution-oriented scholarship. Not only was this historiography 'concerned' and instrumentalist, but many of the social scientists – such as Mykola Hrushevs'kyi, for example – engaged in partisan political activities, and even held government posts when an independent Ukrainian polity came into existence at the beginning of the twentieth century.[9]

Ukrainian Historiography as Social Knowledge: the Pre-Soviet Stage

Ukrainian scholarship was institutionalized quite rapidly by the different, short-lived, independent Ukrainian political regimes of the 1917-20 period. A government-sponsored Ukrainian Academy of Sciences was established in 1919. It and the universities emerged as the official knowledge-bearing institutions, supplementing the pre-World War I private academic/educational organizations. The humanities and the nascent social sciences witnessed a rapid development, primarily within the Academy's Historical-Philosophical and Socio-Economic Branches (*viddily*). The scope and methods of these disciplines allowed, among other things, for an *ukrainoznavstvo* mind-set in the conduct of scholarship on things Ukrainian. With the demise of an independent statehood and the advent of the Soviet regime in Ukraine, émigré scholars, along with those from the now Polish part of Ukraine, established a system of learned societies and higher-education institutions. These were designed to further scholarship begun earlier, but now being pursued in émigré conditions. Ukrainian humanities as well as the emerging social sciences witnessed a development within the confines of these academies. The scholarship that was produced in the realm of historiography continued within the established mental maps, schemata, scripts and myths. The very notion of the legitimacy of an independent Ukrainian statehood was never an issue in this scholarship. The issue was rather why independence had been lost. After all, the Soviet regime was perceived by the Ukrainian émigré public intellectuals as a Russian imposition. In the inter-war years, learned scholarship outside of Ukraine was found in numerous civil-society sites. For example, the Ukrainian Sociological Institute was set up in Vienna in 1919; the Ukrainian Free University was established in the same city in 1921, but later transferred to Prague. The Ukrainian Scientific Institute in Warsaw was organized in 1928; the Ukrainian Scientific Institute in Berlin appeared in 1929; the Ukrainian Historical-Philological Society of 1928 was Prague-based; the Ukrainian Technical and Husbandry Institute was set up in Podebrady in 1932 and the Ukrainian Mohylo-Mazepian Academy of Sciences was founded in Warsaw in 1938. In addition, there was the already existing Shevchenko Scientific Society in L'viv. However, after the first world war the Polish authorities restricted its knowledge-generating activities.

The Institution of Ukrainian Social Knowledge in the Early Soviet Era

The institutionalization of scholarship in the Ukrainian Soviet Socialist Republic (UkSSR) underwent a substantial evolution. The Ukrainian Academy of Sciences, which existed under this name from 1918 to 1921, was renamed during the 1921-36 period as the All-Ukrainian Academy of Sciences, and finally as the Academy of Sciences of the UkSSR. It retained this appellation until the demise of the USSR. During the first decade of the regime it operated as a scholarly body that was quite independent of the public authorities. This establishment, with no Western European equivalent, had the power to determine the cognitive structures and standards for scholarship in the humanities and the social sciences. Even though, over time, the Academy would eventually lose a portion of this prerogative to the political authorities, it would always remain the Soviet Ukrainian centre for co-ordinating research. This institutional peculiarity meant that the Academy would largely pre-empt the role of Soviet Ukrainian universities in the knowledge-generating domain. In order to rein-in the Academy, the authorities first set up an ideologically rival institution in 1922. The Ukrainian Institute of Marxism-Leninism, but especially its Department (*kafedra*) of Ukrainian history, generated quasi-academic social knowledge on things Ukrainian. This politically-coloured social knowledge rivalled that produced by the Ukrainian Academy of Sciences. Government pressure also contributed to the demise of pre-Soviet Ukrainian academic institutional pluralism. The Historical Society of Nestor the Chronicler and the Kyiv Archeographic Commission were integrated into the Academy structures in 1921, and the Ukrainian Scientific Society was merged with it in 1923.

The 1920s were definitely the high point in the development of Soviet Ukrainian social sciences and humanities. This was made possible because of the official party-state nationality policy which favoured 'indigenization' (*korinizatsia*). Moscow instituted this policy in the non-Russian republics, because the regime felt that it lacked sufficient support there. The aim of 'indigenization' was to help the Soviet regime 'take root' among the non-Russians. One of the means used was to foster the development of non-Russian culture and their knowledge-making institutions. In Ukraine, the policy became known as 'Ukrainization' (*ukrainizatsia*). This policy acted, among other things, as an incentive for émigré scholars, for example Mykola Hrushevs'kyi, to return to Ukraine and to become involved in the development of Ukrainian scholarship in general and Ukrainian studies in particular. Ukrainian social knowledge was constructed in various institutions. The most important of them was the Historical-Philological Branch of the Academy. During the Ukrainization interval, this branch, with its 39 commissions and adjunct institutions, played the leading role in fostering fundamental research on Ukrainian issues. The pinnacle of its accomplishments was during the 1924-28 period. The key institutions of the branch were the Chairs of Ukrainian Studies in Kyiv and Kharkiv. The Socio-Economic Branch, with its emphasis on economics, demography, sociology and legal studies, was also important. It allowed for the development of the emerging social sciences, and the production of a country-specific social knowledge, based on Ukrainian socio-cultural knowledge. Ukrainization effectively meant that the broad *ukrainoznavstvo* approach became a mechanism for integrating the humanities and the social sciences into the mainstream.

Diversified historiographical schools appeared during this era of enterprise in Ukrainization and Ukrainian studies. The previous 'populist' or cultural school, and the 'statist' one, witnessed further development. A certain degree of convergence occurred between them. Socio-economic, historical-legal and Marxist schools facilitated the process. Yet this highly pluralist historiography had one factor in common. All schools of thought acknowledged the notion of a singular and linear national historical development as constituting an undisputed social fact. The authorization of this concept meant that all Ukrainian cultural, social, nationhood, political and statehood issues, past and present, could be legitimately analysed as being unequivocally nationally idiosyncratic. The attendant historiographical schemata, narrative scripts and myths, which took this peculiarity for granted, were not a contentious issue, as in tsarist times. The political spin-off of the scholarly accomplishments and social knowledge of the 1920s was that they were instrumental in helping to consolidate not only a horizontal-national Ukrainian identity and national consciousness, but also a horizontal political sense of belonging. Thus, during the Ukrainization era, the social sciences and the humanities ministered not only to the forging of an 'ethnic nation', but also to the construction of a 'civic nation'.[10]

The Demise of Early Soviet-Era Ukrainian Social Knowledge

The advent of Stalinism contributed towards an assimilationist nationality policy and the condemnation of Ukrainization. The national revival of the 1920s was terminated. From 1929 on, the independent regime of the Academy of Sciences was ended. It was transformed into a regional branch of the USSR Academy of Sciences, with limited power and resources. In addition, the entire structure, all-Union and Ukrainian, was made subservient to the political agendas of the regime. The cognitive structures and the social knowledge produced in the 1920s by the Historical-Philological Branch of the Ukrainian Academy were condemned for having fostered a social knowledge allegedly coloured by an ideology of 'bourgeois nationalism'. In fact, all of the Ukrainian studies of the Ukrainization era, but especially historiography, were explicitly singled out as having actually contributed towards some purported Ukrainian separatist movement, intent on seceding from the USSR. The Historical-Philological Branch, as well as most of the Branch commissions, were liquidated in 1930. What remained was absorbed into the remaining Socio-Economics Branch, until it, too, was abolished in 1934. Totally new and much more constricted structures appeared in 1936. The History, Philosophy and Law, and Economics Branches, but also Literature and Language, were lumped together as social sciences, and were placed under the auspices of a new Social Science Section (*sektsiya*) of the Academy. Nevertheless, there was no room in the Ukrainian social sciences for sociology or political science. These were excluded on ideological grounds as being 'bourgeois' in nature. The once rival Ukrainian Institute of Marxism-Leninism, with its Marxist-Leninist frameworks and social knowledge, was also condemned for having produced 'bourgeois nationalist' scholarship in Ukrainian studies. This institute was first transformed, in 1931, into the All-Ukrainian Association of Marxist-Leninist Scientific Research Institutes, and then in 1936 it ceased to exist as a separate entity. It was incorporated into the History Branch of the Social Science Section of the Academy. With the Soviet annexation of Western Ukraine, the Shevchenko Scientific Society which had been established there in the nineteenth century was abolished in 1940 and dissolved into the structures of the Academy. The newly established History Branch of the Academy was therefore an amalgam of the remnants of numerous pre-existing institutions and commissions. It was but a pale version of the former Historical-Philological Branch, as most of its research associates were arrested and executed for allegedly subscribing to the ideologically disavowed mind-set of Ukrainian 'bourgeois nationalism'.[11]

During World War II the Ukrainian social sciences were enjoined to produce 'applied' research deemed helpful in the war effort. This was intertwined with a policy that allowed for a restricted preoccupation with Ukrainian topics. However, at the end of the war, even these lacklustre studies were also assigned the epitaph of 'bourgeois nationalism'. This contributed to the loss in the social sciences, and in the social knowledge that was generated by this field of knowledge, of virtually all national characteristics and content. But while real Ukrainian scholarship was being eradicated in Soviet Ukraine, it continued outside of the USSR. For example, the originally Prague-based Ukrainian Free University was re-established in West Germany. The Ukrainian Free Academy of Sciences was first set up in the same country but later transferred to the USA. Branches of a renewed Shevchenko Scientific Society re-emerged in Western Europe, the USA and Canada. In addition to these and other émigré institutions, Ukrainian studies centres came into being within the confines of western institutions of higher learning, such as, for example, the Harvard Ukrainian Research Institute and the Canadian Institute of Ukrainian Studies, at the University of Alberta. These academic bodies allowed the continuation and development of Ukrainian social sciences and humanities, including historiography.

As to the institutional aspects of Soviet Ukrainian scholarship, the Academy was subject to a complicated system of controls and supervision. These institutional arrangements seriously hampered the development of the social sciences and social knowledge. Not only was the Academy of Sciences of the Ukrainian SSR subordinated to the USSR Academy of Sciences, but it was simultaneously placed under the UkSSR Council of Ministers, as well as under the Communist Party of Ukraine (CPU). It, and not the universities or other institutes of higher education (VUZy), continued as the centre of social-scientific scholarship. The regime favoured 'applied' social research over basic research. This was in order to further its political agenda, even though this social knowledge was but a simulacrum of reality. In fact, it was of little 'practical' value, and lacked academic rigour. The quality of Soviet Ukrainian scholarship also suffered from its isolation from the methodological developments and innovations in the outside world. Unlike in the Russian case, the Ukrainian social sciences were constantly enjoined to be vigilant for manifestations of 'bourgeois nationalism'. Until the demise of the USSR, the Social Science Section of the Academy continued to supervise an amorphous domain of social sciences, which covered the History Branch and Philosophy and Law as well as the Literature, Languages and Fine Arts Branches.[12]

The Specifics of Soviet Ukrainian Historiography as Social Knowledge

The peculiar Soviet social science regime that was instituted after the demise of Ukrainization continued with few 'liberalizing' intervals until the advent of glasnost in the late 1980s. As public policies and scholarship were closely intertwined in the former USSR, the CPSU imposed all-Union directives on the social sciences, and the CPU layered on additional directives specifically relevant to the Ukrainian social sciences. The framework established by the party was meant to be a 'system of significance' designed to control the activities of the social scientists. As such, the scheme laid down rules according to which the social world was to be made intelligible. Methodological positions in the Soviet Ukrainian social sciences were simultaneously political arguments intended to produce an authoritative, 'bureaucratic' and 'politically correct' knowledge. The top-down approach relied on new schemata, narrative scripts, signs and symbols, as well as political myths.

There was also a specific form of discourse in the Soviet social sciences. It reinforced the framework and the bureaucratic form of knowledge itself. The discourse was an 'officialese' and encoded *langue de bois* of power. It emphasized the idea of a total textuality of reality. Only the texts produced by Soviet social scientists were considered to contain an 'authoritative' and an 'authentic' account of reality. There was little concern about whether these texts corresponded to the 'empirical reality' of the real world or not. No concern was shown as to the possibility of textualism distorting reality. This stereotyped language, with its referential signs, symbols and myths, created a social knowledge that was therefore a mere simulacrum of reality. In that respect it contributed towards a curious 'power of emptiness' of the social sciences. Employing the technique of a variety of binary opposites, the Soviet social science discourse actually transformed the social sciences themselves into a 'game'. Nevertheless, it was possible for social scientists to learn ways to manipulate this discourse so as to indicate, to those steeped in the *langue de bois*, disagreements with the top-down imposed frames, interpretations, and so on. This would eventually allow for the development of alternative ways of looking at the social facts, and even frames of analysis, while giving the appearance of conforming to the directives concerning the social sciences, the 'officialese' language and the textual simulation of reality. To sum up, the official cognitive structure of Soviet social science and social knowledge contained normative, explanatory, prescriptive and emotive elements, even though the entire enterprise was divorced from socio-cultural knowledge.[13]

Soviet social cognizance resorted to the repeated restatement of regime-invented 'general tendencies' and 'objective laws' (*zakonomirnos'ti*) allegedly governing socio-historical development, with no concern for proving or disproving them. These apparently Soviet but essentially Russocentric formulations ignored the peculiarities of the non-Russian nations comprising the USSR. In addition, structural determinism and a fixation on collectivities pre-empted a centring on agency and the individual. Not only was the Soviet political regime involved in the politics of social science knowledge, but it also held a monopoly in determining the status of the social scientists. Positions and privileges were distributed along regime-established rules and norms. The above-described institutional arrangements of scholarship ensured a close proximity of the social scientists to the party state apparatus. Thus the Soviet knowledge regime, its cognitive frames and social knowledge itself embodied politics and power relations. The social sciences were claimed to be 'scientific', and 'objective', because, and only because, they supposedly reflected 'class positions' and 'party-mindedness' (*partiinist*) as determined by the CPSU. This notion of 'scientism' had absolutely nothing in common with Western social science notions of 'objectivity' and 'disinterested' inquiry. Consequently, according to the instrumentalist stipulations of Soviet social science, social scientists were expected, among other things, to uphold and defend the party, the regime and the territorial integrity of the USSR as a state.[14]

Most of the directives in the social sciences were applicable to historiography. Aware of its potential power, Soviet authorities placed much emphasis on harnessing and controlling historiography. Ukrainian historiography was singled out as being potentially disruptive of the system. All of Ukrainian scholarship, including historiography of the Ukrainization period, was declared to be not only 'bourgeois nationalist' in nature, but actually conducive to political separatism from the USSR. That is why so much effort was put into undoing the 'nationalizing discourse' of the previous eras, and diligently supervising present-day scholarship. The idea of a singular Ukrainian historical development and the accompanying national solidarity myths were simply reviled. Having condemned the particular nature of Ukrainian social sciences, a standard scheme was imposed in 1934 on non-Russian historiography. However, this total regimentation became fully operational only after the second world war. The CPSU and the CPU directives indicated how Ukrainian history, society and polity ought to be conceptualized; which events, facts, persons and institutions were politically 'acceptable' and which were not. The newly imposed premise specified that Ukrainian socio-historical development was an integral component of Russian development, and that this had been the case even before Ukraine became a part of the Tsarist Empire.[15]

This social science frame was predicated on a new assimilationist nationality policy. The social sciences were to transmute the nationality policy and other directives into social knowledge. This was designed to help undo past scholarly contributions, especially those of the 1920s, in the realm of Ukrainian nation- and state-building. The partiality of the cognitive structure was crucial in determining what constituted a Ukrainian national 'historical memory' acceptable to the regime, and what myths, symbols and icons were politically opportune. The social sciences were expected to contribute towards 'social engineering' by establishing which Ukrainian social facts were to be selectively underlined and which ones were to be ignored, omitted from the collective memory or even deliberately falsified. The Soviet version of the 'amelioration' of Ukrainian society through the social sciences paradoxically meant that the social sciences would now help to 'de-construct' the sense of national belonging, so as to produce a people lacking a distinct horizontal identity. Social cognizance was to contribute towards the transformation of the population of Ukraine into a new horizontal 'imagined community', that of the 'Soviet people' (*radyans'kyi narod*). In addition, this process would also soft-pedal Soviet Ukrainian vertical-political identity. On the contrary, it stressed exclusively an all-Union vertical-political belonging. A cluster of signs, symbols and myths, such as the 'Soviet homeland', 'Soviet fatherland', 'Soviet patriotism', 'Soviet way of life', and the like, were to accompany this Soviet-style 'nation- and state-building'. A 'drawing together' (*zblyzhennya*) of the peoples of the USSR was expected to occur, with Russian as their 'second native language' (*druha ridna mova*).[16]

In order to arrive at this assimilationist end-state, the party directives made it imperative for the Soviet Ukrainian social sciences to develop a politically induced myth of an alleged common ancestry for Ukrainians, Russians and Belorussians. This was the notion of the *drevnorus'ka narodnist'* ('old Rus' people'). Yet, simultaneously, this alleged common Slavic proto-nation or people was often used to mean only 'old Russian'. The principal intimation of this myth was that in contradistinction to the Ukrainian nation, the Russians enjoyed a direct lineage from this *drevnorus'ka narodnist'*. In addition, the genesis of the modern Russian nation was claimed to have preceded that of the Ukrainian one. Consequently, the social sciences were required to subscribe to the idea that the Russian nation was more 'fulfilled' and 'accomplished' than the Ukrainian community. In simplified and vulgarized terminology, the Russians were assigned the role of an 'elder brother' (*starshyi brat*) throughout history. Furthermore, the Russian state was conceptualized as being an immediate successor of the Kyivan Rus' state. At no time could Ukraine claim such political institutional lineage or legitimacy. Finally, this myth of Ukrainian evolution from a single form of communality – that of the 'old Rus' people' – to that of the 'Soviet people' was allegedly governed by one unique and overriding goal: that of an 'eternal and inviolable reunification' (*vozyednannya*) of the Ukrainians with Russia, even when they had become a distinct nation.[17]

This mental frame left no room for any notion of an independent Ukrainian statehood. The subject was made politically taboo by the insistence that the non-Russians, Ukrainians included, had given it up, by entering voluntarily into the Tsarist Empire. This idea was partially covered by the myth of the salutary 'lesser evil' formula. By being absorbed by the Tsarist Empire the non-Russians had supposedly been spared from being incorporated by neighbouring states. The positive aspect of belonging to the empire was that the Russians allegedly 'took care' of the non-Russians. In addition, the myth claimed that, of all the peoples, only the Ukrainians had entered into an exceptionally close melding with Russia. The others had simply 'united' (*obyednannya* or *priyednannya*) with the Russians. In the case of the Ukrainians, it was a 'return to the fold', one of a total 'reunification' (*vozyednannya*). A supposedly 'unbreakable' and 'perpetual' bond had developed between the Ukrainians and the Russians, thereby precluding even any thought of Ukrainian secession. In order to reinforce this point, Stalinist historiography reviled, and in the process de-legitimized, past Ukrainian statehoods, such as for example the seventeenth-century Cossack Hetmanate, Zaporizhs'ka Sich, and the 1917-20 polity. Social sciences were enjoined either to avoid the subject of past pro-independence movements, or to condemn the secessionist attempts of the early eighteenth and twentieth centuries.[18]

According to this official prism for visualizing Ukrainian historical development, the Ukrainians were also presented as having gained from their association with Russian culture, meaning that an 'elder brother' myth was also applicable to cultural matters. In order to make this acceptable it was acknowledged that the Ukrainians were in fact subject only to tsarist, but not to Russian, political and cultural colonialism and oppression. It was denied that the economic colonialization of Ukraine had ever existed at all. This additional dimension explained that since Ukraine formed an integral part of the centralized imperial economy it had benefited from this situation. Furthermore, Ukraine was claimed to have experienced generally positive economic consequences, for the Tsarist Empire had effectively facilitated Ukraine's integration into the world economy. The implication was that an independent Ukraine would have been much worse off — the so-called 'lesser evil' formula. Paradoxically, the integration of the tsarist economy itself into the world economy was decried for having limited Russian independence.[19]

The Emergence of an Alternative Perspective in Soviet Ukrainian Social Knowledge

The partial de-Stalinization that began in the mid 1950s and continued until the early 1970s loosened the general political regimentation of Ukraine, and led to a mild 'national revival'. Even though the bulk of this renewal was oriented towards a preoccupation with the issue of the demise of the Ukrainian language during the Stalinist era, it spilled over onto the humanities and the social sciences. Politicians, public intellectuals and academics ridiculed the pathetic state of Ukrainian scholarship in general and historiography in particular. Ukrainian social knowledge was said to have become entirely 'a-national', to the point where the national history was a 'history devoid of history'. However, unlike in the 1920s, when the majority of Ukrainian scholars in the humanities and social sciences rejected the official tsarist schemes, and turned towards the development of cognitive frames that were rooted in national socio-cultural knowledge, this did not occur in the 1960s. It appears that Soviet political socialization had been successful. In addition, the fresh memory of Stalinism and the regime-specific institutionalization and ideologization of the social science profession all worked in favour of the status quo. Consequently, two unequal groupings emerged in the humanities and the social sciences, during this political 'thaw' and 'national revival'. A comparable differentiation came into existence in the realm of historiography.[20]

The majority continued their position as 'detractors' of anything Ukrainian. They subscribed to the notion of the Ukrainian historical process as found on the Stalinist mental map. These detractors insisted on the need to re-impose rigid administrative controls over the academic institutional structures, so as to weed out any alternative reflections on historiography. This majority orientation maintained that the main task of the social sciences was to be instrumental in supporting the political regime. That is why the detractors stressed that the social sciences in general, and historiography in particular, had to continue to subscribe to the principle of *partiinist'*. Vigilance was to be shown by the social scientists in uncovering manifestations of what was called 'objectivism' (*obyektivizm*) and 'revisionism', as well as of Ukrainian 'bourgeois nationalism'. All of these features were claimed to be evident in the scholarship of those attempting to reassess Ukrainian history, culture, politics and society. In addition, Soviet Ukrainian social sciences, and especially historiography, were to be instrumental in disclaiming and repudiating the cognitive maps and social knowledge of both Western 'bourgeois' scholars and Ukrainian émigré 'bourgeois nationalist falsifiers'.[21]

The minority orientation in historiography was that of the 'rehabilitators' of things Ukrainian. They decried the methodological poverty of the social sciences and the lack of a relational, dialectical and especially a 'concrete' (*konkretnyi*) contextual approach in social knowledge in general. *Partiinist'* was rejected not only as hindering the emergence of a normal and objective social science, but also as stifling the creativity of the social scientists. A plurality of approaches, cognitive frames and even schools of thought was advocated in Ukrainian historiography. The imposed – Stalinist – standard scheme for depicting the Ukrainian historical process was repudiated for its Russian ethnocentrism. Emphasis was now to be placed on the so-called 'concrete' circumstances of Ukrainian historical development. This Aesopic formulation indicated the need to shift from an over-emphasis on structure in social knowledge to some recognition of agency. The social scientists were expected to discover specifically Ukrainian 'law-like regularities' (*zakonomirnosti*) governing Ukrainian development. Failure to accomplish this was said to invoke a future 'judgement of history' on Ukrainian social knowledge. This effectively meant that the hitherto falsified and truncated image of nationhood was totally unacceptable and that a continuation of this endeavour would be seen by future social scientists as unacceptable. The rehabilitators insisted not only on improving the quality of scholarship – they were also concerned that this renewed scholarship, especially in the realm of historiography, ought to contribute to the construction, or the reconstruction, of collective Ukrainian horizontal national identities, damaged by the Stalinist scheme. In this respect, the rehabilitators pursued a 'nationalizing discourse' with a 'national project' in mind. Finally, they may have had a more ambitious design concerning the renewed historiography. They claimed that it would eventually come to constitute a kind of Ukrainian 'political thought' (*politychna dumka*).[22]

The rehabilitative historiography proceeded to resurrect much of the previously acquired social knowledge, including nineteenth-century and early Soviet-era Ukrainian historiography. This historiography insisted on several features essential to the Ukrainian developmental process. The Ukrainian national historical process in general, and nation-building in particular, was claimed to have been a 'bottom-up' one, with culture and political ideas playing a primary role. This was in contradistinction to the allegedly 'top-down', state-centred Russian process. The other singular Ukrainian characteristic was the role of 'national liberation' in Ukrainian historical development. It was claimed that this feature was absent in the Russian case. Finally, unlike in its northern neighbour, there was assumed to have been little class differentiation in Ukraine. This alleged specificity of the Ukrainians implied the idea of national unity. This singular feature of the Ukrainians was then contrasted to the supposed lack of this attribute in the class-ridden Russians. These 'counter myths' debunked the Stalinist ones. Other rejected myths included the 'leading role' assigned to the Russians, their 'elder brother' status, the 'lesser evil', and 'eternal friendship'. The questioning of the 'common origin' myth and that of 'reunification' was rather more calculating. The entire compilation of rehabilitative counter-myths was implied to offer a more 'authentic' cognizance, eminently in line with Ukrainian cultural knowledge. It was thus insinuated that official Soviet social knowledge provided a falsified notion of reality. The historiography's connoted group rights and a community's historical entitlement to culture, as well as to territory, were of the utmost importance.[23]

Ukrainian national liberation was depicted as constituting the very essence of Ukrainian development. This was the case because all Ukrainian history was claimed to have been oriented towards overcoming the political, social, cultural and economic colonial situation imposed on it by its neighbours, especially tsarist Russia. National liberation was considered to have been a truly holistic national experience which united the entire people. This blatant disregard of class analysis was rationalized on the grounds of a supposedly weak class distinction, as well as foreign domination. Hence the idea of a supposedly holistic and undifferentiated 'spirit of the people' (*narodnist*) which imbued the entire nation and its political activity. The notion of *narodnist* implied a latent myth of a superior status for Ukrainian culture, compared with Russian culture. This populist perspective was contrasted to the role of 'great men' in the Russian case. The key aspect of the idea of national liberation was that it allowed the rehabilitators to raise the question as to the end-state of this process. Both Ukrainian nationhood and statehood were presented as having been achieved at different points in time, by means of national liberation. This was the closest that the rehabilitative historiography would come to the question of the outcome of the process of national liberation and the issue of secession. The historiography also hinted at the inherently Ukrainian features of Kyivan Rus'. The seventeenth- and eighteenth-century Cossack statehood (*derzhavnist*) received special attention. Tsarist policies were blamed for the demise of the Cossack polities. There were ambiguous formulations as to the achievement of national liberation with the establishment of the independent statehood of 1917-20, and to some extent the Soviet state that supplemented it. All were implied to have been the end products of a long national liberation process. However, when the Soviet regime was discussed, emphasis was placed primarily on the positive consequences of the Ukrainization era. In a sense, the rehabilitators brought to the fore historical grievances about the lack of specifically Ukrainian political institutions, as well as demands for rectificatory justice.[24]

The Return to 'Normalcy' in Soviet Ukrainian Social Knowledge

In the early 1970s this limited 'national revival' was put to an end. Scholars associated with the revival and the rehabilitative historiography were purged from academic institutions. Not only were they dismissed, but many were also debarred from publishing. 'Bourgeois nationalist' deviation, 'methodological errors' and the 'idealization of the past' were again detected in the Ukrainian social sciences, especially in historiography. The very notion of Ukrainian national liberation as a normative concept was discredited. Care was taken to condemn the role of the Ukrainian Cossacks in this process, and the Cossack statehood itself was ridiculed. The rehabilitative historiography was also denounced for alleged idealization of the acquisitions of nineteenth-century and early Soviet Ukrainian scholarship. According to the detractors, who now fully controlled the social sciences, the rehabilitators had committed a most serious error by failing to extol all the advantages for Ukraine of its reunification with Russia. A neo-Stalinist frame was again re-imposed on all of Ukrainian historiography. The nature of the ever politically sensitive idea of Ukrainian historical development was now more restricted in scope. What emerged was an image of a process lacking any national singularity – at best it was an evolution from the 'old Rus' people', via the 'reunification' with the Russians, to the 'Soviet people'.[25]

The dominant regime of social cognizance that was re-introduced was not only oriented towards scholarship, but was also instrumental in the further alteration of Ukrainian horizontal-national identity. The Russocentric schemata, narrative scripts, myths, signs and symbols inherent in official social knowledge were apparently internalized by a good portion of the general public. This contributed towards a weakening of their sense of national belonging and contributed towards liminality and a somewhat colonized mentality. This social knowledge was instrumental in eliminating significant portions of the national 'we' from Ukrainian collective memory. The remaining fragments of the national 'we' were subject to 'a-Ukrainian', if not 'anti-Ukrainian' interpretations. The end result of all of this was that by the late 1980s a sizeable portion of the Ukrainian population, including the eponymous one, lacked an unproblematic and widely shared national identity. Some inhabitants of Ukraine regarded themselves as being simultaneously Ukrainian and Russian. Others had already undergone an identity shift from Ukrainian to 'Soviet people'. If it is assumed that a sense of collective and personal identity leads to the articulation of certain political values and priorities, the weakly developed national 'belongingness' helped create a population that was characterized by an unarticulated sense of politicized national identity. The very idea of Ukraine's secession from the USSR was probably unfathomable for most of the 'a-national' inhabitants of the Ukrainian Soviet Socialist Republic.[26]

This state of affairs continued in the social sciences and in historiography until the late 1980s. However, the rehabilitative historiographical scholarship did not disappear entirely during the 1970s and 1980s. It continued to exist, but the subscribing social scientists who were allowed to publish were extremely careful in their formulations so as to avoid being labelled 'bourgeois nationalists'. Much of their work consisted in publishing historical Ukrainian archival material. Little annotated, it was intent on having the 'facts speak for themselves'. This oblique process of rehabilitating Ukrainian culture and history was understood only by those initiated in this approach. This rehabilitative endeavour was also a tacit way of disagreeing with the official rhetoric, while going through the motions of apparently following it. The Aesopian language used to dissent from the dominant paradigm, and from social knowledge that denied any national singularity, stressed that the 'Ukrainian social fact' had been 'insufficiently understood' and thus 'required further study'. The nature of the Ukrainian historical process, the connection between Kyivan Rus' and the Ukrainian nation and the essence of the seventeenth- and eighteenth century Cossack polity exemplified these allegedly 'insufficiently understood' aspects of Ukrainian nationhood and statehood. Therefore, the impact of the rehabilitative scholarship was not totally lost. Its knowledge and 'nationalizing discourse' inspired a limited audience, that of the Ukrainian public intellectuals. Some of them operated within the political system, while others were in the dissident movement. Most dissidents extolled the idea of the universal human condition, human rights and justice. A segment of this movement would undergo an evolution from cultural rights to concerns with political autonomy, and even the idea of secession from the USSR. This radicalization of attitude actually occurred during the 1970s, a period of most severe repression. It was then that the dissidents became engrossed with the subject of Ukrainian 'martyrdom' and national 'ethnocide' and, in the process, evolved a lachrymose genre.[27]

Political Changes in Soviet Ukraine

Ukraine demurred as one of the last bastions in the USSR opposed to perestroika (*perebudova* in Ukrainian). The authorities in Kyiv made sure that, compared with other parts of the USSR, glasnost (*hlasnist'* in Ukrainian) and *demokratyzatsiya* were slow to arrive in Ukraine. However, the way the USSR political centre mishandled the Chernobyl disaster, as well as the revelations of Stalinist atrocities in Ukraine, contributed towards a general dissipation of Soviet legitimacy in Ukraine. Notwithstanding, the CPU remained passive in the light of these developments. In fact the party continued to harass societal actors advocating transformation, transparency and democracy. This stance contributed towards the exit of many public intellectuals from the CPU. When the regime did reluctantly allow non-communist civic associations and cultural fronts, public intellectuals along with dissidents forged a national democratic movement. But unlike the situation in other Soviet republics, the CPU originally refused to come to an understanding with the national democrats.

An alteration in party policy would become evident only after a leadership reshuffles in Kyiv in the late 1980s. The new leadership finally accepted perestroika. However, the issue of what was to be done about the erosion of legitimacy and power at the USSR centre, and a similar loss of power and legitimacy in Ukraine, badly divided the CPU. The majority – that is, the 'orthodox' or 'conservative' faction – either refused to face the problem, or remained inactive. The 'liberal' portion of the CPU nomenclature came to the realization that, if left unchecked, the situation would inevitably undermine their privileged position. With the overriding preoccupation of holding onto power, the 'liberal' faction focused on the idea that the UkSSR was not getting its 'fair share'. In practice this implied the advocacy of a greater 'concern' with Ukrainian issues and policies. This furthering of the 'liberal' faction's own agenda inevitably challenged the USSR centre. In the process of flexing their political muscle, these 'national communists' proceeded to appropriate portions of the national democrats' concern with the Ukrainian 'national question'.[28]

A New Reassessment of Ukrainian Social Knowledge

It was in this climate of democratization and transparency that a mildly rehabilitative viewpoint manifested itself among public intellectuals in general, as well as in the social sciences. This attitude would again, as in the 1960s, decry the sorry state of Ukrainian historiography. According to the public intellectuals who subscribed to this orientation, the very image of Ukraine had become totally diluted and unfocused. The public intellectuals claimed that no construction of a positive collective or individual national identity was possible as long as the institutionalized Ukrainian collective memory was presented according to the official Soviet approach. Their main contention was that this rhetoric was a-Ukrainian, if not anti-Ukrainian, in nature. Furthermore, it was claimed that individual or collective national identity-building could not flourish if Ukrainian history was presented as but a series of gaping 'blank spots' (*bili plyamy*). Counter-myths were suggested to displace the imposed ones.

For example, the notion of a common Ukrainian-Russian development was to be replaced by the idea of a singular and specifically Ukrainian historical process. This echoed earlier rehabilitative formulations. The 'brotherhood' myth was to be exchanged for one stressing the adverse nature of Russian, tsarist and Soviet polities. Closely connected to this idea were the notions of the 'martyr-dom' and 'ethnocide' of the Ukrainian nation, which had allegedly been brought about by Russian and Soviet imperialism and colonialism. The 'old Rus' people' myth was questioned as Ukrainian national roots were traced to the Kyivan Rus'. There was a manifestation of a historical grievance caused by the loss of the Cossack Hetmanate and *Zaporizhs'ka Sich*. The goals of the seventeenth-century Ukrainian association with Russia were said to have been limited in scope and not to have included the idea of 'reunification'. More significantly, it was claimed that Russia had failed to respect this original, limited political alliance. In addition, the rehabilitative voices called for a reassessment of all the different past statehoods, including Kyivan Rus', the Cossack polities and the early twentieth-century independent regimes. Historical political figures such as, for example, Mazepa and Hrushevs'kyi, who had each pursued independence-seeking policies in their own era, were to be reinstated. There were even calls for the development of a specifically Ukrainian socio-humanities field of knowledge that would focus primarily on things Ukrainian.[29]

Ukrainian Independence

Ukrainian independence came about almost as an unpredicted contingency of dis-creet Soviet political events. In the period immediately before independence, the 'national communists' made the UkSSR legislature their main political forum, as the CPU Politburo remained in the hands of the 'conservative communists'. With the help of a small group of national democrats, they proceeded to transform this institution into something resembling a real national parliament. In addition, the presidency of the Presidium of the UkSSR Supreme Soviet was made into a de fac-to presidency of the republic. The rhetoric justifying these institutional changes underlined the need for the UkSSR to attain greater latitude from the USSR cen-tre. This CPU faction was crucial in having this institution adopt a law in 1989 making Ukrainian the official state language. Of more consequence was the July 1990 Declaration on the State Sovereignty of Ukraine. Basing themselves on the principle that Ukrainian sovereignty overrode all-Union sovereignty, the parlia-ment and its presidency refused to sign the Union Treaty revised in 1991. The 'national communists' considered the new treaty unacceptable on account of its unjust centralism. At about this time, the UkSSR Supreme Soviet created a new political institution, that of the President of the UkSSR. This institution had the vested power to disregard all-Union legislation. Yet paradoxically, the Kyiv leadership's hesitant stance during the abortive August 1991 coup symbolized well the Ukrainian nomenclature's quandary. Until the very end of the USSR they remained torn between loyalty to the centre and the desire to assert the UkSSR's prerogatives. Nevertheless, in the aftermath of the coup, the 'national communists' did manage to 'reinvent' themselves as a national 'party of power'.[30]

The principle of national determination, inherent in the rehabilitative nation-to-state model of Ukrainian development, was used by the national democrats to justify Ukrainian secession or, as they preferred to call it, Ukrainian 'national liberation'. Much of the national democrats' approach to things Ukrainian echoed the image of Ukraine as expounded both by Ukrainian historiography of the 1920s and by the rehabilitators of the 1960s. As for the 'national communists', the actual decision-makers at the time of independence, their rationalization of this act can be deduced from their pre-independence posture. It rested on the idea that the circumstances in which Ukraine found itself within the USSR were basically 'unjust'. The Ukrainian government therefore affirmed the right of a Soviet administrative unit to escape from an implied situation of injustice. The 'national communists' intertwined this idea of the 'state rights' of a Soviet ethno-administrative unit with those of the right of national self-determination, borrowed from the national democrats. This compounded apology for independence legitimized the self-interest of the 'national communists'. It also helped them to safeguard political power in their own hands. While the 'conservative' faction of the CPU remained indecisive, the 'national communists' proceeded with the August 1991 Declaration of Independence, an act overwhelmingly validated by a nation-wide referendum in December 1991. The referendum, as a political act, gave popular legitimization to Ukrainian secession. Notwithstanding the endorsement of independence, a sizeable portion of the population who voted for Ukrainian independence did so not as an affirmation of their politicized Ukrainian national identity, but as a manifestation of their economic wants and needs. A separate Ukrainian polity was perceived as being more capable of delivering economic benefits than the USSR.[31]

Contemporary Social Knowledge and Politics

Since the newly independent state lacked proper myths, signs and symbols, as the Soviet ones were discredited and debunked, the government resurrected signs and symbols that had until very recently been derided, ridiculed, condemned and forbidden, as being allegedly Ukrainian 'bourgeois nationalist'. In declaring the anthem, the blue-and-yellow flag and the trident associated with the Ukrainian statehood of 1917-20 as national/state symbols, the public authorities established a symbolically effective myth of political continuity. The task of elaborating more malleable symbols of nationhood and statehood was left to public intellectuals. The denouement of this avocation was to be within the general context of what could be described as a 'top-down' induced governmental 'nationalizing project'. It was intent not only on ensuring institutional state-building, but also on inviting a national cultural revival that would comprise the propagation of the humanities and the social sciences, particularly historiography. The malleable symbols that were to be constructed by the public intellectuals would provide an additional legitimization for the new regime. The various pliant symbols of nationhood could also help to mould a common vision and to mobilize the population around agreed principles. Social knowledge containing mouldable symbols would, furthermore, aid in the transmutation of the Soviet-vintage, 'quasi' or 'virtual' statehood into a real one, as well as in the permutation of the Soviet-era nationhood, which was experiencing similar difficulties, into a genuine one. Social cognizance would thus help in the construction of both horizontal-national and vertical-political identities. There was a resemblance in all of this to the Ukrainian public intellectuals' mission during the long nineteenth century, the difference being that their undertaking then had been primarily one of ensuring a nation-to-state mutation, while in the context of an independent Ukraine it was a state-to-nation endeavour.[32]

Numerous reasons have so far impeded the accomplishment of the 'nationalizing project', the achievement of a genuine cultural revival, the development of scholarship, and the elaboration of a 'national ameliorative' standpoint. The emerging Ukrainian civil society has remained characterized by a 'flat landscape', with amorphous and weak societal associations, few of which have managed to promote a national revival or the renewal of social knowledge. The extremely serious and on-going governmental budgetary crisis has meant that the state has been incapable of providing a cultural renewal or a regeneration of scholarship. Instead of the cultural revival that was expected during the brief euphoria following independence, Ukraine has actually witnessed the reverse. The lack of professionalism in certain social science fields has remained a knotty point. For example, Soviet-era economists lacked proper preparation, and the professional training of the contemporary political scientist is wanting. Former advocates of 'scientific communism', as well as those working in the field of history of the USSR or the CPSU, publicists, and so on, have proclaimed themselves political scientists. This has had an adverse effect on the restitution of proper social scientific scholarship. A more serious issue has been the continuity of Soviet-era academic institutions with essentially detractive, Soviet-era research personnel, who basically still possess a Soviet-era mind-set. Few of the formerly dismissed knowledge-generating social scientists of the rehabilitative orientation are likely to be reintegrated into academic institutions. As for the Academy, despite its name changes – first to the Ukrainian Academy of Sciences, in 1992, and then to the National Academy of Sciences of Ukraine, in 1994 – there have been few substantive changes in terms of its structure, direction or approach. Nevertheless, a handful of new institutes have been layered onto the old structure. The new institution-building is illustrated by the Institute of Archeography and Source Studies and the Institute of Oriental Studies. However, the Academy still remains the co-ordinating body for social science and humanities research, even though the universities are starting to affirm themselves in this domain. There are cases where individuals and even entire institutions have undergone some shifts in orientation, from 'class analysis' to a preoccupation with nationhood. For example, those social scientists who were formerly responsible for 'uncovering' alleged Ukrainian 'bourgeois nationalist falsifications' are today the advocates of Ukrainian 'ethno-state studies' (*etnoderzhavoznavsto*). The Institute of History of the CPSU, which throughout the post-war era spearheaded the detractive orientation outside of the Academy of Sciences, has now been renamed the Institute of Political and Ethnonational Studies and has been integrated into the Academy.[33]

Yet, in spite of all of this, it appears at first sight that Ukrainian scholarship has witnessed one of those 'extraordinary' moments in history that heralds a paradigm shift. For example, in much of the historiography there has been an overturning of Soviet-era misconceptions about nationhood as well as the now admitted, Soviet-era blatant deceptions concerning freedom, equality, fraternity of nations, etc. This move has been associated with the resurrection of past schemata, scripts and myths, as markers that make available a more 'preferable' sense of nationhood. The cognition frames and the social knowledge developed by nineteenth-century scholarship, the erudition of the 1920s, and émigré scholarship, appear to be today's principal referentials. There have even been demands for the re-establishment of *ukrainoznavstvo* as an integrative discipline for the entire field of socio-humanities and even of 'scientific nationalism' as a method of scholarship.[34]

Nonetheless, on close reading there is little reason to speak of any paradigm shift. The rehabilitative-oriented humanities specialists and social scientists needed no change in mental maps. Their scholarship was and is in line with their cognitive structures. However, the problem lies with the majority of contemporary social scientists and those in the humanities. They were, after all, detractors in their orientation of the past. Some have remained openly so, others are more covert about it. An important contingent of public intellectuals have not altered their Soviet-vintage system of internalized acquired learning, for it has become something of a habitus for them. Numerous public intellectuals and researchers continue to grasp the world through their past cognitive systems. As in the past, there is much reliance on formal schemes and a collage of quotes. The social knowledge that is produced has but a veneer of rehabilitative schemata, narratives, symbols, and so on. This simulated rehabilitative scholarship therefore retains Soviet-vintage discourse, even though the focus of this rhetoric has cosmetically shifted from class to nation.[35]

Today, consequently, there is still a detractive/rehabilitative type of confrontation evident among public intellectuals. The two distinct cognitive frames have produced types of scholarship that correspond to the assumptions and values of these referentials. Each of these approaches has a built-in 'concerned' point of view, as well as advocacy. The main subject of contention is not the re-assessment of the Soviet past. The nature of the present Ukrainian nation and its statehood are of prime concern. Debates concerning civic and ethnic nationhood issues spill over into the very idea of Ukrainian political independence. The current rehabilitators, even though they indulge in some re-analysis of the Soviet era, are really preoccupied with the advocacy and defence of political independence as an irreversible process. As for the detractors, they are not averse to the idea of undoing this political act, so as to return to arrangements that recall those of the past. Plus ça change, plus c'est la même chose ...[36]

Conclusion

Ukrainian social sciences emerged slowly in rather difficult circumstances. Early nineteenth-century developments were in a socio-humanities vein. Ukrainian studies of that time underlined history as a crucial field of public knowledge. Historical cognizance as social knowledge that was created by public intellectuals was grounded in cultural cognition. Consequently, this social cognition, with its narratives, discourses and myths, was readily acceptable to the Ukrainian community, for it was perceived as corresponding to community cultural knowledge. Ukrainian historiography as a cognitive-normative, explanatory, evaluative and argumentative endeavour was also a manifestation of experiential social knowledge about 'things Ukrainian'. It contributed towards the institutionalization of national memory, Ukrainian nation-building and Ukrainian independence-seeking thought and action.

The advent of the Soviet regime in Ukraine eventually put an end to this form of social knowledge. The Soviet social sciences instituted regime-imposed schemes, narratives and myths. The social knowledge that emerged was politically driven. The institutionalized memory that historiography, for example, offered as social knowledge was a regime-imposed one. Even though the politically governed, Soviet social science cognitive arrangements were essentially in the rationalist tradition, there was more to them. The Soviet hegemonic mental frame and social knowledge tended also to combine abstract, non-representational expressions with 'matter-of-fact' concrete formulations. Eventually, an officially imposed scheme helped to confine the Soviet social scientists' cognizant capabilities concerning the analysis of the past, present and future of Soviet reality. Soviet social knowledge in general, and that of historiography in particular, was a form of 'bureaucratic scholarship'. Even though it was basically deductive, normative, evaluative and prescriptive, and attempted to be instrumental, it was a very peculiar phenomenon. In the last analysis, Soviet social knowledge offered no more than a simulacrum of social reality.

The instrumental aspect of Soviet social science was also quite particular. The social scientists were expected to produce knowledge, with its accompanying myths, that was supposed to reinforce the regime's legitimacy. Consequently, the know-how evolved by the Soviet Ukrainian social sciences explicitly or implicitly extolled the notion of the Ukrainian union, merger or amalgamation with its northern neighbour. This political amalgamation was extolled regardless of whether it was with the tsarist polity or the Soviet one. Soviet Ukrainian historiography was also enjoined to produce scholarship that would not concern itself with the sustenance and reinforcement of a specifically Ukrainian collective identity, outside the context of an all-Soviet one. In order to attain this objective, the official historiography was to truncate and scale down, if not denigrate, the individuality of Ukrainian nationhood and to tone down the thought of a discrete Ukrainian statehood. Ideas of any Ukrainian disaffiliation, separation, breaking away or secession were rebuked by this social knowledge.

Despite the regimented nature of Soviet Ukrainian social sciences, including historiography, some social scientists did break away from the dominant scheme, with its attendant political myths. The alternative mental map was based on past acquisitions of Ukrainian social knowledge, and displayed a high valuation of Ukrainian nationhood and statehood. It was adopted by social scientists intent on rehabilitating things Ukrainian, in contrast to the detractive role played by the official historiography. The social scientists of this mind-set did formulate a positive image of Ukrainianness. The rehabilitative historiography claimed that the detractive orientation was tendentious in its Russian centrism and, as such, was neither truthful nor accurate. Offering Ukrainian centrism, the rehabilitative historiography came to consider the Ukrainian *narod*, Ukrainian culture and national liberation as constituting the basic core of Ukainianness. This historiography therefore offered a 'nationalizing discourse', aimed at promoting the notion of a singular Ukrainian development, and the idea of a distinct nationhood. At the same time, the rehabilitative historiography approached cautiously – and at times only implicitly – the question of Ukrainian political prerogatives. It stressed collective rights, the cultural self-preservation of a people, historical entitlement to a territory and nationhood, and rectificatory justice. The closest it came to the idea of a distinct Ukrainian political entity was when this scholarship expressed the notion of an historical grievance for the lost Ukrainian political institutions of the past.

The essentially deductive, normative, evaluative, prescriptive and committed rehabilitative orientation did suffer periodic reversals and repressions. This partially explains why, by the time of Ukrainian independence in 1991, the rehabilitative social sciences were only a marginal force. The lack of a direct impact of this historiography on the general public may explain why, in that politically crucial time period, Ukraine did not possess a clear, unambiguous and widely shared national identity. In fact, there is little evidence that the official and dominant orientation in the social sciences had any direct bearing on Ukrainian independence. Not only did the official social scientists possess a detractive mind-set towards 'things Ukrainian', but they lacked a positive, policy-oriented instrumental attitude in the realm of public affairs. Instead, the entire bureaucratic social science establishment, as well as the individual social scientists, remained paralysed in the face of the political changes that were taking place in Ukraine. These social scientists were, with rare exceptions, taken unawares by the political events. They followed these events, or at best paralleled them, in the sense that they partially readjusted their rhetorical discourse. However, the Soviet Ukrainian social scientists were not really attuned to the social world or to the Ukrainian 'social fact'. They were prisoners of their carefully constructed and maintained simulacrum of the social world, which passed for social knowledge. Contrary to the official Soviet Ukrainian social sciences, which did not have any impact on the political transformations in Ukraine, the marginalized and often-repressed rehabilitative social knowledge orientation did. The political actions and policies of the political actors who established Ukrainian independence in 1991 were justified and legitimized by the acquisitions of the rehabilitative social knowledge. Therefore this social knowledge may be considered to have been at least a distant cause of Ukrainian independence in the 1990s. In this respect, it was not dissimilar to the impact that early twentieth-century Ukrainian social knowledge had on the Ukraine's first experience of independence in that century.

Today, the rehabilitative schemata, narrative scripts and myths have become commonplace, and enjoy official approval. However, despite the widespread usage of rehabilitative-type formulations, there is little evidence of a profound change in the mind-set of most social scientists. Having learned how to manipulate discourses in the Soviet era, many contemporary Ukrainian social scientists have changed their rhetoric only superficially. They have adopted the officially sponsored discourse, without divesting themselves of the former Soviet mode of thinking. All of this has contributed to the continuation of a basically Soviet style of scholarship, which carries only a veneer of the new, indicating the possibility of cognitive dissonance. This staying power of past social learning is reinforced by the continuity of academic institutional structures, and their staff. A 'bureaucratic' type of social scholarship is still evident, as is the close link between the public authorities and public intellectuals in general, and those in the humanities and the social sciences in particular. The political authorities have imposed on the social sciences the task of formulating policy-oriented social knowledge. This social knowledge is to be politically instrumental in ensuring Ukrainian nation- and state-building. Nonetheless, this venture of linking social knowledge with public policy has been greatly hindered by the general state of crisis in which Ukraine finds itself today. A disparate, traumatized and impoverished society may not be readily receptive or responsive to publicly created social knowledge, narratives, symbols or social engineering.

Notes

1 Bernard Giesen, *Intellectuals and the German Nation*, Cambridge, Cambridge University Press, 1998, pp. 4-10, 28-102; Teun A. van Dijk, *Ideology; A Multidisciplinary Approach*, London, Sage Publications, 1998, pp. 8, 26-28, 34-7; Bjorn Wittrock and Peter Wagner, 'Social Science and the Building of the Early Welfare State. Towards a Comparison of Statist and Non-Statist Western Societies', in Dietrich Rueschmeyer and Theda Skocpol (eds), *States, Social Knowledge, and the Origin of Modern Social Policies*, Princeton, N. J., Princeton University Press, 1996, pp. 91-99.

2 'Ukrainistyka', in *Entsykl'opediya Ukrainoznavstva*, Paris/New York, Molode Zhyttya, 1985, Vol. 11, pp. 203-233.
Note: The word Ukraine will be rendered in English without the definite article, as is the current standard practice. Ukrainian and Russian words are transliterated according to the Library of Congress system. Ukrainian names, when in Ukrainian, are transliterated as such (e.g. Kyiv). However, when a Ukrainian name appears in Russian, it is transliterated in Russian (e.g. Kiev).

3 Yaroslav Isaevych, 'Nashi try vidrodzhennya - ne lyshe zdobutky, ale i vtraty', *Suchasnist'*, No. 12, 1998, pp. 136-143.

4 Omeljan Prytsak and John S. Reshetar Jr, 'The Ukraine and the Dialectics of Nation-Building', in Donald W. Treadgold (ed.), *The Development of the USSR: An Exchange of Views*, Seattle, University of Washington Press, 1964, pp. 211-274.

5 V. H. Sarbei, 'Etapy formuvannya ukrains'koi samosvidomosti (kinets' XVIII - pochatok XX st.)', *Ukrains'kyi istorychnyi zhurnal*, Nos 7-8, 1993, pp. 3-16.

6 Ivan Krypyakevych, *Istoriya Ukrainy*, L'viv, Svit, 1992, pp. 295-299. This is a reprint of a work first published in 1938, *Istoriya Naukovoho Tovarystva im. Shevchenka*, New York/Munich, NTSh, 1949.

7 Van Dijk, pp. 37-51, 66-87, 126-134. Ulf Hedetoft, *Signs of Nations*, Aldershot, Dartmouth, 1995, pp. 178-180, 588; Orest Subtelny, *Ukraine: A History*, Toronto, University of Toronto Press, 1988, pp. 221-331, 237-42, 278-86; Catherine Wanner, *Burden of Dreams*, University Park, Pa., Pennsylvania State University Press, 1998, pp. 37-8, 45-6.

8 Stephen Velychenko, *National History as Cultural Process: The Interpretation of Ukraine's Past in Polish, Ukrainian and Russian Historiography*, Edmonton, Canadian Institute of Ukrainian Studies, 1992, pp. 79-140; N. M. Karamzin's and M. Pogodin's schematas, scripts and myths served as sources for the official tsarist - and, later, Soviet - schemes of history.

[9] Mykhailo Hrushevs'kyi, 'The Traditional Scheme of "Russian" History and the Problem of a Rational Organization of the History of the Eastern Slavs', in *From Kievan Rus' to Modern Ukraine: Formation of the Ukrainian Nation*, Cambridge, Mass., Ukrainian Studies Fund, 1984, pp. 355-364. A reprint of the 1904 work first published in St. Petersburg, Velychenko, *op. cit.*, pp. 141-229.

[10] Subtelny, *op. cit.*, pp. 387-402.

[11] Heorhii Kasyanov, *Ukrains'ka intelihentsiya 1920-kh-30-kh rokiv*, Kyiv, Hlobus Vik, 1992; James Mace, *Communism and the Dilemmas of National Liberation: National Communism in Soviet Ukraine 1918-1933*, Cambridge, Mass., Harvard University Press, 1983, pp. 232-68.

[12] Robert Sullivant, *Soviet Politics and the Ukraine, 1917-1957*, New York, Columbia University Press, 1962, pp. 149-233; K. K. Dubyna, 'Instytut Istorii', in Borys Paton (ed.), *Istoriya Akademii Nauk Ukrains'koi RSR*, Kyiv, Nukova Dumka, Vol. 2, 1967, pp. 17-20.

[13] Patrick Seriot, 'Officialese and Straight Talk in Socialist Europe of the 1980s', in Michael E. Urban (ed.), *Ideology and System Change in the USSR and Eastern Europe*, New York, St Martin's Press, 1992, pp. 202-212; Kathline Verdey, *National Identity Under Socialism*, Berkeley, University of California Press, 1991, pp. 3-18.

[14] Anna Maslennikova, 'The Communist Language: Changes and Paradoxes', in Dane R. Gordon (ed.), *Philosophy in Post-Communist Europe*, Amsterdam, Rodopi, 1998, pp. 93-116; V. L. Vasilenko *et al.*, *Nauchnie osnovy rukovodstva formirovaniem novogo cheloveka*, Kiev, Politicheskaya literatura, 1985.

[15] K. Lytvyn, 'Ob istorii ukrainskogo naroda', *Bolshevik*, No. 7, 1947, pp. 41-56; I. I. Hurzhii, V. Sarbei, V. I. Lenin pro naivazhlyvishi pytannia istorii Ukrainy, Kyiv, Naukova dumka, 1960, pp. 60-70; Lowell Tillet, *The Great Friendship: Soviet Historians on the Non-Russian Nationalities*, Chapel Hill, University of North Carolina Press, 1969, pp. 36-67. Yuri Shapoval, '"On Ukrainian Separatism". A GPU Circular of 1926', *Harvard Ukrainian Studies*, Vol. 18, 1994, pp. 275-302.

[16] Walker Connor, *The National Question in Marxist-Leninist Theory and Strategy*, Princeton, N.J., Princeton University Press, 1984.

[17] N. Yakovlev, 'O shkol'nykh uchebnykakh po istorii', *Kultura i Zhizn'*, 30 Nov. 1946. *Tezisy o 300-letii vossoedineniya Ukrainy s Rossiei (1654-1954 gg.)*, Moscow, 1954. .

[18] M. Braichevskyi, 'Priyednannya chy vozyednannya', in *Shyroke more Ukrainy*, Baltimore/Paris, Smoloskyp, 1972, pp. 21-52.

[19] *Kul'turne budivnytstvo v Ukrains'kii RSR*, Kyiv, Politychna literatura, Vol. 2, 1961.

[20] 'Za glubokoe nauchnoe izuchenie istorii ukrainskogo naroda', *Voprosy istorii*, No. 7, 1955, pp. 3-10.

[21] I. E. Kravtsev, *Razvitie natsional'nykh otnoshenii v SSSR*, Kiev, Akademiya Nauk, 1962.

[22] F. P. Shevchenko, 'Pro stvorennya vstupu do istorychnoi nauky', *Ukrains'kyi istorychnyi zhurnal*, No. 1, 1959, pp. 90-100. M. I. Marchenko, *Istoriya ukrains'koi ku'ltury, Kyiv, Radyans'ka shkola*, 1961, pp. 201-230.

[23] F. P. Shevchenko, 'Chomu Mykhailo Hrushevs'kyi povernuvsya na radyans'ku Ukrainu', *Ukrains'kyi istorychnyi zhurnal*, No. 11, 1966, pp. 24-29; F. P. Shevchenko, 'Pro sud istorii', *Ukrains'kyi istorychnyi zhurnal*, No. 2, 1967, pp. 45-54.

[24] I. D. Boiko, 'Do pytannya pro derzhavnist' ukrains'koho narodu v period feodalizmu', *Ukrains'kyi istorychnyi zhurnal*, No. 8, 1969, pp. 82-86.

[25] 'Pro seriozni nedoliky ta pomylky odniei knyhy', *Kommunist Ukrainy*, No. 1, 1973, pp. 77-82; V. Malanchuk, 'Rastsvet dukhovnoi kul'tury ukrainskogo naroda v bratskoi semie narodov SSSR', *Voprosy filosofii*, No. 4, 1979, pp. 77-82.

26 I. Mykhailyuk, 'Kompleks malorosiistva', *Etnonatsionalnyi rozvytok Ukrainy*, Kyiv, Instytut derzhavy i prava AN Ukrainy, 1993, pp. 64-66; Oksana Hrabowych, 'Kolonial'na spadshchyna v syohodishnii Ukraini: kil'ka kluchovych pytan', *Arka*, No. 1, 1994, pp. 14-17; Ivan M. Myhul, 'Ukrainian Nationalising and Minorities Projects, and Foreign Policy', in Katlijn Malfliet and Ria Laenen (eds), *Minority Policy in Central and Eastern Europe: The Link Between Domestic Policy, Foreign Policy and European Integration*, Leuven, The Institute for European Policy, 1998, pp. 103-104.

27 'Ethnocide of Ukrainians in the USSR', *The Ukrainian Herald*, Nos 7-8, 1974, Baltimore, Smoloskyp, 1977; Anatolii Rusachenko, 'Yak Ukraina zdobuvala nezalezhnist' i shcho z toho vykhodyt', *Suchasnist*, Nos 3-4, 1996, pp. 58-64.

28 Andrew Wilson, *Ukrainian Nationalism in the 1990s: A Minority Faith*, Cambridge, Cambridge University Press, 1997, pp. 97-116.

29 B. I. Kantselyarchuk, D. V. Patlai, 'Aktual'ni problemy natsional'noi polityky v Ukraini', *Ukrainskyi istorychnyi zhurnal*, No. 4, 1991, pp. 20-29; H. K. Vasylenko, *Velyka Skyfiya*, Kyiv, Znannya, 1991; L. Hlibko, 'My slovyany', *Derzhavnist*, No. 1, 1992, pp. 10-15; Yaroslav Dashkevych, 'Natsional'ne pytannya v Ukraini', *Ukraina*, No. 28, 1994, pp. 7-13; M. N. Koval, '40-richchya Ukrains'koho istorychnoho zhurnalu', *Ukrainskyi istorychnyi zhurnal*, No. 4, 1997, pp. 11-19; Volodymyr Kulyk, 'Pys'mennyts'ke vidrodzhennya: ukrains'ka derzhavna ideya v dyskursi 'opozytsii vseredyni rezhymu' pershykh rokiv perebudovy', *Suchasnist*, No. 1, 1998, pp. 54-79.

30 Romain Yakémtchouk, *L'indépendence de l'Ukraine*, Bruxelles, Institut royal des relations internationales, 1993; Ilya Prizel, *National Identity and Foreign Policy: Nationalism and Leadership in Poland, Russia and Ukraine*, Cambridge, Cambridge University Press, 1998, chapter 9.

31 Alexander J. Motyl, *Dilemmas of Independence: Ukraine after Independence*, New York, Council of Foreign Relations Books, 1993, pp. 49-52; Prizel, pp. 362-363.

32 Andrii Hrechko, 'Do pytannya pro natsional'nu symvoliku', *Samostiina Ukraina*, No. 17, 1991, pp. 21-31; Yuri Pakhomov, 'Politychna kul'tura posttotalitarnoi doby', *Politolohichni chytannya*, No. 2, 1992, pp. 39-47; V.M. Lytvyn, A.H. Slyusarenko, 'Na politychnii areni Ukrainy', *Ukrainskyi istorychnyi zhurnal*, No. 1, 1994, pp. 9-30; Mykola Tomenko, 'Osnovy derzhavnoi etnonatsional'noi polityky', *Ukrainska perspektyva*, No. 2, 1995, pp. 61-67; Myhul, op.cit., pp. 103-112.

33 Ivan Varzar, 'Pro politychnu nauku pravdyve promovylo – ne apolohetychne, a istoriohrafichne', Nova polityka, No. 3, 1997, pp. 46-50; Vitalii Chyshko and Nazar Rybak, 'Sotsial' no-humanitarni nauky v Ukraini: perspektyvy rozvytku', Pamyat' stolit', No. 6, 1997, pp. 112-116; Viktor Tancher, 'Sotsiolohichna dumka Ukrainy na tli svitovoi sotsiolohii', *Sotsiol'ohiya: teoriya, metody, marketinh*, Nos 1-2, 1998, pp. 18-27.

34 Evhen Bestryts'kyi, 'Chomu natsionalizm ne mozhe buty naukoyu', *Politychna dumka*, No. 2, 1994, pp. 31-32; *Khto ye khto v ukrains'kykh suspil'nykh naukakh*, Kyiv, Vydavnytstvo K.I.S., 1998, pp. 451-505, 511-518; V. Baran, *et al.*, 'Ukraina, ukraintsi, *ukrainoznavstvo*: dumky, problemy, rishennya', *Osvita*, 14-21 April 1999.

35 Yaroslav Dashkevych, 'Dorohamy ukrains'koho klio', pamyat' stolit', No. 3, 1996, pp. 2-9; Petro Kononenko, '*Ukrainoznavstvo* v systemi osvity i nauky. Problemy upravlinnya', *Osvita i upravlinnya*, Vol. 1, No. 1, 1997, pp. 71-76;

36 Ya. Ryabchuk, 'Hromadyans'ke suspil'stvo i natsional'na emantsypatsiya', *Fil'osofs'ka I sotsiol'ohichna dumka*, No. 12, 1991, pp. 11-12; P. Tolochko, 'Imeyet li Ukraina natsional'nuyu ideyu?', *Kievskie novosti*, 20 October 1995; Yakiv Dubrov, 'Dukhovne vidrodzhennya i stanovlennya ukrains'koi natsii yak emerzhytna evolyutsiya', *Natsional'ni interesy*, No. 1, 1996, pp. 50-61.

Alexei Zverev

2. 'The Patience of a Nation is Measured in Centuries'. National Revival in Tatarstan and Historiography

Introduction

The Tatars have always been part of Russian history and politics, yet distinct from them. Historical self-perceptions have kept the Russians and the Volga Tatars[1] apart. The Russians cannot forget the ravages of the Golden Horde, which allegedly shut Russia off from Europe for 240 years[2] and, as some believe, has left a lasting 'Oriental' mark on its polity ever since. For the Tatars, this is a 'black legend' that does not correspond to reality. In their view, the Horde actually kept Russia from falling apart and defended it from the invasions from the West, preventing Russia from being colonized by the Teutonic Order, Lithuania, Poland or Sweden. In fact, a salient tradition of Russian thinkers – from the historians Nikolai Karamzin and Georgi Vernadsky to the ethnologist Lev Gumilev – concurred with this view to a certain extent. For their part, the Tatars cannot forgive the Russian state for their defeat and the destruction of the Kazan Khanate at the hands of Tsar Ivan the Terrible in 1552, and the forced Christianization and Russification that followed.[3]

Mutual wounds inflicted in history and enshrined in folk memory are hard to forget. It is equally true that after the Russian conquest the Tatars gradually found a modicum of co-existence with the Russians. Tatar blood flowed in the veins of many outstanding figures of Russian history and culture – from the tsar Boris Godunov to the poet Anna Akhmatova, as it did in the veins of the world-famous ballet dancer Rudolf Nureyev.

Russian armies of the tsars and Bolsheviks were sometimes commanded by Tatar generals. Just as, on the eve of 1917, the well-off section of the Tatar population identified themselves with the tsarist monarchy (despite all its wrongdoing against the Tatars), in 1991 the Tatar ruling élites could not but feel a certain affinity with the October Revolution (despite all its unfulfilled promises). After all, it was the Bolsheviks that gave the Tatars their first (Soviet) republic in 1920.

It is to be remembered that it was Tatar revolutionaries with impeccable Tatar patriotic credentials who helped install Soviet power in Tatarstan in 1918, and that what these people were acting out – even if they could only partly achieve it – was the Tatar (and Muslim) political agenda as they understood it at that particular juncture. What these revolutionaries dreamed of was a self-governing Republic of Turan which would include the entire Turkic-populated areas of the Soviet Union, and would be a spearhead of revolution in the colonial East, complete with its own army, a separate Communist Party and a Colonial International independent of the Komintern. What they achieved, however, was an Autonomous Tatar Republic (the Tatar ASSR) controlled by Moscow and cut off from the Muslim East.

Many Tatar historians nowadays create a vision of history in which a full set of historical arguments for the Tatars as a distinct oppressed nationality is mustered, so that the question of independence begs itself, even if it is not directly posed. One gets an impression of rather acute discomfort, among some sections of the nationally-conscious Tatar intelligentsia, at living in Russia, and of the huge difficulty of preserving their cultural and historic identity – but it is a discomfort that, in their view, has to be patiently endured for lack of a better outcome. As one Tatar author has put it, 'the patience of a nation is measured in centuries'.[4]

Nevertheless, both politicians and scholars in present-day Tatarstan deny harbouring secessionist objectives. Tatarstan's major ideologist, the Director of the Kazan-based Institute of History and one of the founders of the Tatar Public Centre (TPC) – an umbrella Tatar nationalist organization, which emerged in the general context of Gorbachev's perestroika – Republic of Tatarstan (RT) Presidential Advisor Rafael Khakimov, has denied that the ultimate objective of the Tatar national movement is independence: 'To suppose that, say, Tatarstan pursues a "false-bottomed" policy is not serious; the republic is not interested in secession, and there are valid reasons for this. Suffice it to say that 75 per cent of Tatars live outside Tatarstan, and that, incidentally, they live mostly in their historic homeland, that is, on the territory of the former Kazan, Astrakhan, Kasimov and Siberian Khanates. Thus a substantial part of Russia is Tatar to the same extent as it is Russian. It is in the interest of Tatarstan to conduct a policy of enhancing its influence on Russian matters for the purpose of preserving a treaty-based status for the republic and developing the culture of Russia's Tatars.'[5] The message here is clear: we do not advocate secession, but we do intend to increase our influence. This does not mean that in the event of a denial of 'what is due', the Tatars may not remember their 'historic rights' and put secession on the agenda. The protean character of nationalism, which is contingent on the conditions in which the given ascriptive group lives and on how these people perceive these conditions, implies that radical changes in the formulation of political goals cannot be excluded.

In the following we will analyse the unstable, transient and recurrent character of Tatar nationalism and the role of historiography in the legitimization of nationalist objectives. We will first analyse the three periods of the Tatar national revival over the last century or so, with particular emphasis on the third, which is currently under way. We will dwell on the reasons for the initial rise and subsequent decline of the radical Tatar nationalism of today. We will then deal with the shifting attitudes of Tatar intellectuals towards Tatarstan's place in Russia, the correlation between Soviet, Tatar émigré and post-Soviet Tatar historiography and the difficult problems engendered by the incompatible nature of Russian and Tatar state-centred historical narratives.

The Three Attempts at a Tatar National Revival

The latest spell in the Tatar national revival (roughly 1989 to the present) is the third in a series since the end of the nineteenth century. The first was associated with the activity of Islamic reformers (the Jadids), Tatar cultural figures and politicians of ca. 1880-1918. This period may be said to have started at the time when the Tatar educator and historian Shigabutdin Marjani opened his first reforming *medresse* in Kazan and another educator, Kayum Nasyri, wrote the first textbook in the Tatar vernacular. The period saw the first Tatar political parties which attempted to guide the Muslim national movement in the whole of Russia. Their agenda included cultural-national autonomy, i.e., autonomy in matters of religion and education, without an army or a territorial administration other than that dealing with religious and educational matters (and the financing thereof).

In 1917, under the Kerensky government in Russia, the Russian army disintegrated, with soldiers of various nationalities deserting from the front in their millions. Amid general anarchy, some national movements began forming their national units even before they put forward the slogan of independence for their nations. By the end of 1917, Tatar politicians were divided between the advocates of a non-territorial, cultural-national autonomy for Russia's Muslims, and the so-called 'territorialists', who were proponents of territorial autonomy for the Turkic peoples of the Volga-Ural region. Both denied an intention to secede. The former, led by Sadri Maksudi, were largely composed of anti-Bolshevik, liberal and moderate socialist parties which controlled the parliament of the Muslim cultural-national autonomy. This non-territorial autonomous entity of the Muslims of inner Russia and Siberia – without the Muslims of Central Asia and the Caucasus, who had their own political plans – had been proclaimed in July 1917, and its parliament convened in November the same year. By the end of 1917, the parliament had some troops under its command. The 'territorialists' (*tufrakchylar*) mostly consisted of non-Bolshevik leftist parties that controlled the Tatar Military Council, the Harbi Shuro, which was also in command of some troops. In early 1918, the Harbi Shuro scheduled the proclamation of an autonomous Turco-Tatar state of Idel-Ural (the Volga-Ural State) within the RSFSR for 1 March 1918.

The Bolsheviks feared that the two factions and their armed units would merge and that the anti-Bolshevik parliament would assume command over them. Had it had time to do this and mobilize the entire Tatar population under the nationalist slogans, the Bolsheviks might have had a major conflict on their hands. The local Russian Bolsheviks of the Kazan Soviet were opposed to the creation of Idel-Ural and were prepared to fight it by force of arms (Lenin's generous promises to Russia's nationalities were not always shared by local Bolshevik leaders). The logic of struggle might sway even the conciliatory, leftist Tatar elements into the anti-Bolshevik camp. On the eve of the proclamation of Idel-Ural, therefore, the Bolsheviks, led by Mirsaid Sultan-Galiev, first arrested the Harbi Shuro leaders and then released them on condition that they refused to proclaim Idel Ural. Soon after, the Bolsheviks disarmed the Tatar units and dispersed the Turco-Tatar parliament, but promised to set up a Soviet Tatar-Bashkir Republic within the borders of Idel-Ural. This defused the situation, and the conflict between Tatars and the Soviets was nipped in the bud. Some Tatar politicians who had planned the creation of Idel-Ural (Galimjan Sharaf and Ilias Alkin, among others) would later co-operate with the Soviet government. A recent Tatar textbook for students expresses relief that the Muslim movement of Idel-Ural did not then become a hotbed of civil war.[6]

The second attempt at national revival is associated with the activities of the Tatar National Bolsheviks (Mirsaid Sultan-Galiev and others) after the Bolshevik Revolution of 1917 in Russia. Owing to the opposition of the Bashkir national movement led by Akhmet Zaki Validov, the Bolsheviks could not make good their promise of a Tatar-Bashkir Republic, and they set up separate Soviet republics for the Tatars and the Bashkirs.[7] The Tatar Autonomous Republic, established in 1920, was the first Tatar state (although a part of Soviet Russia and with restricted functions) since the fall of the Kazan Khanate to the hosts of Ivan the Terrible in 1552. The period was marked by a more lenient policy on the part of the Tatar Bolsheviks towards members of the local cultural and religious élite than that practised under the tsars or, later, under Stalin. This period came to an end in 1928, with the second and definitive arrest of Sultan-Galiev.

In the years that have passed since the start of the latest upsurge of the Tatar national movement in 1989, the latter has had its ups and downs. It gained a certain momentum in the years just preceding the break-up of the USSR. The TPC (Tatar Public Centre) mobilized certain sections of the Tatar population under the slogan of upgrading the Tatar Autonomous Republic, a second-level territorial entity in the hierarchy of Soviet republics, to the status of a Union republic – a long-standing Tatar demand common to both the élite and the intellectuals. Being a Union republic meant direct entry into the USSR by a Union Treaty, on a par with the Russian Federation.[8] According to the Soviet Constitution, Union republics were sovereign and had the right to withdraw from the Union. Under pressure from below, the Tatar communist leadership effectively adopted this programme as its own, and the movement secured the passing by Tatarstan's parliament of the republic's Declaration of State Sovereignty in August 1990. At that time, the nationalist publications did not distinguish between the sovereignty proclaimed in the above Declaration and complete independence. According to them, Tatarstan would be a Union republic of the USSR for as long as it suited its interests. Let us note in passing that after the Declaration was adopted, the USSR had little more than a year to live.

As Gorbachev was losing and Yeltsin asserting control over the Kremlin, the Tatar national movement was growing more radical, losing touch with public opinion and political realities in the process. The second TPC programme (February 1991) accused the RSFSR, then under the democratic leadership of the early Boris Yeltsin, of 'embarking on the path to creating a state of a unitary and totalitarian type'. At that time the TPC claimed that Tatarstan's parliament had to delegate to the Union (not RSFSR) bodies only those powers that were needed to further the republic's sovereignty, and had the right to withdraw these powers from the centre and reclaim them at any time. 'History shows', the programme went on, 'that neither Russia nor the USSR can act as guarantors of human rights; for the Tatars, it is only the state in the person of the Tatar Republic that can guarantee them'. Even more radical groupings, such as the Ittifak ('Alliance') party, the Sovereignty Committee, the Iman ('Faith') Youth Islamic Culture Centre, the Azatlyk ('Freedom') Union of Tatar Youth, and others, strove for immediate and complete independence for Tatarstan, with Azatlyk, at its second Kurultai (congress), in a resolution of entitled 'On Territorial Demands to the Russian Empire Named the RSFSR' (October 1991), demanding a 'reunification of all the native Tatar lands that existed before the conquest of the Kazan Khanate (1552) by the Russian colonialists, enlisting historians and the general public in that task'.[9] The latter point underscores the importance of history for the nationalist enterprise.

A fairly high level of Tatar nationalist mobilization in 1990-91 pushed the ex-communist Tatar leadership into a more assertive policy vis-à-vis Russia. This circumstance, along with a certain disorientation in Moscow in a period just after the break-up of the USSR, caused great perplexity among the Russian leaders. But the Tatar leadership generally managed to contain the nationalist upsurge. Relations between the intellectuals grouped in the Tatar national movement and the official Tatar leadership contained elements of both rivalry and co-operation. The balance of forces at the time may be represented by a rectangle composed of 1) Moscow, 2) the Tatar nationalists, 3) the ethnic Russian 'democrats' in Tatarstan and 4) the Tatarstan leadership. In this constellation, Moscow, with the help of the Russian 'democrats' in Tatarstan, attempted successfully to woo the Tatarstan leadership to its side with threats and material benefits. The Tatar nationalists opposed both Moscow and the local Russians and put pressure on the Tatarstan leadership when it seemed to succumb to pressure from Moscow, but defended that leadership when it opposed Moscow. The Tatarstan leadership embroiled both the ethnic Russian and the Tatar opposition with each other and succeeded in asserting itself as the only valid partner for Moscow.

Thus from the very start the paths of Tatarstan's leadership and the Tatar national movement ran at times counter, at times parallel to each other. The former was reaping the political benefits from the movement, extending and entrenching its power in the sovereign state that Tatarstan became. This combination of factors led Moscow and Kazan to agree on a devolution of powers between the centre and the Republic of Tatarstan. In February 1994, the devolution process led to the conclusion of a Power-Sharing Treaty between Moscow and Kazan. This treaty between the two seats of government – the Kremlins of Moscow and Kazan – were largely based on informal agreements between the two respective presidents, Yeltsin and Shaimiev. The Treaty did not come under public scrutiny, nor was it ratified by the two parliaments, which makes some observers wonder if it will survive under President Vladimir Putin. But the Treaty did establish *de facto* dual sovereignty based on the acceptance of inconsistencies between the constitutions of Russia and Tatarstan. In the process, the Tatar government side invoked the fact that the Russian Constitution provides that the republics are states. A state is sovereign by definition. Hence Tatar sovereignty, in Tatarstan's opinion, does not run counter to the Russian Constitution even though the latter makes no mention of republic sovereignty. The Treaty did much to calm spirits in both Kazan and Moscow. After 1993, the already weakened Tatar national movement dwindled almost to nothing as a political force.

The Changing Fortunes of the Tatar National Movement

This third attempt at national revival, at the start of the 1990s, may be explained by various factors. As sociologists point out, in the 1960s a process of stepped-up urbanization ushered in a relative increase in the specific weight of the Tatar intelligentsia and administrators in the republic compared to their ethnic Russian counterparts. In average educational level the Tatars began to approach local Russians, the social status of the Tatars rose more dynamically than that of ethnic Russians, and Tatar administrative personnel came to occupy a predominant position in the republic.[10] Their rising social status led to an increased Tatar national awareness. The upper strata of Tatar society, firmly established by that time, had begun to feel that the republic's Soviet-type autonomous status, involving restricted budgets and fewer possibilities for developing local culture, was too narrow for them. The Tatar national revival of the early 1990s was formed within the state and academic institutions created in the Soviet era. It probably involved more intellectuals than the previous two revivals but its potential was short-lived, with the result that it registered only partial gains.

While the Tatar party and government élite was more concerned about channelling greater resources from the centre to the republic, the intellectuals were naturally more concerned with culture and history. They were thus acutely aware of the fact that the Soviet nationalities and demographic policy had left three-quarters of the Tatar population beyond the republic's borders. At the same time, communist construction projects like the giant Kamaz plant in Naberezhnie Chelny (in Tatar: Yar Chally) in Tatarstan absorbed great masses of Tatar village youths who were feeling ill-at-ease in the Russophone urban environment (let us add that these newcomers were also lower-skilled and underpaid), and such new urban centres were thus to become the future focal points of nationalist mobilization. In sum, by the end of the 1980s, Tatar nationalism had acquired both a growing number of oracles and an expanding circle of followers.

The rise of Tatar nationalism and secessionism was also linked to a particular political conjuncture, and its decline to the change in that conjuncture. What we are referring to is the internal split in Soviet society that led to the break-up of the USSR at the end of 1991. Secession may be facilitated by internal strife, civil war, world war, revolution or foreign occupation. Some of the contending forces in the metropolitan power may become an ally of a secessionist force. So the Tatar nationalists had (or thought they had) an unmissable historic chance of jumping on the bandwagon of the republics seceding from the Soviet Union.

The role of social science in the process of legitimizing sovereignty was twofold: first, social scientists – historians, economists, jurists, sociologists and political scientists – together with teachers, doctors and writers, provided the nucleus of the movement for sovereignty; second, recourse was made to science in trying to ensure distributive justice, set legal safeguards and restore historical truth. The demand for distributive justice could be illustrated by the widely-held, if naive, belief that if the proceeds from all the oil pumped from Tatarstan's oil-wells since 1946 had gone into the republic's exchequer, Tatarstan would have been a 'second Kuwait'. The naivety lay in forgetting that the Tatar ASSR would not have been able to finance its oil production alone, while export routes lay through Russian territory and could be cut off at any moment. Legal standards to ensure Tatar sovereignty were said to be necessary owing to the fact that the Tatar ASSR, set up by Bolshevik decree in 1920, had its prerogatives curtailed in the 1930s precisely because the republic had been set up 'from above' and not by a legally binding agreement. What had been granted 'from on high' could be withheld in an arbitrary manner. Historical truth required the cleaning of the Augean stables of Soviet historiography and the re-establishment of a national narrative.

Thus, as the 1990s began, radical sections of the Tatar intelligentsia raised the banner of national independence. However, Tatar society was politically fragmented from the start, and the more radical the nationalists became, the less support they received from the general public and academia. Dmitry Gorenburg has analysed the data obtained by two groups of US sociologists who randomly polled selected groups of the population in four Russian republics, including Tatarstan, in 1993. Signalling the key influence of the Institute of Language, Literature and History[11] in Kazan as the founder of the contemporary Tatar nationalist movement (intellectuals, including academics, accounted for half of the delegates at the first two TPC congresses), Gorenburg found that, among the population groups, those supportive of Tatar nationalism included certain groups of Tatar intellectuals (mostly those educated in the Tatar language: academics, members of the creative intelligentsia, doctors and teachers, especially those from the countryside), and migrant Tatar workers who had come to the big cities from the villages, while those not inclined to support it included the party élite, factory and agricultural workers, practising Muslims and women.[12] A Tatar youth journal also lists 'petty and middle-ranking officials, teachers and students in Tatar schools, and the intelligentsia' among the 'strata close to the national idea', and 'Tatar businessmen, workers, commercial and service-sector personnel, and rural dwellers, as well as mixed-marriage and Russified Tatars' as 'pro-Soviet strata' who were not in favour of it.[13]

To this should be added the fact that roughly half of the population was ethnic Russian, who could only be enlisted to the Tatar cause by a discourse of so-called 'parity nationalism' (Tatarstan as a sovereign but polyethnic society with equal rights for ethnic Russians and Tatars,[14] not one based on Tatar privilege) — and also the fact that 42 per cent of all marriages in Tatarstan in 1993 were mixed Russo-Tatar marriages.[15] Nationalists in Tatarstan often claim that the language spoken in such families is almost invariably Russian and that children born of such marriages also more frequently speak Russian than Tatar, which adversely affects the potential for Tatar nationalist mobilization.

The Tatar movement has so far not found the means to integrate the various existing groups of Tatars and their possible allies into an overall political strategy for secession. These include: the Tatars living in the Republic of Tatarstan (1.765 million); the inhabitants of Tatarstan of various nationalities (3.638 million); the Tatars generally (including those of the Urals and Siberia) (5.543 million); the Tatars in conjunction with other Turkic (and possibly Finno-Ugrian) peoples of the Volga-Urals region (8.853 million); and the total population of the Volga region, including the area of habitation of the Kazan Tatars (roughly 17 million).[16] This population mosaic discourages rather than encourages any possible Tatar plans to achieve secession, although it may stimulate both interethnic communication and qualified forms of autonomy or sovereignty.

Especially since the end of 1991, leadership in the national movement has passed into the hands of the Tatar *nomenklatura*, which, Gorenburg believes, is not nationalist-minded. We would describe it as either pro-Russian, Soviet-style 'internationalist' or parity-nationalist in the sense outlined above, but not secessionist. The French researcher Jean-Robert Raviot likewise denies that this élite has separatist leanings, believing Tatarstan 'sovereignty' to be a form of adaptation of the Tatar Soviet-era élite to post-Soviet reality. He characterizes the Tatarstan regime as an 'enlightened oligarchy' and a regime of President Mintimer Shaimiev's personal power.

From this perspective, Kazan's bargaining with Moscow may be seen not as just another symptom of the crumbling of the Soviet system but as an established mode of that system's functioning.[17] Incidentally, in Russia as a whole, after the defeat of the hard-line 'putsch' of August 1991, the 'mass-meeting democracy' of the 'democrats' gave way to a new version of rule by various strata of the *nomenklatura*. The Gaidar reforms, begun in 1992, and the decline of living standards sapped the influence of the 'democrats' even more, as the people became less preoccupied with politics than with their own survival.[18] As popular pressure dwindled, the Tatarstan post-Soviet élite seized the nationalist banner from the nationalists, institutionalized their demands in the referendum to confirm the Declaration of State Sovereignty of March 1992 and the Tatarstan Constitution of November 1992, and then made a deal with Moscow, enshrined in the 1994 RF-RT Power-Sharing Treaty. The opposition Tatar nationalists were excluded from parliament and government at all levels.

The change of fortunes of the Tatar national movement may be illustrated by one example: in May 1991 its members staged a successful hunger strike in a square in Kazan, demanding that the parliament of Tatarstan rescind its decision to allow the Russian presidential election to be held in Tatarstan. The nationalists were supported by a 50,000-strong demonstration by the Tatar population in the streets of Kazan. The Tatarstan parliament's decision was rescinded and the election disrupted. The hunger strikers were carried into the parliament building and showered with flowers. In summer 1999, the same nationalists and some other opposition figures went on hunger strike in a Kazan square, but this time they demanded the introduction in Tatarstan of Russian electoral laws, which, in their view, were more democratic than those introduced by President Shaimiev's regime. Almost no one in either Kazan or Moscow paid any attention to this hunger strike. The former TPC leader Fandas Safiullin, who did not support it, was elected to the Russian Duma in December 1999 in contradiction to the strongly defended slogans of his organization in 1991 or 1993; he now sees independence for Tatarstan as a position of last resort in case the centre takes an expressly anti-Tatar line; and in January 2000 a 'common front' of about fifteen parties in Tatarstan – Tatar nationalist and non-nationalist alike – called on Russia's acting President Vladimir Putin to send an RF representative to the republic, similar to those serving in other regions and republics, in order to combat the abuses of rights and freedoms stemming from disparities between the RF and RT constitutions, and to bring the latter into conformity with the former.[19] Thus nationalism in Tatarstan has come full circle and turned against itself, which leads one to agree with a thesis advanced by Rogers Brubaker, namely that in many cases 'moments of high nationalist mobilization – where they did occur – proved ephemeral; "nation" was revealed to be a galvanizing category at one moment, but not at the next'.[20]

The Contingency of the Tatar Nationalist Mobilization – A Historical Outline

The fluidity, transience or intermittent character of Tatar nationalism is linked among other things to the difficulty of sustaining nationalist mobilization at boiling-point. This is a further explanation for the failure of radical demands to become embedded in the Tatar nationalist movement. Radical changes in the mobilization potential of emancipatory objectives can be observed throughout Tatar history. Scholars note, for example, that rebellions aimed at liberation from Russia kept breaking out among the Tatars (often jointly with the Bashkirs and Finno-Ugrian peoples, and sometimes with Russian peasants and Cossacks in social revolt) for more than two centuries after the capture of Kazan by Ivan the Terrible in 1552. Nonetheless, at the end of the Time of Troubles, in 1612, Tatar warriors took part in Kuzma Minin and Dmitri Pozharsky's militia formed to recapture Moscow from the Polish interventionists, and in the following year, 1613, the Tatar nobles took part in the election of the first tsar of the Romanov dynasty by the convention of all Russian estates (the Zemski Sobor). The contemporary Tatar political scientist Aidar Khabutdinov points out that in the eyes of the upper strata of Tatar society this latter fact served as a legitimization of the Tatars' presence in Russia's fold right up until the revolution of 1917.[21]

Periodic campaigns to Christianize the Tatars, especially in the first half of the eighteenth century, did nevertheless draw forth new rebellions. After the repeal by Catherine II of a number of anti-Tatar restrictions (a ban on the building of mosques, Muslim schools, and commercial activity), Russia experienced no more Tatar rebellions for the whole of the first half of the nineteenth century.

Afterwards, the constraints (in the field of education and trade) resumed, which again led to Tatar unrest, the appearance of anti-Russian sects and the Tatars' partial emigration to Turkey in the second half of the same century.

The Tatar intelligentsia took an active part in the pan-Russian opposition movement before and during the revolution of 1905. However, after that revolution, when many censorial restrictions were lifted and new possibilities for the development of Tatar culture opened up (along with the suppression of pan-Turkist propaganda in a number of Tatar *medresses*), the Tatar nationalist movement almost died out from 1907 until 1917. Tatar sentiment changed again during the October Revolution of 1917 and the Civil War of 1918-20, when a far greater number of Tatars fought on the side of the Bolsheviks than on the side of their opponents – the Whites who stood for 'Russia single and indivisible'. The Tatar masses viewed the latter as their enslavers of yesterday and allies of Western imperialists. The Tatar revolutionaries wished to rouse the Oriental countries to rebellion against Western colonialists and to play a pre-eminent role in that struggle. The separatist movement is thus contingent and experiences now a phase of ascendancy, now a phase of decline. All of the above also illustrates the difficulty of making a straightforward, 'nationalist' interpretation of history, especially if one tries to preserve the standards of objectivity.

Tatar Historiography in the Soviet Period

Shifting meanings of the concept of a Tatar nation and of the place of the Tatar nation in Russia are to be found in twentieth-century historiography. Soviet and dissident émigré interpretations of historical traditions were followed in the second half of the 1980s by historians eager to explore parts of Tatar history that had previously been suppressed.

In the Soviet period, Tatar historiography became the 'history of the Tatar ASSR', which narrowed the scope of research chiefly to the early Middle Ages on the territory of present-day Tatarstan. In practice this meant devoting primary attention to the history of the Bulgars and the Bulgar Khanate[22] examined in an ethnographic spirit, as a branch of study of the local lore of one of Russia's regions. Scholars were in effect forbidden to study the history of those ancestors of modern Tatars who lived outside Tataria and did not belong to the Bulgar ethnos. The resolution of the Communist Party Central Committee of 9 August 1944 'On the Present State of Mass Political and Ideological Work in the Tatar Party Organization and Measures for its Improvement' placed a ban on independent Tatar studies of the Golden Horde that touched on subjects of Tatar national concern. Also banned was the national epic *Idegei*, which made reference to the wars of the Tatar epic hero Idegei against Russia. This epic, whose text had been restored prior to the second world war by Tatar and Russian scholars, was not published in Kazan until 1990. It was prescribed that the conquest of Kazan by Russia in 1552 was to be regarded as a voluntary affair. Tatar history was studied, by the Tatar scholars among others, mostly from Russian chronicles, and was inscribed into the framework of Russian history. The Jadid enlighteners - especially those of the early twentieth century, who had dissented from the reigning orthodox Marxist ideology (for instance by lapses into pan-Turkism) or had committed transgressions against the Soviet regime - were proclaimed to be reactionaries, and ritualistically denounced, and Tatar scholars were discouraged from carrying out research in their political and cultural activity. The uncomfortable subjects in Tatar history (such as the ideas and role of Mirsaid Sultan-Galiev) were omitted. It is clear that under such ideological pressure Tatar historians could not pursue open, public debates on autonomy for the republic or ground such autonomy using historical material. What remained for them to do was mostly to study the local problems of history and culture of the Bulgar period without any broad theoretical scope and to stress the Tatars' positive role in all the 'historic feats' of the Soviet period.

The Uses of History Made by Émigré Tatar Nationalists: the Case of Gayaz Iskhaki

The émigré Tatar nationalists, for their part, while striving to play the role of custodians of undistorted historical memory, nonetheless sometimes created no less rigid and slanted patterns of Tatar history bearing the hallmark of the 'telos of the oppressed'. Among the émigrés who wrote on historical subjects, a prominent place is held by Gayaz Iskhaki (1878-1954). This is due to the following reasons. First, although not a professional historian, he was the first to give a clear-cut substantiation of Tatar nationalism. Second, being an émigré, he was free to express his thoughts and be explicit in saying what others could not or did not want to say. Third, his work was republished in Kazan in 1991 and his personality has received acclaim in present-day Tatarstan – among other things, Iskhaki's works are classics of Tatar literature and his is a household name among his own people.

In an essay entitled *Idel-Ural*, which was published in Paris in 1933, Iskhaki conveys a number of themes and motifs that run throughout the Tatar nationalist narrative. To start with, it is not the Tatar people that is the subject of secession for him, but the Turco-Tatar people of Idel-Ural – a vast region stretching in the form of a misshapen triangle between the Volga, the Urals and Turkestan, that is, the historic zone of habitation of the Tatars, Bashkirs and neighbouring Finno-Ugrian peoples. Implicit in this conception is the idea of the domination of the Tatar element – as the one most highly educated and best prepared for state administration – over the Bashkirs and the Ugro-Finns in the Idel-Ural State. In 1917-20, different sections of the Tatar political élite had already raised the subject of unification with Bashkiria in the form of the Volga-Ural State as the territorial autonomous state referred to above, and in the form of the Tatar-Bashkir Republic as a federated state within the 'greater' RSFSR, before the latter's partition into Union and autonomous republics. But as far back as the period of the Civil War of 1918-20 the Bashkirs had shown an unwillingness to go along with the plans of Tatar politicians to form a common Tatar-Bashkir state, and they developed their own, Bashkir nationalism, with an anti-Russian and anti-Tatar colouring.[23] This attitude left unresolved the question of how Tatarstan would achieve independence without the support of allies.

Another keynote idea of Gayaz Iskhaki's, which is echoed by present-day Tatar historiography, concerns the deep-rooted traditions of Turco-Tatar statehood, and the continuity of the people's struggle for liberation after it had been lost. The version of Tatar history he provides rekindles the nation's pride and imparts it assurance of its own strength. The history of the Turco-Tatars is ancient and majestic. The Huns, the Kypchaks, the Khazars, the Volga Bulgars and the Ugro-Finns all took part in the genesis of this people. On their long historic path they created a number of powerful, rich and highly civilized states – the Turkic and Khazar Khanates, the Bulgar Khanate, the Turkicized Golden Horde and the Kazan Khanate. These states enjoyed thriving handicrafts and arable farming, carrying on extensive commerce with the countries of East and West. Islam, embraced by the Bulgars and, later, after the Mongol invasions, entrenched in the Golden Horde, was tolerant of other religions. The Kazan Khanate guaranteed freedom of belief and custom to its non-Muslim inhabitants, the Chuvash, the Mari, the Udmurt and the Mordva.

All this was crushed after the conquest of the Kazan Khanate by the Russians, whose role in history is described by Iskhaki in an exceptionally negative light.[24] The recurring periods of oppression of the Tatars by the Russian state are shown in bold relief, while the periods of a more favourable attitude to them on the part of the latter, and any progress in Tatar life under Russian conditions generally, are explained by the national struggle of the Tatars themselves and by the concessions Russia's ruling classes were making to the Tatar national movement. This kind of 'state Tatar history' has found a champion in today's Tatarstan in the writings of the academician Indus Tagirov, while other Tatar historians often make a point of emphasizing the contribution made by the Tatars to the Russian language, culture and history.

Iskhaki concludes his essay with a eulogy about the enterprising and hard-working people of Idel-Ural who, once independent and in possession of their mineral-rich region, would be able to develop industry and agriculture to a high degree and compete successfully with Europeans. 'Despite the long years it spent under the Russian yoke, that people had never lost hope of restoring its former greatness, and there is no doubt that at the first opportunity it will take the administration of its native land into its own hands and very soon re-establish order and legality therein, so as – together with other peoples – to free itself from the Muscovite yoke and follow the path of progress and freedom.'[25] Such were the ideals of Tatar nationalism.

Tatar Historiography During and After Perestroika

In the early perestroika years many historians used the new-found opportunities to fill in the 'blank spots of history'. Here again they confronted the need to restore historical truth, a major preoccupation of the Tatar national movement. Somewhat like their counterparts in Moscow vis-à-vis the Bolshevik leader Nikolai Bukharin, the Tatar historians of perestroika portrayed the images of liberal Tatar communists who died in the Stalinist purges. Foremost among them was the long-vilified Sultan-Galiev. Although a thorough analysis of his views still remains to be made, his biography as reconstructed by the historian Bulat Sultanbekov and the published excerpts from his pre-trial confession made it possible to modify and even disprove the image of Sultan-Galiev as it had been drawn by Western historians of the 1970s and 1980s, who seemed to have taken the Stalinist accusations at face value.

While Sultan-Galiev has not been found by modern Tatar historians to be an opponent of revolution and Soviet power, he did oppose Stalin on the question of the diminished status of Soviet autonomous republics – an issue of great political importance for Tatarstan in the early 1990s. He was gravely concerned at the prospect that Great-Russian chauvinism would defeat the revolution. It may be said that he was experiencing a nationalism that was growing in direct proportion to his ebbing belief in the revolution's capacity to keep its internationalist spirit intact. Towards the end of the 1920s he came to the conclusion that if (or when) the revolution was defeated, he would be ready to make common cause with the most extreme pan-Turkist nationalists and fight the resurgent Russian empire in the guise of the Soviet Union, whose demise he predicted.[26] Of course, we know that confessions made in prison are not always reliable, and this case awaits critical study. Everything that happened to Sultan-Galiev was and remains very topical for the Tatars of today (and not for them alone).

Tatar historians have made a study of the leaders of the first national revival – the Islamic reformers, pre-1917 politicians and the leaders of the national movement. The study of the Jadids has made it possible to coin the concept of 'Euro-Islam' – a specifically Tatar version of Islam characterized by religious tolerance and openness towards European values. As Tatarstan negotiators were bargaining with Moscow over the nature of federalism and the extent of substate sovereignty, Tatar historians were rediscovering the debates at the first Muslim congress in 1917 over territorial federalism (as championed by the Azeris or Bashkirs) or cultural-national autonomy (as championed by the Tatars at the time). This gave a solid historical background to the contemporary Tatar demands for treaty-based federalism from below.

The advent of sovereignty in Tatarstan posed the question of 'upgrading' Tatar history from a study of local lore to the study of a country, albeit one situated within a larger state, and of the relationship between Russian and Tatar versions of history. The teaching of the history of Tatarstan was introduced in a number of Tatar institutes of higher learning. 'Russia is simultaneously a country of many peoples (a multinational country)', wrote the Tatar historian Y. Sharapov, 'and, so to speak, a country of many countries, a federation of many republics [having the status of] states ... The history of Tatarstan is called on to reflect independently the place of the country and its people in world history, to show their contribution to world civilization. Tatarstan's history can only be understood in the context of the history of Russia, which should be freed from ideological stereotypes. For Tatarstan and the Tatar people, Russia and the Russian people have been and remain their nearest neighbours and partners, although their relationship in history included both confrontation and co-operation'.[27]

We have already noted that the Soviet regime imposed on Tatar historians the patterns of the past that were comfortable for the Russians' self-perception and corresponded to perceived Russian national interest. Even if we ignore the purely Soviet requirements of the historian (in the form of 'class struggle', 'proletarian internationalism' and so forth) and the falsifications involved in adjusting Tatar history to fit the Russian pattern, still the question remains of the incompatibility between certain aspects of the two state-centred visions of the world – Russian and Tatar.

To take one example: the Russians generally tend to show indifference to the life of their Muslim (and Tatar) compatriots; for a Tatar historian, to look at his republic with the eyes of his mainstream Russian counterpart would probably mean viewing Tatarstan as a province that is secondary from the standpoint of Russia's overall development. At least traditionally, it means seeing the ancestors of today's Tatars as barbarous invaders who swept across Russia with the hordes of Genghis Khan, and seeing the conquest of Kazan by the Russians in 1552 as a felicitous event marking the end of one of the last vestiges of the Golden Horde. Surely, were the Tatar historian to think along these lines, some of his colleagues would say that he was perpetuating the provincialism of his 'sovereign republic' and cultivating the mentality of a conquered, colonized people among the

Tatars. As things now stand, this Tatar historian would rather portray the era of the Golden Horde as a colourful and eventful historical period of Tatar life when Russia was merely a not-very-interesting provincial adjunct of the Golden Horde. In sum, he would centre not on what the Tatars meant in the Russian context, but rather on what Russia meant when viewed through the prism of Tatar interests (including the interests of 'own truth' and prestige). Different national priorities lead to a different emphasis. Thus a Russian cultural studies expert would describe St Basil's Cathedral in Red Square in Moscow as a monument of Russian architecture of the period of Ivan the Terrible. He would say that it was built to celebrate the capture of Kazan by that tsar, a worthy deed in the eyes of the Russian people of that time. A Tatar historian would say that that temple was a direct replica of the Kul Sharif mosque in Kazan, destroyed by the Russians during the capture of the city. For the Tatars, Kul Sharif is a symbol of the lost Tatar culture and the need to rebuild it.

Conclusion

The protean character of Tatar nationalism is primarily linked to shifting attitudes towards Russia. Ever since Kazan was conquered, with two-thirds of the Tatar population now dispersed across Russia outside present-day Tatarstan and the territorial link with the Muslim world severed by tsar and Bolshevik alike (by the latter more than the former), the fate of the Tatars has been decided in the Kremlin. Independence remains a dream, and Tatar thought presents not a blueprint for separation from Russia, but rather a sequence of disparate strategies for securing equal rights for the Tatars in Russian society. Each generation of Tatar thinkers picks up where the previous one left off in disillusion, struggling against unequal odds, confronted with a geopolitical situation not of its own choosing, which cannot be radically changed. But they have to try again and again if the Tatar nation is to survive. In the process, the Tatars are contributing to both their own and the Russians' liberation from the legacy of empire.

Secession studies cannot be free from prescribed policy goals or from value orientations, nor can they always do without a certain dose of teleology. In the hands of 'late nations' still in the making, such as Tatarstan, the social sciences turn into a battlefield. Cognitive frames conceived by scholars from the metropolitan powers do not satisfy the intellectuals of such nations, if only because they have to create their own history, their own culture, their own vision of the world. The scholars of newly independent states (including substates that have proclaimed their sovereignty) act under some kind of public compulsion: to prove that their nation (or at least the ethnos living on the same territory) has always existed, that their state has deep historical roots. Thus history becomes the history of struggle for independent statehood, loss of statehood, regaining statehood.

Scholars of metropolitan powers may look down on the sometimes biased, precocious strivings of their colleagues from the 'new nations' – but they do not have to prove the very existence of their own ethnic groups, nations and states and therefore do not have to tackle the numerous difficulties inherent in this question. For the latter scholars, in contrast, the wish to 'uphold' their place in history, to 'redeem' past wrongs, to 'prove' the justice of their struggle *urbi et orbi* become a permanent object of search and endeavour. And only with the passage of time can such a partisan image of the world give way to a more balanced discourse, devoid of providential telos. The Quebecois historical narratives, for instance, gradually changed their character from being pastoral pictures of rural Francophone society devoted to the values of Catholicism, whose untainted nature was threatened by the onslaught of the modern Anglophone civilization, to quite a different view of the world where businessmen, farmers and entrepreneurs from Quebec compete on equal terms with their counterparts from Anglophone Canada and the USA.[28] It is possible that the same prospect also lies in store for the scholars of Tatarstan.

Notes

[1] The word 'Tatar' or 'Tartar' as applied to the Turkic peoples is in fact a historical misnomer. According to many Orientalists, this was originally the name of an awe-inspiring, warlike Mongol tribe at the time of Genghis Khan which left its trace in the Chinese chronicles of the thirteenth century as 'ta-ta' or 'ta-tan'. Although Genghis Khan destroyed that tribe, its name became associated with the Mongol hordes of Genghis Khan himself. When news of the Mongol invasions reached Europe, the Europeans, fearing the dreadful invaders, blended the word 'Tatar' with the Greek 'Tartaros', the realm of the dead. From here flowed the designation 'Tartary', still used on Western maps well into the eighteenth century, as the broad land-mass east of the Caspian Sea and reaching to the Pacific Ocean, inhabited by 'Tartars' – a collective name for the Turks and Mongols of Eurasia. The contemporary Oxford Dictionary, for instance, still lists 'Tartar' (also 'Tatar') as 'a member of a group of Central Asian peoples including Mongols and Turks', and also (in the form of 'tartar') as a 'violent-tempered or intractable person'. See *Concise Oxford Dictionary*, Eighth Edition, Oxford, Oxford University Press, 1990, p. 1249. The Tatar historian Abrar Karimullin thought that the name 'Tatar', originally signifying 'Mongol', was first applied to the Bulgars of the Kazan Khanate by the Russians after they conquered that khanate in the mid-sixteenth century. The Turks of the Volga region, according to Karimullin, used the name 'Bulgar' and not 'Tatar' as their own designation until the very end of the nineteenth century. See Abrar G. Karimullin, *Tatary: etnos i etnonim*, Kazan, Tatarskoe knizhnoe izdatel'stvo, 1989, pp. 62-67. In the Russian language, the word 'Tatar' is used for both the Mongol-Tartars and the Turkic Tatars of today. This results in a situation where the opprobrium associated with the former is involuntarily or intentionally laid at the door of modern Tatars. This, in part, has even prompted a section of Tatar public opinion nowadays to

dissociate themselves from the name 'Tatars' in favour of 'Bulgars'. See Viktor Shnirelman, 'Ot konfessional'nogo k etnicheskomu: bulgarskaya ideya v natsional'nom soznanii kazanskikh tatar v XX veke', *Vestnik Yevrazii – Acta Eurasica*, No. 1-2, 1998, pp. 137-159.

2 While the Westernizing tradition in Russian political thought laid the blame for Russia's separation from the rest of Europe on Mongol-Tartar rule, historians such as Robert Wipper and Sergei Platonov held that the Tartars had little to do with it. In their view, keeping Russia from Europe was an age-old concern of those European powers – Lithuania, Poland, the Baltic German monastic orders and Sweden – that had prevented Russia from reaching the Baltic Sea until the eighteenth century. See *V poiskhakh svoego puti: Rossiya mezhdu Yevropoi i Aziei*, Moscow, Logos, 1997, p. 6. It should be stressed that the issue of how closely the Kazan Tatars relate to the Turkicized population of the Golden Horde and its domination of Russia is a matter of debate between historians. The forebears of the Kazan Tatars, for example, did not take part in the early Mongol campaigns against Ancient Rus in the 1230s, nor in the famous battle at Kulikovo Pole in 1380, which formed a rallying-point for the resurgent Russian spirit in its struggle against Tartar domination.

3 On the Tatar cultural and economic regression wrought by the Russian conquest, see the work written in the 1920s by a Soviet historian, professor Mikhail Khudyakov, a native of Kazan – and one which, despite the author's Russian descent, is currently regarded in Tatarstan as part of Tatar historiography: Mikhail Khudyakov, *Ocherki po istorii Kazanskogo khanstva*, Moscow, INSAN, 1991, pp. 154-155, 162-163.

4 The expression is taken from a Tatar author, Zufar Fatkutdinov. See Zufar Fatkutdinov, 'Terpenie naroda izmeryaetsya stoletiyami', *Idel*, No. 11-12, 1995, pp. 20-23.

5 Rafael S. Khakimov, 'Ob osnovakh asimmetrichnosti Rossiiskoi Federatsii', in Leokadia Drobizheva (ed.), *Asimmetrichnaya federatsiya: vzglyad iz tsentra, respublik i oblastei*, Vol. 2, Moscow, Institut antropologii i etnologii RAN, 1998, p. 45.

6 Bulat F. Sultanbekov *et al.*, *Istoriya Tatarstana. Vol IV. XX vek. 1917-1995 gg.*, Kazan, Khater, 1998, p. 40.

7 In the view of Tatar historians, this Bashkir nationalist opposition to unification with Tatarstan facilitated Soviet Russia's 'divide and rule' policy aimed at splitting the two nations.

8 See first TPC programme adopted in February 1989 in Mikhail N. Guboglo (ed.), *Suverennyi Tatarstan*, a collection of documents of the Tatar national movement compiled by the Kazan historian Damir M. Iskhakov, Vol. 2, Moscow, TSIMO, 1998, p. 103.

9 *Ibid.*, pp. 133, 137, 262.

10 Lev S. Perepelkin, 'Istoki mezhetnicheskogo konflikta v Tatarii', *Mir Rossii*, Vol. 1, No. 1, 1992, (quoted from a computer file version kindly provided by the author).

11 Since 1996, the institute has been divided into the Institute of Language, Literature and Art and a separate Institute of History of the Tatarstan Academy of Sciences.

12 Dmitry Gorenburg, *Nationalism for the Masses: How Nationalist Elites Mobilize Their Followers*, a paper prepared for the annual meeting of the American Political Science Association, 28 August 1998 (manuscript).

13 'Tatarstan? Ili Tatarskii stan?', *Idel*, No. 5-6, 1995, p. 23.

14 We have borrowed the expression 'parity nationalism' from Damir Iskhakov, in Guboglo (ed.), *op. cit.*, p. 25.

15 S. Abashin, 'Situatsiya v Respublike Tatarstan (itogi 10-letnego "su_____veniteta" i dal'neishie perspektivy', to be published in *Konflikt - dialog - sotrudnichestvo*, No. 1, 1999, Moscow, Centre for Strategic and Political Studies, p. 115.

16 Numbers derived from census data for 1989 and the following sources: Damir M. Iskhakov, 'Gde zhivut tatary', *Tatarstan*, No. 5, 1993, p. 37; *Rossiiskie regiony nakanune vyborov-95*,

Moscow, Yuridicheskaya literatura, 1995, passim; Lev Perepelkin and Tatyana M. Mastyugina, *Etnologiya*, Moscow, Znanie, 1997, quoted from a computer file version kindly provided by the authors).

[17] Jean-Robert Raviot, 'Fenomen Tatarstana i federativnoe stroitel'stvo v Rossii', *Vestnik Yevrazii – Acta Eurasica*, No. 1-2, 1998, pp. 196-197.

[18] Lilia F. Shevtsova, *Rezhim Borisa Yeltsina*, Moscow, ROSSPEN, 1999, pp. 66-69.

[19] *Izvestia*, 15 January 2000.

[20] Rogers Brubaker, 'Myths and Misconceptions in the Study of Nationalism', in Margaret Moore (ed.), *National Self-Determination and Secession*, Oxford, Oxford University Press, 1998, p. 243.

[21] A. Khabutdinov, 'Problema istoricheskoi samoidentifikatsii tatarskogo sotsiuma v nachale XX v.', in *Sotsial'no-istoricheskoe znanie v Tatarstane: istoricheskie traditsii i sovremennost'*, Kazan, AN Respubliki Tatarstan, 1995, p. 64.

[22] The Bulgar Khanate existed from the eighth to the first third of the fifteenth century AD (capital: Bulgar). Bulgar was in the territory of present-day Tatarstan, not far from Kazan. In fact, the Bulgar tribe once lived in the North Caucasus, and from there one part of it, under Khan Asparukh, went to the Balkans in the seventh century AD to found Bulgaria (mixing with the Slavs there), while another group went to the banks of the Volga and Kama rivers, where they still live today. After being devastated by the Mongol-Tartars in 1236, the Bulgar Khanate became, like the Russian principalities, a vassal of the Golden Horde. The city of Bulgar itself was destroyed in 1361 by one of the khans of the Golden Horde and the place was abandoned as a settlement in the fifteenth century. The successor to the Bulgar Khanate was the Kazan Khanate (1439-1552).

[23] The question of Bashkiria (Bashkortostan) still retains its urgency and is a key one from the standpoint of the conceivable secession of Tatarstan. The contemporary Tatar political scientist Engel Tagirov notes that, in adopting the Declaration of State Sovereignty in 1990, Tatarstan hoped that a similar declaration would be passed by Bashkortostan and that both republics would then march towards independence together. See Engel R. Tagirov, *Tatarstanskaya model': mif i real'nost'*, Kazan, Ekopolis, 1997, p. 5. It was for this reason that the above-mentioned declaration did not refer to Tatarstan as being part of Russia or mention that the Tatar SSR had been proclaimed a Union republic within the USSR. But, independently of the 'Bashkortostan factor', Tatar scholars are acutely aware that Tatarstan is too small and the Tatars are too dispersed across Russia's territory for them to attain their goals single-handed.

[24] Iskhaki pays no attention to the phenomena of the Russo-Tatar 'historical symbiosis', such as those referred to in the works of Russian Eurasianist scholars. See Georgi V. Vernadsky, 'Dva podviga sv. Alexandra Nevskogo', in *Russkii uzel yevraziistva*, Moscow, Belovodie, 1997, pp. 227-249; by the same author, 'Mongol'skoe igo v russkoi istorii' in *Ibid.*, pp. 250-264; Pyotr N. Savitsky, 'Step' i osedlost'', in *Kontinent Yevraziya*, Moscow, Agraf, 1997, pp. 332-335.

[25] Ayaz Iskhaki, *Idel-Ural*, London, The Society for Central Asian Studies, 1988, pp. 59-60.

[26] Bulat F. Sultanbekov (ed.), *Mirsaid Sultan-Galiev, Statyi. Vystupleniya. Dokumenty*, Kazan, Tatarskoe knizhnoe izdatel'stvo, 1992.

[27] Ya. Sharapov, 'Kontseptsiya natsional'noi istorii Tatarstana', in *Sotsial'no-istoricheskoe znanie v Tatarstane: istoricheskie traditsii i sovremennost'*, Kazan, AN Respubliki Tatarstan, 1995, p. 56.

[28] See the chapter by Ronald Rudin in this volume.

Bruno Coppieters

3. In Defence of the Homeland: Intellectuals and the Georgian-Abkhazian Conflict[1]

The origin of the people inhabiting the eastern coast of the Black Sea has always exercised a strong fascination for historians. For Herodotus, known as the 'Father of History', the Colchian population of this region was related to the Egyptians: 'There can be no doubt that the Colchians are an Egyptian race. Before I heard any mention of the fact from others, I had remarked it myself. After the thought had struck me, I made inquiries on the subject both in Colchis and in Egypt, and I found that the Colchians had a more distinct recollection of the Egyptians than the Egyptians had of them. Still, the Egyptians said that they believed the Colchians to be descended from the army of Sesostris'.[2] Herodotus, who wrote his *Histories* in the fifth century BC, based his findings on linguistic affinities and on some common cultural practices, such as circumcision and weaving techniques. Other Greek and some Roman scholars, on the contrary, asserted that the inhabitants of this region came from the Pyrenees in present-day Spain. Georgian authors in the middle ages had a more religious interest in the question and traced the origin of its people to the bible. Kartlos, a descendent of Noah, was said to be the 'Urvater' of the Georgian people.[3]

The French historian César Famin, who published a contribution on the Caucasus in an encyclopaedia of geography in 1824, passed critical judgement on all previous attempts to retrace the ethnic origin of the various peoples of the Caucasus. Ancient authors had gathered precious knowledge on these peoples but had failed to decipher the noble past of the region, as they lacked the modern critical methods of historiography and geography: 'In the steppes of the Caucasus one could more easily find the grains of primitive sand that were successively deposited there by the desert winds than one could disentangle the genealogical chaos of the ancient inhabitants of the Caucasian region. Herodotus, Thucydides, Diodorus, Pliny and Strabo undoubtedly provide most precious information in this regard; but, at the time when these venerable historians were writing, they lacked all the resources that, a number of centuries later, the development of human knowledge has placed at the disposal of geographers and historians'.[4]

Historians from Greece, Rome and Byzantium had made the mistake of giving the same name to different peoples who had consecutively inhabited the region, and of giving different names to one and the same people. Critical historiography has had to re-examine the truthfulness of narratives such as those of the ancient Greek authors. The establishment of colonies gave the Greeks an opportunity to gather substantial knowledge about the peoples inhabiting the Caucasus, but their poetical genius (*'génie poétique'*) covered the historical facts with a veil of mythical knowledge. The difficulty of retracing the origins of the various nationalities of the Caucasus – Famin counted no fewer than twenty in his own time[5] – was also caused by objective factors. There were hundreds of different tribes in antiquity to whom it would be difficult to ascribe clear territorial boundaries. Moreover, successive foreign invasions disrupted domestic economic and political processes. Critical historiography was therefore confronted with an extremely difficult task in trying to unscramble what had really happened in this region.[6] Famin's contrasting of modern critical analysis with ancient poetical and religious imagination, in retracing the origins of the nations of the Caucasus, reflected the values of a scholar from the first half of the nineteenth century. Even though the question of the origin of the nations of the Caucasus was relevant before the modern age, in order to justify dynastic claims,[7] it had never had a direct bearing on political mass mobilization. It carried a very different significance a century later, under the Soviet regime, when it became part of a highly politicized discussion on the socialist transformation of the region.

The present chapter is devoted to the use of history – in particular, the methods of ethnogenesis – and other scientific disciplines as mobilizing tools in the conflict between the Georgian and Abkhazian communities. In the wake of de-stalinization in the 1950s, the discussion of ancestral rights on the territory of Abkhazia became one of the main issues in the conflict between the two national communities. It was closely linked to the repeated attempts by the Abkhazian national movement to secede from the Georgian Soviet Socialist Republic. The political and institutional settings in which scientific debates took place in the Soviet period and their transformation as a result of the war is a further topic of interest for the comparative analysis attempted in this volume. This chapter describes the kind of arguments and scientific disciplines to be found in the Georgian-Abkhazian conflict over the political status of Abkhazia, and the way in which scholars in both national communities have reflected on questions such as the moral responsibility of the intelligentsia in the mass mobilizations leading to the war, and criteria for truthfulness in scientific debates.

The following chapter is divided into three parts. The first focuses on the history of the conflict up to the 1992-93 war. The issues mentioned above – the institutional setting in which scientific debates took place, the use of scientific arguments and disciplines and the critical self-reflection of intellectuals – will all be addressed in this part, but the various explanatory factors at work in this intellectual conflict will be analysed in chronological order as interrelated elements. The second part deepens this understanding through a separate analysis of the individual factors. The third part briefly depicts the changes that have taken place in the intellectual communities in Georgia and Abkhazia since the war, and assesses the ways in which intellectuals have reflected on the role they played in the pre-war period.

The History of the Conflict

The 1930s were fateful years for the Soviet Union.[8] Stalinist terror was directed against possible dissent in Soviet society and in the Communist Party itself, regardless of the nationality of its members,[9] and against any form of thought that might somehow be branded as nationalism. The policies of repression went hand in hand with a reform of the ethno-federal Soviet institutions. In 1936, the Transcaucasian Soviet Federated Socialist Republic was split up into Armenia, Azerbaijan and Georgia. These three states became Soviet Socialist Republics (SSRs). The so-called 'titular nations' of these states (the Armenians, Azeris and Georgians, respectively, who gave their names to the republics) had the right to self-determination, up to and including the right of secession. The 1936 constitution declared Union republics to be sovereign states with the right to secede. Such rights remained highly formal as long as the Communist Party retained its leadership of the overall state and exercised centralized control of all its subordinated units, but it had more than symbolic significance for the nationalities concerned. This is particularly true of some of the nationalities that received only a lower status. The Autonomous Soviet Socialist Republic of Abkhazia (Abkhazian ASSR) was not granted sovereignty or the right to secede, nor did it have the right to demand an upgrading of its political status, which would have implied secession from Georgia. According to the Soviet constitution, the territory of the Union republics could not be changed without their consent.[10] So, as part of the Georgian Union Republic, Abkhazia became dependent both on the communist leadership in Moscow and on the authorities in Tbilisi.

The Stalinist terror acquired a specific meaning in Georgia and Abkhazia. Nestor Lakoba, the communist leader of Abkhazia, was poisoned in December 1936 by Lavrenti Beria, Head of the Georgian Communist Party[11] and Stalin's most powerful lieutenant in the region. The fact that Beria was a Mingrelian, originating from the village of Merkheuli, which is located not far from Abkhazia's capital Sukhum(i),[12] gave a particular significance to the policies he implemented in the name of the Soviet state.[13] Age-old conflicts between the Abkhazian ethnic community and the Mingrelians – a sub-ethnic Georgian community with its own language and culture – had been overlayered but not suppressed by the Soviet regime.[14] From the Abkhazian perspective, Beria's actions were seen as part of the Georgian attempt to take full control of Abkhazia. Beria started a purge of Abkhazian officials and replaced them by putting Mingrelians in leading positions in the Abkhazian ASSR. A campaign was launched with the apparent aim of suppressing Abkhazian culture as a separate entity. The fact that the Abkhazian population was small (as a result of forced emigration to the Ottoman Empire, under the tsarist regime in the nineteenth century) could explain why Stalin's regime had ready to hand an alternative to their deportation to Central Asia, which had been the fate of other peoples of the Caucasus, like the Chechens and the Ingush. The small size of the Abkhazian population (56,000 out of a total population of 311,000 for the whole of Abkhazia)[15] would indeed have facilitated its total assimilation over a few generations. After 1937, Abkhazian publications were to be published only in Georgian script – a ruling which was not suppressed until 1954, after the death of Stalin.[16] Abkhazian schools were closed from 1944 to 1953.[17] In the same period, the Tbilisi government launched a programme to colonize the Abkhazian region. The immigration waves of Georgian, Russian and Armenian workers changed the demographic situation dramatically. Georgian immigration was not very significant from 1926 to 1939, but it rose sharply between 1939 and 1959.[18] During this latter period the Georgian – and especially Mingrelian – population of Abkhazia increased by 66,000, compared with 5,000 for the Abkhazian population.

These events exacerbated the already deep antagonism that existed between the two communities. The political motives behind the decision to bring in a massive new workforce to Abkhazia cannot easily be dissociated from the economic ones, and indeed both kinds of motives were strongly interlinked in the Soviet type of planned economy. Moreover, migration movements are a normal consequence of the modernization of traditional societies and of economic development. But the Abkhazian community had good reason to believe that the influx of Georgian settlers was due not only to economic causes but also to the determination of Tbilisi to establish more direct control over their country. This perception was reinforced by historical memories of the Russian programmes of forced migration and colonization in the Caucasus region. In the second half of the nineteenth century, Russia had achieved the political pacification of this restive region at the cost of the forced migration to the Ottoman Empire of a large section of the population of Abkhazia and other parts of the Caucasus.[19] Whereas a multi-national population has been a traditional feature of the Caucasus, co-habitation with Georgians subsequently became resented by the Abkhazian population as a threat. They feared that their neighbours might end up stripping them first of their status as a titular nation and then of their territory. From this perspective, the Abkhazian élites perceived any academic debate about the ancient history of this territory or the origin of its inhabitants or their languages as a dangerous terrain affecting the survival of their community. Under Stalin or Khrushchev, it was not possible to voice this perception of a deep danger publicly, or to translate it into a political programme, but it gradually gave rise to a coherent intellectual and political discourse.

In 1954, the literary historian Pavle Ingoroqva[20] published a book on the origins of the people inhabiting Abkhazia in which he denied that the Abkhazian community was indigenous to the region. In his view, they had migrated from the Northern Caucasus to Abkhazia in the seventeenth century, taking over the ethnonym of the 'real' Abkhazians, while these 'real' Abkhazians, as depicted in ancient sources, were in fact Georgians. This thesis was based on his interpretation of historical documents and his linguistic analysis of geographical terms. Ingoroqva's interpretation was adopted by other scholars in Georgia, leading in August 1956 to loud protests from the Abkhazian side, including from the president of the Abkhazian Council of Ministers and other Abkhazian communist officials. This espousal by Georgian academics of the thesis of the non-indigenous character of the Abkhazians came at a time when Stalin's deportation of numerous national minorities was still fresh in all memories. The Abkhazians had good reason to believe that such actions might one day be repeated. Ingoroqva's thesis not only lent legitimacy to the Georgian policy of colonization of Abkhazia, but might have provided some kind of justification for the forced removal of the Abkhazians from their lands.[21]

The publication of Ingoroqva's book could indeed be interpreted as a sign that the Georgian authorities were ready to challenge the rights and privileges of the Abkhazian titular nation on its territory. There was no academic freedom or freedom of publication in Soviet Georgia. Historical research was a highly political activity, strictly controlled by the Georgian authorities, who would not tolerate any kind of publication that questioned its policies or endangered the ideological dominance of the Communist Party. According to Soviet practice, publications fostering inter-ethnic conflicts were forbidden. The refusal to censure Ingoroqva's book was therefore a political act.

The Abkhazian idea of a nation was based on the belief that the links between a community, its ethnic origin and its ancestral land were sacred. Ingoroqva's thesis was perceived as an insult to the nation. Soon after the Abkhazian protests against its popularization by Georgian scholars, the first appeals in support of secession were made to the Soviet authorities. In a letter addressed to the Moscow leadership in April 1957, a series of prominent Abkhazian signatories requested that the Abkhazian SSR should accede to the Russian Federation. This request was based on the presupposition that it was the exclusive right of the titular nation to determine the political status of its homeland. The request was refused, but the Soviet authorities exerted serious pressure on the Georgian Communist Party to change its policies, and in June 1957 Tbilisi distanced itself from Ingoroqva's thesis.[22]

The death of Stalin and de-stalinization improved the position of the Abkhazian community: measures were implemented to enhance the status of the Abkhazian and Russian languages, and a new teacher-training course in 'Abkhazian and Russian language and literature' was introduced in 1954 at the Sukhum(i) Pedagogical Institute.[23] In addition, the Central Committee of the Georgian Communist Party admitted, in August 1956, that it had followed erroneous policies towards the republic's numerous minorities. This included a divide-and-rule policy that had increased ethnic tensions, and an attempt to destroy the national culture of these minorities through repression or assimilation: 'In Abkhazia and South Ossetia, the conflict between Georgians, Abkhazians, Armenians and Ossetians was artificially fomented and a policy leading to the liquidation of the national cultures of the local Abkhazian, Ossetian and Armenian peoples and their forced assimilation was deliberately pursued.'[24] This radical self-criticism did not, however, lead to more effective ways of integrating the Abkhazian community into the Georgian political framework. The fact that Ingoroqva's thesis was repudiated only in 1957 – one year after the self-criticism by the Georgian communist leadership – was a clear indication of the difficulty of achieving Georgian-Abkhazian reconciliation.

The view that the Abkhazian community was not indigenous to Abkhazia was not destined to disappear. Ten years after its publication by Ingoroqva, N. A. Berdzenishvili published a similar thesis, and the Tbilisi authorities likewise failed to condemn it. The review published in the Communist Party newspaper in March 1967 honoured his analysis as 'an important contribution to Georgian historical science'.[25] Abkhazian intellectuals and students protested against this publication and the lack of condemnation by the Georgian leadership. A new Abkhazian request for secession from the Georgian SSR and integration into the Russian Federation was sent to the Soviet authorities. At a meeting of the Bureau of the Georgian Central Committee in March 1967, the complaints by the Abkhazian delegates were discussed but did not meet with any approval. According to the statement issued on behalf of the Central Committee by its Secretary, Sturua, Berdzenishvili's work did not include 'anything insulting for the Abkhazians' and should not be used to legitimize any kind of trouble. Ingoroqva's thesis was not to be silenced. In 1978, the Abkhazian historians G. Dzidzaria and Z. Anchabadze presented a study to the Georgian Communist Party, claiming that no less than 32 publications, most of them scientific, included Ingoroqva's thesis in a modified form.[26]

In January 1976, at the 25th Congress of the Georgian Communist Party, party leader Eduard Shevardnadze made an appeal for increased efforts to reduce existing educational and cultural inequalities between the ethnic communities in the Georgian Republic. Substantial economic investments were promised for Abkhazia. Such policies addressing the material causes of ethnic conflicts were, however, far from sufficient to prevent secessionist strivings in Abkhazia. This approach was not adequate for addressing the problem of an increasingly nationalist mood in both Georgia and Abkhazia.

In Georgia, new conflicts emerged in 1977 during the discussions on education policies and a new Soviet constitution. There were fears in the Georgian Communist Party and among the Georgian intelligentsia that the development of bilingual education (Russian and Georgian) in Georgia itself would lead to a decay in knowledge of the Georgian mother tongue. The draft constitution put forward by the Soviet leadership envisaged abolishing the privileged status of Georgian as a 'state language' and giving equal standing to all the languages used in the Georgian Republic. This challenge to the privileges of the titular nation, which at the time constituted about 68 per cent of the population of the Union republic,[27] was perceived by the Georgian communist leadership and public as an attempt at the further Russification of their homeland. The Georgian Writers' Union played a prominent role in opposing this draft. After strong movements of protest, including demonstrations by several thousand people (the majority of them students and youth), the new constitutional regulation was cancelled in April 1978. Georgian remained the official state language of the republic. [28]

In Abkhazia, in a letter in December 1977, 130 prominent intellectuals and party officials accused the Georgian authorities of continuing Beria's policies and of 'Georgianizing' their republic[29] – a letter which, by the same token, implied a criticism of the Abkhazian communist leadership for co-operating in the process of 'Georgianization'. They requested once more that Abkhazia should join Russia. In spring 1978 a number of demonstrations took place in Abkhazia. In May, 12,000 people assembled in the village of Lykhny, the traditional gathering-place where the Abkhazian community elders discussed public affairs, and there they signed an appeal for secession. Troubled by these disturbances and the waning legitimacy of the local communist leaders, the Moscow leadership decided to intervene. The local party leader was dismissed, and the Soviet authorities rejected the secessionist request to include Abkhazia in the Russian Federation. They also opposed the suppression of Georgian as an official language in Abkhazia. Moscow considered, however, that some of the other Abkhazian claims were legitimate. It was convinced that much could be achieved by working on material conditions in the autonomous republic, such as improving the local infrastructure or creating new industries. Even more than in the past, leading positions were to be allocated to ethnic Abkhazians. The concessions also included greater institutional autonomy in the fields of science, education and the media. After the protest meetings of 1978, Sukhum(i) got its own university – the Pedagogical Institute was transformed into the Abkhazian State University, designed to serve the needs of the whole of western Georgia. It had an Abkhazian, a Georgian and a Russian section. The Abkhazian Republic also got its own television station, which every week broadcast a few hours of (mainly news) programmes in the Abkhazian language.[30]

The Georgian communist leadership then tried to avoid further conflicts by making the Abkhazian question taboo.[31] Complaints raised in either community about the privileges granted to the other could not be discussed either within the party or in the media. It was argued that such discussions would only fan the flames of existing conflicts. Forbidding public discussion of the Abkhazian question, however, did not prevent it. Fears of Russification, which had come to the fore during the discussions on the new Soviet constitution, were voiced by Georgian intellectuals in discussing the future of Abkhazia. The strong, even dominant, position of the Russian language – it was used as a *lingua franca* between Abkhazia's various communities – was perceived as a threat to Georgian culture. In this way, the Georgian-Abkhazian conflict became part of the increasingly tense Russo-Georgian relations. The fact that Georgian-Abkhazian relations could not be discussed openly left dissident literature as one of the few outlets for fears and complaints. From the beginning of the 1980s, Georgian *samizdat* literature protested against the living conditions of the Georgian population residing in Abkhazia.

From the perspective of the Georgian national movement, the Soviet form of economic modernization was directly responsible for the creation of a multicultural society in Georgia, challenging the leading position of the ethnic Georgians as its titular nation. The Soviet plans in the second half of the 1980s to create a new Transcaucasian Railway, linking Tbilisi to Vladikavkaz (known as Orjonikidze until 1990) in the Russian Federation, were opposed because of their consequences for the ecological balance in northern Georgia. Cultural monuments would moreover have to be sacrificed. Some nationalists also saw this railway as an incentive to further immigration into Georgia by a foreign workforce.[32] A declaration, dated 3 June 1987 and signed by 800 writers, artists and scientists (among them Merab Kostava and Zviad Gamsakhurdia), and addressed to Secretary-General Gorbachev, considered this project to be a breach of Georgia's sovereignty. The letter included some statements on the status of the minorities. The signatories declared that the right of a people to a particular territory was a sacred right which, in principle, could not be shared. They compared a country to a home where there is only one landlord and all the other inhabitants are guests. The fact that the ethnically Georgian part of the population had fallen below 70 per cent was seen as a consequence of the creation of autonomous entities by the Russian authorities. The majority of the Georgian public and political élite did not question the autochthonous status of the Abkhazians on their territory.[33] But a strong trend in the Georgian nationalist movement supported the idea that political autonomy for Abkhazia and its status as a privileged titular nation could quite well be replaced by cultural autonomy.[34]

Since 1957, protest movements whose demands included secession had erupted in the Abkhazian Republic every ten years.[35] In 1957, 1967 and 1977 these movements were closely linked to academic polemics. The fourth wave of protest movements came in the wake of the democratization of Soviet state structures. Political reforms made new kinds of political mobilization possible and brought to the fore the question of redistributing power among élites and national groups. Previously, key posts in Abkhazia had been distributed according to a complicated system based on ethnic criteria. Certain posts could only be held by ethnic Georgians, while for others only ethnic Abkhazians or Russians were eligible. This distribution of power had given a certain stability to the political system, but its lack of transparency and democratic legitimacy had also exacerbated the tensions between the ethnic communities.

In the so-called 'Abkhazian Letter', written in June 1988 at the initiative of the Writers' Union of Abkhazia and addressed to the Soviet Communist Party, 60 well-known personalities from the Akbhaz community – all members of the Communist Party, including even some high-ranking officials – once more demanded the secession of Abkhazia from the Georgian SSR.[36] They wanted the re-establishment of Abkhazia's Union republic status, which had been granted after the establishment of the Soviet regime. The letter stated that in 1931 Abkhazia's status had been unjustly downgraded to that of an autonomous republic within Georgia. In the authors' view, the Tbilisi authorities had followed colonialist policies in relation to Abkhazia, before and after the establishment of a Soviet regime in the region in 1921. In this respect, there was no basic difference between the policies of the Menshevik government, which had ruled Georgia in the period 1918-21, and those of the Georgian government after the take-over by the communists. They were both regarded as expressions of Georgian colonialism. The letter did not envisage any possibility of overcoming the conflict with Georgia, and put forward secession as a last resort. In March 1989, about 30,000 people gathered in Lykhny. Representatives of national minorities in Abkhazia, such as the Greek, Armenian and Russian communities, took part in this mobilization. Their appeal, addressed to party leader Mikhail Gorbachev, was a rewording of previous demands.

The capacity to mobilize popular support was not confined to the Abkhazian leadership – the Georgian national movement too was receiving increased public support – and intellectuals and scholars played a prominent role in these mobilizations. The involvement of the intelligentsia in the public dispute had taken a new turn thanks to an escalating 'media war' between the two communities. Series of articles denigrating each other's point of view were published in the

Georgian and Abkhazian press. The polemics were addressed to a domestic audience as part of a mobilization campaign in each community, and the historical arguments making scientific claims were popularized by journalists or by scholars themselves. The origins of the present population of Abkhazia and Georgian-Abkhazian relations in the period 1918-21 were the most prominent historical themes. In the Georgian media, Ingoroqva's ideas were fully rehabilitated, including by Gamsakhurdia himself.[37] Georgians' conviction that the conflict with the Abkhazian community was primarily the result of manipulation by Russia was supported by historians, who stated that political autonomy had been granted to both Abkhazian and Ossetian revolutionaries as a reward for their support to the Bolsheviks in the annexation of Georgia.[38]

In 1989, the Georgian national movement was focused on the conflict with the leadership of the South Ossetian autonomous region,[39] but meanwhile the conflict between Tbilisi and the Abkhazian officials in Sukhum(i) continued to escalate. On 14 May 1989, the Georgian Council of Ministers decided to form a branch of Tbilisi State University in Sukhum(i) by splitting up the existing multilingual Abkhazian university. This problem then became one of the main sources of discord between the Georgian and Abkhazian communities in Abkhazia itself. The Abkhazian national movement linked the question of a united Abkhazian university to the survival of Abkhazian culture, declaring that its rights as a nation were being 'strangled on its own soil'.[40] The attempt to divide the university structures led to violent clashes, first in Sukhum(i) on 15 July 1989 and, the day after, in Ochamchira.

The population gathered weapons. The Georgian authorities feared that Moscow would make use of the spread of violence to declare a state of emergency in the Abkhazian Republic and that authority over Abkhazia would consequently be withdrawn from Tbilisi. According to this scenario, local conflicts and riots would pave the way for future secession by Abkhazia. This fear did not lead to steps favouring de-escalation. A 'State Programme for the Georgian Language', stipulating the compulsory teaching of Georgian in all the republic's schools, became law in August 1989. Passing a test in Georgian language and literature would now be an essential qualification for admission to higher education throughout the republic. The consequences of such a ruling for minorities like the Abkhazians, amongst whom knowledge of Georgian was virtually non-existent,[41] cannot be overstated. It revived the memory of Stalinist repression.[42]

Among the intelligentsia of the Georgian and Abkhazian communities, however, there was no consensus on the slogans used by their leaderships. In 1990, the two most famous intellectuals of Georgia and Abkhazia opposed the choices made by their people. The Georgian philosopher Merab Mamardashvili, who up to his death in 1990 enjoyed a high reputation in the Soviet Union as an independent scholar, openly criticized the nationalist mobilization of the Georgian population. Fazil Iskander, an Abkhazian novelist, whose books (written in Russian) were extremely popular in the Soviet Union, could be heard as a voice of moderation in the escalating conflict. In his literary writings, he had described the prejudices of the Abkhazians towards their Mingrelian neighbours with a certain amount of irony.[43] In 1990, he distanced himself from the Lykhny Appeal and from secessionist strivings. He warned that Abkhazia could be turned into a new Nagorno-Karabakh. He was not taken seriously by either side in the conflict. He was criticized, for instance, by the Georgian historian Giorgi Paichadze because in his appeal he had mentioned the previous oppression of Abkhazians by the Georgian authorities. In Paichadze's view, such oppression had never existed.[44]

The events leading up to the war of 1992-93 were to follow one another at high speed.[45] In March 1990, Georgia declared its sovereignty. It declined to participate in the referendum of 17 March 1991 on the renewal of the Soviet federal framework as proposed by Gorbachev. The non-Georgian population of Abkhazia, however, did take part in this referendum, and voted by an overwhelming majority in favour of preserving the Union. Yet two weeks later it took no part in the referendum on Georgia's independence, which was supported by a huge majority of the population of Georgia. Independence was declared in April 1991, and Zviad Gamsakhurdia was elected president the following month, with over 86 per cent of the vote. In Abkhazia, the conflicts between the two main national communities made it impossible to agree on the functioning or legitimacy of a common institutional framework. The Abkhazian parliament became paralysed by the formation of two blocks.

In Tbilisi, political support for Zviad Gamsakhurdia waned, and he was ousted in the winter of 1991-92 by a *coup d'état* mounted by his former supporters among paramilitary groupings. Eduard Shevardnadze, the former leader of the Georgian Communist Party and Soviet Minister for Foreign Affairs, returned to his country in March 1992. He managed to ensure respect for a ceasefire in South Ossetia, but did not support a de-escalation of political tensions in Abkhazia. In July of the same year, the Abkhazian parliament – in the absence of the Georgian deputies, who were boycotting its proceedings – re-instated the constitution that had been adopted by the All-Abkhazian Congress of Soviets in 1925, and which provided for treaty ties with Georgia and the right to secession.[46] The Abkhazian deputies argued that this step was a response to a unilateral action taken by the Georgian parliament to rescind all constitutional acts of the Soviet period and to re-establish the Georgian constitution of 1921, which included only a vague clause on Abkhazian autonomy.

On 14 August 1992, the Georgian National Guard – a Georgian paramilitary organization, whose leader Tengiz Kitovani was a member of the Georgian State Council (which was presided over by Shevardnadze) – entered Abkhazia and occupied its capital Sukhum(i). Russian-mediated ceasefires did not hold. She-vardnadze's appeals for Western support received no response. Support from volunteers from the Confederation of Mountain Peoples of the Caucasus, and Russian military assistance, made it possible for the Abkhazian forces to repulse the Georgian troops from Abkhazia, and the Georgian defeat was sealed in October 1993.

The UN report on the Secretary-General's fact-finding mission in October 1993 to investigate human-rights violations in Abkhazia stated that atrocities and human-rights violations had been committed by both sides in the conflict. According to this report, most Georgians living in the region between the Gumista and Inguri Rivers had tried to flee before the arrival of the Abkhazian forces. Their motive was fear, and this fear was actively fuelled by the Abkhazian side. According to the UN report, those who stayed behind were said to have been either killed outright or warned by the first Abkhazian units entering southern Abkhazia that other troops engaged in looting, burning and killing were on their way. The report also listed serious war crimes committed by the Georgian side during the conflict.[47]

Despite the ending of the war, by the start of the new millennium only a little progress had been made towards reaching an agreement. A United Nations Military Observer Mission in Georgia (UNOMIG) was sent to monitor the ceasefire. Russian (formally CIS) troops were deployed along the conflict line and Russia was called on to act as a facilitator in the conflict. Negotiations took place under UN auspices but by the end of 2001 had failed to lead to any agreement on political status or the return of refugees. Abkhazia adopted a new constitution in 1994, declaring itself sovereign. Under Georgian pressure, Russia imposed a blockade of Abkhazia. Georgia adopted its new constitution in 1995. The federalization of the country was postponed pending a peace settlement for the Abkhazian and South Ossetian conflicts. In the Georgian-Abkhazian negotiations concerning a so-called 'common state', the Abkhazian authorities proposed a confederal arrangement, whereby the equality and sovereign status of both entities would be respected. This was regarded as unacceptable by the Georgian authorities, who claimed that a confederation would act as a stepping-stone to full independence for Abkhazia. In their view, Abkhazia should retain the status of a federated unit within the Georgian state. These opposing views led to a deadlock in the negotiations. In the meantime, large numbers of Georgian refugees returned to their homes in the Gali region – without, however, receiving sufficient guarantees for their security. Confidence-building measures likewise failed to lead to results that were considered satisfactory by either side in the conflict. In 1999, Abkhazia declared its independence. This has not been recognized by the international community.

Factors at Work

The Privileges of a Titular Nation

Several factors have to be taken into account in an analysis of the widening cleavage between the two ethnic communities.[48] The first is the strengthening of the privileged position of the titular nations of Union and autonomous republics, and of their leaderships. This was typical of the entire Soviet Union but, according to Grey Hodnett, the over-representation of the titular nation in the state structures of the Georgian Republic was exceptionally high by any Soviet standards. In the period 1955-72, 97.2 per cent of all nomenklatura positions were occupied by Georgian nationals.[49] Georgians were greatly over-represented in the regional administration, economic management, party leadership, ministerial offices and civil service of the Union republic. This was also reflected in education.[50] The indigenous intelligentsia was able to consolidate its position through preferential access to higher education, and through the establishment of a hegemonic position in cultural activities.[51] In 1985, 91 per cent of book production and 83 per cent of newspapers were in Georgian. Two television stations and 11 radio stations broadcast Georgian programmes. The language barrier effectively excluded the minorities from the State University of Tbilisi. In 1987, the conservative Politburo member Ligachev complained that 98 per cent of the students at this top university were of Georgian nationality.[52]

This particular form of self-government, which was accompanied by a number of phenomena such as corruption, nepotism and a shadow economy at the various levels of the Soviet hierarchical framework, led to heightened tension between the Georgian and Abkhazian national nomenklaturas. The distribution of power between the leadership of the Union and that of the autonomous republic, and between the leaderships of the two main nationalities in Abkhazia itself, was in fact linked to the distribution of political privileges and material wealth. Abkhazia managed to extract concessions from Moscow and Tbilisi in order to enforce its position in cultural and educational policies. These concessions provoked strong feelings of resentment among the Georgian community of Abkhazia. This population, which constituted a relative majority of 39 per cent of the total population of Abkhazia in 1959 and 45 per cent in 1989, felt itself to be a victim of discrimination, which increased the tension between the two communities and between the two republics.

Most national minorities in Georgia did not actively oppose the privileged status of its titular nation. Members of the minorities played an active part in Georgia's rich intellectual and artistic life, without, however, engaging themselves in the construction of a separate identity for their national community. According to Mark Saroyan, the cultural and political practices of these minorities 'reflect an operational code that largely precludes the construction of minority national culture outside the home republic'. Armenian writers active in Georgia, for instance, did not use the genre of the historical novel, which has served as an indispensable vehicle of ethnic history in Armenia itself.[53] Things were different, however, for intellectuals from minorities which, like the Ossetes and the Abkhazians, themselves enjoyed the status of a titular nation. The Abkhazian University, for example, was one of the most important projects in the Soviet authorities' attempt to pacify the restive region. Together with the Institute for Language, Literature and History, it was the most important institution of the Abkhazian intelligentsia, while Georgians condemned it as an instrument of Russification, since many of its courses were given in Russian.[54]

It is interesting to note that many Georgian scholars criticized the privileged status of the Abkhazian nationality, without reflecting on the hegemonic role of their own community in the Georgian Union Republic. In a book published during the war, the Georgian historian Mariam Lordkipanidze perceived the privileges accorded to the titular nation of Abkhazia as unjust. She accused her Abkhazian ('Apsua')[55] colleagues of defending the thesis – which directly mirrors that of Ingoroqva – that only the Abkhazians were indigenous to the region: 'More newspapers and magazines were published for the Apsua population (17 %) than for the Georgian population (47 %). The Apsua had their own theatre and their own branch of the Writers' Union; they published books and had their own radio and television centre (broadcasting largely in Abkhaz and Russian), and they had the Abkhaz Research Institute for Language, Literature and History (a branch of the Academy of Sciences of the Georgian SSR), whose scholars were almost exclusively of Apsua nationality and where research involved only Abkhaz themes. For decades, Abkhaz and Russian historians wrote a "history" of Abkhazia that distorted reality. The basic aim of these "historical writings" was to present Abkhazia as the primordial country of the Apsua while the Georgians were conquerors who had deprived them of their land, language, writing and culture.'[56]

Despite the apparent symmetry in the privileged position of the titular nationality in state structures and in scientific and educational institutions, the Abkhazian community was in an inferior position not only where access to political and economic decision-making at the all-Union level was concerned, but also with regard to the Soviet scientific and educational system. This reflected the relations of subordination between Union republics and autonomous republics and the privileged status, in both political units, of their titular nation. It was not possible, for instance, to defend a candidate or a doctoral dissertation[57] in Abkhazia itself. Scholars from the region could receive a doctoral degree only in Moscow, which meant going through a difficult process of selection on the basis of qualifications and other criteria, or in Tbilisi, which meant adapting to the standards set by Georgian scholars. For this reason, close links with research institutions and publishing houses in Moscow became an issue of strategic importance for Abkhazian scholars.[58]

Both Georgians and Abkhazians found support in the positions of the liberal reformers in Moscow. In Moscow in the late 1980s, one of the main issues in the academic and political debate on the future of Soviet federalism was the type of relations to be established between the various units within the Soviet framework. Some scholars, such as the late Galina Starovoitova, an ethnographer and member of the Congress of People's Deputies, advocated giving equal standing to all titular nations. She favoured a kind of confederal arrangement, which would reject the formal hierarchical division of major ethnic groups. Authority would then be delegated from the bottom up, with each subject of the federation determining, by itself, the degree of sovereignty it wished to delegate to the Soviet centre. The reformed Union should even allow the emergence of new political entities for national communities demanding statehood.[59] The deputies of the democratic Inter-Regional Group, to whom the nuclear scientist and human-rights activist Andrei Sakharov belonged, were influenced by these views, which also came close to the Abkhazian position on the issue. Other political reformers, however, feared that this approach would weaken the rights of the existing Union republics and play into the hands of the conservatives at the centre.[60] This was also the view defended by Tbilisi.

In the opinion of Georgian critics, the Abkhazian D. Gulia Institute of Language, Literature and History became the spearhead for Abkhazian separatism, especially after Vladislav Ardzinba's appointment as director in 1988. A large majority of its researchers were ethnic Abkhazians. Ardzinba himself was a specialist in the Hittites and the history of the ancient Near East. He became a People's Deputy to the USSR Supreme Soviet and, a year later, Chairman of the Supreme Soviet of Abkhazia.[61] The great importance of scientific institutions as a mobilizing force and a marker for national identity has been perfectly understood by all sides in the conflict. In October 1992, the National State Archive of Abkhazia and the Abkhazian D. Gulia Research Institute of Language, Literature and History were burnt down by Georgian troops.[62]

The Politicization of History and the Social Sciences

The high degree of politicization of history and the social sciences in Georgia and Abkhazia is a second factor to be taken into account in analysing the intellectual conflict between the two communities. This politicization gradually took on more radical nationalist traits. It is linked to the types of political discourse on nation-building to be found in Georgia and Abkhazia, both of which stress the importance of objective national characteristics in national identity-building.

Such characteristics include tangible facts, such as language or the presence on a particular territory 'from time immemorial'.[63] As explained by Oliver Reisner, 'because national identity is not conceived of as the subjective identification of individuals but rather as an objectively binding definition of belonging, this means that those groups which ultimately succeed in implanting their definition of national identity will also determine the interests of the national state'.[64] Both communities share the subjective sense of having Abkhazia as a homeland or – from the Georgian perspective – as an inalienable part of their homeland.[65] The denial by some Georgian scholars of the indigenous character of the Abkhazian population implied exclusive claims to the Abkhazian territory. There was no agreement among Georgian historians on this particular thesis, but a far greater convergence existed concerning the view that Georgians had constituted the dominant group or cultural entity from time immemorial.[66] Exclusive claims to the Abkhazian territory were also put forward by those Abkhazian intellectuals who were striving for secession. They saw Abkhazian political and cultural history as either separate from Georgia, or opposed to it. Their subjective sense of homeland, supported by their interpretation of the objective evidence of historiography, in their view justified both exclusive privileges as a titular nation and their claim that they were entitled to secession as an expression of their right to self-determination.

The debate on the origins of the inhabitants of Abkhazia is a good illustration of the high degree of politicization of all scientific debates on territory and ethnicity in the Soviet Union. The linking of the territorial dimension of national identity to a hierarchical federal framework – within which the titular nation could claim exclusive privileges over a particular territory inhabited by a multiethnic population – dramatized all discussions on the historical nature of this territory. A view of Abkhazia stressing that there was a need to acknowledge properly the diverse origins of its population, the equal rights of all its inhabitants and the consequences of socio-economic development for migration processes, was *a priori* excluded from academic and political discussions.

Scientific debates on the history of Abkhazia have frequently had recourse to the method of ethnogenesis ('the formation of peoples'), which is particularly important in the context of an analysis of the relationship between scientific methodology and politics. Already in the nineteenth century, discussions on the rights to particular territories had paralleled the creation of modern nationalism in the Caucasus.

By the end of the 1930s, studies of ethnogenesis had become increasingly important in Soviet scholarship.[67] This intellectual interest was fuelled not only for academic purposes – it was dictated largely by political motives. In the 1930s, an important paradigm shift in Soviet views on historiography and linguistics had taken place, reflecting profound transformations in the political environment. After the 1917 revolution, the thesis of the historian Mikhail N. Pokrovski and the linguist Nikolai Y. Marr – that attention should mainly be devoted to the stages common to all Soviet nations – had dominated Soviet historiography, and had received protection from the highest authorities. In the 1930s, however, Pokrovski and Marr's views were challenged by research focusing on the individual histories of the various nations constituting the Soviet Union. This approach was more in line than the previous one with the new national policies of the communist leadership. The introduction of the new paradigm was facilitated by the purges and reorganization that decimated the defenders of the previous approach to history and archaeology. A strong national focus was also facilitated by the rehabilitation of Russian history – which had previously been identified by Pokrovski and his followers with the history of a colonial power – in 1934.

The methods of ethnogenesis were further favoured by the emergence of new intellectual élites in the various republics, which became particularly relevant after the death of Stalin in 1953. When Ingoroqva's thesis on the non-indigenous character of the Abkhazian people became widely discussed in 1954, a whole generation of Soviet scholars had already been educated in these particular notions and methods of ethnogenesis. The local élites then selected new research programmes in line with their own traditions, value systems and political objectives. The strengthening of the privileged position of the 'titular nations' in the various republics of the Soviet Union, after the death of Stalin, went hand in hand with a growing need to prove the convergence of their present dominant position in the state with the existence of an age-old homogeneous settlement of ancestors on the same territory, and their autochthonous development throughout history. This ethnocentric attitude is closely linked to the essentialist view of the nation present in many studies on ethnogenesis, whereby cultures are seen as resembling crystallized minerals: once they have been formed, their shape is fixed once and for all.[68] This approach determined the scientific programmes carried out and the relative importance of particular disciplines followed in the individual republics. In the late Soviet period, Georgia had one of the highest numbers of practitioners of archaeology in the world, for its population size.[69]

The politicization of historical research on the basis of an ethnocentric attitude led to a situation where definitive answers were given to complicated scientific problems without any firm evidence.[70] There is, of course, great unevenness in the quality of ethnogenetic research on Abkhazia, but it is striking that terms such as 'undoubtedly', 'indisputably' and similar expressions are used far more commonly in this type of research than might be expected, taking into account the fact that the material sources used in the reconstruction of the ethnic map of the region allow room for different interpretations. This is particularly the case with history before our era. Many researchers in Georgia and Abkhazia seem to be no less confident in the validity of their interpretations than Herodotus when he asserted 'There can be no doubt that the Colchians are an Egyptian race'. Certainty is claimed in the interpretations concerning the proto-Abkhazian or proto-Georgian character of the ancient population on the territory of present-day Abkhazia, or concerning the reconstruction of a historical continuity in the ethnic composition of the population in the region, as if the archaeological material or classical texts spoke for themselves.[71] The high political value attached to such interpretations, and the lack of academic freedom in discussing research results, made it difficult to achieve much methodological progress in critical historiography.[72]

An even clearer sign of the high politicization of the humanities in Georgia and Abkhazia is the direct involvement of intellectuals in the political conflict between the two communities. The number of historical themes and scientific disciplines involved in the justification of Georgia's and Abkhazia's right to national self-determination increased significantly in the 1980s, and it was often difficult to distinguish the boundaries between scholarship and political propaganda. Zviad Gamsakhurdia, a senior researcher at the Institute for Literature at the Georgian Academy of Sciences[73] and internationally the best-known leader of the dissident movement, was active in discussing language myths. He defended the thesis that the Georgian language had been humiliated and thrust into obscurity throughout history, but predicted its resurrection and elevation to spiritual leadership. He was at home in the worlds of both professional research and political dissent. Gamsakhurdia was able to make use of research done by philologists and medievalists who wrote in specialized publications – focusing, for example, on the interpretation of ancient Georgian manuscripts in their historical context – in order to defend political theses in which the unique character of the Georgian language and culture took a prominent place.[74]

After his appointment as director of the Abkhazian Institute of Language, Literature and History, the Abkhazian scholar Vladislav Ardzinba likewise belonged to the worlds of both politics and scientific research. The Georgian historian Teimuraz Mikeladze had argued that iron had been first invented by the Chalybs, who were regarded as the 'ancestors' of the Georgians. They had introduced the Iron Age, he claimed, thereby making a massive contribution to human culture. Ardzinba argued that iron was in fact discovered by the ancestors of the Abkhazian-Adyghe peoples who lived, in the second millennium BC, precisely where Mikeladze located the Chalybs.[75] The political significance of this thesis cannot be overestimated.

A differentiation should be made, however, between the scholars who were also active as public intellectuals and those who did not share such political interests. In Georgia, language myths were most energetically defended by artists, journalists and teachers, whereas – with significant exceptions – professional linguists were more reluctant to defend such views, especially when they had no political interests. These language myths were both 'extrinsic myths' focusing on the origin and destiny of the Georgian language and 'intrinsic myths' focusing on features such as elegance, purity and lexical resources which gave Georgian a superiority over other languages.[76] An indication of the degree of professionalization of this discipline is the extent to which Georgian linguists were reluctant to defend such myths. In this context, Graham Smith and his co-authors draw a comparison with Western Europe, where language myths belonged to linguistic orthodoxy in the sixteenth and seventeenth centuries, before being stigmatized by scholars as the products of amateurs and eccentrics.[77]

The absence of open political discussions between the two communities on issues related to nation-building and secession may help to explain the type of scientific polemics on these issues. Both communities had been building up separate institutions, which were unable to enter into an open and critical dialogue with one another. The lack of objectivity in academic discussions touching on Georgian-Abkhazian relations has to be situated in this context. Objectivity is not necessarily to be seen only as a property of understanding, but can also be analysed as a property of the understander. Objectivity may be characterized, with Theodore R. Schatzki, as a set of character traits such as a willingness to revise judgments when they appear to be illegitimate, openness enough to learn from others and the capacity to dialogue in an even-handed and sincere manner with the people one studies.[78] Put into the Soviet context of Georgian-Abkhazian relations, objectivity as a kind of scholarly behaviour would have favoured the use of a set of inter-subjectively acceptable criteria in all debates on Abkhazia and its history. For all the reasons mentioned above, such a form of objectivity had been made impossible in Soviet times.[79]

Coming to Terms with the Stalinist Past

The incapacity of post-Stalinist leaders to assess the tragic consequences of the campaigns of terror and repression of the 1930s and 1940s for inter-ethnic relations in Georgia and Abkhazia is a further aspect of the Georgian-Abkhazian conflict. From the perspective of the Georgian leadership, there were no objective historical reasons to assume any responsibility for Stalin's or Beria's actions. In its view, the repression of the Georgian political élite had been no less severe than that of the Abkhazian one. The Georgian intelligentsia pointed out that Stalin and Beria had been acting primarily in their capacity as Soviet politicians, and not as Georgian nationalists, but it failed to assess how and to what extent their actions were embedded in a historical pattern of conflictual relations between the two communities. From the Abkhazian perspective, Georgian nationalistic motives were inherent in the methods used to repress their culture and population. Even though all Soviet nationalities had suffered from the Stalinist purges, the types of repressive regime and the motives of those implementing them had varied widely. In this respect, there was no radical distinction to be made, in their view, between the Soviet and the Georgian identities of political figures such as Stalin or Beria.

Orthodox and Unorthodox Nationalism

A fourth factor is constituted by the specific interaction between the authorities and the dissident movement of the 1970s. There was greater intellectual freedom in Georgia than in the rest of the Soviet Union in the 1970s and 1980s.[80] A further characteristic of intellectual life there was the fact that the 'orthodox' nationalism of the party leadership, which strove for a hegemony of Georgian national culture in the republic,[81] and the 'unorthodox' nationalism[82] of the *samizdat* movement, interacted in a way that led to a radicalization of both. The orthodox nationalism of the local party leadership ensured legitimacy in Georgian public opinion. But it also lent legitimacy to the struggle of the unorthodox nationalists for a new cultural and language policy. Indeed, it made it easier for the dissident movement to fight on this than on other issues, such as democracy or human rights. Compared with the Russian dissident movement, Georgian dissidents were less exercised about individual human rights and more concerned about the fate of the nation. As a further feature of this non-orthodox nationalism, Jürgen Gerber notes that none of the *samizdat* documents defended the language or cultural rights of non-Georgian minorities in Georgia. This shows that the Georgian dissidents shared the orthodox nationalists' aim of enforcing a hegemonic position for the Georgian language throughout the republic.[83] In fact they were even more radical in this respect, as they criticized the granting of concessions to minorities.[84] Safeguarding the language and national culture was a more consensual issue for the Georgian public, and a more immediate concern[85] than the far more abstract struggle for human and individual rights. This may also help to explain the great popularity of Zviad Gamsakhurdia during the presidential election of May 1991.

Looking Back

The involvement of intellectuals was decisive in the mobilization leading to the Georgian-Abkhazian war of 1992-93. On this point, there is a general consensus among all parties involved. The Georgian leader Eduard Shevardnadze, in his foreword to a book published during this war, described the use of historical arguments as one of the basest aspects of the conflict. He stressed the responsibility of historians, but gave no indication whatsoever of the particular kind of arguments he had in mind. In his view, the perversion of scientific knowledge was part of an orchestrated campaign to sow the seeds of hatred between the two communities (he also left open the question of who might have orchestrated this campaign): 'First of all, the battleground was thoroughly prepared by an orchestrated stream of propaganda. It is said that when cannons are firing, the Muses fall silent, but here the Muse of History, Clio, has been deliberately perverted. Pseudo-historians with their pseudo-history have falsified the past and poisoned the present. The seeds of hatred have been intentionally sown'.[86] George Hewitt, Professor of Caucasian Languages at the University of London, who has come to be seen as a partisan of the Abkhazian cause, pointed to the sole responsibility of Georgian scholars in his condemnation of the abuse of scientific tools for the sake of nationalism: 'And perhaps the basest aspect of the long-running confrontation is the way that some academics in Tbilisi have been prepared over the years to prostitute their disciplines in the service of local chauvinist politics'.[87] Paul B. Henze, a senior researcher at the Rand Corporation, proposed an opposite view in a travel report on Abkhazia written after the war, where he wrote that the Abkhazian leadership was entirely lacking in popular support. Its motives were inspired by intellectual abstractions and were completely foreign to the concerns of its own community. In his opinion, 'Abkhaz separatism has been almost entirely an intellectual phenomenon'.[88]

Shevardnadze's statement – that the involvement of intellectuals in the Georgian-Abkhazian conflict was part of a bigger plot to set both communities against each other – reflected a widespread assumption in Georgia. According to one of the variants of this type of interpretation, Gamsakhurdia and his followers were 'involuntary assistants of imperial forces that sought to form an anti-Georgian coalition on ethnic and religious grounds by uniting all non-Georgians residing in Georgia, and partly Muslim Georgians (Ajarians, Meskhetians) too, through a common fear of Georgian nationalism and fanaticism'.[89] Other interpretative variants refer to provocation against Shevardnadze himself, who is said to have miscalculated the possibility of pacifying Abkhazia by sending in troops in August 1992. Such conspiracy theories have the ideological consequence of shifting responsibility from Georgia's leadership to the Russian authorities. As historical myths, they are not entirely devoid of truth. The Soviet and Russian authorities have indeed played an active role in Georgian-Abkhazian relations, in order to defend a hegemonic position. A further variant of the analysis of the conflict in terms of Russia's involvement and primary responsibility is illustrated in Naira Gelashvili's book, which was written during the 1992-93 war. She describes the common history of the Georgians and Abkhazians as a relationship which was harmonious in principle but was destroyed by Russia's treacherous role in choosing to follow a divide-and-rule policy. In the past, Georgians had attempted to create a common front against Russian imperial policies. Gelashvili points out a number of Georgian intellectuals from the nineteenth and twentieth centuries who opposed the Russian policy of cultural assimilation and favoured the emergence of Abkhazian culture.[90] Such an analysis fits with Georgia's self-image as a nation longing, for two whole centuries, for national emancipation from Russian rule, but is hardly convincing to Akbhaz historians who, on the contrary, draw largely on examples of Georgian intellectuals and politicians who supported the Russian and Soviet policies of assimilation and oppression.

Georgian-Abkhazian relations constitute long-term cycles of victimization in which the perpetration of aggression or the refusal to redress historical injustices is justified by a previous victimization, so that every community considers that it has objective grounds for seeing itself as a victim and refusing to acknowledge guilt.[91] Intellectuals have a particular responsibility in the perpetuation of such historical memories and in designing ways to overcome them. Introspection, however, is difficult for the Georgian and Abkhazian intellectuals who were directly involved in the conflict. For many of them, further involvement in political debates on Georgian-Abkhazian relations have been made impossible by the war itself and its consequences. The collapse of economic activities has seriously affected scientific and educational institutions, leaving scholars with more pressing material concerns than the legitimization of territorial or political claims. Both communities are now far less receptive to ideological mobilization than before the war. Their governments are less in need of ideological legitimization than practical know-how for rebuilding their shattered societies. Intellectuals who previously played a prominent role in guiding popular mobilization have at present little or no access to the ruling circles or to political decision-makers.[92]

Insofar as the scholarly legitimization of political demands in international forums are concerned, yesterday's discourses on the region's history are not particularly useful. International security organizations have no great interest in questions such as the territorial location of proto-Georgian or proto-Abkhazian identities. Georgian and Abkhazian scholarly communities are ill prepared to address the political issues facing their communities. Intellectuals have not played a significant role in the negotiations on sovereign rights for Georgia and Abkhazia or on the creation of a common state. This is partly due to the lack of local expertise in the particular fields that are relevant to these negotiations. Modernizing the political system in order to overcome ethnic conflict would necessitate an apprenticeship in certain scientific skills, especially in the legal and administrative fields, for which no resources are available at present. This is particularly true for Abkhazia, with its small population, which is also suffering the consequences of its isolation from the outside world. Only some resources can be drawn from co-operation with foreign NGOs and academic institutions, which generally focus on building trust between the two national communities.

The Abkhazian community in Abkhazia is not politically homogenous. Abkhazian scholars, however, wish to remain loyal to their community. Many of them view the strength of this small community as residing largely in its capacity to speak with a single voice. The negative consequences of such apparent unity for the public debate on future alternatives for Abkhazia are all too apparent.

Particularly difficult is the issue of the consequences of the war for the cohabitation of the various national communities in Abkhazia. Georgian refugees had been able to return only to the Gali region in Abkhazia, which is populated almost exclusively by Mingrelian Georgians. Confronted with the accusation of ethnic cleansing, which has been raised regularly in UN Security Council discussions and was included in the final declarations of OSCE summits,[93] a number of Abkhazian scholars have taken a position on this issue. They deny the responsibility of the Abkhazian authorities for the fate of the displaced persons. In the view of the Abkhazian authors involved in this discussion, the mass repatriation of Georgian refugees to the whole of Abkhazia without international guarantees for the Abkhazian community itself could only be allowed after a peace agreement. The early return of all refugees would lead to new clashes and new military intervention by Tbilisi. Political concessions from the other side are expected, whereas no answer is offered by Abkhazian intellectuals to the key question of how and with what institutional guarantees the Georgian population can be included in Abkhazia's political future. The Abkhazian perception of the Georgian community of Abkhazia as an instrument of colonization and foreign rule is no less decisive in the design of common political institutions in Abkhazia than the Georgian view of Abkhazia as being primarily a Georgian land. In both communities, it will probably remain difficult to achieve a critical assessment of the history of Georgian-Abkhazian relations as long as their future remains unsettled.

Notes

1   The following chapter is based on a number of interviews in Georgia and Abkhazia. I have to thank Emil Adelkhanov, Tamaz Beridze, David Darchiashvili, Stanislav Lakoba, Mariam Lordkipanidze and Avtandil Menteshashvili for sharing their views with me on this matter. George Hewitt and Viacheslav Chirikba have sent me precious documentation. I am also grateful to Rachel Clogg, David Darchiashvili, J. Paul Goode, Michel Huysseune, Richard Reeve, Xiaokun Song and Alexei Zverev for comments on the first draft of this paper.

2   *The History of Herodotus*, Second Book. The English translation, by George Rawlinson, is available on the *Internet Ancient History Sourcebook*:
    http://www.fordham.edu/halsall/ancient/herodotus-history.txt On the views of Herodotus see Otar Lordkipanidze, *Archäologie in Georgien. Von der Altsteinzeit zum Mittelalter*, Weinheim, VCH Acta Humanoria, 1991, p. 4.

3   *Ibid.*

[4] César Famin, 'Région Caucasienne', in *L'Univers, ou Histoire et description de tous les peuples, de leurs religions, moeurs, coutumes, etc.*, Weimar, Grossherzogl. Sächs. Priv. Landes-Industrie-Comptoirs, 1824, p. 16.

[5] *Ibid.*, p. 19.

[6] *Ibid.*, pp. 17-19. In reconstructing the past history of the Caucasus, Famin makes extensive use of ancient sources and mythical and religious narratives, despite the author's criticism of these sources as being highly speculative.

[7] On the use made of history under the rule of the Bagrationi see Thorniké Gordadzé, 'La réforme du passé. L'effort historiographique de construction de la nation géorgienne', *Revue d'études comparatives Est-Ouest*, Vol. 30, No. 1, 1999, p. 75.

[8] On the following see Richard Sakwa, *Soviet Politics in Perspective*, London, Routledge, 1998; Jürgen Gerber, *Georgien: Nationale Opposition und kommunistische Herrschaft seit 1956*, Baden-Baden, Nomos Verlag, 1997, pp. 123-124; Stanislav Lakoba, 'History: 1917-1989', in George Hewitt (ed.), *The Abkhazians*, Richmond, Surrey, Curzon Press, 1999, pp. 94-96; Naira Gelaschwili, *Georgien. Ein Paradies in Trümmern*, Berlin, Aufbau Taschenbuch Verlag, 1993.

[9] Of the 644 delegates to the Tenth Georgian Party Congress in May 1937, 425 were arrested and shot. See Amy Knight, *Beria. Stalin's First Lieutenant*, Princeton, N.J., Princeton University Press, 1993, p. 84.

[10] See Vernon V. Aspaturian, *The Union Republics in Soviet Diplomacy. A Study of Soviet Federalism in the Service of Soviet Foreign Policy*, Geneva and Paris, E. Droz and Minard, 1960, p. 126.

[11] On Beria's party career see *Lavrentii Beria, 1953. Dokumenty*, Moscow, Mezhdunarodnyi fond 'Demokratiya', 1999, pp. 429-430.

[12] Georgian authors would generally use the transliteration 'Sukhumi' in English texts, whereas Abkhazian scholars would drop the 'i' and write 'Sukhum'. I refer to 'Sukhum(i)' in order to avoid choosing between the Georgian and the Abkhazian preferences.

[13] Knight, *op. cit.*, p. 14.

[14] In his study cited above, César Famin describes how the Abkhazians were involved in conflicts with the neighbouring communities and settlements of the Russians, Mingrelians and Cherkessians: 'The Georgians call the Abases by the name of *Abkassi*; several geographers call their country *Abkassia*, and even *Avogasi*; they themselves, finally, have adopted the name *Abzné* ... The Abases live in a state of perpetual hostility with their neighbours, the Russians of *Soudjouk-Kalé* and the Mingrelians; but they have no more redoubtable enemies than the very people they would seem most likely to get along with – the Cherkessians.' Famin, *op. cit.*, p. 33.

[15] According to the 1939 census data. Cf. Daniel Müller, 'Demography', in Hewitt (ed.), *op. cit.*, pp. 235-6.

[16] From 1926 to 1954, Abkhazian orthography was changed four times: in 1926 the alphabet based on Russian characters was replaced by one with Latin characters. This was then replaced by another Roman-based alphabet in 1928. This was in turn changed in 1937 into an alphabet based on Georgian characters and finally, in 1954, into the current Cyrillic-based one. See Vasilij Avidzba, 'Literature & Linguistic Politics', in Hewitt (ed.), *op. cit.*, p. 177.

[17] G. Hewitt (author's name was withheld in the publication), '"Guests" on their own territory', *Index on Censorship*, 1/90, p. 23.

[18] Müller, *op. cit.*, p. 235; Darrell Slider, 'Crisis and Response in Soviet Nationality Policy: the Case of Abkhazia', *Central Asian Survey*, Vol. 4, No. 4, 1985, p. 52. During the period 1926-39, the immigration of the Russian, Greek and Armenian population was far higher than that of Georgians.

[19] On this issue see Lakoba, *op. cit.*, pp. 81-85.

20   On Ingoroqva see 'Appendix to Documents from the KGB Archive in Sukhum. Abkhazia in the Stalin Years', translated by B.G. Hewitt, *Central Asian Survey*, Vol. 15, No. 2, 1996, p. 267; George Hewitt, Introduction to Hewitt (ed.), *op. cit.*, pp. 18 ff.; Lakoba, *op. cit.*, pp. 15-18; Gerber, pp. 125-126. The thesis that Abkhazians were relative latecomers in the region was first propounded by the Georgian historian Davit Bakradze in 1889. See George Hewitt, 'The Role of Scholars in the Abkhazians' Loss of Trust in the Georgians and How to Remedy the Situation', in Mehmet Tütüncü (ed.), *Caucasus: War and Peace*, Haarlem, Sota, 1998, p. 118.

21   According to George Hewitt (personal communication), plans to deport the Abkhazians in 1948 were cancelled at the last minute. Ingoroqva's thesis had originally been published in a journal in the late 1940s.

22   Gerber, *op. cit.*, p. 126.

23   Graham Smith, Vivien Law, Andrew Wilson, Annette Bohr and Edward Allworth, *Nation-building in the Post-Soviet Borderlands. The Politics of National Identities*, Cambridge, Cambridge University Press, 1998, p. 171.

24   Quoted in Gerber, *op. cit.*, p. 125.

25   Quoted in *ibid.*, p. 127.

26   *Ibid.*, p. 132.

27   According to the figures reproduced in Revaz Gachechiladze, *The New Georgia. Space, Society, Politics*, London, UCL Press, p. 74.

28   Gelaschwili, *op. cit.*, pp. 148-149; Gerber, *op. cit.*, pp. 93-95.

29   On the following see Slider, *op. cit.*, pp. 59-61; Gerber, *op. cit.*, pp. 130-135; Ronald Grigor Suny, 'On the Road to Independence: Cultural Cohesion and Ethnic Revival in a Multinational Society', in R. S. Suny (ed.), *Transcaucasia, Nationalism, and Social Change. Essays on the History of Armenia, Azerbaijan, and Georgia*, Ann Arbor, The University of Michigan Press, 1996, p. 395.

30   Lakoba, *op. cit.*, p. 98. In the early days of this television station, there was even less broadcasting in the Abkhazian language.

31   Gerber, *op. cit.*, p. 135.

32   *Ibid.*, pp. 153-160.

33   See Ghia Nodia, 'The Conflict in Abkhazia: National Projects and Political Circumstances', in Bruno Coppieters, Ghia Nodia and Yuri Anchabadze (eds), *Georgians and Abkhazians. The Search for a Peace Settlement*, Sonderveröffentlichung des Bundesinstituts für Ostwissenschaftliche und Internationale Studien, Cologne, Oktober 1998, p. 25.

34   Gelaschwili, *op. cit.*, p. 88.

35   Svetlana Chervonnaya, *Conflict in the Caucasus. Georgia, Abkhazia and the Russian Shadow*, London, Gothic Image, 1994, p. 32.

36   On Abkhazian-Georgian relations during perestroika see Gerber, *op. cit.*, pp. 136-147.

37   Hewitt, 'The Role of Scholars in the Abkhazians' Loss of Trust in the Georgians and how to Remedy the Situation', *op. cit.*, p. 120; Hewitt (ed.) p. 19.

38   Gerber, *op. cit.* p. 139; Chervonnaya, *op. cit.*, pp. 55-56.

39   On the conflict with South Ossetia see Alexei Zverev, 'Ethnic Conflicts in the Caucasus 1988-1994', in Bruno Coppieters (ed.), *Contested Borders in the Caucasus*, Brussels, VUBPRESS, 1996, pp. 13-71, also on http://poli.vub.ac.be/

40   B.G. Hewitt, 'A Reply to Paul Henze's Views on Georgia', 1993, on the website www.apsny.org; Yuri Anchabadze, 'History: the Modern Period', in Hewitt (ed.), *op. cit.*, p. 133; Viktor Popkov, 'Soviet Abkhazia 1989: a Personal Account', in Hewitt (ed.), p. 105; Naira Gelaschwili, op. cit., pp. 96-98; Zaira K. Khiba, 'An Abkhazian's Response', *Index on Censorship*, 5/90, pp. 30-31.

41 Lakoba, *op. cit.*, p. 101.

42 Gueorgui Otyrba, 'War in Abkhazia. The Regional Significance of the Georgian-Abkhaz Conflict', in Roman Szporluk (ed.), *National Identity and Ethnicity in Russia and the New States of Eurasia*, New York, M.E. Sharpe, 1994, p. 286.

43 See for instance Fazil Iskander, *Sandro of Chegem*, London/Boston, Faber and Faber, 1993.

44 Gerber, *op. cit.*, p. 139.

45 On the following see the chronology published in Jonathan Cohen (ed.), 'A Question of Sovereignty. The Georgia-Abkhazia Peace Process', *Accord. An International Review of Peace Initiatives*, Issue 7, 1999, pp. 80-87.

46 Otyrba, *op. cit.*, p. 287; Lakoba, p. 93. On the 1925 Constitution see Gerber, *op. cit.*, pp. 123-124.

47 On the following see Bruno Coppieters, 'Shades of Grey. Intentions, Motives and Moral Responsibility in the Georgian-Abkhaz Conflict', in Coppieters, Nodia, Anchabadze (eds), *op. cit.*, pp. 157-164.

48 See Gerber's explanations of the growing tensions between the Georgian and Abkhazian communities in the post-Stalinist period. Gerber, *op. cit.*, pp. 127 ff.

49 An exceptional political over-representation of the titular nation was also characteristic of the Armenian republic. G. Hodnett, 'Leadership in the Soviet Republics. A Quantitative Study of Recruitment Policy', Oakville, 1978, pp. 98-114, quoted in Gerber, *op. cit.*, p. 42.

50 *Ibid.*, pp. 42-43.

51 Smith *et al.*, *op. cit.*, p. 6.

52 Gerber, *op. cit.*, p. 99.

53 Mark Saroyan, 'Beyond the Nation-State: Culture and Ethnic Politics in Soviet Transcaucasia', in Suny (ed.), *op. cit.*, p. 408.

54 Gerber, *op. cit.*, p. 141.

55 Lordkipanidze refers to the Abkhazians as 'Apsua' to differentiate them as an ethnic group among the inhabitants of Abkhazia.

56 Mariam Lordkipanidze, *Essays on Georgian History*, Tbilisi, Metsniereba, 1994, pp. 207-208.

57 According to the Soviet tradition, the first step in a research career is the defence of a 'candidate's dissertation', while the second is the defence of a doctoral dissertation. This second doctorate can be compared to a 'doctorat d'État' in France or a 'Habilitation' in Germany.

58 Svetlana Chervonnaya even went so far as to depict the Moscow Institute of Ethnology and Anthropology, for instance, as 'the ideological headquarters' of the Abkhazian secessionist movement. Chervonnaya, *op. cit.*, p. 2.

59 Galina Starovoitova, 'Nationality Policies in the Period of Perestroika: Some Comments from a Political Actor', in Gail W. Lapidus, Victor Zaslavsky with Philip Goldman, *From Union to Commonwealth. Nationalism and Separatism in the Soviet Republics*, Cambridge, Cambridge University Press, 1992, p. 120. On this discussion see Robert J. Kaiser, *The Geography of Nationalism in Russia and the USSR*, Princeton, N.J., Princeton University Press, 1994, pp. 351-353.

60 Gail Lapidus, 'The Impact of Perestroika on the National Question', in Lapidus, Zaslavsky with Goldman, *op. cit.*, p. 61.

61 Anchabadze, *op. cit.*, p. 136.

62 *Ibid.*, p. 141.

63 On the objective dimension of the meaning given to 'homeland' in the former Soviet Union see Kaiser, *op. cit.*, pp. 6-10.

64 Oliver Reisner, 'What Can and Should We Learn From Georgian History? Observations of Someone Who Was Trained in the Western Tradition of Science', *Internationale Schulbuchforschung/ International Textbook Research*, Vol. 20, No. 4, 1998, pp. 418-419.

65   Kaiser defines the homeland as 'the geographical cradle of the nation and also the "natural" place where the nation is to fulfil its destiny': Kaiser, *op. cit.*, p. 10.

66   Smith *et al., op. cit.*, p. 55.

67   See Victor A. Shnirelman, 'From Internationalism to Nationalism: Forgotten Pages of Soviet Archaeology in the 1930s and 1940s', in Philip. L. Kohl and Clare Fawcett (eds), *Nationalism, Politics and the Practice of Archaeology*, Cambridge, Cambridge University Press, 1995, pp. 120-138.

68   A criticism of essentialism in the archaeology of the Caucasus is to be found in Kohl and Tsetskhladze, *op. cit.*, pp. 150-151.

69   Philip L. Kohl and Gocha R. Tsetskhladze, 'Nationalism and Archaeology in the Caucasus', in Kohl and Fawcett, *op. cit.*, p. 158. This estimation was confirmed to me by archaeologist Viktor Loginov from Abkhazia. There are, however, no precise figures which would make it possible to make a comparion with Israel, for instance.

70   Smith *et al., op. cit.*, p. 58.

71   'There is no consensus in the scholarly literature regarding the oldest ethnic map of Western Georgia, particularly its Black Sea coast. However, this refers to an extremely remote period (6th-5th millennia BC), about which there cannot be any discussion of a concrete ethnos, whereas from the second millennium BC, when the picture is relatively clearer, a mainly Kartvelian population is presumed to inhabit Western Transcaucasia. From this latter period up to Classical times, the archaeological material suggests the existence here of a common Colchian, i.e. Kartvelian, culture. (…) In the second and first millennia BC the Kartvelian (properly Svan) ethnic element was widespread in the mountainous and lowland regions of Western Georgia. This conclusion is supported by the evidence of ancient Greek mythology (the expedition of the Argonauts to Colchis) and linguistic research, which points to the existence here of a Kartvelian language by the time of the earliest contacts between Greeks and Colchians. Such a view is fully backed by the evidence of Classical written sources…' Mariam Lordkipanidze, *op. cit.*, p. 190. In this quotation, Kartvelian is a synonym for Georgian, and includes the sub-ethnic groups of Mingrelians, Svans and Laz. Mariam Lordkipanidze writes that she is not sure whether or not there were any non-Georgian tribes along the west of what is now Georgia, but she has no doubt about the predominance of Georgian culture in that region.

72   According to Philip L. Kohl the 'constructivist' perspective in Western scholarship would regard ethnogenesis as a minor matter compared with the study of ethnomorphosis, or the study of the changes that ethnic groups experience over time. See Philip L. Kohl, 'Nationalism and Archaeology: On the Constructions of Nations and the Reconstructions of the Remote Past', *Annual Review of Anthropology*, Vol. 27, 1998, pp. 223-246.

73   Gerber, *op. cit.*, p. 62.

74   Smith *et al., op. cit.*, p. 182.

75   *Ibid.*, pp. 53-4.

76   *Ibid.*, p. 175.

77   *Ibid.*, p. 174.

78   Ted Schatzki refers to Hans-Georg Gadamer. Ted Schatzki, 'Objectivity and Rationality', in Wolfgang Natter, Theodore R. Schatzki and John Paul Jones (eds), *Objectivity and Its Other*, New York, The Guilford Press, 1995, pp. 137-60.

79   Stanislav Lakoba defines scientific objectivity in Georgian-Abkhazian relations negatively, by identifying it with not defending a pro-Georgian point of view. Lakoba, *op. cit.*, p. 98.

80   *Ibid.*, pp. 59-60.

81   *Ibid.*, p. 88.

82 On the distinction between an orthodox nationalism, loyal to the political system, and an unorthodox nationalism, challenging the system, see Rakowska-Harmstone quoted in Sakwa, *op. cit.*, p. 243.

83 Gerber, *op. cit.*, p. 101.

84 *Ibid.*, p. 64

85 *Ibid.*, p. 73.

86 Eduard Shevardnadze, 'Foreword' to Chervonnaya, *op. cit.*, p. xxii.

87 Hewitt, Introduction to Hewitt (ed.), *op. cit.*, p. 17.

88 Paul B. Henze, 'Abkhazia Diary – 1997', in Tütüncu (ed.), *op. cit.*, p. 102.

89 Chervonnaya, *op. cit.*, pp. 54-55.

90 See Gelaschwili, *op. cit.*, pp. 61-66.

91 See Ronald D. Crelinsten, 'Prosecuting Gross Human-Rights Violations from the Perspective of the Victim', in Albert J. Jongman (ed.), *Contemporary Genocides: Causes, Cases, Consequences*, Leiden, PIOOM, 1996, pp. 175-185 and Coppieters, *op. cit.*, p. 164.

92 The number of books and brochures on the history of the region published in Georgia and Abkhazia continues to be significant: Georgian Academy of Sciences. Research Centre for Relations between Nations, *Historic, Political and Legal Aspects of the Conflict in Abkhazia*, Tbilisi, Metsniereba, 1995; Avtandil Menteshashvili, *Istoricheskie predposylki sovremennogo separatizma v Gruzii*, Tbilisi, Tipografiya Tbilisskogo Universiteta, 1998; Grigorii Lezhava, Mezhdu Gruziei i Rossiei. Istoricheskie korni i sovremennie faktory abkhazo-gruzinskogo konflikta (XIX-XX vv.), Moscow, Tsentr po izutscheniyu mezhnatsional'nykh otnoschenii, 1997; Spartak Zhidkov, *Brosok maloi imperii*, Maikop, Aligeia, 1996; Stanislav Lakoba, *Stoletnyaya voina Gruzii protiv Abkhazii*, Gagra, Assotsiatsiya 'Intelligentsiya Abkhazii', 1993; Stanislav Lakoba, *Abkhaziya. Posle dvuch okkupatsii*, Gagra, Assotsiatsiya 'Intelligentsiya Abkhazii', 1994; Yermolai Adzhindzhal, *Iz istorii abkhazskoi gosudarstvennosti*, Sukhum, Assotsiatsiya 'Intelligentsiya Abkhazii', 1996; Yu. Voronov, *Abkhazy: kto oni?*, Gagra, Assotsiatsiya 'Intelligentsiya Abkhazii', 1993.

93 http://www.osce.org/docs/english/summite.htm

Moshe Gammer

4. Nationalism and History: Rewriting the Chechen National Past

The sudden, drastic (and, to a great many, traumatic) dissolution of the USSR in 1991 left all its components facing a vacuum in many fields. One of the more important voids was in the sphere of ideology. Looking urgently for new ideologies instead of the defunct 'Marxism-Leninism' to legitimize their claim to power, most of the political players turned to nationalism. Here, however, a great many of the components of the ex-USSR have been facing another major problem: under Soviet nationality policy the different peoples of the USSR were trapped in the midst of three incompatible processes – nation-building by the different titular groups, the construction of 'Soviet patriotism' and the forging of 'proletarian internationalism'. Thus none of those peoples who had begun national consolidation under the Soviets had a chance to complete it. All of them now therefore need either to redefine existing identities or to replace them by new ones. The redefinition of an identity or the construction of a new one involves re-shaping collective memory and re-writing history.

Consequently, all the components of the ex-USSR – first and foremost among them, the fifteen previous Union republics (Soviet Socialist Republics or SSRs)[1] which on 1 January 1992 found that they were now separate sovereign states – have been involved in a massive re-writing of their past. This need has been even more crucial in Chechnya, which was the only autonomous republic (Autonomous Soviet Socialist Republic or ASSR) within the ex-RSFSR (Russian Soviet Federal Socialist Republic, now turned into the Russian Federation) to secede – a move not allowed by either the Soviet or the new Russian constitutions. One reason (among quite a few) for Chechnya's more crucial need to rewrite history is that it is the only ex-Soviet political unit where nationalists have permanently replaced the ex-Communist Party *apparatchik*s. Ichkeria (the official name of Chechnya) was not the only autonomous entity in the Russian Federation to claim special status.[2] Only Grozny (Chechnya's capital, renamed Johar in 1997), however, has stuck to its claim to full independence, rejecting any solution that would make it look as if it were losing independence and entering the Russian Federation. For that purpose it was even willing to fight a full-scale war, the first round of which (1994-96) it won, at least militarily. Furthermore, in order to achieve independence the Chechen nationalist movement, or at least major parts of it, have had to give up the dream of Vainakh[3] unity and accept the existence of a separate Ingush republic, which has chosen to become a 'subject'[4] of the Russian Federation.

All this has called for both a radical re-moulding of Chechen national identity and a thorough revision of its collective past. The Chechen authorities, the national movement, and in fact all the Chechen intelligentsia – that is, both professional historians and (even more so) many other persons with higher education – have been involved in this revision of their national past and rewriting of their history on both the academic and popular levels. It all began in 1989, when Gorbachev's *glasnost* reached the periphery, and has been steadily growing in momentum ever since. The main milestones in its development have been 1) in 1990, the appointment of a Chechen as republican secretary of the party for the first time since the second world war;[5] 2) what many call the 'Chechen Revolution' – the seizure of power by the national movement in September 1991;[6] 3) the war of 1994-96 and 4) the war that began in 1999. The new version of the Chechen past has had to tackle two challenges: the immediate, political need to justify independence and counter the Russian arguments – legal and other – against secession;[7] and the deeper requirement of de-colonizing, or in this case de-Sovietizing, the nation's psyche, mentality and culture. The arguments of the former and the concepts of the latter are in many cases intertwined.

According to a little-known, adroit proverb, 'even when one walks away from Rome, one is still on the road to Rome'.[8] Indeed, in many cases in the past the first stage of decolonization occurred with the umbilical cord still solidly tied to the colonial metropolitan power. The Chechen case is no exception: the new Chechen historical narrative conducts an ongoing dialogue, or rather an argument, with both its Soviet counterpart and the new official narrative in Moscow. This argument with Moscow is still to a great extent within the Soviet paradigm, amongst other things because the participants on both sides – the authors of the new narrative included – were schooled in the USSR. Thus, while striving to de-Sovietize, the new Chechen historical narrative is still strongly linked to Soviet narratives, ways of arguing and moulds of thinking. It tries to prove, for example, that its national heroes were 'progressive' and 'popular', not 'reactionary'. It tends, like its progenitor, to be openly political, to make value judgements and moralize and to overlook facts inconsistent with its thesis. Moreover, even emotionally it is still very much connected to the ex-USSR, and tries, for example, to prove the Chechens' loyalty and heroism in the 'Great Patriotic War', as the Second World War is still called in the ex-USSR.

The main arguments and concepts which the Chechen nationalist narrative tries to counter are:[9]

(1) The Checheno-Ingush ASSR, as an autonomous republic within a Union republic – the RSFSR – had no sovereignty, no right to self-determination and, therefore, no right of secession from either the RSFSR or the USSR.[10]

(2) The Checheno-Ingush ASSR was formed by and within the USSR where no previous Chechen state existed, which should strengthen the previous argument.

(3) The Chechens were, to use Marxist (in fact Hegelian) terminology, a *'geschichtslose Nation'*.[11] This supplies the previous argument with additional historical depth, since one can argue that the state finally formed for the Chechens was not of their own making but was granted to them by the Soviet authorities. Also, it is part of a broader, typically colonialist attitude.

(4) The Chechens, like all other non-Russian (and especially non-European) peoples of the USSR, had been 'savages' until enlightened by the Russian people who brought them the benefits of civilization, the most important of which was the 'proletarian revolution'.[12] Thus the Soviet authorities aimed to create a 'Homo Sovieticus' by changing the values and mores of the Chechens – and in fact all non-Russians – and this involved, among other things, transforming them into what one might call 'Chechen-speaking Russians'. Seventy years of Soviet brainwashing, coming on top of sixty years of similar (though far less effective) tsarist indoctrination, had some measure of success: the Chechens – especially the urban and educated strata – were Sovietized, although far less than most other peoples of the USSR.

(5) Contained within the previous concept, and resulting from it, is the notion of the 'eternal friendship of the family of peoples of the USSR led by their elder brother, the Russian people'. According to this, each of the non-Russian peoples was drawn to the 'elder brother' from their very first contact, until finally each of them 'voluntarily' joined the Russian state. The resistance to tsarist Russia (and by implication to the USSR) was thus reduced to a handful of 'reactionaries' and 'criminal elements' who acted against the interests and the will of the overwhelming majority of their peoples.[13]

(6) An independent Chechen state is not viable on many grounds (including economic ones) and the Chechens are not able to sustain it. This idea is hinted at in the three immediately preceding points.

In their efforts to construct a de-Sovietized Chechen identity and history the nationalists (and later also the authorities) have been drawing on two pre-Soviet and pre-Russian layers – the Islamic, mainly Sufi Qadiri[14] heritage and the

Chechen national traditions, many of them pre- and some un-Islamic. In this process, Chechen written and oral sources, which were banned in the Soviet period, have been published and used. In the main, however, Chechen historians and writers have been using Russian and Soviet sources (archival and other) and studies (historical, ethnographic, archaeological and other) to find and quote facts and opinions consistent with their approach. This heavy dependence on Russian sources reflects the above-mentioned 'umbilical cord'. But it also demonstrates the fact that Russian is both the main working language of most educated Chechens and the only foreign one they know.

The main motifs in the emerging Chechen historical narrative are:

(1)   The Chechens (or the Vainakhs) are an ancient civilized nation. They are descendants of the Hurrians, the founders of the ancient Kingdoms of Mittani and Urartu[15] and are, therefore, one of the civilizations of the ancient Near East. Since antiquity they were in contact with, and influenced, the peoples of the steppes.[16] The Soviet narrative is, thus, reversed: the Chechens are the Russians' elders in age and civilization and, by implication, are also the ones who indirectly civilized them.

(2)   The Vainakhs have inhabited their present territory continuously since at least the 4th century BC.[17] The northern districts, now populated by Russians, had also been settled by the Chechens until Russian colonization dislodged them. This argument aims to counter the Soviet thesis that the Chechens migrated from the mountains into the lowlands only in the 17th and 18th centuries,[18] and the possible political implications of this.

(3)   They have formed states and polities over the ages. A Vainakh state – Durzuketi – existed in the Northern Caucasus in the 4th and 3rd centuries BC and one of its princesses was the first queen of Georgia.[19] Other states of which they were part included Serir (5th-9th centuries AD), Alaniya (10th-11th centuries) and Simsim (16th century). Before Russian encroachment they formed a democratic society and their *Mehk Khel* – the 'Council of the Land' – was the seat of sovereignty and took all major internal and external decisions. Finally, in the nineteenth century the Chechens voluntarily became part of the *Imamate* – the Islamic state constructed by the leaders of the resistance to Russia. Thus not only do the Chechens form an 'historic nation', but Russian conquest was downright imperialism and an act of aggression.

(4)   The Chechens like to compare their national character to that of a wolf (*borz*) –whose importance in Chechen culture is demonstrated by the fact that it is the emblem of the Republic of Ichkeria. Like the wolf, the Chechens are freedom-loving and untamed and would rather die resisting than surrender; like their lupine ideal they are fearless and do not hesitate

to take on larger and stronger rivals; like the wolf they are loyal to their kin and are ready to sacrifice their lives for them. True to their national character, the Chechens (Vainakhs) have always defended their freedom against foreign invaders, be they the Sasanids, the Byzantine Empire, the Arab Caliphate, the Khazars, the Chingisids, Timur Leng,[20] Nadir Shah, the tsars or the Soviets. Their three-hundred-year-long resistance to Russia is but the most recent chapter in this history of struggle for their liberty. And during this struggle, as in ancient and medieval times, the Chechens have never submitted to Russian rule and have never been resigned to either the *Pax Russica* or *Pax Sovietica*. This narrative thus disregards the fact that generations of Chechens lived normal and peaceful lives under Russian and Soviet rule even though they were never resigned to it.

(5)   Russian and Soviet conquest were blatant cases of aggression and imperialism, followed by colonization and the displacement of the Chechens from their most fertile lands.[21] Furthermore, both empires attempted to carry out the spiritual, cultural, psychological and physical genocide of the Chechens. These latter two themes – resistance and genocide – are the ones most intensively used in Chechen nationalist discourse and will be discussed here at greater length.

The 'Three-Hundred-Year-Long War'

To the Chechen authorities and national movement, the armed conflict of 1994-96 was but the latest round in an ongoing war that had started three centuries before. Although Russian 'robbery raids' against peaceful Chechen (and other Caucasian) villages started under Ivan IV ('the Terrible', 1530-1584),[22] it was under Peter I ('the Great', 1682-1725) that a systematic conquest was attempted and the long war began: during Peter's Persian campaign of 1722, Russian regular troops for the first time encountered the Chechens 'in their native forests, and the result' – the complete destruction of the Russian unit – 'was ominous of what was to take place on numerous occasions'.[23] The narrative constructed in Grozny lists nine peaks of resistance:[24]

1. **The 'First Gazavat' (i.e. Holy War, 1785-92)** under the leadership of Imam Mansur was the first organized and united resistance to the fully-fledged, systematic conquest of the Caucasus started by Catherine II ('the Great', 1763-1796).[25]

2. **The Revolt of 1825-27** led by Shaykh Muhammad of Mayortup, the chief religious authority in the land, and Beybulat (Taimiev), its greatest and most famous war leader,[26] was in reaction to the extremely brutal policy of Aleksei

Yermolov (the omnipotent governor of Georgia and Commander-in-Chief of the Russian forces in the Caucasus, 1816-1826).

3. **The 'Great Gazavat' (1829-59)** led by the three Daghestani Imams of the Naqshbandi-Khalidi Sufi tariqat:[27] Ghazi Muhammad (1829-1832), Hamzat Bek (1832-1834) and the greatest and most successful of them, Shamil (1834-1859).[28]

4. **The Uprising of 1863** broke out in several places in what seemed to be an opportunity to shake off Russian rule provided by the Polish revolt of that year. A significant fact is that it was led by the Qadiri Sufi tariqat.[29]

5. **The 'Lesser Gazavat' (1877-78)** was an attempt to re-establish Shamil's Imamate under Daghestani leadership, made during the Russo-Ottoman war in those years.[30]

6. **The 'Last Gazavat' (1918-21):** following the two revolutions of 1917, an independent, secular 'Mountain Republic' was established on 11 May 1918 but was soon crushed by Denikin, the 'White' Russian general who controlled large areas to the north and east of the Black Sea. It was replaced in September 1919 by Sheikh Uzun Hajji's 'North Caucasian Emirate', which was dissolved by the 'Red Army' in February 1920. In September 1920, a large-scale revolt broke out against the Bolsheviks, led by Shaykh Najm al-Din Hutsali, who assumed the title of Imam and intended to re-establish the Imamate. This lasted until 1921.[31]

7. **The Revolt of 1929-30** in reaction to the Stalinist persecutions of religion and 'collectivization'.

8. **The Israilov Revolt (1940-42)** led by Hasan Israilov, a poet turned resistance leader who, inspired by the Finnish victories in the 'Winter War' of 1939-40, called on his people to rise and turn the Caucasus into a 'second Finland'.[32]

9. **The Current Conflict (1991-)**, beginning with Moscow's attempt to depose the newly elected president Jokhar Dudaev by paratroopers in November 1991, and escalating into a full-scale invasion in December 1994. The Accords of May 1997 temporarily put an end to hostilities but have not resolved the conflict, as the second full-scale invasion of September 1999 has clearly demonstrated.

In between these 'rounds', runs the new narrative, low-intensity resistance (to borrow from modern military jargon) never stopped. During the tsarist period it took the form of what the authorities termed 'widespread banditry'. It was usually aimed at well-to-do Russians, Georgians, Ossetes, Armenians – never at poor fellow-Caucasian Muslims or Western travellers. In the Soviet – mainly Stalinist – period, acts of what was officially reported as 'political banditry' included the assassination of Soviet servicemen, officials and Chechen collaborators (such as kolkhoz chairmen), the destruction of official and military vehicles, derailing of trains and ambushes against military or militia/GPU[33] units. The last *abrek* (that is, warrior against Soviet rule) was killed in 1976.

The main external political goal of this narrative is fairly clear: if the Chechens have never submitted to Russian rule, then their declaration of independence is not secession. On the contrary: the Russian attempts to prevent this independence, culminating in the invasion of 1994, are imperialism and acts of aggression. That is why the Chechen leadership have consistently demanded that a peace treaty should specifically affirm that it is ending a three-century-old war.[34] Yeltsin's statement to that effect at the signing ceremony of the May 1997 Russo-Chechen accord was to them the most precious victory.

The main internal political goals are no less transparent. One is to legitimize the current nationalist regime and its leaders – Johar Dudaev and, after his death, Zelimkhan Yandarbiev and Aslan Maskhadov. Another is to sanction the regime's course of action – insistence on independence even at the cost of confrontation and full-scale war with Russia. A third aim is to augment national cohesion and pride, and through them to mobilize the people to support the regime and its aims. In some ways, the historical periods and heroes it has chosen to highlight point to these aims. Out of the long history of resistance, the new national narrative speaks little about the Soviet period and deals briefly with three out of the five 'peaks' of resistance to tsarist Russia. It has chosen to concentrate on only two of these five 'peaks' – the first (1785-92) and the third (1829-59). Accordingly, even though other resistance leaders are discussed, the two major national heroes are Imams Mansur and Shamil.

Imam Mansur (1760?-1794) was the title assumed by Ushurma in 1785, when he began to call on the Chechens and other Caucasians to resist Russian encroachment. A Chechen from the *aul* (village) of Aldi, on the outskirts of present-day Grozny, Ushurma was, according to tradition – though no documentation is available to confirm it – a Naqshbandi Shaykh. He fought the Russia of Catherine the Great for seven years with varying degrees of success, and was finally captured on 3 July 1792 in Anapa, when Russian troops took the city from the Ottomans. On 26 October 1792 he was sentenced by Catherine to life imprisonment and died in prison on 24 April 1794. The official cause of death was consumption.

While his immediate success was fairly limited, Imam Mansur's imprint on the Caucasus and its history has been enormous. One of the best – and least appreciated – books on the Russian conquest of the Caucasus summarized Imam Mansur's significance in the following words:

> He was the first to preach and lead the [...] Holy War against the infidel Russians in the Caucasus [... and] in his endeavour to unite [...] the fierce tribes of mountain and forest, he it was who first

taught them that in religious reform lay the one chance of preserving their cherished liberty and independence.[35]

Indeed, in many fields Imam Mansur marked the way to be followed by his successors – the Imams of 'the Great Gazavat' in the nineteenth century. Even a superficial glance would reveal that in many, if not all, of their strategies, tactics and methods they were imitating him. More importantly, the changes he introduced into the lives of his people, even if not completed in his own lifetime, would have a lasting effect.

While Russian and Soviet historiography have used nothing but pejoratives to describe Imam Mansur,[36] to the Chechens he has always been a saint and a hero. However, with a single exception[37] they were compelled to keep silent about him, which best suited the post-Stalin Soviet authorities. Nevertheless, in the 1970s a Chechen historian managed to 'sneak in' and publish positive descriptions of Mansur.[38] As Gorbachev's policy of *glasnost* reached the Checheno-Ingush ASSR, Chechen historians started a campaign to rewrite the description of Mansur in both professional-historical forums[39] and the popular mass media.[40]

Since the proclamation of independence, in November 1991, Mansur has become one – and in many ways the more significant – of the two most important heroes in the official Chechen pantheon. Among the first acts of the new government were the renaming of Grozny airport and one of the city's two main squares after him. There was also a suggestion of erecting Mansur's statue instead of that of Yermolov, which had been pulled down in 1990.[41]

What might be called the 'homecoming' of Mansur reached a peak in May 1992, when an international conference to discuss him was convened in Grozny.[42] It was attended by major political figures – including President Dudaev, who addressed it – and enjoyed massive media coverage. The publication of a major work by a Chechen historian[43] had been timed to coincide with the conference, as was the issue of the first postage stamps of the independent Chechen Republic, one of which carried an image of the Imam.[44]

The choice of Mansur is a fairly obvious one. On the home front Imam Mansur, being a Chechen, helps to boost Chechen identity and pride. Outside, Chechnya has been aware that in order to secure its own independence it needs to spread 'decolonization from Russia' to other parts of the Northern Caucasus. The Chechen authorities under Dudaev publicly promoted the idea of North Caucasian unity. The Chechen Republic had the only government represented in the Confederation of the Caucasian Mountain Peoples.[45] Chechen volunteers fought on the side of the Abkhazians against the Georgians – a fact widely publicized by Grozny. The war of 1994-96 served to substantiate this awareness among wider circles in Chechnya. In 1998, for example, 157 different political parties, movements, foundations and organizations of different kinds, all dedicated to Caucasian unity in one form or another, were active in the Chechen Republic.[46] Making Mansur a national hero lends legitimacy both to the Chechen call to other 'mountaineers' to join their struggle and to their claim to lead it. After all, he was the Chechen progenitor of the resistance to Russia and of the state based on the *shari'a* (Islamic law) – the *Imamat* – and he was the first to call on all the people of the Northern Caucasus to unite.

The other historical hero has been included by overwhelming popular accord, although dissident voices have been heard: ***Imam Shamil (Shamuyil, i.e., Samuel)*** (1797-1871) was the third and most successful leader of the 'Great Gazavat'. During his twenty-five years of leadership (1834-59) he managed to unite Daghestanis and Chechens and to build a state – the Imamate – with an orderly administration, systematic taxation and a regular army. All this he achieved while continuously fighting the Russians and dealing them quite a few painful blows. However, the odds against him were such that in 1859 he was finally left with no choice but to surrender. After ten years in a 'golden cage' in Russia, Shamil was allowed by Alexander II (1855-81) to set off on the *hajj* (the pilgrimage to Mecca, one of the five 'pillars', or basic commandments, of Islam). In 1871 he died in Medina.

Unlike Mansur, Shamil was described in quite approving terms in Russian historiography. In the Soviet Union he was first celebrated as a leader of a national liberation movement, then vilified as a Turkish and English spy, until he finally emerged as a bizarre hermaphrodite, at once 'progressive' and 'reactionary'.[47] To the Chechens, Shamil has always been one of the prominent heroes and symbols of their resistance, notwithstanding the fact that he was not a Chechen. They were therefore, alongside the Daghestanis, his most fervent defenders in Soviet historiography. In fact, when they had been denied the option of mentioning other national heroes, writing about Shamil became almost the only outlet for Chechen nationalism.

After the declaration of independence the Chechen nationalist authorities clearly demonstrated Shamil's place in their pantheon of heroes in the above-mentioned issue of stamps in May 1992. This was confirmed on 21 July 1997 when the Republic of Ichkeria officially celebrated Shamil's bicentennial.[48] In the central ceremony President Maskhadov unveiled a memorial complex for Shamil in Vedeno, the Imam's capital between 1845 and 1859. The complex includes a mosque with a minaret 25 metres high (symbolizing Shamil's 25 years of leading the resistance), a *Madrassa* (traditional Muslim institute of higher education, where *'ulama* – authorized experts on Islamic law and religious leaders – are trained and given a certificate) and a wall from his fortress, destroyed by the Russian Army.[49]

Yet the nationalist historical narrative under construction does not speak at length about Shamil himself.[50] In fact the heroes of this narrative are neither

Mansur nor Shamil, but rather the Chechen people. Thus emphasis is laid on the centrality of Chechnya and the Chechens to Shamil's struggle and rule: on the fact that the Chechens supplied him with many of his bravest soldiers,[51] his ablest generals, governors and engineers, his best advisors and his most loyal lieutenants;[52] that the bitterest, hardest, bloodiest fighting took place in Chechnya – here Shamil gained his greatest victories[53] and here he was finally beaten after a long war of attrition; that Chechnya was the bread basket of his dominions and strategically its most important part[54] – which is highlighted by the fact that between 1840 and 1859 Shamil chose to locate his 'capitals' there.

More importantly, the emphasis is on the *continuing resistance*. Shamil was but one leader, and the struggle he led but one phase in this ongoing 'three-hundred-year-long war'. Thus, in some cases, promoters of the Chechen historical narrative have berated Shamil for his surrender in 1859.[55] An extreme expression by a diaspora Chechen, totally unacceptable to those constructing the nationalist narrative in Chechnya itself, stated:

> Imam Shamil was a Dahgistani. He led the uprising against the Russians. The Chechens joined him in his struggle. But when he surrendered, the Chechens called him a traitor [...] The Chechens consider Shamil a traitor. They do not consider this [his surrender – MG] as an acceptance of Russian rule.[56]

As a counter to Shamil and a symbol of 'true' resistance to the bitter end, some builders of this historical narrative promote one of his *na'ibs* (lieutenants) – Baysungur from Benoy – who, 'extremely crippled in combat' and 'able to move and take part in battles only tied to his horse', continued to fight the Russians for almost two years after the Imam. 'He represented', wrote a modern Chechen author, '*a model symbol of the Chechen people's physical shape and insubordination at that period of time*' [emphasis mine – MG].[57] Nevertheless, Shamil remains one of the major heroes of the emerging nationalist and official historiography, a fact that can be explained by several reasons.

First, Shamil just could not be ignored. After all, he was the most successful and famous of the resistance leaders and, although not a Chechen himself, he led the Chechens for far longer than any other chief.[58] Second, he was the founder of an Islamic state – the *Imamat* – based on the *shari'a*, to which the Chechen authorities have been committed since independence and more fervently since the end of the war. Third, although not one of themselves, to many Chechens Shamil was a national hero. This phenomenon gathered momentum in the Soviet period when Shamil was the only hero the Chechens could publicly identify with in order to give vent to their national grievances and nationalist feelings. Fourth, Shamil is the national hero of the Daghestanis, particularly the Avars.[59]

He is thus a central link with the neighbour that is so important to Chechnya on numerous levels, first and foremost that of North Caucasian unity.[60] This became very clear in the above-mentioned ceremony to mark Shamil's bicentennial, on 21 July 1997, when president Aslan Maskhadov praised Shamil's contribution 'to the liberation struggle of the Caucasian peoples' and called on his listeners to 'remember at all times' that 'all the people living in the Caucasus constitute one "Caucasian" nation'.[61]

In the early 1990s the two heroes complemented each other as the precedents, legitimization and role models for the leader of the current struggle of the Chechen national independence movement, and the first president of the republic. Already, he was put on an equal footing with them.

Johar Dudaev (1944-96) was the first Chechen to reach the rank of general in the Soviet Air Force. In the late 1980s and early 1990s he commanded a division of strategic bombers stationed in Estonia where, in January 1991, he stopped Soviet special forces from moving in on Estonian nationalists demanding independence. In March 1991 he was elected leader of the Executive Committee of the All-National Congress of the Chechen People (*ispolkom Obshchenatsional'no-go kongressa chechenskogo naroda*, that is, the national movement) and in May he resigned from the Air Force. On 27 October 1991 Dudaev won the presidential election.[62] Four days later, on 1 November 1991, he signed the 'Act of Sovereignty of the Republic'. He led the struggle for independence, which deteriorated into full-scale war following the Russian invasion of December 1994. On 14 December 1995 the All-National Congress of the Chechen People extended his term of presidency until 'proper democratic and internationally monitored elections can be held'.[63] On the night of 21-22 April 1996 he was reported to have been killed by a Russian air-to-ground missile which homed in on his satellite telephone.

Like Mansur and Baysungur (both Chechens) and unlike Shamil, Dudaev died sword in hand as a *shahid (*martyr, one who was killed in a *Jihad*). Unlike them, however, his death is denied by many.[64] In that, he resembles the man most venerated by the overwhelming majority of the Chechens: *Shaykh Kunta Hajji* (1830?-1867), who introduced the Qadiriyya into the Caucasus in the early 1860s, following the collapse of Shamil's Imamate. Within several years he made the Qadiriyya into the dominant Sufi *tariqa* in the social, economic and political life – in fact in the daily life – of the Chechens. The Russian authorities, always suspicious of any movement not fully controlled by them, took Kunta Hajji by surprise and arrested him on 15 January 1864, transferred him to a military prison and 'resettle[d him] for life under police supervision' in a remote town in the province of Novgorod, where he died on 31 May 1867. His followers deny his death. They believe to this very day that he is in a state of hidden existence, from which he intervenes on their behalf and guides their actions.[65]

While not in any way an official hero, Kunta Hajji is in fact far more than that. To most Chechens he is their *ustadh* (spiritual guide and master), and his significance is far greater than that of all the above-mentioned heroes combined. This in itself would be enough to explain the great number of publications about him since the declaration of independence.[66] There is, however, another reason for Kunta Hajji's importance: the Qadiriyya withstood Soviet efforts to uproot it, and after the declaration of independence it came to play a leading role in the public life of the republic. It has, in fact, been aligned with Chechen nationalism at least since the 1940s, and has been a major support base for the nationalist regime in Chechnya since 1991.[67] Thus the slightest hint, by implication – nothing else would be acceptable – comparing Dudaev to him, would give a strong boost to the legitimization of the nationalist regime and greatly expand support for it among different sectors of the population.

The Chain of Attempts at Genocide

According to the nationalist narrative, Russian military and political authorities conducted a war of extermination against the Chechens from their very first attempts at the systematic conquest of the Caucasus. The reason for this was the obstinate resistance of the Chechens and their refusal to accept Russian rule. But even the threat of genocide did not stop Chechen resistance. The nationalist narrative lists four attempts at genocide, laying greatest emphasis on the third:

1. **The Russian Conquest (18th-19th Centuries).** Already Potyomkin, Catherine II's commander in the Caucasus, had suggested that 'it is impossible to subdue the Chechens unless one exterminates them completely'. Some forty years later the Emperor Nicholas I (1825-55) instructed his commander in the Caucasus 'to tame forever the mountain peoples, or *exterminate the insubordinate*' [emphasis mine – MG].[68] Present-day Chechen writers hold that Chechen losses, direct and indirect (that is, the loss of the potential descendants of those killed), during the nine decades of struggle to conquer Chechnya and then to establish Russian rule there, exceeded 1,000,000(!).[69] The Chechens count three specific Russian methods of genocide, which have been used also by both Soviet and post-Soviet Russia:
   • *Systematic Campaign of Starvation:* The Russian authorities blockaded the unconquered areas and refused to allow the Chechens import essential goods; they developed the tactics of 'punitive raids', which as a rule involved systematically destroying and burning villages and hamlets, ruining all supplies and gardens, stampeding and burning fields and seizing livestock and movables. By these and other means, including the destruc-

tion of forests, they pushed the population from its most fertile lands into the mountains, where many died of deprivation and hunger.[70]

- *Exile:* In the late 1850s, the authorities considered transferring the Chechens from their homeland to inner Russia.[71] In the mid 1860s they actively 'encouraged' them to follow the Circassians and emigrate *en masse* to the Ottoman Empire. Some 5,000 families, all in all about 23,000 people – 'the most energetic, the most freedom-loving part of the population' – emigrated, as a present-day Chechen historian laments. 'It was an ethnic catastrophe which deprived the people of its finest sons.'[72] Also in later periods, most notably the late 1880s and early 1910s, Russian 'encouragement' resulted in waves of emigration to the Ottoman Empire.

- *Massacre:* Many of the 'punitive raids' ended in massacres, especially if the population was caught unawares and defended itself. The usual excuse of the Russian officers was that 'the exasperated soldiers went out of control'. There were also, however, deliberate massacres of entire villages. The most notorious of these was the massacre of Dadi Yurt on 27 September 1819. On specific orders from Yermolov, Russian troops surrounded the village and slaughtered all its inhabitants – men, women and children.

The slaughter of Dadi Yurt has remained a symbol of genocide and resistance to this very day. Its impact is almost as strong nowadays as it was 180 years ago. It is commemorated by numerous folk traditions and songs as well as by works of art and literature, which tell of the heroic defence of the village by its men, encouraged by the dancing and singing of the girls in the village square. Once all the men were killed, the women and maidens took their place – dagger in hand. To the Russians' astonishment the surviving young women preferred to cut their own throats rather than be taken prisoner. The few women who had been captured and distributed among Russian officers jumped from the ferry into the river, each taking 'her' officer with her.[73]

2. **The Soviet Conquest (1920s-1930s)** was achieved by similar methods of systematic terror, mass arrests and exile to the Gulag, starvation and forceful retaliation against entire villages. The Soviet regime was far more effective at mass killing than the tsarist government because of the advanced technology at their disposal (machine-guns, aircraft, etc.). Thus, according to Soviet statistics quoted by a Chechen writer, in 1937 the Chechen population numbered 200,800 fewer than in 1929.[74] But, more important than the physical genocide, says the Chechen narrative, the Soviet campaigns against the so-called 'Kulaks', the religious persecution, the double change of alphabet (first into Latin and then into Cyrillic) amounted to spiritual and cultural genocide. To them it was a deliberate attempt to 'de-Chechenize' the Chechens so as to pave the way for their Russification.

3. **The 'Deportation' (1944-57).** In 1944 on Soviet Army Day, 23 February, all
Chechens (and Ingush) were rounded up from all over the USSR (including
soldiers from the front) and 'deported' to Central Asia, where they were settled under a 'special regime'. The Checheno-Ingush ASSR was abolished and
demoted to the Grozny District, while parts were annexed to the neighbouring Georgian SSR and North Ossetian ASSR. Thus Stalin finally carried out
the proposal of many past officials and generals, which the tsarist authorities
had never adopted.

The official reason for the 'deportation' was given as mass 'treason' and collaboration by the Chechens with Nazi Germany though the *Wehrmacht* had
hardly set foot on the territory of the Checheno-Ingush ASSR).[75] Although
they were exonerated by Khrushchev, this accusation of treason remained in
common use and continued to be taught in schools, even in the Checheno-
Ingush ASSR, until the dissolution of the USSR.[76] In an apparent internal
contradiction (not uncommon in nationalist – indeed all politically-related –
historiographies), the Chechen nationalist narrative puts a great deal of effort
into disproving this charge of 'treason' against the empire it claims the
Chechens have never been part of.[77] Numerous memoirs by Chechen soldiers
in the Red Army and documents related to their heroism and loyalty in the
battles against the *Wehrmacht* have been published.[78] The most frequently
quoted event is the defence, to the death, of the fortress of Brest-Litovsk by a
Chechen unit.[79]

To the Chechens, the so-called 'deportation' is the worst catastrophe in their
collective memory. It is also the most recent (or was until the war of 1994-96
and the one which started in 1999), and is still a living memory to a great many
of them. After a long time in which commemorations of the deportation were
restricted, in 1989 people's memories, evidence and documents began to be
published, and this process gathered momentum after the declaration of independence.[80] According to the nationalist narrative it was the most comprehensive and blatant attempt to wipe the Chechens off the face of the earth as a
nation and, as such, a crime unprecedented in the entire history of humanity.

- *Physical Extermination:* The rounding up and transportation of the depor-
tees was carried out with great brutality. Those unable to move – old people,
hospitalized patients, or simply those who did not understand the instruc-
tions because they did not speak Russian – were murdered. Many died in the
trucks and cattle trains in which they were transported. Others perished at
their places of resettlement – of starvation, disease, sheer fatigue and weakness or exposure to the extremes of a climate they were not used to. According to one source, chemicals and poisons were added to the food supplied to
the Chechens during their deportation.[81] This source calculates that roughly
60-65% of the deported Chechens perished during those years.[82]

The most hideous mass murder happened in Khaybakh, the highest and most isolated Chechen *aul*. Since it was impossible to bring in trucks, the NKVD colonel commanding the operation decided not to bother moving the population. Instead, they were lined up and shot, together with those Soviet soldiers who refused to shoot civilians. Having become a forceful imprint on the Chechen collective memory and consciousness, Khaybakh reinforced and gave special significance to previous massacres, first and foremost that of Dadi Yurt. In the years between the declaration of independence and the war of 1994-96, an association was established to dig out and bury the remains and to make Khaybakh into a memorial.[83]

- *Cultural and Spiritual Obliteration:* The deported were prevented from having an education in their own language – a policy continued as far as possible after rehabilitation and repatriation. In all the schools in Grozny, for example, the language of instruction was Russian only. That is why a large proportion of those under the age of fifty have not mastered Chechen as a literary language. The practice of religion was severely punished when discovered and any cultural activity discouraged, though not completely prevented.

- *Wiping Out Their Trace:* To ensure that the Chechens would never return, others, mainly Russians and Ukrainians, were settled in their homes. But the regime went further than that. The names Chechnya and Chechens disappeared from official publications and textbooks. All the geographical names were changed to Russian ones. Mosques, mausoleums of saints and any other monuments connected to the Chechens were destroyed. Chechnya was to become a Russian land and the Chechens were to be forgotten. Most painful to the Chechens, however, was the destruction of the graveyards.[84] 'What could be more loathsome', wrote a British journalist who covered the war of 1994-96, 'to a people who consider ancestors as important as the living, who still rise out of their car seats in respect as they drive past cemeteries?'[85] Indeed, 'as soon as they got a chance they gathered all the stones up again and built a memorial, a garden of death in the centre of Grozny. Dignity was restored'.[86]

Although rehabilitated by Khrushchev in 1956 and allowed to return to their homeland and to re-establish the Checheno-Ingush ASSR, the Chechens (and the Ingush) continued to be suspected by the authorities. They were strictly controlled by Moscow and therefore not allowed to settle again in many of the mountain villages where it would have been extremely difficult to keep them under supervision. One manifestation of this mistrust and control was the fact that, until Gorbachev's policy of *glasnost'*, a Russian had always been the first party secretary of the republic.

4. **The War of 1994-96.** To Chechen spokesmen, the war was but another such attempt at genocide.[87] The indifference to civilian casualties in the indiscriminate bombardment of Grozny, the use of aircraft and helicopter gunships to wipe out entire villages without warning the population, the mass arrests of men in concentration camps where they were subjected to torture, the smear campaign against the 'Chechen mafia' by the authorities and the subsequent harassment – by the police as well as by hooligans – of so-called 'persons of Caucasian origin' in the main urban centres of Russia – these and many other deeds point (according to the Chechen narrative) to genocidal aims on the part of the Russian authorities. Of all the indiscriminate killing of civilians during this war, the most atrocious occurred in Samashki in April 1995, when Russian Internal Ministry troops murdered scores of civilians.[88] Samashki has thus joined the chain of symbols of genocide beginning with Dadi Yurt and including Khaybakh.

Furthermore, in the indiscriminate bombing of Grozny in the winter of 1995, the most important institutions of cultural and historical significance were destroyed. Among them were the monument to the deportation, mentioned above; the Central State Archives, where irreplaceable collections of documents and manuscripts were held;[89] the Humanities Research Institute;[90] the university, and the museum. The Chechens strongly believe that this was not merely one of the effects of the bombing but a deliberate attempt to complete the task, begun by Stalin, of wiping out all traces of the Chechens.

The theme of genocide has two clear, immediate political goals: internationally, it aims to raise support and gain recognition for Chechnya's right to independence on moral and emotional grounds. After all, how can one allow Russia to continue to rule Chechnya, if it is guilty of genocide against the Chechens? Furthermore, how can one refuse the victims of genocide the redress of independent statehood?[91] Internally it has powerful mobilizing appeal, the deportation in particular being, according to some historians, a case of 'chosen trauma'.[92] Indeed, a large body of evidence points to the fact that fears of a second 'deportation' and the resolve never to let such a thing happen again seem to have played a pivotal role in the bitter Chechen resistance to the Russian forces.

In a broader sense, these two motifs – genocide and resistance – are specific cases of the general themes of victimization and heroism, which practically all nationalist historiographies use extensively.[93] In the Chechen case, as in so many others, they are mutually-reinforcing sides of the same coin: the memory of genocide brings to the fore the sense of victimization and thus stiffens the resolve to resist. The memory of resistance, especially in face of genocide, generates pride and sets a standard of behaviour to be followed. And that, according to the Chechen narrative, is what makes the Chechens unique in history: even in the Gulag, as Solzhenitsyn testified (Chechen authors quote this with particular pride):

> (…) there was one nation which did not surrender to the psychology of submission – not distinct individuals or a few mutineers but the entire nation as a whole. These were the Chechens.[94]

Notes

1. The USSR was a federation of several dozen autonomous entities, all with different areas and population sizes and different levels of authority. They were arranged on five levels: Soviet Socialist Republics (SSR), Autonomous Soviet Socialist Republics (ASSR), Autonomous Provinces, Districts and Sub-Districts. According to the Soviet constitution, only the fifteen SSRs were 'sovereign' states which had joined the USSR voluntarily and had the privilege of seceding. They were thus the only direct members of the USSR. All other 'autonomies' were parts of the SSRs in which they were included, lacked 'sovereignty' and had no right to secede either from their SSR or from the USSR.

2. Tatarstan, for example, refused to sign the Federation treaty, and instead signed a bilateral treaty with Moscow in 1994. Others, like Khakassia, waited on the sidelines to see what Tatarstan (and Chechnya) would achieve.

3. Vainakh is the common name for the Ingush and Chechens. The Ingush are very close to the Chechens ethnically, linguistically and otherwise. In fact most Chechens consider them to be part of their own people. However, different historical backgrounds – 'the Ingush did not participate either in the Shamil movement in the nineteenth century or in the great rebellion of 1920-22' (Alexandre Bennigsen and S. Enders Wimbush, *Muslims of the Soviet Empire. A Guide*, London, Hurst, 1985, p. 189) – strongly cultivated by Russian and Soviet authorities, created separate identities for them. While most Ingush nationalists insisted on their own statehood, a great many Chechen nationalists wanted a united Vainakh state.

4. This is the official Russian title of members of the Russian Federation. Subjects (*subyekty*) are not only the autonomous republics but also the different regions (*oblast*) and 'lands' (*krai*).

5. From their 'rehabilitation' by Khrushchev, in 1957, until Gorbachev's policy of *glasnost*, a Russian had always been the first party secretary of the republic. This was in strong contradiction to the usual Soviet practice of having a member of the titular nationality as first secretary (while a Russian was the second secretary and had real power), and it thus underlined the degree to which Moscow distrusted the Chechens and Ingush.

6. There are, however, those who object to this term on the ground that it might be reminiscent of the 'Communist [i.e. Bolshevik – MG] coup' and thus be tantamount to a recognition of 'Communism as a worthy enemy' (private communication).

7. This study concentrates on the rewriting of the past. Other activities and fields, such as international law, are outside its scope.

8. Robert Silverberg, *Nightwings*, Part I: 'Nightwings'. In the original, in a distant future the city is called 'Roum'.

9. The following is an attempt to systematize and unify different and sometimes contradictory individual approaches. A great many of the terms used here are mine, and not necessarily those of Chechen writers.

10 Chechnya declared its independence on 1 November 1991, before the official dissolution of the USSR on 31 December 1991.

11 'Non-historical' (literally: 'history-less') nation is the term used by Friedrich Engels. Cf. Michael Lowy and Claudine Weil, *Les Marxistes et la question nationale, 1848-1914*, Paris, Maspero, 1974.

12 Correspondingly any signs of non-Russian culture were disregarded. Thus, for example, in the cards prepared for each deported family in 1944 (and tirelessly collected and saved by the Chechens until their destruction during the bombardment of Grozny in 1995), many Chechen heads of families were described as 'illiterates', which did not prevent them from signing in Arabic at the bottom of the card ...

13 For the emergence of the formula and its development up to the mid 1960s, see Lowel R. Tillet, *The Great Friendship. Soviet Historians on the Non-Russian Nationalities*, Chapel Hill, N.C., University of North Carolina Press, 1969. For later developments as well as for the implications of the formula for Chechnya and Daghestan, see Moshe Gammer, 'Shamil in Soviet Historiography', *Middle Eastern Studies*, Vol. 28, No. 4, 1992, pp. 729-777. Publications in this spirit continued to be printed in Groznyi well into Gorbachev's *glasnost'*, up to 1989. E.g.: *Istoki velikoi druzhby*, Groznyi, 1978; *Istochnikovedenie istorii dorevolyutsionnoi Checheno-Ingushetii*, Groznyi, 1988; *Ukreplenie druzhby i internatsional'nykh svyazei trudyashchikhsya ChIASSR v protsesse sotsialisticheskogo stroitel'stva*, Groznyi, 1988; *Progressivnoe vliyanie Rossii na sotsial'no-ekonomicheskoe i politicheskoe razvitie narodov Checheno-Ingushetii (dorevolyutsionnyi period)*, Groznyi, 1989.

14 Sufism is the mystical dimension of Islam, and also has an important role in popular religion. The Qadiriyya is one of the four oldest and most prestigious *tariqat*s (brotherhoods) and is one of the most widespread, perhaps even *the* most widespread. Unlike most *tariqat*s, who are concentrated in specific areas, the Qadiriyya is present all over the Muslim world.

15 L. O. Bubakhin and Dolkhan A.-A. Khozhaev, 'Potomki Nefertiti', *Komsomol'skoe plemya*, 11 February 1989, p. 10; Lema Usmanov, *Nepokorennaya Chechnya*, Moscow, 1997, pp. 32-33. Khozhaev was head of the archives administration under the Dudaev government. At the time of writing (summer 1999) he is secretary of the committee for drafting the new constitution. Ahmadov was professor of history at the University of Grozny. Usmanov is the representative of the Republic of Ichkeria to the USA.

16 Yakub Vagapov, *Vainakhi i sarmaty. Nakhskii plast v sarmatskoi onomastike*, Groznyi, 1990. Gapurov is professor of history at the university of Grozny.

17 Usmanov, *op. cit.*, p. 34.

18 For example, N. G. Volkova, *Etnicheskii sostav naseleniya Severnogo Kavkaza v XVII - nachale XX veka*, Moscow, 1974.

19 This version thus claims indirectly that the Vainakhs civilized the Georgians, which reverses the usual Georgian (-originated) and Russian/Soviet version according to which the Georgians were the ones to bring the torch of civilization to the 'barbarian' tribes north of the main Caucasus range.

20 Hajji Khizriev, 'Bitva na Tereke Khulagidov s Dzhuchidami i bor'ba gortsev Zakavkazya protiv inozemnykh zakhvatchikov v XIII-XIV vv.', in A. I. Khasbulatov *et al.* (eds), Checheno-Ingushetiya v politicheskoi istorii Rossii i Kavkaza v dorevolyutsionnom proshlom, Groznyi, 1990, pp. 101-114. *idem, Kavkaztsy protiv Timura. (Bor'ba gortsev Severnogo Kavkaza protiv ekspansii Timura)*, Groznyi, 1992. Khizriev is a former senior researcher at the Institute of Humanities of the Chechen Republic.

21 A. I. Khasbulatov, 'Agrarnyi vopros v politike tsarizma v Checheno-Ingushetii vo II pol XIX - nach. XX v.', in Khasbulatov *et al.* (eds), *op. cit.*, pp. 5-28; Sharpudin Ahmadov, 'K voprosu o

pereselencheskoi politike tsarizma v Terskoi oblasti v poreformennoe vremya', in *ibid.*, 1990, pp. 29-48; Kh. S. Ahmadov and G. A. Gorchkhanova, 'Soslovno-pozemel'nyi vopros v poreformennoi Checheno-Ingushetii', in *ibid.*, pp. 48-61; E. D. Muzhokhoeva, 'Checheno-Ingushetiya v administrativno-politicheskoi sisteme upravleniya Terskoi oblasti v 40-60-e gody XIX veka', in *ibid.*, pp. 61-76.

22 For a description from this point of view see, for example, Kh. A. Akiev and A. T. Khashagul'-gov, 'K politicheskoi situatsii na Tereke v 1651-1652 godakh', in Khasbulatov *et al.* (eds), *op. cit.*, pp. 67-86. From 1991 to 1994 Akiev was head of the Institute of Humanities of the Chechen Republic. Khasbulatov is a professor at the University of Grozny and brother of the former chairman of the Russian parliament.

23 John Frederick Baddeley, *The Russian Conquest of the Caucasus*, London, 1908, p. 25. For later battles from the Chechen perspective see, e.g., Yavus Z. Akhmadov, 'Politicheskie sobytiya na Severnom Kavkaze v XVI - 40-kh godakh XVII veka', in A. I. Khasbulatov *et al.* (eds), *op. cit.*, pp. 87-101; *idem*, 'Vzaimootnosheniya Chechni i Rossii (vtoraya polovina XVI - seredina XIX vv.)', in Yu. A Aydaev (ed.), *Chechentsy: Istoriya i sovremennost'*, Moscow, 1996, pp. 145-150; Dolkhan Khozhaev, 'Khankal'skoe srazhenie (1735 g.)', *Zavety Ilyicha* (Grozny district local newspaper), 8 December 1998.

24 For the most comprehensive and articulate exposition of this narrative, see Usmanov, *op. cit.*, pp. 68-85. And cf. Moshe Gammer, 'The Russo-Chechen Conflict in Historical Perspective', in Mehmet Tütüncü (ed.), *Caucasus – War and Peace: The New World Disorder in Caucasia*, Haarlem (The Netherlands), Sota, 1998, pp. 43-57.

25 *'Al-Imam al-Mansur'* means in Arabic 'the Victorious Leader'. The best and most comprehensive study of Imam Mansur is still Alexandre Bennigsen, 'Un mouvement populaire au Caucase du XVIIIe siècle: la guerre sainte de Sheikh Mansur (1785-1794). Page mal connue et controversée des relations russo-turques', *Cahiers du Monde Russe et Sovietique*, Vol. 5, No. 2, 1964, pp. 159-205.

26 The first piece to published about Beybulat was Alvi Musaev and Dolkhan Khozhaev, 'Slavnyi Beibulat – groza Kavkaza', *Komsomol'skoe plemia*, 5 October 1989. Two years later a book was dedicated to this hero: L. N. Kolosov, *Slavnyi Beibulat. Istoriko-biograficheskii ocherk*, Groznyi, 1991.

27 The Naqshbandiyya is one of the most widespread Sufi *tariqat*s in Islam. 'Strictly orthodox' from its beginning, the Naqshbandiyya spread from its area of origin in Central Asia to India where, in the seventeenth century, it was transformed into 'the vanguard of renascent Islamic orthodoxy' (Bernard Lewis, *The Middle East and the West*, New York, Weidenfeld, 1966, p. 96). From India its 'militant revivalism' (*ibid.*, p. 97) spread to other parts of the Muslim world and influenced both resistance to foreign encroachment and conquest and so-called 'fundamentalist' Islamic movements. For the Naqshbandiyya, see Hamid Algar, 'A Brief History of the Naqshbandi Order', in Marc Gaborieau, Alexandre Popovic and Thierry Zarcone (eds), *Naqshbandis. Historical Development and Present Situation of a Muslim Mystical Order*, Istanbul, Isis, 1990. For its Khalidi branch, which dominates in the Caucasus, see Butrus Abu-Manneh, 'The Naqshbandiyya-Mujaddidiya in the Ottoman Lands in the Early 19th Century', *Die Welt des Islams*, Vol. 12, 1982, pp. 1-12. For its emergence in the Caucasus, see Moshe Gammer, 'The Beginnings of the Naqshbandiyya in Daghestan and the Russian Conquest of the Caucasus', *Die Welt des Islams*, Vol. 34, 1994, pp. 204-217.

28 For Shamil and his two predecessors, see Moshe Gammer, *Muslim Resistance to the Tsar: Shamil and the Conquest of Chechnia and Daghestan.* London, Frank Cass, 1994.

29 The Qadiriyya surfaced in the Caucasus in the 1850s, preaching peace and submission to Russia. This is why it was banned by Shamil. After Shamil's surrender the overwhelming majority

of the Chechens, driven by war fatigue and their disappointment with the Naqshbandi Imams, became (and have remained until the present) adherents of the Qadiriyya. That this pacifist movement (to use modern terminology) was driven to lead a rebellion is in itself a statement about Russian rule. For further details, see Moshe Gammer, 'The Qadiriyya in the Northern Caucasus', *Journal of the History of Sufism*, Vol.1, No. 2, 2000 (October 2000; Special Issue: The Qadiriyya Sufi Order), pp. 275-294.

[30] In the last days of Gorbachev's USSR a source on that uprising was finally published after having been forbidden for half a century – Goytakin Rasu of Benoy, 'Istoriya o tom, kak Albik-Khadzhi stal imamom', *Respublika*, 8 August 1991, pp. 6-7. Translation from Arabic into Chechen by A. Nazhaev (in 1928). Translation from Chechen into Russian by D. Khozhaev.

[31] See Alexandre Bennigsen, 'Muslim Guerrilla Warfare in the Caucasus, 1918-1928', *Central Asian Survey*, Vol. 2, No. 1, 1983, pp. 280-294; Marie Bennigsen-Broxup, 'The Last Gazavat. The 1920-1921 Uprising', in Marie Bennigsen-Broxup (ed.), *The North Caucasus Barrier. The Russian Advance Towards the Muslim World*, London, Hurst, 1992, pp. 112-145.

[32] See Abdurahman Avtorkhanov, 'The Chechens and Ingush during the Soviet Period and its Antecedents', in Marie Bennigsen-Broxup (ed.), *op. cit.*, pp. 146-194.

[33] The police in the USSR was called 'Militia'. The GPU was the secret police, successor of the ChK. Its acronym was later changed to NKVD, MGB and then to KGB.

[34] See, for example, Dudaev's speech at the All-National Congress of the Chechen People on 8 June 1991, as reported in *Bart* (Groznyi), No. 6 (010), June 1991, p. 3.

[35] Baddeley, *op. cit.*, p. 47.

[36] For a short summary of the historiography of Mansur, see Moshe Gammer, 'A Preliminary to Decolonizing the Historiography of Shaykh Mansur', *Middle Eastern Studies*, Vol. 32, No. 1, 1996, pp. 191-202.

[37] Z. Sheripov, 'Sheikh Mansur. (Kratkii istoriko-biograficheskii ocherk)', in *O tekh, kogo nazyvali abrekami*, Groznyi, 1925. This had been published before the Stalinist regime gained full control over the writing of history in the USSR.

[38] Sharpudin B. Ahmadov, 'Ob istokakh antifeodal'nogo i antikolonial'nogo dvizheniia v Chechne v kontse XVIII v.', *Izvestiia Checheno-Ingushskogo nauchno-issledovatel'skogo instituta*, Vol. 9, No. 3, 1974, Ser. 1; *idem*, 'K voprosu o klassovoi bor'be v Chechne XVIII v.' in *Voprosy istorii klassoobrazovaniya i sotsial'nykh dvizhenii v dorevolyutsionnoi Checheno-Ingushetii (XVI-nachalo XX v.)*, Groznyi, 1980. Ahmadov was a senior researcher at the Institute of Humanities of the Chechen Republic.

[39] Shahruddin A. Gapurov, 'Nekotore voprosy istoriografii dvizheniya gortsev pod predvotitel'stvom Mansura vo vtoroi polovine 80kh godov XVIII v.', in *Voprosy istoriografii dorevolyutsionnoi Checheno-Ingushetii*, Groznyi, 1988. In another article, together with his co-author Gadeev he even broke a long-standing taboo in Soviet historiography by daring to compare Mansur's struggle to that of other anti-colonial leaders resisting Western powers – Shahruddin A. Gapurov and Vaha Iu. Gadeev, 'Sravnitel'nyi analiz nekotorykh aspektov dvizheniia gortsev severnogo Kavkaza pod rukovodstvom Mansura v kontse XVIII v veka i narodnykh dvizheniiakh v stranakh zarubeznogo Vostoka', in *Aktual'ne problemy istorii dorevoliutsionnoi Checheno-Ingushetii. Regional'naia nauchnaya konferentsiya. Tezisi dokladov i soobshchenii*, Groznyi, 1991.

[40] Dolkhan Khozhaev, 'Pravda o Sheikhe Mansure', *Groznenskii rabochii*, 16 August 1989; Vaha Gadeyev and Shahruddin Gapurov, 'Istorin Tsqhayolu qovsame ag'onash', *Orga* (Groznyi), No. 4, 1989, Shahruddin Gapurov and Vaha Gadeyev, 'Znat' istoriyu svoego naroda', *Politicheskii sobesednik* (Groznyi), No. 1, 1990.

[41] Yermolov's statue which had been erected in Groznyi in tsarist times was removed by the Bolsheviks in deference to Chechen feelings. In 1944, following the 'deportation' of the Chechens and Ingush, the statue was re-erected and it remained in place throughout the rest of the Soviet period until 1990. The symbolic meaning of this is obvious.

[42] See *Sheikh Mansur i osvoboditel'naya bor'ba narodov Severnogo Kavkaza v poslednei treti XVIII veka. Tezisy dokladov i soobshchenii mezhdunarodnoi nauchnoi konferentsii*, Groznyi, 1992.

[43] Sharpudin B. Ahmadov, *Imam Mansur (Narodno-osvoboditel'noe dvizhenie v Chechne i na Severnom Kavkaze v kontse XVIII v.)*, Groznyi, 1991 (in fact 1992). The book was an act of personal devotion as it had been written over many years in the knowledge that its publication would never be allowed. See also, *idem*, 'Narodno-osvoboditel'noe dvizhenie v Chechne i na Severnom Kavkaze pod predvoditel'stvom Imama Mansura (1785-1791)', in Aydaev (ed.), *op. cit.*, pp. 150-176.

[44] The issue included five stamps. One depicted the state arms (the wolf), and another the presidential palace. The three remaining stamps portrayed three national heroes – Imam Mansur, Imam Shamil and General Dudaev. Naturally enough, these stamps have never gone into official use because the Russian postal services refused to recognize them.

[45] On the CCMP, see Moshe Gammer, 'Unity, Diversity and Conflict in the Northern Caucasus', in Yaacov Ro'i (ed.), *Muslim Eurasia: Conflicting Legacies*, London, Frank Cass, 1995, pp. 163-186.

[46] Zulfiye Kadir, *The Rise of Political Islam in Russia* (unpublished paper), p. 7.

[47] For Shamil's description in historiography, see Moshe Gammer, 'Shamil in Soviet Historiography', *Middle Eastern Studies*, Vol. 28, No. 4, 1992, pp. 729-777. For developments since the dissolution of the USSR, see *idem*, 'Collective Memory and Politics: Remarks on Some Competing Historical Narratives in the Caucasus and Russia and their Use of a "National Hero"', *Caucasian Regional Studies*, Vol. 4, No. 1, 1999, to be found on internet: http://poli.vub.ac.be/publi/

[48] The Chechen authorities chose to celebrate the bicentennial in July – not in October like elsewhere in the CIS – as a demonstration of the republic's independence.

[49] RIA [Russkoe Informatsionnoe Agentstvo] - Novosti, 21 July 1997. The fortress referred to is probably the one popularly known as 'Shamil's Fortress' which was damaged in Russian bombardments during the recent war. In fact it is a fort built by the Russian forces after the capture of Vedeno in 1859. Shamil's original 'Capital' – New Dargo – was destroyed completely after its capture. Its ruins are now covered by a mound, several kilometres south of the present fort. And cf. Dolkhan Khozhaev, 'Krepost' Shamilya', *Komsomol'skoe plemya*, 1 November 1990, p. 8.

[50] Dolkhan Khozhaev, 'Gordyi syn Kavkaza', *Groznenskii rabochii*, 26 April 1990, p. 3; Gasym Kerimov, 'Islam i Shamil', *Respublika*, 30 May 1991, p. 8. Kerimov is a Moscow-based Azerbaijani historian.

[51] Dolkhan Khozhaev, 'Armiya Shamilya', *Golos Checheno-Ingushetii*, 24 March 1992, p. 3; *idem*, 'Artilleriya imamata, ili kto strelyal iz derevyannoi pushki?', *Respublika*, 2 November 1991, pp. 6-7.

[52] Dolkhan Khozhaev, 'Naiby Chechni', *Respublika*, 6 March 1992, pp. 5, 8; *idem*, 'Marshal lesnogo boya', *Komsomol'skoe plemya*, 17 May 1990, pp. 6-7; *idem*, 'Eshche raz ob Udi Mulle', *Respublika*, 15 February 1992; *idem*, 'Pervyi sredi naibov', *Leninskaya pravda* (local newspaper of Urus Martan), 15, 29 April, 1, 4 May 1990; *idem*, 'Medal' Shamilya', *Golos Checheno-Ingushetii*, 15 October 1991, p. 4; Abdul Gagaev and Dolkhan Khozhaev, 'Geroi iz pesni', *Komsomol'skoe plemya*, 6 September 1990, pp. 6-7.

[53] Like the battle on the river Valerik in 1840, preserved for posterity in a poem by Lermontov – Dolkhan Khozhaev, 'Bitva pod Valerikom', *Komsomol'skoe plemya*, 25 October 1990, p. 8; *idem*, 'Orstkhoitsev uvidel Lermontov', *Komsomol'skoe plemya*, 14 December 1989, p. 7 – and

the campaign in Kabarda in 1846 – *idem*, 'Pokhod Shamilya v Kabardu', *Golos Checheno-Ingushetii*, 22, 28, 29 November 1991, p. 3 (of each issue).

54 Dolkhan Khozhaev, 'Chechenskaya oblast' imamata', *Golos Checheno-Ingushetii*, 23 November 1990, p. 4. And cf.. Yavus Ahmadov, 'Imamat Shamilya – gosudarstvo gortsev Chechni i Dagestana', in Aydaev (ed.), *op. cit.*, pp. 177-184.

55 Thus a review by Aslanbek Kadiev of several books on the recent war in Chechnya sent over several e-mail discussion lists. Kadiev is the representative of the Republic of Ichkeria to several West European states.

56 Eiman Jafar's (ejafar@csd.uwm.edu) message on the Discussion List about Chechnya (chechnya@Plearn.bitnet) of 24 January 1995.

57 Usmanov, *op. cit.*, p. 71. And cf. Dolkhan Khozhaev, 'Baysungur Benoevskii', *Komsomol'skoe plemya*, 17 August 1989; *idem*, '"Svoboda ili smert" ili "intrigi imamskogo dvora"', *Komsomol'skoe plemya*, 21, 28 June 1990, pp. 10, 8 respectively; *idem*, 'Rytsar' svobody', *Groznenskii rabochii*, 8 November 1989, p. 3.

58 A Chechen historian expressed the opinion that the Chechens have been unable to unite unless led by an external (i.e., non-Chechen) leader – Mayrbek Vachagaev, *Chechnya v kavkazskoi voine, 1816-1859* (unpublished thesis, Moscow, 1995), pp. 84-85. Shamil's 'foreignness' may have supplied legitimization for Dudaev in another sphere: Dudaev belonged to a clan which is partly Chechen and partly Ingush. He could, therefore, have been depicted by some of his opponents as an outsider. The example of Shamil and interpretations like Vachagaev's might have turned his dubious Chechen credentials into an advantage. Vachagaev was formerly Press Secretary to President Maskhadov. In July 1999 he was appointed Chechen representative in Moscow. He was arrested in October 1999 by the Russian authorities.

59 The Avars form about 27% of the population of Daghestan, and are the largest and most dominant of its 12 autochthonous titular nationalities. Shamil, like his two predecessors, was an Avar.

60 Daghestan is the most favoured candidate for union with Chechnya on several counts: (1) it is the largest of the republics of the Northern Caucasus in terms of territory as well as population and – numerically as well as proportionately – has the smallest Russian population; (2) it is the historical centre of Islam in the Northern Caucasus. Daghestan therefore carries more weight than any other republic in the region and may sweep others along in its wake. (3) Daghestan is in the throes of an acute economic and social crisis; (4) it also shares with Chechnya the memories (and perhaps the ethos) of the long, joint resistance to Russia and of the united Imamate under Shamil. It might, therefore, be more easily persuaded to separate from Russia than other republics in the Northern Caucasus. (5) Last but not least, Daghestan is adjacent to Chechnya and borders on the Caspian Sea. A decolonized Daghestan – whether independent or united with Chechnya – would grant Chechnya an outlet to the sea, enhance its political and economic independence and multiply its chances of achieving recognition for its sovereignty.

61 RIA-Novosti, 21 July 1997. For further details, see Moshe Gammer, 'Islam and Politics in the North Eastern Caucasus (Daghestan and Chechnya)', in Muhiaddin Mesbahi (ed.), *Islam in Central Asia and the Caucasus* (tentative title; forthcoming).

62 Dudaev won with 90% of the votes, representing 64.6% of the electorate.

63 Reuters, 14 December 1995.

64 The fact that Dudaev's burial took place under a shroud of secrecy and the body was not shown caused many to doubt the official announcement of his death. According to some rumours he was wounded and spirited away for medical treatment abroad. According to others, his death was staged so as to allow negotiations between the nationalist authorities and Moscow (which

refused to negotiate with Dudaev). There are still people who believe that Dudaev will return when the time is ripe.

[65] See Gammer, 'The Qadiriyya in the Northern Caucasus', *op. cit.*

[66] Yavus Ahmadov, '"Syn Kishi" (O znamenitom dvizhenii Kunta-Khadzhi)', *Respublika*, 11 July 1991; Vahit Akaev, 'Ilskhan-Yu'rtara Hazha', *Daymohk*, 14 January 1992; *idem*, 'O religiozno-nravstvennykh vozzreniyakh sheikha Kunta-Khadzhi', *Golos Chechenskoi Respubliki*, 16 September 1992; *idem*, 'Religiozno-nravstvennie vozzreniya sheikha Kunta-Khadzhi Kishieva', in Vahit Akaev *et al.* (eds), *Iz istorii Islama v Checheno-Ingushetii*, Groznyi, 1992, pp. 45-52; *idem*, 'Sheikh Kunta Khadzhi – velikomuchenik', *Golos Checheno-Ingushetii*, 26 March 1991; *idem*, *Sheikh Kunta Khadzhi: Zhizn' i uchenie*, Groznyi, 1994; *idem*, 'Zikrizm i zikristy', *Respublika*, 16 September 1992; K. Chokaev, 'Kunta-Haja a, ts'unan zama a', *Leninan Neq*, 1990; D. Kagermanov, 'Ustazan h'oq'eh' diytsa…', *Daymokh*, 16 January 1991; S.-Kh. Nunuev, 'Kishin Kunta-Haja a, tahanlera de a', *Leninan Neq*, 20 May 1990; Tutuev, V., 'Vovshashka h'ovsa…', *Daymohk*, 17 July 1991; A. Utsiev, 'Qhin tsqa a Kunta-Ha'jekh la'tsna', *Daymohk*, 31 May 1990.

[67] For the place of the Qadiriyya in politics see Gammer, 'Islam and Politics in the North-Eastern Caucasus (Daghestan and Chechnya)', *op. cit.*

[68] V. G. Gadzhiev and Kh. Kh. Ramazanov (eds), *Dvizhenie gortsev Severo-Vostochnogo Kavkaza v 20 - 50kh gg. XIX v. Sbornik dokumentov*, Makhachkala, 1959, p. 58, document No. 32, Letter from Nicholas I to Paskevich, 25 September [7 October] 1829.

[69] Usmanov, *op. cit.*, pp. 71-72. Vachagaev calculates Chechen losses between 1830 and 1860 at over 500,000 – *op. cit.*, p. 35.

[70] The destruction of the forests is regarded by many Chechens as an act of 'ecologicide'.

[71] 'Pis'ma Rostislava Andreyevicha Faddeyeva k rodnym', *Russkii vestnik*, 1897, No. 10, pp. 63-64.

[72] Yavus Ahmadov, *Dvizhenie Kunta Khadzhi*, paper delivered at the First International Conference on Shamil and the Anti-Colonial Struggle in the Caucasus, Oxford, March 1991, p. 11.

[73] Vachagaev, *op. cit.*, pp. 72-73.

[74] Usmanov, *op. cit.*, p. 83.

[75] For the deportation of the Chechens and other nationalities, see Robert Conquest, *The Nation Killers: The Soviet Deportation of Nationalities*, London, MacMillan, 1970; Alexandre M. Nekrich, *The Punished Peoples*, New York, 1978. For further sources, see Brian Glyn Williams, *Commemorating 'The Deportation'. The Role of Memorialization and Collective Memory in the 1994-96 Chechen War*, Paper Presented at the Fourth Annual World Convention of the Association for the Study of Nationalities, Columbia University, 15-17 April 1999.

[76] As late as 1988, the Chairman of the Supreme Soviet of the Checheno-Ingush ASSR stated in an article in the ideological journal of the Communist Party of the Soviet Union that 'a good many […] traitors and enemies of Soviet power,' in the ChIASSR 'formed terrorist gangs, committed acts of sabotage and assassinated party and Soviet activists'. This 'insignificant minority […] stabbed primarily their own people in the back' since their 'dirty crimes were among the causes of the tragedy which befell the Chechens and Ingush – their expulsion from their homes' – Kh. Kh. Bokov, 'Formirovat' internatsionalistskie ubezhdeniya', *Kommunist*, No. 3, February 1988, p. 89.

[77] E.g., Yu. Aytbaev, 'O belom skakune, kotorogo chechentsy ne darili Adol'fu Gitleru', in Yu. Aytbaev (ed.), *op. cit.*, pp. 278-284.

[78] See, for example, Kh. Gakaev, 'Chechentsy v boyakh protiv nemetsko-fashistskikh zakhvatchikov', in Aydaev (ed.), *op. cit.*, pp. 235-242; A. Oleinik, 'Doblestnyi rytsar' Kavkaza', *ibid.*, pp. 245-251; Yu. Aydaev, 'Pobratimstvo (o vstrechakh s geroyami Sovetskogo Soyuza P. P. Brikelem i M. A. Visaitovym)', *ibid.*, pp. 251-256.

79 E.g., Khalid Oshaev, *Brest – oreshek ognennyi. Khudozhestvenno-dokumental'naya povest'*, Groznyi, 1990.

80 The first publication to appear in print was Mahomed Jurgaev and Oleg Jurgaev, *Krugi ada*, Groznyi, 1989, published at the expense of the authors. In 1991 books were published by the government of the republic and by the association of Chechens and Ingush in Kazakhstan – Ministerstvo kul'tury ChIASSR and Checheno-Ingushskii gosudarstvennyi ob'edinennyi muzei, *Zhivaya pamyat'. O zhertvakh stalinskikh repressii*, Groznyi, 1991 and L. Yahyaev (ed.), *Belaya kniga. Iz istorii vyseleniya chechentsev i ingushei, 1944-1957 gg. Vospominaniya, arkhivnie materialy, fotodokumenty*, Groznyi and Alma Ata, 1991. Also see Hamzat Yandarbiev, *Prestuplenie veka*, Groznyi, 1992; *Repressirovannie narody: istoriya i sovremennost'. (Tezisy dokladov i soobshchenii Rossiiskoi nauchno-prakticheskoi konferentsii, 28-29 maya 1992 g.* Elista, 1992; E. Isaev, 'Iz 'osoboi papki Stalina.' O deportatsii chechentsev i ingushei', in Aytbaev (ed.), *op. cit.*, pp. 261-274. For further publications, not available to me, see Williams, *op. cit.*

81 Usmanov, *op. cit.*, pp. 83-84.

82 *Ibid.*, p. 83; Yu. Aytbaev and A. Aytbaev, 'Tyazhkii put' k millionu', in Yu. Aytbaev (ed.), pp. 228-232.

83 It only managed to publish an account of the massacre: *Khaibakh: sledstvie prodolzhaetsya*, Groznyi, 1994. See also Said-Emin Bitsoev, 'Khaibakh – aul, kotorogo net', in Yu. Aytbaev (ed.), *op. cit.*, pp. 275-277. For the commemoration of the 'deportation' see Williams, *op. cit.*

84 According to testimonies by Chechens this was done only in places where Slavs were settled. In places settled by other Caucasians, the graveyards were not only preserved but looked after.

85 Sebastian Smith, *Allah's Mountains. Politics and War in the Russian Caucasus*, London, Tauris, 1998, pp. 1-2.

86 *Ibid., loc. cit.*

87 See, for example, the title of Usmanov's introduction (*op. cit.*, pp. 5-31): 'Chetvertyi genotsid' (The Fourth Genocide). And see a list of Russian war crimes on pp. 168-220.

88 See A. Blinushov, *By All Available Means: the Russian Federation Ministry of Internal Affairs Operation in the Village of Samashki*, Moscow, 1996.

89 The Dudaev administration concentrated all the Soviet archives – historical, government, party and KGB – under one roof at the State Archives. The collection included the files on the 'deportation' and the lives of the Chechens and Ingush in Kazakhstan, saved from the archives of the Kazakh SSR in the 1970s (where they were destined for destruction).

90 For its collections and their importance, see O. P. Orlov and A. V. Cherkasov, *Rossiya-Chechnya: tsep' oshibok i prestuplenii*, Moscow, 1998, p. 261.

91 No doubt the experience of other peoples (such as the Jews and the Armenians) who had been victims of genocide and then tried – with varying degrees of success, it must be remembered – to get international sympathy and support for their statehood must have played a part.

92 Williams, *op. cit.* The term was coined by Vamik D. Volkan, 'On Chosen Trauma', *Mind and Human Interaction*, Vol. 4, No. 1, 1992, pp. 3-19. According to Volkan, if a victimized community is unable to overcome a traumatic event it passes on this task to future generations, together with the resolve 'never again!'.

93 In fact, almost any attempt to shape group identity is bound to use these motives, a fact which should be interpreted by the tools of social psychology rather than those of history.

94 Aleksandr Solzhenitsyn, *Arkhipelag GULag, 1918-1956. Opyt khudozhestvennogo issledovaniya*, Part 6, Chapter 4.

Robert Stallaerts

5. The Disintegration of the Yugoslav Intellectual Community

Introduction

Secession in Yugoslavia is an expression of deep-rooted nationalism. In his *Vie et mort de la Yougoslavie*, published in 1992, the French Slavist Paul Garde was one of the first to describe the life cycle and tragic end of Yugoslavia. Books and articles followed, but relatively few concentrated on the specific role of scientific institutions and Yugoslav intellectuals.[1] The first aim of the following contribution is to depict the institutional framework of the social sciences in Yugoslavia. The Yugoslav, Croatian and Serbian Academies are important in this respect. These Academies were intended to support the national culture of Yugoslavia as a whole and that of the individual federated republics. Particularly important disciplines were linguistics and history. The evolution of the Academies reflected changes in scientific politics, as the authorities attempted to control and to influence research at these institutions. Immediately after taking power, Yugoslav communists were eager to silence nationalist forces. Both nationalists and scientists, however, fought for their freedom, and gradually, with the erosion of the centralist system, nationalism was to find a home in the official scientific institutions.

Second, we also subject to scrutiny a major dissenting philosophical current, which was long regarded as a counterweight to rising nationalism: the Praxis group. Most of its members were partisans during the second world war and became members of the Communist League of Yugoslavia. In that respect, these left-wing critics of Tito's regime were very different from most of the other opposition groups and the émigré intelligentsia who fought the socialist revolution and the communist regime. The break-up of the Praxis group and the subsequent – strongly nationalist – stand taken by some of its leading members exemplifies the disintegration of the Yugoslav intellectual community.

Third, the Memorandum of the Serbian Academy will be analysed in some detail. This Memorandum, which was publicized in the Serbian press in the autumn of 1986, started the definitive transition of the country's leading ideology from communism to nationalism. The Memorandum was not immediately applauded in Serbian political circles. Only later did it become useful to Milošević in his rise to power, when he adopted the national programme included in the Memorandum as his own. But the use made of this scientific document by the new authorities has to be seen in a complex relationship between scientific and political practices. Refuting the thesis of pure instrumentality in Serbian social science – which holds that scientists and academicians merely serve and justify the interests of the politicians – in the case of the Memorandum, as with the Praxis group or the activities of the academies and other scientific institutions, we observe a looser interconnection (and at times even an opposition) between scholars and the political establishment.

The Academies of Science and Arts

A Yugoslavian Academy (*Jugoslavenska Akademija Znanosti i Umjetnosti*, JAZU) was established in the nineteenth century, before the foundation of Yugoslavia itself. It appeared in the wake of the so-called Illyrian Movement, an expression of Slavic feeling under the Austro-Hungarian Habsburg monarchy. The Illyrian Movement defended the idea that Croats, Serbs and Slovenes were members of a common Slav stock. This idea of a community of all Southern Slav peoples was conceived by intellectuals in the nineteenth century who lived mainly in the Croatian part of the peninsula. The name 'Illyrians' referred to the population groups who had lived on the borders of the Adriatic Sea before the sixth and seventh centuries. The main inspirer of the idea of a Yugoslav Academy was the 'Croatian' Catholic Bishop, Josip Juraj Strossmayer (1815-1903).[2] The Austrian authorities approved its creation only in 1867. The Academy was set up in Zagreb as a Yugoslav, or a Southern Slav, Academy which intended also to direct its work towards Bulgaria as a so-called Southern Slav people (Yugo meaning 'south' in the Serbo-Croat language). Strossmayer was considered to be both 'a truly nationalist Croat' and 'a genuine Yugoslav'. He favoured the romantic idea of conciliating Catholic Croats and Orthodox Serbs in a common Slav cultural nation. In practice, however, Croat members of the Academy tried to use it to spread Croat nationalism. In 1868, the Academy started publishing a series on Croatian historical sources, called *Monumenta spectantia historiam Slavorum Meridionalium.*

In the first Yugoslavia, which was founded after the first world war as a kingdom and was dissolved with the country's occupation during the second world war,[3] the Yugoslav Academy had to repel centralist attacks from the Royal Academy of Belgrade. The president of the Yugoslav Academy, Gavro Manojlović, managed to retain the seat of the Academy in Zagreb. But at the end of the 1930s, under the influence of nationalist and authoritarian pressure, the Yugoslav Academy transformed its programmatic orientation and changed its name to Croatian Academy. This was confirmed by the new Ustaša regime during the second world war. A new management board of five Academicians was then installed, better suited to the fascist brand of nationalism propagated by the regime.[4]

After the second world war, the communists came to power and reorganized the Academies in line with their Marxist views. Besides the Croatian Academy, there also existed the Serbian Academy (*Srpska Akademija Nauka*, SANU), the immediate heir of the Serbian Royal Academy of Sciences and Arts founded in Belgrade in 1886,[5] and the Slovenian Academy (*Slovenska Akademija Znanosti i Umetnosti*, SAZU), which had started its activities in 1938.[6] New social science institutes were being founded. General guidelines were being provided for interpreting history in accordance with the Marxist point of view.[7] Prominent leaders of the socialist revolution, such as Milovan Djilas and Edvard Kardelj, were eager to participate in the activities of these academies. In the late 1940s, Tito lectured on historiographical subjects – with great success, according to official reports – before the Slovene and Serbian Academies.[8]

Croatian historiography reconstructed the existence of a separate Croatian people and an independent Croatian state in various periods of history. At the end of the 1960s there were serious debates among Yugoslav historians on Croatia's national history. In 1968, four Croatian historians – Šidak, Gross, Karaman and Šćepić – published their interpretation of the history of the Croatian people during the period 1860-1940.[9] Official Yugoslav historians criticized it for neglecting the Yugoslav component. In turn, when Božić, Dedijer and Ekmević produced their History of Yugoslavia (*Istorija Jugoslavije*, 1974), the Croats Gross and Šidak condemned the unbalanced treatment of Croatian and Serbian history. Croatian historians not belonging to the academic establishment and working in the Institutes for the Study of the Partisan War or Labour Movement,[10] such as Vlado Gotovac and Franjo Tudjman, expressed even more nationalistic views. In the beginning of the 1970s, such problems were initially dealt with by repression.[11] Criticism of the unitarist line was labelled Croatian extremism, and banned. One of the Croatian historical journals, Trpimir Macan's *Povijest hrvatskog naroda* (History of the Croatian People), was taken out of circulation in 1972.

At the same time as this repression was taking place, the view prevailed at the top of the communist leadership that the unity of Yugoslavia could be preserved only by transforming its institutions and giving more autonomy to its constituent parts.[12] This was achieved by the new Constitution of 1974. All republican institutions, including the scientific ones, took full advantage of these decentralizing initiatives which were taking place at various levels of the Yugoslav federal structure. The Academy of Sciences and Arts of Kosovo and the Academy of Vojvodina (both Kosovo and Vojvodina had been granted the status of provinces of Serbia) went through a period in which they expanded their range of activities to an unforeseen scale. Thanks to these reforms, official academies and historical and social science institutes could publish and organize their research along nationalist lines without interference from the centre. Highly sensitive themes, previously labelled as nationalistic, became topics of research. At the same time, federal scientific institutions such as the Institute of Economic Sciences – earlier a scientific organ supporting the Federal Planning Institute – withered away.

At the beginning of the 1980s, with the death of Tito in 1980 and the downturn in the economy, the communist party experienced a serious legitimacy crisis. Previously taboo themes were aired in the press and in scientific publications. The dark sides of the communist regime, such as the existence of internment camps or abuse of power, were openly discussed. Publications rehabilitated nationalistic forces that had been fighting against the communist regime. Nationalism pervaded politics and historiography.

When Milošević took control of power in Serbia at the end of the 1980s, he closed down the Provincial Academies of Kosovo and Vojvodina. Their activities were absorbed by the Serbian Academy in Belgrade. It was argued that the functioning of the Provincial Academies involved a risk of secession and constituted a danger for Serbian culture. The Serb authorities pointed out that by accepting the Tosk language variant – spoken in central and southern Albania – the Ghegspeaking Kosovars left the door wide open to cultural and political penetration from Albania, since handbooks in the Tosk language variant were effectively brought into Kosovo.

Nationalistic revisionism also took a firm lead in Croatian historiography. National figures and movements and the role of religion and the church in Croatian history[13] became favourite topics of research. A revised history of the Independent State of Croatia just before and during the second world war was presented to the public. Criticism of the history of the partisan movement during the second world war, which had previously been voiced exclusively in dissident circles, was now officially sanctioned.

The Sabor (House of Parliament) passed a new law on the Academy on 26 June 1991, providing the Croatian Academy of Sciences and Arts (CANU) with a more nationalist profile. The catholic Cardinal Franjo Kuharić became one of its honorary members. The old and respected scientist Ivan Supek, president of the Academy and a liberal opponent of Tudjman, tried to protect the autonomy of the Academy against major intrusions by party politics, in particular by the dominant nationalist party *Hrvatska Demokratska Zajednica* (HDZ). But he could not prevent President Tudjman from becoming a member of the Academy, however dubious his scientific achievements. Tudjman tried to replace Supek as head of the Academy with one of his own supporters, but Supek managed to retain the presidency for a further term. There were also other signs of resistance against the dominant nationalist ideology. Some historians in autonomous research institutes, grouped around an historical journal, refused to be instrumentalized by the new regime.

The Critical Intelligentsia of the Praxis group

Praxis was founded in September 1964. The group created a special bond between the main scientific centres of Yugoslavia (Zagreb, Ljubljana and Belgrade), reinforced by the organization of a summer school in Korčula. Its review *Praxis* was originally published in Serbo-Croatian, and from 1965 on also in three Western languages. The journal developed a left-wing critique of the regime and its scientific policies. The chief editors of *Praxis* were Danilo Pejović and Gajo Petrović. Despite the fact that the authors defended individual positions, it was possible to discern a theoretical hard core, which was based on a few common theses.[14] The philosophical concept of 'praxis' was central to this theory. This concept, which had been defined and discussed in the first issue of the journal,[15] was strongly influenced by the philosophical writings of Karl Marx.[16] The members of the Praxis group defended a normative, universalist conception of human emancipation.

According to their vision, humankind is continuously transforming itself and its social environment through the creative transformation of outward reality – a process that will finally lead to the achievement of its essential nature. This view of humanity and society justified the implementation of the Yugoslav institutions of self-management as a step towards true democratic socialism. The Yugoslav self-management institutions were based on an attempt to bring key decisions concerning the organization of human work and politics within the reach of the working people and the citizen. This ideal was to a degree put into practice in industry by the so-called 'work councils', which had a range of areas of competence in the management of their enterprises. The idea of self-management was not shared by communist ideology in the Soviet Union. From that perspective, the theses put forward in Praxis reflected the Yugoslav regime's break with the Soviet political system at the end of the 1940s and the beginning of the 1950s. At the same time, of course, given the orthodox communist inheritance in their own country, it was not to be expected that the Praxis group's theory on self-management could be implemented in Yugoslav society, dominated by the monopoly of one party, without causing major problems.

The precise content that individual Praxis members gave to the philosophical conceptualization depended on their discipline and methodology. Even the level of abstraction depended on the chosen discipline. The sociologist Rudi Supek, for instance, was relatively concrete in his criticism of Yugoslav society, unlike many philosophers. The latter embedded their views in different traditions. The Zagreb-based Milan Kangrga, for example, influenced by German phenomenology, and especially Heidegger, differed in approach and style from the Belgrade-based Mihailo Marković, who had been schooled in Anglo-Saxon neopositivism.

Another basic tenet of the group, also derived from the early theoretical writings of Marx,[17] was the thesis that 'praxis' (practice) implied 'a relentless criticism of all existing reality'.[18] This statement implied continuous criticism of Yugoslav society and in particular of the Communist League of Yugoslavia. Praxis members criticized widespread unemployment and growing social inequality in 'socialist' Yugoslavia. They complained about the lack of democracy and true self-management, and defended the right to freedom of opinion. The communist establishment was invariably labelled as 'bureaucrats'. They were seen as constituting a particular social stratum, or even a special class.[19] The League of Communists was divided on the issue of how to deal with this kind of dissident opinion. On the one hand, members of Praxis were at times heavily criticized, yet on the other, the journal was officially subsidized.

The communists seemed to need a universalist theory of humanity and a progressive justification of self-management as a theoretical counterweight to the growing influence of nationalism. The active participation by most Praxis philosophers in the communist revolution, and the fact that official ideological documents mostly incorporated progressive views, which had a certain similarity to the opinions of Praxis members, compounded the ambiguity in relations between Praxis and the party leadership. Little by little, however, the Praxis philosophers overstated their case and went far beyond the practical needs of the official Yugoslav ideologues. The group's scathing criticism of the communist leadership prompted the leading ideologue Edvard Kardelj – seen at the time as the second most powerful figure in the regime after Tito – to write a counter-criticism of the theses of the Praxis group, which was published in 1966.[20] After several unsuccessful attacks, at the beginning of the 1970s the 'bureaucrats' finally managed to silence the Praxis group in Zagreb. This coincided with the repression of nationalist intellectuals in the Croatian capital – confirming the idea that in the eyes of the party leadership Praxis constituted a theoretical counterweight to nationalism. This repression was a fatal blow to the group, which had already been weakened by growing dissension internally.

In 1981, the founding of the journal *Praxis International* – which was presented as the international continuation of *Praxis* – led to controversies. Its main editor was Mihailo Marković, a Belgrade philosopher who had been editor-in-chief of the old *Praxis*. He worked on the new journal together with Richard J. Bernstein. Only a few other former Praxis members agreed to sit on the editorial board of the new publication.[21] Zagreb-based philosophers were absent.

Disagreements arose within the Belgrade group of former Praxis members. One was between those who had previously been victims of repression. At the end of 1974, eight professors and assistants of the Faculty of Philosophy at the University of Belgrade had been removed by the authorities. The professors dismissed were Mihailo Marković, Ljubomir Tadić, Miladin Životić, Zagorka Pesić-Golubović, Svetozar Stojanović, Draguljub Mićunović, Triva Indjić and Nebojsa Popov.[22] They had been accused of 'spoiling the youth' and 'undermining the Yugoslav system of self-management'. In particular, their alleged role in the 1968 student revolt and their participation in Praxis group activities had made them a prime target for the Yugoslav authorities. For several years thereafter, their common fate had been unemployment or a closely watched scientific career. The strong solidarity initially felt within this 'Group of Eight' was broken in 1988 by the reintegration into the establishment of Miladin Životić, who accepted a chair in the philosophy faculty.[23] In addition, ideological divergences arose between members. Ljubomir Tadić highlighted the qualities of the nineteenth-century bourgeois Serbian order. Mihailo Marković, on the other hand, continued to praise the value of social property and to reject privatization strategies. He became for a time the theoretician of the Milošević regime. In the early 1990s a Serbian nationalist viewpoint, completely opposed to the universalist conception of humanity favoured by the Praxis group, was common to all three former members of the group – Mihailo Marković, Ljubomir Tadić (who became members of the Serbian Academy) and even Miladin Životić.[24] It is difficult to explain this fundamental turnaround,[25] except in very general terms by the fundamental regression of economic and political life and climate in Yugoslav society.

The Debate on the Memorandum of the Serbian Academy

In the 1980s, intellectual and academic circles in Yugoslavia debated on the future of the state, and deployed arguments that would later be used in the debate for and against the right to secession. A major turning-point in this debate came with the Memorandum of the Serbian Academy. At a meeting on 23 May 1985, the Academy accepted a proposal by the economist Ivan Maksimović that it should write a memorandum to address the 'most acute social, political, economic, welfare and scientific and cultural problems' of Serbia and Yugoslavia.[26] First drafts were discussed at various meetings in 1986. On 24 September 1986, the Belgrade evening paper *Večernje Novosti* launched an overt attack on the Memorandum, publishing selected excerpts from the text.[27] The

Academy reacted by stating that this publication was totally unauthorized and was in fact a theft of an uncompleted version of part of a larger scientific document.[28] Only half of the text could be regarded as final. On 5 October 1986, the Committee decided to stop its work on the document and to assign responsibility for its fate to the Presidency of the Academy. The turmoil caused by the newspaper article alarmed the political authorities and particularly the Presidency of the Socialist Republic of Serbia, which asked for a report. The Executive Board of the Academy denied that the intention of the Memorandum was 'fratricidal' and 'warmongering'. It also repeated that the publication of the excerpts had been unauthorized.[29] In a letter sent on 3 October to Dušan Kanazir, the President of the Academy, Serbian Vice-President Bulatović asked to be sent the version of the Memorandum that had become public. The Executive Board replied that no one in the Academy had the right to release material that had not been approved by the competent bodies.[30]

This history of the origins of the Memorandum demonstrates that the relationship between scholars and politicians was not free from tension. The text itself was a radical reassessment of the programme of the Serbian political leadership. The first part dealt with the crisis in the economy, the defects in the confederal organization of Yugoslavia, the privileged position of Slovenia and Croatia, the dominant position of the party in the state and the moral crisis in society. It defined some principles for redressing the economic, political and moral situation: the introduction of a more efficient economic system, the implementation of the principle of self-determination for the peoples of Yugoslavia and a guarantee of human rights. The Memorandum proposed centralization as a response to the so-called confederal tendencies of the 1974 Constitution. It was claimed that these confederal tendencies had destroyed the unity of the economic system and had led to the downfall of the republics' national economies.

In the second part of the Memorandum, the position of the Serbian people and state was further analysed and a new Serbian programme presented. A recurring theme was the disadvantaged legal position of Serbia as a consequence of the Constitutional reform of 1974. The establishment of the autonomous provinces of Kosovo and Vojvodina within the Republic of Serbia was said to have led to a loss of sovereignty for the Serbian republic itself. In the view of the authors, Serbia could not take autonomous decisions, unlike the two autonomous regions, Kosovo and Vojvodina, whose assemblies had autonomous rights and could at the same time make decisions on their own affairs and also contribute to decision-making at the Serbian and Yugoslav federative levels. According to the authors of the Memorandum, the national integrity of the Serbian people had to be restored, regardless of where they lived, whether within or outside the present Republic of Serbia. This could be interpreted as a threatening appeal for secession[31] and the construction of a Greater Serbian State.

The most comprehensive criticism of the Memorandum came in 1987 from émigré intellectual circles of the Croatian diaspora, articulated by the members of the Croatian National Congress (*Hrvatsko Narodno Vijeće*). The Croatian academic émigré milieu had a long tradition of producing critical accounts of the communist Yugoslav regime.[32] Mate Mestrović and Radovan Latković of the *Hrvatsko Narodno Vijeće* acknowledged the accuracy of the Memorandum's general description of the Yugoslav economy as being in crisis. But they disagreed with its authors on the causes of the economic débâcle and on the proposed solutions. From the point of view of the Croat émigré writers, the command economy (increasingly under the authority of the republics), state control of society, the non-existence of private ownership and, especially, the destruction of private forms of agriculture, had to be seen as the main causes of the present crisis. They reproached the Memorandum writers for ignoring the need for economic liberalism and decentralization. Nor did the Croats agree with the Memorandum's description of confederal tendencies as going against historical progress. In their view, the constitutional reform of 1974 had led not to a 'real' confederation, but to eight state bureaucracies.

At this point, the Croats were pleading for a rational coordination policy within the framework of a non-bureaucratic confederation. They pleaded for a real confederation, adding that it was following the natural course of history for peoples or nations to acquire their own statehood. Usually, Croat émigré intellectuals at the time defended the right of the Croats to an independent state, but here the more moderate option of a confederation was clearly chosen for tactical reasons. In order to be included in the debate, it was better to plead for a confederation and thereby achieve a gradual loosening of the bonds of the Yugoslav state. Among the human rights they championed, the Croat critics included the right to self-determination and the right to secession – rights that were formally provided for in the Constitution. They agreed with the Memorandum's assertion that sovereignty 'comes forth from the free will of the peoples', but disagreed with the proposal from the Serbian Academy to implement an integral, democratic federalism. Such a policy was perceived by the Croat critics as a return to unitarism and the hegemony of the Serbian people over the other Yugoslav nations. The Croat scholars rejected the central thesis of the Memorandum, which stated that the Yugoslav authorities had followed discriminatory policies in relation to the Serbian economy. They defended the contrary thesis of malicious treatment of the Croatian economy by the Yugoslav regimes, both in the Kingdom of Yugoslavia and in the second Yugoslavia under Tito's communist regime.

The situation in the first Yugoslavia was a highly contentious issue in the polemics between Croat and Serb scholars. The Croats rejected the Memorandum's thesis that the Serbs had not had a privileged position under this regime. The Croatian counter-arguments were based on a pre-war study by Rudolf

Bičanić, who had studied the economic performance and political representation of Croatia in the first Yugoslavia. In this study, which was first published in 1938, Bičanić had highlighted the monopoly position of the Crown and the Belgrade political élite, which was reflected in the under-representation of the Croats in the higher ranks of the military. This political domination had led to economic exploitation. Economic policy measures, such as an undervaluation of the dinar and an unjust tax policy, had favoured the Serbian economy. The taxes on agricultural estates and on houses, for instance, were twice as high in Croatia as in Serbia. All this was true at least up to 1928, when a more centralizing policy was introduced. The Croat critics of the Memorandum pointed to more recent indices to show the constant decline of the Croatian economy and the concomitant rise of the Serbian economy between 1925 and 1971: in industry, Croatia's 33% share fell to 18% while Serbia's rose from 20% to 35%. A similar trend could be perceived in banking and commerce.

In a new publication, published in 1995, the Serbian Academy answered the Croatian criticisms. It first condemned the separatist aspirations of the Croatian 'Anti-Memorandum'. Then it rejected the allegations in the 'Anti-Memorandum' concerning the subjugated and dependent status of Croatia in the economic and political fields. From the perspective of the Serbian Academy, a confederation would inevitably lead to a separation of the various republics; moreover, the efficiency of the economy required a unified policy. The offer by Slovenia and Croatia on 4 October 1990 to form a loose confederation was described by the Serbian Academy as a transitional strategy towards independence. The Serbian Academy reaffirmed its view that only an integral, democratic federalism could overcome nationalism and separatism, and rejected the depiction of Serb positions as Greater-Serbian nationalism. The Serbs pleaded for a more centralist and unitary system.

The Academy dealt in detail with the Croatian allegations concerning the so-called privileged position of Serbia. Yugoslav leaders such as Tito, Kardelj or Bakarić, it claimed, had been at least as anti-Serbian as they had been anti-Croatian. The policy of these leaders had to be seen as a legacy of the inter-war Comintern policy which, in order to destroy the social order had stigmatized the Serbian bourgeoisie as hegemonistic. Federalism had been used by the communists to keep Serbia powerless. The constitution of Kosovo and Vojvodina as two independent provinces within the Republic of Serbia, in 1974, had turned these provinces into states within a state. The federalization of Yugoslavia had led to the formation of an anti-Serbian coalition, in which Croatia – itself a victim of the communist policy during the Croatian spring – was an active member.

The Serb Academy characterized the data used by the Croatian side to prove economic exploitation by the Serbs as outdated. These data were indeed based largely on the book by Rudolf Bičanić, which had been published in 1938. In the view of his Serbian critics, the author of this book had used the wrong indicators and base years. This had already been demonstrated at the time by Serbian economists, but their writings had been largely ignored by the economic profession in Yugoslavia, and especially in Croatia. Moreover, Bičanić himself had not used his earlier findings in a book published after the war, which seemed to prove that he had understood his errors. According to the Serbian Academy, the only reliable disaggregated statistics were those adjusted for industry in 1938 by the Economic Institute of Serbia. Bičanić had ignored these data in his first book, as by then it had already gone to press. Taking the reliable data into account, the growth of industry in Croatia was 1.9 times faster than in Serbia proper. Moreover, whereas in Croatia 481,000 dinars had been invested per 1,000 inhabitants, the figure was only 281,000 for Serbia.[33] The per capita GNP of Croatia had quadrupled between 1947 and 1971, which contradicted the Croatian claim that the position of Croatia had declined. From the Serbian perspective, Croatia had shown a higher growth rate than Serbia.

The Serbian Academy further criticized the analysis made by the former president of the Yugoslav Academy of Sciences and Arts, the Croatian Jakov Sirotković.[34] He had depicted the 1938 statistical analysis of industry by the Economic Institute of Serbia as 'statistics-juggling', and had fallen back on Bičanić's figures. Sirotković had argued that Croatia had been discriminated against, citing GNP indices for a 35-year period, from 1952 to 1987.[35] These figures allegedly proved that Serbia had higher and Croatia lower indices than the Yugoslav average. The Academy criticized these projections on two key points: if per capita data were given, the situation was reversed. Moreover, the selection of the base year was critical. The selection of 1952 was unjustified, as the GNP in that year had been exceptionally low owing to bad weather conditions in agriculture and a total transformation of industry because of the conflict with the Soviet Union (industries had had to be dismantled and relocated in other parts of Yugoslavia in order to protect them from possible Soviet aggression). According to the first column of figures in Table 1, which were used by Sirotković, Croatia had been a victim of economic discrimination, with a growth index of only 640 as against 701 for Serbia. This would not be the case, however, if per capita data were used for the same period, as the figures in the second column demonstrate (536 for Croatia as against 498 for Serbia). The use of 1947 as a base year would also prove that Croatia was relatively privileged in comparison with Serbia.[36]

Table 1 – GNP indices of Yugoslavia, Croatia and Serbia (in dinars, 1972 prices)

	1987/52		1988/47	
	Total	Per capita	Total	Per capita
SFRY	675	484	730	486
Croatia	640	536	745	598
Serbia	701	498	702	464

Source: Kosta Mihailović and Vasilije Krestić, Serbian Academy of Sciences and Arts. Presidency. *Memorandum of the Serbian Academy of Sciences and Arts. Answers to Criticisms*, Belgrade, SANU, 1995, p. 62. Period 1987/52 – column 1 – based on Sirotković, other columns are based on Statistical Yearbook of Yugoslavia, Belgrade, Federal Statistics Office, various years.

Sirotković argued in relative terms, while it seemed more logical to the Academy to compare absolute levels. It could then be shown that Croatia, already starting from a slightly higher level, had considerably increased its advantage in the period 1947-1988, and the per capita income span widened considerably (See Table 2).

Table 2 – Per capita GNP, absolute levels in dinars, 1972 prices

	Per capita GNP		Increment
	1947	1988	1988/1947
SFRY	3,460	16,814	13,354
Croatia	3,610	21,587	17,977
Serbia	3,274	15,183	11,909

Source: Mihailović and Krestić, p. 64. Based on Federal Statistics Office, 1986 and Statistical Yearbook of Yugoslavia, 1990.

The Academy further observed that a comparison for 1988 of the levels of development in both current prices and constant prices clearly showed the underprivileged position of Serbia compared with that of Croatia (see Table 3).

Table 3 – Per capita GNP in 1988

	Prices in dinars		Indices	
	Constant	Current	Constant	Current
SFRY	16,814	62,939	100.0	100.0
Croatia	21,587	82,063	128.4	130.4
Serbia	15,183	54,201	90.3	86.1

Source: Mihailović and Krestić, p. 67. Based on Statistical Yearbook of Yugoslavia, 1990, Belgrade, Federal Statistics Office.

A quarter of Serbs were at that time living outside Serbia. The Memorandum had argued that Serbs in Croatia lived in the least developed parts. Sirotković contradicted this statement by arguing that 80% of them lived and worked in urban areas. The Serbian Academy replied to this criticism using statistics prepared by Kosta Mihailović (1990) for 1981. According to these figures, the per capita income of the Serbs in Croatia was significantly lower than that of the Croatians of Croatia (see Table 4).

Table 4 – Per capita national income by republic and by ethnic group. (in dinars, 1981 prices)

	National	Croats	Serbs
SFRY	89,466	105,16	85,051
Croatia	114,660	114,461	98,906
Serbia	82,660	108,997	88,672

Source: Mihailović and Krestić, p. 69. Based on Kosta Mihailović, *Regionalna stvarnost Jugoslavija*, Belgrade, Ekonomika, 1990, p. 153.

The Academy concluded this debate by observing that in 1947 Slovenia and Croatia accounted for 34.7% of the population of Yugoslavia and 39.9% of its GNP, whereas in 1988 they had 28.1% of its population and 44.8% of its GNP. With a constant proportion of 41.5% of the population, Serbia's share in GNP had declined from 39% in 1947 to 35.5% in 1988.

From this discussion between Croatian and Serbian economists one may conclude that both parties select data and methodology on the basis of political objectives. They are clever in pointing out that their adversaries have used the wrong methodology. It is difficult for an outsider to make a final judgment on this debate, partly thanks to the lack of reliable data. In strictly economic terms, however, the Serbian side seems to put forward more plausible arguments. But both parties neglect the fact that the growth of one Yugoslav republic produces a number of spin-offs for the others. In this respect, the Yugoslav economy should be seen instead as a co-operative system. The Croatian and Serbian economists ignore this point, preferring to use a simplified model of the economy as a zero-sum game in which all one player's gains are made at the expense of the others.

The explanation of economic discrimination against the Serbs as a result of the evil intentions of a communist leadership is a product of the imagination, and lacks any foundation. In this respect, there seems to be a remarkable dissonance between a certain rationality in discussing methodological issues, for instance, and the ease with which prejudices are underwritten. The Serbian Memorandum defends a programme of Serbian renaissance but refuses to be regarded as being inspired by nationalism. The Memorandum stresses that the Serbs in Croatia are discriminated against economically and that the secession of Croatia would leave them unprotected. In this way the Serbian Academy has actively contributed to the growing nationalist climate in the country and has provided an intellectual and academic rationale for the programme for a Greater Serbia.

In its critique of the causes of Yugoslavia's economic decline, the Serbian Academy misses the main point. It concentrates on regional economics and the relations between the republics, but does not take into account the general nature of the Yugoslav economic crisis. This is partly because the Memorandum was largely inspired by Kosta Mihailović, an economist specializing in regional development economics. The exclusive focus on the thesis that Yugoslav economic policies had disadvantaged Serbia has drawn attention away from the general structural causes of the crisis in the Yugoslav economy, such as low productivity, inefficient organization and the serious debt problem. These structural weaknesses in the self-managed economic system were aggravated by the competitive investment policy of republican bureaucracies, which pointlessly duplicated industrial capacity in each republic. Moreover, the lack of restraint and self-discipline in the self-managed enterprises – for example the diversion of resources from investment to wages and collective consumption – common to all Yugoslav enterprises, were certainly even more serious in the underdeveloped regions. It handicapped the developed republics by the useless transfer of resources to the funds of less developed regions.

Much of Yugoslav expansion was financed by foreign debt and, with high interest and increased energy costs to be paid at the beginning of the 1980s, the economic system collapsed. An effective diagnosis of this situation should have taken all arguments into account without prejudice, but in the early 1980s the ideological conditions for such fruitful debate on the causes of the economic crisis were not present. Yet it is also true that the highly critical evaluations of the economic performance of the self-management system made by Western observers was not free from ideological prejudice either. It is our personal opinion that a gradual reform of the system of self-management would have been workable. But such a reform would only have been possible if based on a correct diagnosis.

In Place of a Conclusion

Yugoslav authors like to use this formula in drawing conclusions, and we would like to honour this tradition. In this contribution, we have explored the basic attitude of the Yugoslav intelligentsia towards the main political problems of state organization. In the first part, we described the roles and functions of their Academies and the development of historiography. We find here a high degree of autonomy and dissidence.

Apart from the brief period immediately after the communist take-over, which has generally been characterized as the Stalinist period, scientists had a certain amount of freedom to express their views. Dissident thought could flourish in the discussion forums of the Praxis group. Originally constituted as a reformist socialist current, its radical positions came to be rejected by the regime as oppositional. It is striking, however, how the positions of some of the leading members of the group later evolved towards nationalism. In the second half of the 1980s, nationalism found academic expression in Serbia and Croatia in the discussion on the so-called Memorandum. In this debate, an analysis of the general structural deficiencies of the Yugoslav economy was neglected. The exclusive focus on the relatively disadvantaged position of the republican economies and particular national interests made an objective analysis of the economic crisis impossible.

Notes

[1] Paul Garde, *Vie et mort de la Yougoslavie*, Paris, Fayard, 1992. A recent overview of intellectual debates in Serbia is given in Aleksandar Pavković 'From Yugoslavism to Serbism: the Serb National Idea 1986-1996', *Nations and Nationalism*, Vol. 4, No. 4, 1998, pp. 511-528.

[2] Stevan K. Pavlowitch, *Yugoslavia*, New York, Praeger, 1971, p. 43; Robert Stallaerts & Jeannine Laurens, *Historical Dictionary of the Republic of Croatia*, Lanham, Md, London, The Scarecrow Press, 1995, p. 205.

[3] The second Yugoslavia was built up by the communists after their victory in the second world war. At the beginning of the 1980s, after the death of Tito, there was much talk about a third Yugoslavia in a non-communist era. This never actually had a chance to emerge because the country disintegrated.

[4] Ivan Božić, Vladimir Dedijer, Sima Cirković and Milorad Ekmević, *History of Yugoslavia*, New York, McGraw-Hill, 1974.

[5] Werner Markert, *Jugoslawien. Osteuropa-Handbuch*, Köln/Graz, Böhlau-Verlag, 1954, p. 195.

[6] In fact, it was the heir of the venerable 'Društvo za Humanističke Vede' (Society of the Humanities). Its oldest roots can even be traced back to the Jesuit and theology schools of the sixteenth century and the *Academia Operosorum*, founded in Ljubljana in 1693.

7   Of course, because the theory – still less the practice – were not set in stone, there was always a wide margin of interpretation. There was a continuous discussion on the limits of the paradigm. Classical historians who graduated before the war continued their work more or less on their old premises. Moreover, the diaspora disputed the communist theses as often as possible.

8   For the further 'history of Yugoslav historiography', see Ivo Banac, 'Historiography of the Countries of Eastern Europe: Yugoslavia', *American Historical Review*, Vol. 97, 1992, pp. 1084-1104.

9   Šidak, Gross, Karaman and Sčepić published their interpretation in Jaroslav Šidak, Mirjana Gross, Igor Karaman and Dragovan Sčepić, *Povijest hrvatskog narodag, 1860-1940* (History of the Croatian People, 1860-1940), Zagreb, Školska knjiga, 1968.

10   The same pattern could later be seen in Belgrade. Although scientists were removed from teaching positions at the university in the early 1980s, they were allowed to continue their work in research institutes – such as the Belgrade Institute of Social Sciences – and there produce fundamental criticism of Yugoslav society. The case of Miladin Životić was an indication to some observers that a transformation to a more democratic society was still possible at the end of the 1980s, just before Milošević came to power.

11   It is more than symbolic that immediately after the take-over of the new regime by Tudjman, a second edition of this national history was published (Trpimir Macan, *Povijest Hrvatskoga Naroda*. Zagreb, Školska Knjiga, II. izdanje, 1992). In fact, it was one more expression of the emergence of a new ideological mainstream.

12   Here, the opinion of 'first thinker and ideologue' Edvard Kardelj was decisive. He also prepared the draft of the new constitution of 1974, which institutionalized the (con)federation.

13   For example, Jure Krišto, *Prešušena povijest – Katolička crkva u hrvatskoj politici. 1850-1918* (The Suppressed History – The Catholic Church in Croatian Politics, 1850-1918), Zagreb, Hrvatska sveč ilišna naklada, 1994.

14   The editorial committee of the international edition of *Praxis* consisted of Branko Bošnjak, Danko Grlić, Milan Kangrga, Danilo Pejović, Gajo Petrović, Rudi Supek and Predrag Vranički (*Praxis*, 1965, 1). The local Serbo-Croat edition was launched in 1963.

15   Pedrag Vranički, Gajo Petrović, Rudi Supek, Danko Grlić and Branko Bošnjak, *Praxis, International edition*, No. 1, 1965.

16   For a short, systematic description of the basic philosophical views of the Praxis Group, see Mihailo Marković and Robert S. Cohen, *Yugoslavia: The Rise and Fall of Socialist Humanism. A History of the Praxis Group*, Nottingham, Spokesman Books, 1975, pp. 30-40.

17   In his theses on Feuerbach.

18   Marković and Cohen, *op. cit.*, p. 38.

19   The labels were of course reminiscent of the theses of Yugoslavia's greatest dissident, Milovan Djilas, who had earlier clashed with the bureaucracy and had been removed from power. This is also the reason why some critics of the regime called the Praxis philosophers 'Djilasists'.

20   One of the main reproaches levelled at the Praxis group was its supposed anarcho-liberal character. Moreover, its intellectualism and supposed élitism were not in line with the concrete phase of development of Yugoslav self-management. This all meant that Praxis members were accused of alienating power for themselves from the Yugoslav masses and labourers and from its avant-garde, the League of Communist of Yugoslavia. (See Edvard Kardelj, *Beleške o našoj društvenoj kritici*, Beograd, Kultura, 1966).

21   Rudi Supek and Veljko Rus from Ljubljana, and Svetozar Stojanović, Ljubomir Tadić and Zagorka Pesić-Golubović, from Belgrade (*Praxis International*, Vol. 1, No. 1, 1981).

22   Marković and Cohen, *op. cit.*, pp. 42-43.

23 Životić himself played down the disagreement. But it is typical of the change in the press that the once high-quality magazine *NIN* should report the news under a sensational headline: 'My Conflict with the Group of Eight' (Moj spor sa 'grupom 8'). The 'Group of Eight' refers to the eight professors who were dismissed from Belgrade university.

24 The Zagreb professor of economics, Branko Horvat, also a collaborator of the Praxis group, remained closer to an universalist position. He became president of the Croatian Social Democrats. He defended both a certain form of social property and at the same time a strict guarantee of civil and human rights.

25 The 'relentless criticism of all existing reality' implied an eventual revision of one's own conceptions. This, however, is but a poor motivation for what seems to be a conforming attitude to power-politics designed to secure one's own position. Such a change of attitude was a general trend among intellectuals. Among my personal acquaintances, scholars (and assistants of Branko Horvat) at the *Institut Ekonomskih Nauka* (Institute of Economic Studies in Belgrade) changed over to Serbian nationalist positions.

26 *Memorandum*, Serbian Academy of Sciences and Arts, 1995, pp. 95-140 (p. 13).

27 *Ibid.*, p. 14.

28 The original text contained 73 typewritten pages, of which 30 can be considered to have been approved by the Committee (*Ibid.*, p. 15).

29 However, alternative visions were never formulated, and later most academicians referred to the Memorandum as an authoritative document. Incidentally, one member of the Academy distanced himself from the content and main theses of the document. On this, see further the detailed analysis by the Belgrade philopher Oliveira Milosavljević, 'Populistička upotreba autoriteta nauke. Javna politička delatnost srpske Akademije Nauka i Umetnosti (1986-1992)' (Populist Use of the Authority of Science. Public political activities of the Serbian Academy of Sciences and Arts (1986-1992)), *Republika*, 1-31 July, Nos 119-120, 1998. Partially translated into French as 'Du mauvais usage de l'autorité scientifique', in Nebojsa Popov (ed.), *Radiographie d'un nationalisme. Les racines serbes du conflit yougoslave*, Paris, Editions de l'Atelier, 1998, pp. 205-238.

30 Cfr. Pavković, *op. cit.*, p. 513.

31 This is observed also in a short remark on Serbian secession in the Memorandum by Oliviera Milosavljević, in Popov, *op. cit.*, p. 74.

32 For a short overview of the intellectual production of Croatian nationalist émigré groups in the United States, ending finally with massive support for Tudjman, see Jure Prpić, 'Američki Hrvati i oslobodjenje Hrvatske', in Jure Prpić, *Hrvati u Americi* (The Croatian Immigrants in America), Zagreb, Hrvatska matica Iseljenika, 1977, pp. 357-399, especially pp. 357-399.

33 In these figures, Croatia includes Slavonia and Dalmatia and Serbia Vojvodina (but not Srem) (Kosta Mihailović and Vasilije Krestić, Serbian Academy of Sciences and Arts. Presidency. *Memorandum of the Serbian Academy of Sciences and Arts. Answers to Criticisms*, Belgrade, SANU, 1995, p. 35).

34 Mihailović and Krestić, pp. 60-76.

35 The indices were constructed by converting current prices for each year into prices for the base year 1972.

36 According to statistics from the Federal Statistics Office, GNP in Croatia had increased by 17.5% (the per capita increase being 12.8%) over the period 1947-1952, while the increase in Serbia's GNP amounted to only 1.3% (and per capita GNP decreased by 5.1%). The Serbian Academy also argued that in 1947 Croatia's GNP was 10.3% higher than the Serbian GNP, and that this difference had increased to 31.2% by 1952.

Ronald Rudin

6. Bargaining from Strength: Historical Writing and Political Autonomy in Late-Twentieth-Century Quebec[1]

Introduction

Over the past thirty years, political discourse in Quebec has been dominated by those interested in expanding the autonomy of this Canadian province. Ever since the creation of the Canadian federation (normally referred to as Confederation) in 1867, there have been those in Quebec who have sought to maximize the autonomy allowed to the province under the terms of the constitutional arrangements of the mid-nineteenth century. However, since the 1960s the major Quebec political parties have been dedicated to securing greater autonomy, within the confines of Canada through a fundamental renegotiation of the Confederation pact if possible, or through Quebec's separation from Canada and the creation of some new relationship between two sovereign states if need be. There have been two bitterly fought referenda on the question of Quebec's sovereignty since 1980. While those in favour of Quebec remaining part of Canada won in both cases (albeit by the smallest of margins in 1995), they did so only by advocating a profound reassessment of the province's ties to Canada, thus dramatically reflecting the depth of support for autonomy, however defined, in late-twentieth-century Quebec.

Over roughly the same period, there has been an equally noticeable shift in the nature of Quebec historical writing. Prior to the 1960s, most Quebec historians concentrated on what made Quebec a distinct society in the context of North America. These historians, writing from a number of political perspectives, particularly focused upon the factors responsible for the relative powerlessness of the French-speaking majority. Although constituting roughly 80% of the population of Quebec, French-speakers traditionally wielded relatively little power in both the political and economic arenas, and Quebec historians devoted considerable energy to explaining why this should have been the case. Since the 1960s, however, historians have turned away from this emphasis upon difference to explore, instead, the ways in which Quebecers had long been much like most

North Americans. In short, the historians were interested in showing Quebecers to have constituted a 'normal' people.[2]

On the face of it, these changes in terms of both political discourse and historical writing in Quebec would appear to have been at odds with one another. In the period since the 1960s, the emphasis upon autonomy frequently led political leaders to emphasize the exceptional nature of Quebec society due to its linguistic and cultural characteristics. This emphasis upon difference took on its most concrete form in a proposal to change the Canadian constitution in the 1980s so as to recognize Quebec as having constituted a 'distinct' society. At the same time historians were intent on placing Quebecers, as one observer remarked, 'in the mainstream of developments both in North America and across the western world. From this perspective, Quebec was as industrial, as capitalistic, as liberal, as developed, in short as modern as other societies'.[3]

This paper is designed to analyse this paradoxical situation through a closer analysis of political and social circumstances, on the one hand, and the nature of Quebec historical writing, on the other. To that end, the first part of this chapter focuses upon the nature of historical writing in the context of Quebec's social and political history from Confederation to the 1960s, when the Quebec government took unprecedented steps to promote the social and economic interests of the province's French-speaking majority. With the support of the state, the position of French-speakers was dramatically improved with the result that this period of profound change tends to be referred to as having constituted a 'Quiet Revolution'. The greater economic and political power of French-speaking Quebecers ultimately helped shape both political discourse and historical writing over the past thirty years. As we will see in the second part of the paper, the political search for autonomy by emphasizing Quebec's exceptionalism and the historians' search for 'normalcy' were really parts of a single process of late-twentieth-century social change. Since this linking of historical writing with political discourse touches directly upon the issue of objectivity in the historical profession, the concluding section of the paper will address the apparent conflict between the inherently political nature of historical writing and the pretensions to objectivity held by many historians.

Society and Historical Writing in pre-1960 Quebec

The Social and Political Context[4]

Over the course of a century, from roughly the moment at which Canada was created as a country to the start of the 1960s, Quebec shared in many of the processes that shaped much of the western world. The European colonization of the St-Lawrence River valley, which runs through the heart of Quebec, was begun by France in the seventeenth century. Under French rule, relatively few immigrants made the journey across the Atlantic, with the result that a relatively small French-Catholic population existed in 1763 when control of the territory passed from France to England following the Seven Years' War. This population earned its living from the land, a situation that did not greatly change until the mid-nineteenth century when changes in technology and transportation brought the industrial revolution to Quebec, at roughly the same moment that it was spreading through other parts of North America.

Industrialization left its mark on Quebec in various ways. On one level, it resulted in the slow drift of the French-speaking population from the land to the cities, most notably Montreal which emerged as a major industrial, commercial and financial centre. By the time of World War I, the majority of the residents of Quebec were living in cities, a situation which paralleled the growth of the urban population in the rest of Canada. As the twentieth century continued, so too did the urbanization of the population, with the result that 74% of the population of Quebec was living in cities by the start of the 1960s, a figure that has continued to rise over the past thirty years.

On another level, the emergence of an industrial economy had significant consequences for Quebec as it facilitated the creation of Canada as a country in 1867. Prior to Confederation, much of the territory that would become Canada was divided among a number of relatively self-governing colonies, which were collectively known as British North America. By the mid-nineteenth century, England had little strategic interest in maintaining very much control over the internal workings of the colonies. Accordingly, it was attracted by the idea of a federation of the various colonies so that they might look after themselves. At the same time, the business leaders of the colonies were interested in the considerable economic advantages that such a union might offer. In particular, the business leaders in Montreal, most of whom were English-speakers even though they resided in a largely French-speaking territory, looked forward to the creation of a large common market (there had previously been some tariff barriers between colonies) within which industrial goods might be sold and across which railways might be built. Accordingly, when the representatives of the various British North American colonies sat down to negotiate the terms of the new federation, business concerns were given a good deal of consideration.

Had the business leaders (amply represented by the two leading politicians of the time, John A. Macdonald and George-Etienne Cartier, both of whom had served as corporate lawyers) had their way, Canada would have been a country with a single, central government with the power to facilitate the development of the industrial economy that was taking shape.[5] These leaders soon realized that such extreme centralization, however desirable, was impossible in the face of Quebecers' insistence that they maintain control over their distinctive Catholic institutions that provided education and social services to the bulk of the population. Ever since the French regime, the Catholic church had been in charge of these services, and Quebecers were opposed to allowing such matters to fall under the control of a Canadian government, dominated by English-speaking Protestants, who would constitute the majority in the new country as a whole. Accordingly, the framers of Canada's constitution, the British North America (BNA) Act, established a two-tier system of government. The power to build a transcontinental economy was to be within the competence of the central government, while the various provinces would control such matters as education and social services. In the case of Quebec, this meant that the provincial government would allow the Catholic church to play a central role in the provision of services to the population. While other provinces were busily creating state-run ministries of education, in Quebec this was viewed as unnecessary as the Catholic church was to have the mandate to administer most of the schools.[6]

Over the first hundred years of Confederation, Quebecers expressed considerable insecurity about the political arrangement of 1867, but largely manifested this feeling in repeated demands that the central government respect the province's constitutional responsibilities. Blessed with superior resources, central governments, particularly in the period immediately following World War II, tried to exert some control over areas within Quebec's competence. In reaction, Quebec governments regularly pointed to the distinctive linguistic and cultural make-up of Quebec which required that it remain in control over the few matters left in its hands. This sense of insecurity was particularly heightened by the influx of a significant number of immigrants in the post-war period. Most of these immigrants chose to live their lives in English, the mother tongue of roughly 15% of the population of the province, thus raising the spectre that Quebecers might succumb to the force of anglicization, always a danger for a French-speaking people in the North American sea of English-speakers.

Writing a 'Different' Past

Most Quebec historical writing from the mid-nineteenth century to the 1960s was designed to help Quebecers understand why they had long been poorer and less powerful than English-speakers in Canada. There were some significant changes over this century, primarily due to the emergence of history as a professional discipline in the early twentieth century. Nevertheless, nearly all historians presented a French-speaking and Catholic population that had long been fundamentally different from the English-speakers who surrounded them in North America. Moreover, nearly all historians made little secret of the fact that they hoped that their writings would somehow contribute to '*la survivance*' (the survival) of their people.

This tradition began in the 1840s, with the publication of the first comprehensive history of the French-speaking population of Quebec. François-Xavier Garneau wrote his *Histoire du Canada depuis sa découverte jusqu'à nos jours* (The History of Canada from its Discovery to the Present) in the late 1840s, at a time when hope for survival seemed bleak. In 1837-38 there had been a rebellion against British rule, which was followed by the imposition of a new political system designed to assimilate French-speakers into the English-speaking population that surrounded them. In this context, Garneau set out to chronicle the history of a people marked by the fact that it had been forced to make its way in the world on its own. In the final analysis, France had abandoned Quebecers, following which England threatened them with the prospect of 'suffering and humiliation'.[7] The history of Quebec, then, was one of a resilient people who had been true to their roots so as to fend off the forces of assimilation.

While Garneau presented a saga designed to stiffen the resolve of Quebecers, his work was found wanting in certain regards by Abbé Lionel Groulx, easily the most important French-language historian in Canada over the first half of the twentieth century. Groulx, who became the first professor of Quebec history at the university level in 1915, described Garneau as his model for the way in which he had used history to give his people hope. Nevertheless, Groulx, a priest, could not accept Garneau's frequent marginalization of Catholicism as a positive force in having encouraged survival. In counterpoint to Garneau's overly secular vision of Quebec's past, Groulx produced a large body of work that focused upon the spiritual values of Quebecers, a rural people who had managed to stave off assimilation by following a way of life at odds with the currents of secularization and modernization across North America. Groulx's characterization of Quebecers as a rural people was contradicted by the steady movement of the population to the cities. Nevertheless, he stressed the distinctive characteristics of Quebecers so as to give them the strength to avoid assimilation. Although Groulx flirted with the idea of Quebec's separation from Canada, he was in the mainstream of Quebec intellectual and political leaders during the first half of the twentieth century who recognized that their society was too poor to achieve any new political status. While the politicians tried to hold on to the autonomy that had been granted in 1867, intellectuals such as Groulx tried to give Quebecers the hope to survive until they were strong enough to achieve a new constitutional status.

This recognition of weakness was still evident in Quebec historical writing as a new generation, much better trained than Groulx's, came to occupy leading positions in Quebec's two French-language universities after World War II. For these young historians, however, Quebecers' weakness, particularly in the world of business, was no longer a virtue, as it had appeared in Groulx's writing, but was instead a problem that needed to be fixed. This changed perspective had been prompted by the spectacular growth of the North American economy after World War II. During these years, Quebecers watched the emergence of the consumer society thanks to the introduction of television, all the while remaining incapable of sharing in its fruits owing to their relative poverty. In this context, historians focused upon the causes for Quebecers' economic marginalization.

Those historians who came to succeed Groulx at the Université de Montréal argued that Quebecers' economic inferiority had been the result of the takeover of the French colony in the St-Lawrence valley in the mid-eighteenth century. One of these historians, Guy Frégault, argued that Quebec had constituted a 'normal' society prior to the Conquest. There had been a time when all Quebecers could hope to succeed in the world of business, but after 1763 such hope was gone and all that was left was a 'broken' people.[8] Another group of historians, this one at the Université Laval in Quebec City, also focused on the way in which Quebecers had long been different because of their economic weakness. However, in the hands of historians such as Fernand Ouellet the responsibility rested with the Quebecers themselves who had followed the dictates of Catholicism too readily to make it in a world where individual initiative was required.[9]

These contrasting views on the economic inferiority of French-speakers reflected differing perspectives upon Quebec's relationship with the rest of Canada. The Montreal historians, with their emphasis upon the tragic dimensions of the Conquest, suggested that Quebecers required a fundamental re-negotiation of their place within Canada if they were to regain the power they had wielded during the French regime. As for the Laval historians, their emphasis upon the shortcomings of Quebecers seemed to call out for the revamping of Quebec's institutions, but provided little comfort for those who saw the problem as resting with the Canadian federation.[10] In spite of these differences, however, both the Montreal and Laval historians, like Garneau and Groulx before them, focused upon what had made Quebecers different. Moreover, they all accepted the role of the historian as a public figure who could provide some direction for his society. Both the nature of historical writing and its relationship to public life would change, however, following the 1960s, with the fundamental transformation of many aspects of life in Quebec thanks to the direct intervention of the Quebec state in order to respond to the long-standing weakness, both economic and political, of the province's French-speaking majority. So successful were these reforms in changing both the objective circumstances of French-speakers and the way in which they viewed themselves that the 1960s are commonly referred to in Quebec as having brought about a 'Quiet Revolution'.

Social Change, Political Autonomy, and the Search for a 'Normal' Past

Quebec Society after the Quiet Revolution

During the first century of Canada's history as a country, Quebec had experienced urbanization, industrialization and immigration, forces that were also central to the experiences of many other societies across the western world. Nevertheless, however 'normal' Quebec's experience may have appeared, the marginalization of French-speakers from positions of power, both political and economic, led various leaders – historians included – to look for the roots for Quebecers' relative weakness in the years following World War II. Ordinary Quebecers, anxious to share in the fruits of the consumer society, were prepared to see some fundamental changes in the way their province functioned – but they had to wait until the 1960s, when the political will finally emerged to challenge the English-speaking elite of the business world and the hierarchy of the Catholic church, which had long encouraged the Quebec government to play a relatively passive role in the province's affairs.

That the Quebec state was now prepared to intervene in order to deal with the relative powerlessness of French-speakers was evident in two actions taken by the government of Jean Lesage, leader of the Quebec Liberal Party, whose rise to power in 1960 is usually viewed as marking the start of the Quiet Revolution. In 1962 the Quebec government nationalized the various hydroelectric companies, all owned by English-speakers, which had controlled the most important source of power in the province since the start of the century. By creating Hydro-Québec, the provincial government hoped to create a technologically advanced corporation where French-speakers, who had not always had easy entrée into the corporate world, would be able to get their feet in the door. Similarly, in 1964 the Lesage government created a state-run Ministry of Education to push aside the Catholic church which had been in a dominant position since the mid-nineteenth century, but whose insistence upon a classical education was now viewed as part of the cause of Quebecers' economic weakness.

The nationalization of both hydro-electricity and education reflected the determination of French-speaking Quebecers to use the one government that they could hope to control, the government of Quebec, to achieve levels of wealth and power that had long been held by English-speakers. However, these nationalizations were just the start of a programme, pursued by various governments over much of the past thirty years, to use the Quebec state as a tool to improve the status of French-speakers. On one level, Quebec governments intervened whenever they could to create new programmes within the jurisdictions that had been consigned to them as part of the Confederation arrangements of

1867. In this regard, in 1974 the Quebec government passed legislation making French the official language of Quebec, compelling most immigrants to attend French schools, and making French the normal language of business. All of these actions were designed to enhance further the place of French-speakers in the economy, with the result that by the end of the 1970s the long-standing wage gap between French and English-speakers had been closed. The world of business, long viewed as the preserve of English-speakers, now became part of the mainstream of Québécois culture, with the result that business school enrolments boomed and support for free trade with the United States among French-speakers far exceeded that among English Canadians.

On another level, Quebec governments sought to expand the range of actions that they could initiate by seeking a fundamental renegotiation of Quebec's place within the Canadian federation so that the province's distinctive language and culture might be allowed to flourish. Within only a few years of Lesage's rise to power, he was already at the bargaining table with Lester Pearson, the Canadian prime minister at the time, seeking a new relationship between Quebec and Canada that might transfer some federal powers to the province. Since the start of the 1960s, every government of Quebec, regardless of its party affiliation, has been committed to this expansion of Quebec's autonomy. However, in spite of this constant commitment to autonomy, there has been no formal amendment to the Canadian constitution in response to Quebec's demands to be recognized as having a 'special status' or constituting a 'distinct society', to use only two of the numerous formulations that have been proposed. Against the background of this failure to achieve further autonomy, the late 1960s saw the rise of a mainstream political party, committed to Quebec's independence, albeit in conjunction with the preservation of economic links with the rest of Canada.

René Lévesque, the founder of the Parti québécois (PQ), had been the Liberal cabinet minister responsible for the nationalization of hydro-electricity in the early 1960s. He was convinced that a new relationship had to be forged with the rest of Canada, but ultimately concluded that such change would never occur through normal negotiations. Accordingly, he left the Liberals in order to create a political party dedicated to the sovereignty of Quebec along with the forging of a new relationship with the rest of Canada. Lévesque's idea of sovereignty-association became the guiding principle for the PQ, which he took to power in 1976. Since he was advocating a reformulation of Quebec's ties to the rest of Canada, and not simply the severing of all connections, there is much that his party and the Liberals (the only other significant political party) have shared over the past thirty years. Both parties have reflected the spirit of the Quiet Revolution, which was to make Quebecers, to use a Liberal Party slogan, *'maîtres chez nous'* (masters in our own house).[11] Each has wanted to make Quebec more autonomous, in the process reflecting a profound transformation of the self-image of Quebecers, a change that was encouraged by the similarly dramatic transformation of Quebec historical writing.

Writing a 'Normal' Past

Prior to the Quiet Revolution, historians focused largely upon what had made Quebecers somehow different from, and usually weaker than, their North American neighbours. This paradigm of difference no longer had very much appeal to historians, however, as Quebecers became central players in public life wielding significant economic and political power. Rather, historians, living in a society which appeared to be in the mainstream of developments, now looked to the past for evidence that Quebecers had long been a modern people. This perspective proved particularly attractive to the generation of historians, which came to occupy newly created positions in the rapidly expanding French-language universities of the late 1960s and early 1970s.

As part of the commitment of the Quebec state to improving the status of French-speakers, government funds were invested in both the expansion of the existing universities and the creation of an entirely new one, the Université du Québec, with campuses scattered across the province. When it came to staffing the new or growing history departments, the universities mainly looked to young scholars, baby-boomers who had been born in the years after World War II, who had attended university during the heady years of the Quiet Revolution, and who were just finishing doctoral degrees as the new positions were opening up. As one of the most influential of these historians, Paul-André Linteau, has observed, 'Coming of age in a Quebec where everyone was talking about modernization, living in an urban-industrial society, it was natural that we would want to understand the roots of contemporary Quebec'. Earlier historians had looked to the French regime or the early years of British rule in order to make sense of the impact of the Conquest which had contributed to Quebec's distinctiveness. However, as Linteau put it, such 'historical writing … was not responding to our concerns. Accordingly, we set off to explore the various factors that led to the emergence of an industrial, capitalist society in Quebec by the middle of the nineteenth century'.[12]

So completely has Linteau's generation shaped Quebec historical writing over the past thirty years that there have been relatively few dissenters from a paradigm that focused upon the emergence of an urban, secular and entrepreneurial Quebec, and which insisted that there was little to distinguish Quebec from the neighbouring societies of North America. Because this generation so profoundly reshaped Quebec historical writing, I have elsewhere labelled them as revisionists.[13] Their perspective found its clearest expression in the most widely read work of history published in Quebec since the Quiet Revolution. Written by

Linteau along with René Durocher and Jean-Claude Robert, *Histoire du Québec contemporain* was a synthesis of the various studies that their generation had been carrying out since the late 1960s.[14]

Linteau, Durocher and Robert dealt exclusively with the period since Confederation, thus setting themselves apart from Quebec historians, going back to Garneau, who had been preoccupied with an earlier period where the roots of Quebecers' inferiority might be found. These earlier historians had focused upon a rural society, in which French-speakers had been strongly influenced by Catholicism and little interested in issues pertinent to the world of business. Concentrating upon the period since 1867, Linteau, Durocher and Robert were insistent upon presenting a profoundly urban people. Accordingly, in the section of *Histoire du Québec contemporain* dealing with the period from 1867 to 1896, the authors gave considerably more space to urban issues than to rural ones, this in spite of the fact that, as they admitted, 'Quebec society was made up largely of rural inhabitants'.[15] However, they wanted to dispute the way in which 'Quebec [had] long been characterized as a society which was largely rural and relatively homogeneous, and in which the family was the central institution'.[16]

Once they established the pedigree of Quebecers as an urban people, Linteau, Durocher and Robert went on to show that they had been important players in the economy, this in contrast with the long-dominant assumption that French-speakers had been pushed aside from, or had become uninterested in, positions of economic power in the aftermath of the Conquest. Linteau and his colleagues pointed to the 'dynamism of a French-speaking bourgeoisie' by showing a francophone presence in the industrial, commercial, financial, and real-estate sectors.[17] From the revisionists' perspective, if English-speakers had long dominated the Quebec economy, it was simply a function of their superior access to capital markets controlled by fellow Anglophones. In spite of this dominance, Linteau and his colleagues insisted on the on-going role of French-speakers in positions of economic influence, albeit not at the very highest levels.

Moreover, this emphasis upon the entrepreneurial talents of Quebecers served to contradict the emphasis in earlier historical writing upon the role of Catholicism in blocking the involvement of Quebecers in the world of business. More generally, Linteau and his colleagues pushed to one side the impact of the Catholic Church which was depicted as only one institution among many vying for control over the Quebec people. Even if the Church sought 'to assert a leading role in society', it was unable to overcome the 'social and ideological changes linked to the development of capitalism'.[18] Moreover, the church was shown as having been incapable of blocking the growth of the role of the state in Quebec, this in spite of the failure to create a state-run Ministry of Education until the 1960s. Nevertheless, in the context of the Quiet Revolution, the revisionists were eager to show that, even in the field of education, Quebecers had been in the mainstream of efforts in most western societies to employ the state as an agent of development. Accordingly, Linteau, Durocher and Robert observed that Quebec governments going back to the 1920s had been involved in the 'modernization of the educational system'.[19]

Here, then, was a Quebec in the mainstream of various developments such as urbanization, industrialization and secularization that had been central to the history of most western nations. Moreover, the revisionist historians constructed a narrative of normalcy by concentrating their attention resolutely upon the territory of Quebec, in contrast with earlier historians such as Lionel Groulx, who entitled his own synthesis of his people's past, *Histoire du Canada français*.[20] In employing the term 'Canada français' (French Canada), Groulx dealt primarily with the French-speaking population of Quebec, as would Linteau, Durocher and Robert thirty years later. At the same time, however, he also took into account the experiences of the relatively weak French-speaking minorities in the other Canadian provinces, with the result that he, and other pre-Quiet Revolution historians, tended to focus upon the sad plight of a linguistic minority.

By the late 1960s, however, in the midst of the Quiet Revolution, when institutions such as Hydro-Québec or the Quebec Ministry of Education were being constructed to serve the population residing in the province, historians began to give their studies a more territorial orientation. In order to emphasize the distance between their conception and that of earlier historians such as Groulx, Linteau and his colleagues began their volume with a lengthy statement of purpose that, to a large extent, defined revisionist historical writing: 'The Quebec that we are studying here is defined in territorial, rather than ethnic, terms. We are interested in phenomena, which were experienced by the men, and women who inhabited this territory. We have consistently used the word "Québécois" in a very precise sense. It pertains to all residents of Quebec, including those whose ancestors came from the northwest thousands of years ago, those who came from France in the time of Jean Talon, those who came from Scotland in the late eighteenth century or from Ireland during the Great Famine, those Jews seeking refuge from the pogroms of Eastern Europe, and those emigrating from a southern Italy which had little to offer them'.[21] This formulation served not only to emphasize the territorial dimensions of the revisionists' conception, but also to place Quebec in the context of the process of immigration, which had been central to the experience of other parts of North America.

While Groulx had written about French Canadians, the revisionists now dealt with Québécois, a term which was coined during the Quiet Revolution. This term, however, was not without its ambiguity. On the one hand, it had a territorial definition that brought all residents of Quebec into the picture. At the same time, the revisionists' preoccupation with establishing the modern credentials of 80% of the population of that territory led them to focus upon the members of a particular ethnic group. This unresolved tension in the writings of the revisionists was similarly evident in the use of the term 'Québécois' by the Parti québécois. On the one hand, this party, from its founding in 1968, has claimed to be interested in representing the interests of all the residents of the territory of Quebec; on the other hand, its policies in such areas as the promotion of the French language have been attractive almost exclusively to members of the French-speaking majority. Very few non-francophones support the Parti québécois, with the result that the party's occasional appeals to a civic form of nationalism tend to be overpowered by the ethnic basis of its political support. In the end, the term 'Québécois' applies most convincingly to the French-speaking population as it came to view itself following the Quiet Revolution. As Jocelyn Létourneau has put it, the French Canadian, 'conquered, humiliated, and demoralized', was replaced in the historical record by the Québécois, 'successful, entrepreneurial and ambitious'.[22]

Revisionism, Objectivity and Autonomy

In addition to the substantive differences between the revisionists and their predecessors, there was also a significant shift in style. Prior to the Quiet Revolution, most Quebec historians, in addition to explaining the past, were prepared to be explicit about the political implications of their work. Both Garneau and Groulx wrote about the past in order to steel the resolve of their people to survive culturally. As for the historians writing after World War II, they were interested in providing lessons about the direction that Quebecers should follow in light of the rise of the consumer society. By contrast, the revisionists went out of their way to avoid giving the impression that they were for one political option or another for Quebec, no mean feat in a society whose French-speaking population is fairly evenly divided over whether to remain part of Canada.

In explaining the intellectual forces that shaped the revisionists, Linteau recognized a particular debt to the American historians of the 1960s and 1970s who were interested in using the techniques of the social sciences to deal, in a rational, scientific manner, with such 'modern' phenomena as urbanization and class conflict.[23] There was something fitting about this American identification since, as we have seen, much revisionist writing was designed to depict Quebecers as a normal North American people. More significantly, however, Linteau and his colleagues were attracted by the seemingly value-free nature of the Americans' approach, which seemed to provide them with the opportunity to distance themselves even further from their predecessors who had worn their political views on their sleeves. Serge Courville, Jean-Claude Robert and Normand Séguin, three leading revisionists, distinguished themselves from previous Quebec historians whose work had been deformed by 'preconceived notions and value judgements'.[24] For his part, Yves Gingras argued that Quebec historians since the 1960s had turned from polemical writing to scientific research so as to avoid 'being overly influenced by current social or economic concerns'.[25]

This self-image of the Quebec historian as objective observer has endured remarkably well into the late twentieth century, in spite of the trend throughout the wider profession to question the pretensions to objectivity of any historical writing. Over the past twenty years, under pressure both from various groups interested in explicitly using history as a tool to advance political agendas and from post-modernists prepared to see works of history as scarcely distinguishable from those of fiction, there has been much debate about the nature of historical writing. As Joyce Appleby, Lynn Hunt and Margaret Jacob have remarked, the only thing that is certain about the historical profession in the 1990s is that 'it rarely has been such a subject of controversy'.[26]

By and large, however, such debates have not made much of a dent in Quebec. Accordingly, Jocelyn Létourneau observed, 'One can count on the fingers of one hand the number of historians in Quebec who seem interested in understanding the assumptions underlying the conceptual model that they [the revisionists] have constructed'.[27] In general, Quebec historians have been comfortable with the way in which they have provided an appropriately modern view of their people's past and have not overly troubled themselves about the implications or the limitations of the revisionist approach. Normand Séguin, a revisionist referred to above, had no difficulty in remarking in 1991, long after the scientific pretensions of the discipline had been thrown into doubt, that history constituted 'a scientific exercise' designed 'to correct mistaken impressions and to fill the gaps in our knowledge'.[28] Séguin's statement, on its own, was not very exceptional. There are numerous historians across the profession at century's end who would be prepared to support his article of faith, but in most contexts such a statement would have been greeted with considerable cynicism. In Quebec, however, Séguin's faith in the scientific mission of historians met with little opposition, as it expressed the conviction, shared by most revisionists, that they were engaged in an exercise relatively free of distortion through value judgements.

This objective stance can be understood both as a reaction to the self-consciously political nature of their predecessors' writings and as a reflection of the manner in which the highly-trained 'expert' became a much respected figure in Quebec in the aftermath of the Quiet Revolution. Accordingly, there was a rapid rise to prominence of individuals who seemed to have the tools to resolve problems in a rational way, 'free of passion and value judgements'.[29] Business people became persons worthy of respect precisely because they projected the image of the modern Quebecer who was capable of succeeding on the international stage.

Similarly, in the public sector, highly-trained technocrats were hailed as the successors to the various representatives of the Catholic Church who had for so long managed the province's educational and social service systems. These civil servants contributed to the new image of the Quebecer by helping to provide the trappings of the modern interventionist state. In this context, the revisionist historians had every reason to see themselves as experts easily distinguishable from predecessors such as Groulx, whose works had been explicitly polemical, and thus deemed insufficiently scientific. The revisionists both looked for a modern past and marketed themselves as thoroughly modern in their own right.

When the revisionists' approach to the past is viewed in this manner, their work becomes less objective than they would claim it to have been. However, this remark is not meant as one of criticism since, as Peter Novick has argued in a penetrating study of the role of objectivity in the American historical profession, historical writing cannot help but be, to some degree, subjective. As Novick observed, 'I think [the idea of historical objectivity] promotes an unreal and misleading invidious distinction between, on the one hand, historical accounts "distorted" by ideological assumptions and purposes; on the other, history free of these taints. It seems to me that to say of a work of history that it is or isn't objective is to make an *empty* observation; to say something neither interesting nor useful'.[30] One might conclude from this disclaimer that Novick was prepared to accept any historical account as legitimate because objectivity was unattainable. In fact, however, he responded to those who would consign history to the ranks of fiction by noting that the pursuit, if not the attainment, of historical objectivity was a form of '*salutary nonsense*'; it was indefinable and unachievable, but just the same it provided some direction for historians.[31] As several commentators have observed, Novick indicated his own faith in the value of trying to get close to some well-documented, reasoned truth by producing a 650-page monograph grounded in years of painstaking research.[32]

Viewed from Novick's perspective, revisionist writing constituted a body of work based upon considerable, conscientious research, but which still reflected, in terms of both its style and substance, certain aspects of Quebec society in the late twentieth century. Accordingly, the revisionists' emphasis upon the normality of the Quebec past has been paralleled by what François Ricard has called 'the "normalization" of Quebec literature'. Ricard observed that since the 1970s there has been 'a weakening of the distinctive characteristics of Quebec literature and a growing tendency for it to resemble the literature of other industrial nations'.[33] Moreover, the revisionist approach to the past has been compatible with the general emphasis upon autonomy in Quebec political discourse since the Quiet Revolution. As we have seen, Quebec's political leaders over the past thirty years have emphasized the ways in which Quebec society is somehow different, usually in linguistic or cultural terms, from other societies in North America in order to provide support for the province's increased autonomy, either within the Canadian federation or outside of it as a sovereign state.

In the Quebec provincial election of 1998, the two major political parties played upon this sense of difference to advance their respective programmes. The Quebec Liberal Party, interested in the re-negotiation of the terms of federation so as to provide Quebec with additional powers, referred repeatedly to the 'unique character' of the province. As for the Parti québécois, which continues to support the sovereignty of Quebec in conjunction with a new relationship with the rest of Canada, its advertising proclaimed: 'Yes, we are different.... We are distinguishable from the rest of North America, not by our weaknesses, but by our strengths'.[34] While earlier Quebec historians such as Lionel Groulx had emphasized the distinctiveness of Quebecers in order to show their vulnerability, the leaders of both the Parti québécois and the Quebec Liberal Party now point to markers of difference in order to convey a sense of pride and even strength.

As a matter of political positioning, nearly all Quebec leaders since the Quiet Revolution have emphasized the 'difference' of Quebecers in order to explain, particularly to potential bargaining partners in the rest of Canada, that there was cause for revamping the way in which Canada was structured. Given the successes of Quebecers over the past thirty years, this emphasis upon Quebec's linguistic or cultural distinctiveness has not been a plea for protection by a weak people, but rather a demand for respect by a different, yet vibrant society. For their part, the revisionist historians, free of practical political concerns, presented Quebecers as a 'normal' people who, within the confines of the territory of Quebec, had long been in the mainstream of developments in the western world. Such a characterization freed Quebecers from being perceived as somehow inferior to their counterparts in English Canada, a perspective that could easily have been absorbed from most Quebec historical writing produced before the Quiet Revolution. English Canadians had little reason to bargain seriously with a people made up of 'poor farmers, who were devout Catholics, with little interest in the modern world'.[35] Rather, the revisionists presented a population that warranted serious consideration at the bargaining table because it had long been 'successful, entrepreneurial and ambitious'.[36]

The transformation of the Quebecer in the historical record from an object of oppression to an agent of success parallels, in certain regards, the treatment of women (as well as other groups which had traditionally held relatively little power) at the hands of historians over the past thirty years. With the expansion of universities across the western world, a process that had also occurred in Quebec in the context of the Quiet Revolution, women assumed a significant presence in history departments for the first time. Many of these new professors were interested in studying the history of women, at first in order to show the ways in which women had been oppressed throughout history. However, they soon shifted their attention from 'subordination and victimization to [an emphasis upon women's] agency and autonomy'.[37] By moving beyond the depiction of women as victims, women's historians – like the revisionists in Quebec – were showing their subjects to have been central players in history, and by connection individuals worthy of consideration in the organization of society. As Joan Scott has put it, 'Feminist history then becomes not the recounting of great deeds performed by women but the exposure of the often silent and hidden operations of gender that are nonetheless present and defining forces in the organization of most societies'.[38] Here was the intersection of history and politics as 'feminists demand[ed] the right to know and understand the experience of women, and to have it analysed, taken into account, recorded and valued, equally with the experience of men'.[39]

While women's historians came to their depiction of women fully aware of its political implications, the revisionist historians, in reaction against their politically involved predecessors, did not think in such terms. These historians did not necessarily calculate that their presentation of Quebecers as a modern people would serve the interests of political leaders trying to expand the province's autonomy. More likely, given the value-free pretensions of the revisionists, few probably gave much thought to the political implications of their approach to the past. Committed as they were to the possibility of understanding the past 'as it was', untainted by the agendas of previous Quebec historians, most revisionists could not imagine that their work might have contained a political message. In any event, their inability to appreciate the subjective aspects of their studies does not free them from the subjectivity shared by all historians. Moreover, the value judgements that they communicated, however implicitly, have allowed Quebecers to go to the bargaining table from a position of strength in their demand for recognition of the province's linguistic and cultural differences.

Lucien Bouchard, the former leader of the Parti québécois and former prime minister of Quebec, once observed that the distinctive identity of Quebecers could only be secured through sovereignty that might give his people 'the normal tool box of a normal state'.[40] In Bouchard's conceptualization, there was no contradiction between his goal for Quebecers to accede to a 'normal' status and the reasons for seeking that goal, namely the preservation of a set of distinctive linguistic and cultural attributes. In a similar manner, there has been no contradiction between the discourse of Quebec's political leaders and the writings of its historians. Both the politicians and the historians have been shaped by the altered contours of Quebec society since the Quiet Revolution, and both, in their own ways and within the limits of their chosen professions, have sought to advance the interests of a people who have been self-conscious about the changes their society has undergone over the past thirty years.

Notes

1 An earlier version of some of the ideas in this paper can be found in my *Making History in Twentieth Century Quebec*, Toronto, University of Toronto Press, 1997. I am grateful to the Social Sciences and Humanities Research Council of Canada for its financial support of my research on Quebec historical writing.

2 Throughout this paper, unless otherwise noted, I have used the term Quebecer to refer to the French-speaking population of Quebec. Although roughly 20% of the population, this author included, are residents of Quebec who do not have French as their mother tongue, the term 'Quebecer' and its more recent French version 'Québécois' (discussed below) are usually applied to the French-speaking majority. Moreover, when referring to Quebec historical writing, I have taken into account only the works of French-speaking historians. This is not to deny the role of non-francophones, such as this author, who have written about Quebec's past. However, since this essay deals with the way in which historical writing reflected social change within the French-speaking population, I chose to focus upon historians who formed part of that linguistic community. This choice should not lead the reader to conclude that there is little interchange between French- and English-speakers interested in Quebec. On the other hand, there is relatively little contact between historians (nearly all of whom are English-speaking) who are interested in English Canada and those (the vast majority of whom are French-speakers) who study Quebec.

3 Gérard Bouchard, 'Sur les mutations de l'historiographie québécoise: les chemins de la maturité', in Fernand Dumont (ed.), *La société québécoise après 30 ans de changements*, Québec, Institut québécois de recherche sur la culture, 1990, p. 262. This and all subsequent quotations originally in French have been translated by the author.

4 The reader who wants to know more about the Quebec context might consult Paul-André Linteau, René Durocher and Jean-Claude Robert, *Quebec: A History, 1867-1929*, Toronto, Lorimer, 1983, and *Quebec Since 1930*, Toronto, Lorimer, 1991. These volumes are translations of the first edition of *Histoire du Québec contemporain*, a work which is discussed at length below.

5 Macdonald and Cartier, as the two leading architects of the Canadian federation, represented not only the leading business interests of the day, but also the two linguistic groups within Canada. Macdonald was an English-speaking Protestant from what would become Ontario, the largest English-speaking province after 1867, while Cartier was a Quebecer, who had taken part in a rebellion by French-speakers against English rule in 1837.

6 There was also a parallel structure to administer schools for the Protestant population. This denominational structure was called into question when Jews, who fit into neither camp, began arriving in Quebec in large numbers at the turn of the century.

7 François-Xavier Garneau, *Histoire du Canada depuis sa découverte jusqu'à nos jours*, Montreal, Beauchemin & Valois, 1882 (4th ed.), II, p. 396.

8 Guy Frégault, *Canada: the War of the Conquest*, trans., Toronto, Oxford University Press, 1969, pp. 342-343.

9 This was made abundantly clear in Fernand Ouellet, *Economic and Social History of Quebec*, Toronto, Gage Publishing Limited, 1980.

10 The political implications of these interpretations are explained in Michael Behiels, *Prelude to Quebec's Quiet Revolution*, Montreal/Kingston, McGill-Queen's University Press, 1985.

11 This slogan was used initially by the Liberals in the 1962 Quebec election which served as an informal referendum on the government's planned nationalization of hydro-electricity.

12 Linteau, 'La nouvelle histoire', *Liberté*, No. 147, 1983, pp. 44-45.

13 Ronald Rudin, 'Revisionism and the Search for a Normal Society: A Critique of Recent Quebec Historical Writing', *Canadian Historical Review*, Vol. 73, 1992, pp. 30-61.

14 Linteau, Durocher and Robert, *Histoire du Québec contemporain: de la Confédération à la crise*, Montreal, 1979; Linteau, Durocher, Robert and Ricard, *Histoire du Québec contemporain: le Québec depuis 1930*, Montreal, 1986; a new and revised edition of the two volumes was published by Boréal in 1989. All references here are to the second edition of the work. I have translated the quotes taken from this updated version, but there is an English translation of the original edition on the market which was cited in footnote 4.

15 *Histoire du Québec contemporain* (hereafter *HQC*), I, p. 197. In the chapter outlining 'the social structure' during this period, only five out of twenty pages focused upon rural life.

16 *HQC*, I, p. 181

17 *Ibid.*, I, pp. 191-192.

18 *Ibid.*, I, p. 267

19 *Ibid.*, I, p. 407.

20 Lionel Groulx, *Histoire du Canada français depuis la découverte*, 4th ed., 2 vols, Montreal, Fides, 1960.

21 *HQC*, I, p. 7

22 Jocelyn Létourneau, 'La production historienne courante portant sur le Québec et ses rapports avec la construction des figures identitaires d'une communauté communicationnelle', *Recherches sociographiques*, 1995, 36, p. 12.

23 Linteau, 'La nouvelle histoire', *op. cit.*, p. 45.

24 Serge Courville, Jean-Claude Robert and Normand Séguin, *Atlas historique du Québec: le pays laurentien au 19e siècle, les morphologies de base*, Québec, Presses de l'Université Laval, 1995, p. 2.

25 Yves Gingras, 'Une sociologie spontanée de la connaissance historique', *Bulletin d'histoire politique*, Vol. 4, 1995, p. 41.

26 Joyce O. Appleby, Lynn Hunt and Margaret C. Jacob, *Telling the Truth About History*, New York, Norton, 1994, p. 4.

27 Létourneau, 'La production historienne', *op. cit.*, p. 1.

28 Normand Séguin, 'Faire de l'histoire au Québec', *Présentations à la Société royale du Canada*, 1990-91, p. 100.

29 Jean-Jacques Simard, *La longue marche des technocrates*, Montreal, Editions coopératives Albert Saint-Martin, 1979, p. 25.

30 Peter Novick, *That Noble Dream: The Objectivity Question and the American Historical Profession*, Cambridge, Cambridge University Press, 1988, p. 6 (his emphasis). The question of objectivity is a complex and highly contentious issue that cannot be addressed at length in this brief essay. The various ways in which objectivity can be conceptualized are discussed by Allen Megill in his introduction to *Rethinking Objectivity*, Durham, N.C./London, Duke University Press, 1994. Megill defines the form of objectivity most relevant to historians as 'disciplinary objectivity', by which the practitioners of a particular discipline recognize that their explanations of particular phenomena may differ from those presented by researchers in other fields. Nevertheless, those within a discipline such as history would, if adepts of disciplinary objectivity, be prepared to recognize the existence of 'a court of appeal that will support objectivity claims; not an absolute court of appeal, but one that will serve within a particular community at a particular time' (p. 7). While claims to the establishment of some eternal truth in this regard were less pretentious than those of individuals who believed in 'absolute objectivity', there was still the idea that certain shared standards might distinguish 'objective' research from work that was somehow tainted. I would join Novick in being uneasy about setting up such a distinction.

31 Novick, *op. cit.*, p. 7. One is reminded here of Sisyphus rolling the rock up the hill, but never quite getting to the top.

32 See, for instance, Thomas Haskell, 'Objectivity is Not Neutrality: Rhetoric and Practice in Peter Novick's "*That Noble Dream*"', *History and Theory*, Vol. 29, 1990, pp. 129-157; James T. Kloppenberg, 'Review Article: Objectivity and Historicism: A Century of American Historical Writing', *American Historical Review*, Vol. 94, 1989, pp. 1011-1030.

33 Ricard, 'Remarques sur la normalisation d'une littérature', *Ecriture*, Vol. 31, 1988, p. 12.

34 The French version has an even more assertive ring than my English translation: 'Oui, nous sommes différents ... Ce qui nous distingue du reste de l'Amérique, ce ne sont pas nos faiblesses, ce sont nos forces'. *Le Devoir*, 24 October 1998.

35 Serge Courville, Jean-Claude Robert et Normand Séguin, 'Un nouvel regard sur le XIXe siècle québécois: l'axe laurentien comme l'espace central', *Interface*, Vol. 14, 1993, p. 23.

36 Létourneau, 'La production historienne', *op. cit.*, p. 12.

37 Novick, p. 500. Needless to say, the issues and debates regarding the writing and politics of women's history (not to mention such fields as working-class or native-American history) are much more complicated than I can communicate in this relatively short essay. Suffice it to say that the impulse, evident in such fields as women's history, to present a previously marginalized group as capable of wielding power was also relevant to revisionist writing about Quebec's past.

38 Joan Wallach Scott, *Gender and the Politics of History*, New York, Columbia University Press, 1988, p. 27.

39 Ruth Pierson and Alison Prentice, 'Feminism and the Writing and Teaching of History', *Atlantis*, Vol. 7, 1982, p. 38.

40 *Montreal Gazette*, 22 October 1994.

Louis Vos

7. Reconstructions of the Past in Belgium and Flanders

In the eyes of some observers, the forces of nationalism are causing such far-reaching social and political change in Belgium that they threaten the cohesion of the nation-state, and may perhaps lead to secession. Since Belgian independence in 1831 there have been such radical shifts in national identity – in fact here we could speak rather of overlapping and/or competing identities – that the political authorities have responded by changing the political structures of the Belgian state along federalist lines. The federal government, the Dutch-speaking Flemish community in the north of Belgium and the French-speaking community – both in the southern Walloon region and in the metropolitan area of Brussels – all have their own governments and institutions.[1]

The various actors in this federal framework each have their own conceptions of how to take the state-building process further, underpinned by specific views on Belgian national identity and on the identities of the different regions and communities. In this chapter, the shifts in the national self-image that have taken place in Belgium during its history and the present configurations of national identities and sub-state nationalism will be described. Central to this chapter is the question whether historians have contributed to the legitimization of this evolving consciousness, and if so, how. It will be demonstrated that the way in which the practice of historiography reflects the process of nation- and state-building has undergone profound changes since the beginnings of a national historiography. We will first focus on the links between the process of nation- and state-building in Belgium after independence, and its legitimization by historiography in the 19th century. Secondly, the impact of the emergence of the Flemish and Walloon Movements (which perceived themselves primarily as movements for cultural and political emancipation) on the conception of the nation adopted in historiography will be analysed. Thirdly, attention will be paid to the institutional setting in which scientific work such as the practice of history has been taking place since the federalization of Belgium. In this case too, the process of state-building has affected the way historians review the past.

The Legitimization of the Belgian Nation

Although Belgium as a nation-state did not come into existence until 1830, its establishment was not the beginning, but rather the culmination, of a process of nation-building. The Netherlands were split up as a result of the Dutch revolt against Spanish rule in the sixteenth century and the resulting war, which formally ended in 1648. Consequently in the territory under Habsburg rule – roughly the area of modern-day Belgium, with the exception of the prince-bishopric of Liège, which remained an independent and sovereign state until the French revolution – a distinct Southern Netherlandic identity developed. It was based on a common culture within which a role was played by the Catholic counter-reformation, historically developed institutions and the political allegiances of a land that functioned in the ensuing period as a buffer zone between the great powers.[2]

This 'identity' grew into modern nationalism during the so-called Brabant revolution in 1789. The revolution was directed against the enlightened but authoritarian rule of the Habsburg emperor Joseph II. It resulted in the setting up of an independent Belgian state. However, this state was to survive for only one year before falling to Austrian troops. Shortly afterwards the French armies conquered the Southern Netherlands, and in 1795 France annexed the territories, which it incorporated as *départements* and which – together with the former prince-bishopric of Liège – were completely integrated into the French state, first by the French republicans, and later by Napoleon.

The Congress of Vienna in 1815 created the United Kingdom of the Netherlands, a conglomeration of lands which are now the Benelux states. Its king, William I, tried to weld North and South together but failed to create a new nation. His state survived for only 15 years. Belgian Catholics and liberals, seeing this new dispensation as domination by Holland, united under the banner of freedom. Dissatisfaction led in the summer of 1830 to a rebellion, which in turn developed into a national revolution, in which liberty was declared to be the highest value. Out of this revolution came a modern nation state – constitutional, liberal, democratic and centralized. Its constitution vested sovereignty in the Belgian people. Once the revolution had succeeded and independence was established, many patriots committed themselves to building a national identity.

A common interpretation of Belgium's national past, propagated by a new national historical school, served as the cornerstone for this national identity. As Jo Tollebeek has emphasized in his analysis of the interpretation made by this school, which had strong romantic overtones:

'These earliest national histories were meant as a contribution to the formation, consolidation and confirmation of a national identity.

Their writers had to lend unity, specificity and continuity to the national past. Their work was less a matter of reconstruction than of construction'.[3]

In the case of Belgium, whose emergence as a nation preceded its political independence, there already existed a 'Belgian' national historiography before 1830. It evolved within the framework of the Austrian Netherlands, and gained momentum from 1780 onwards. Already under French occupation, and within the United Kingdom of the Netherlands, books providing a synthesis of national history were published. It was self-evident that the patriotic and romantic atmosphere following independence stimulated writers, artists and – above all – historians to make their contribution to the national culture. These contributions aimed to provide an historical foundation for the right of the new nation – Belgium – to exist. What they sought above all was:

> 'to strip the freedom they had won of its revolutionary character. The élite wanted to be liberal, not revolutionary. Therefore they did not call the Revolution of 1830 a revolution, but a restoration, or rather a renaissance. In 1830 the "hour of awakening" of the Belgian people had come, and nothing more, the nation was not created then, but only wakened from a deep "sleep of the spirit" (…) or to use another metaphor (…) the old Belgium had risen like a phoenix from its ashes. The country was young, but old as well'.[4]

There were of course some problems to be solved in the interpretation of history. The two major obstacles were on the one hand the geographical diversity of pre-independence Belgium (autonomous principalities, and an entirely separate prince-bishopric of Liège), and on the other the lack of a narrative and chronological continuity in Belgian history.[5] The problem of geographical diversity was solved by choosing a particular principality as the heart of the Belgian Fatherland. Several principalities have been selected for this purpose over the years – Flanders has been chosen several times, and was presented as the core of what later became Belgium. This was the case for instance in Conscience's *History of Belgium* (1845), in which the Flemish medieval cities – prosperous, patriotic and powerful – were presented as the cradle of Belgian nationality.

The lack of unity in Belgian history, due to the constant changes of regime and dynastic rule, was addressed in various ways. Some historians chose a suprahistorical and a-prioristic solution by invoking (or inventing) a 'national genius', a *Volksgeist* as Herder called it, or *une âme belge*, a Belgian soul. It would later serve as one of the major sources for Belgian nationalist ideologies, especially when linked with a defence of the French language or bilingualism. A variation on this 'national genius' solution was to emphasise the history of the common people: the historian could use their customs, way of life and attitudes as the more constant mainstream of an *histoire de longue durée* (history of long-term developments) embedding the – so variable and eventful – political history. Other historians opted for a less a-prioristic solution. They found a way out of the problem presented by the lack of political unity by searching for recurring themes in the national history. These themes then served as a backbone for national identity over time. One solution here was to depict Belgium as the battlefield of Europe. Another – more widespread – option was to describe the Belgians as an ancient people, oppressed for centuries by foreign rule. This approach was even officially dignified in 1860 when a new text was accepted for the national anthem, beginning with the words: 'Après des siècles d'esclavage, Le Belge sortant du tombeau...' ('After centuries of slavery, The Belgian, rising from the grave...'). The problem with such solutions, however, was that they did not cover the whole history of Belgium. To make this history of conquerors and conquered more dynamic, in his history of Belgium (1840) the historian Theodore Juste introduced a dramatic conception of Belgian history as 'a succession of periods of struggle for freedom and periods of prosperity and cultural bloom warranted by a righteous royal government (...). In 1830 the two streams which had permeated Belgian history (...) had indeed reached their end point'.[6] The question of whether 1830 had really marked the 'end of history' still remained, i.e., whether the evolution towards a 'national identity' had reached its final and complete form, or whether this was only the start of a new historical epoch. It became clear in the second half of the century, with the emergence of new social, ideological and linguistic conflicts, that the Belgian construct had not yet been completed.

The new national historiography of the first two decades of the independent Belgium formed only one part of a much broader historical culture, aimed at presenting the national past to the general public. Side by side with the historians, painters, sculptors and writers were also active in raising national consciousness.[7] This was achieved through the publication of numerous historical novels (Hendrik Conscience, Pieter Geiregat), through book illustrations,[8] the organization of historical processions and the erection (in large numbers between 1830 and 1850) of statues of historical heroes. The visual representation of appealing episodes in national history was the result of teamwork by a 'Belgian School of Painting', (Gustave Wappers, Louis Gaillet and Ferdinand de Braeckeleer) which presented itself as both old and new at one and the same time. It was old in the sense that it followed the tradition of the 17th-century artists Rubens and Van Dyck, but also new, because its major concern was the use of a 'national colour', painting a glorious past, and creating a national iconography.[9] In literature, Francophone and Flemish writers pursued the same goal, and between 1830 and

1850 they created a Belgian literature with national authors, literary journals in both French and Dutch, and literary criticism. But because the political and cultural élite spoke French, they could only appreciate the French literature, leaving the literature written in Dutch – or rather in 'Nederduytsch' (Flemish Dutch), as opposed to 'Hollandic' – to the Flemish middle class.[10] As a result, Flemish literature – which was initially perceived as merely Belgian – eventually led this middle class to an increasing awareness of its Flemish identity. This was especially encouraged by the romantic work of Hendrik Conscience. He was the first to create an important *oeuvre* in Dutch, in which 'the anti-French element assumed a central position (…) from then onwards, Flemish literature would be inextricably associated with the development of the Flemish Movement whose anti-French support it would continue to inspire'.[11]

The Francophone writers who wanted to respond to the demand for a national culture after independence faced a double difficulty. First of all, 'the idea underlying the notion of *Volksgeist* crucially relied on the unity of language and culture'.[12] As a consequence some Belgian Francophone writers campaigned for a Belgian variant of the French language, as did Charles Decoster in his *La légende d'Ulenspiegel* (1867). Decoster deliberately interspersed his text with literal translations of Flemish words.[13] A second strategy for solving this problem of a Belgian *Volksgeist* was to dissociate language and culture. Decoster – and other Belgian writers, who preferred to write standard French – were fascinated by the symbolism of the Flemish cultural past, which they presented as highlights of Belgian history. In their effort to create a Francophone literature distinct from that in France, they fell back on Belgian themes that were essentially Flemish.

From Belgian Cultural Nationalism to Flemish Sub-Nationalism

The marginalization of the Flemish language constituted a basic problem in the attempt by these romantic cultural nationalists to build a national Belgian culture. They wanted to bring about the moral renaissance of the Belgian people, to give them their own national history, their own art and their own literature, but were confronted by a language problem which made such a reconstruction extremely problematic. Throughout Belgium, the upper classes spoke French, even in areas where Dutch was the mother tongue of the majority of the population. Shortly after independence, French had been declared the official language of the Belgian state, of its parliament, higher courts, central administration and army. It was felt that using just one language would strengthen state centralization. Despite the fact that Flemish was the vernacular of the vast majority of the population in the northern part of the country, it was then used only in primary education, in the lower courts of justice, and in the councils of smaller munici-palities. Flemish-minded writers and intellectuals deplored this situation and proposed an alternative view of Belgian culture. As they saw it, Belgium would be the poorer if all that was Flemish was to be reduced to a second-class culture. They strove for the official recognition of two national languages, believing that the interaction of the Germanic and Romance traditions within Belgium would lead to a new cultural synthesis. They regarded Belgium as a nation 'with one soul but two voices'.

These intellectuals became the founding fathers of the Flemish Movement. They initiated the constitution of various cultural organizations and societies, whose aims were largely political. The Movement's active membership com-prised students, priests and intellectuals from the Flemish middle class.[14] It evolved into a new type of national movement, in which the middle classes closed ranks against the ruling class. It remained, however, within the Belgian constitutional framework and without any anti-Belgian sentiments (without *anti-belgicisme,* as it is called in Flanders). The revolutionary wave of 1848 in var-ious European countries provided the Flemish Movement with a democratic impetus. At the time, it did not wish to divide the country into monolingual lan-guage areas, but pleaded for bilingualism, at least in Flanders. In the 1870s it succeeded in obtaining some facilities for non-French speakers from Flanders in the administration and in the courts, and a limited bilingual regime in secondary education.

In the last quarter of the nineteenth century a Flemish ethnic and national identity began to manifest itself, as a sub-nation within the greater Belgian nation. This indicated an important shift in national identity since the start of Belgian independence. In 1830 there was merely a Belgian nation. At that time, a 'Flemish' community or sub-nation simply did not exist. But over almost five decades the constant references by writers and intellectuals to the right to speak one's own language worked as a mobilizing tool. Gradually, the idea of 'a lan-guage of one's own' gave way to the idea of 'the language of one's own people'. Around the turn of the century, the idea that language formed the basis of a dis-tinct ethnic group, a people, the 'Flemish people' – as a sub-nation of the Belgian nation – became accepted as referring to an existing reality. This idea was first adopted by some Flemish intellectuals, and gained increasing popular support in the first decades of the 20th century.

Flemish Identity Revisited

The Flemish Movement did not appear at the forefront of Belgian politics for the whole of the nineteenth century. The major antagonism in political life was then between Catholics and liberals, who had been fighting bitterly for power since the 1840s. In the 1880s, a working-class movement with strong socialist overtones also came to the fore. Against this background, the enthusiasm of the first decades for the Belgian national idea had waned. Moreover in the 1890s historiography was gradually gaining scientific recognition. Writing history became an academic profession. It was Henri Pirenne, a professor of history at the State University of Ghent — then still a Francophone institution — who marked this step from a mainly politically-inspired history of the Belgian nation towards a scientific view of national history. In 1900 he published the first volume of his four-volume *Histoire de Belgique*.[15]

Pirenne covered the history of Belgium from Roman times up to the beginning of the Great War. It was a masterpiece of historical synthesis, an attempt to explain the emergence of the Belgian nation and its national identity by a careful reconstruction of its different economic, cultural and political steps in the past. He considered the geo-political and geo-cultural position of the later 'Belgian' territories in Europe — on the edge of the Romance and Germanic parts, acting as a link between Germany and France, even resembling a microcosm of European civilization — to be a primary factor in the specific nature of this Belgian nation. As second factor he emphasized that the Belgian people had constituted a national unit even before political unity was established through Belgian independence. As the third and last factor, he referred to the existence of the *pax belgica*, the peaceful coexistence and cohabitation of different ethnic groups, Flemings and Walloons, in one national cultural space.[16] In his book, Belgium was no longer simply a 'battlefield' of Europe, or the plaything of the great European powers, but a genuine community rightfully aiming to put a political roof over its national identity, and representing a specific form of the greater European civilization. Nor was Belgian independence the 'artificial' creation of international diplomacy. It was the outcome of a lengthy process which had started in the Middle Ages when the principalities of the Low Countries developed mutual economic and political connections, on the basis of common interests. These interests merged with those of the Burgundian dukes, and so was created the Burgundian state, which was later to be more developed institutionally, by the Habsburg dynasty, into a distinct political entity, which went under the name of 'the 17 Provinces'. It comprised the territory of modern-day Belgium, the Netherlands and Luxembourg, with the prince-bishopric of Liège still left out.

Pirenne's work was published in a period of heightened conflicts between various interpretations of the national identity. These conflicts took place primarily on the political level. Flemish people were increasingly aggrieved at the secondary position of their language, which contrasted with the modernization of Flanders. The growth of the tertiary sector in Belgium, for instance, was particularly impressive, and this also affected Flanders. Around 1900, about thirty percent of the Belgian professional population was employed in the administration, trade or the public services. This was the highest percentage in continental Europe, and was as high as in Britain or the USA.[17] This expansion of services and administration was to the advantage of the French-speakers, since French was used as the working language in the service sector in Flanders. It was in this particular context that the Flemish middle classes increased their support for the language demands of the Flemish Movement, and the basis for support for that movement grew. From that time on, the social dimension of the Flemish language struggle became more apparent.

The Czech historian Miroslav Hroch has distinguished three stages in the national movements that emerged in the 19th century among national minorities, 'awakening' in opposition to older, official national identities. He describes a phase A of 'scholarly interest' in which intellectuals (re)discover the cultural content of the new national identity. Then comes phase B of patriotic agitation, in which students and intelligentsia try to convince 'the people' of the importance of their own national identity, followed by phase C in which the movement gains 'mass support'. He links these stages to major periods of modernization: industrial revolution, 'bourgeois revolution' and the formation of a nation[18]. Each period in the development of Flemish nationalism also corresponds to one of these stages.[19] Phase A of scholarly interest can be identified in Flanders up to 1840. Phase B of patriotic agitation took place in Flanders between 1840 and 1890. During that time – starting in the 1870s – the first language laws were passed in parliament, granting the non-Francophones in Flanders some possibility of using Dutch in approaching the authorities, before the courts and in secondary schools. But the legislation was so limited that dissatisfaction among Dutch-speakers grew throughout the century to become a mass movement in the last decade of the nineteenth century: the beginning of phase C, the final phase. The support for this mass movement came mainly from christian-democratic organizations representing the interests of farmers, workers and the middle class, and which were fully organized on a national scale by the turn of the century. Their commitment to the Flemish Movement was the main catalyst for growing popular support.[20] Notwithstanding this merging of Flemish and christian-democrat demands, there were also some groups of non-Catholic Flemish activists in the Flemish Movement. Mass support led also to a broadening of the agenda of the Movement. Instead of simply demanding equal rights for their language, the Flemish activists wanted to create a Flemish-Belgian culture, which would make its own unique contribution to European civilization.

In this last decade of the century, the success of the Flemish Movement led to a whole series of language laws that put the use of Dutch in Flanders on an equal footing with French. A symbolic highlight was when – at the end of the century, in 1898 – Dutch was recognized as an official language of the Belgian nation alongside French, which had already been given that status in 1831. But despite these gains on the legal front, the linguistic programme of the Movement became more radical. By the end of the nineteenth century it had become obvious even to moderate Flemish activists that the French-speaking citizens would never accept bilingualism in Brussels and Wallonia, so that in everyday life Dutch would never be on a par with French. The only way to achieve that would be to have two monolingual areas: a French one in Wallonia and a Dutch one in Flanders, with bilingualism in the centre of the country. So the Flemish activists progressed to wanting territorial (Dutch) monolingualism in the public sphere, hoping that as a result Flanders would become a Flemish homeland in Belgium – not with any anti-Belgian intention, but as a sub-nation.

The existence of a sub-nation clearly manifested itself through several cultural signs. There was the change of the meaning of the term 'Flanders'/'Flemish': this no longer referred to the historical county of Flanders, along the coast of the Low Countries of the *ancien régime*, but to the five provinces of Northern Belgium – from east to west – and its Dutch-speaking population. There was also the appropriation of medieval history by the Flemish, and the dwindling of any Belgian connotation. The new sub-national identity also manifested itself through the creation of several new institutions, labelled 'Flemish', and the increasing significance of – still mainly unofficial – Flemish symbols, such as a Flemish national holiday (11 July), a Flemish national anthem and a Flemish national standard (a black lion in a yellow field). The peculiar thing about this sub-nation was that, according to the self-image of the Flemish, it was still smoothly embedded within the Belgian nation. Anti-Belgianism did not exist before the first world war.

The growing antagonism within the Belgian community, and the diverging concepts of the nation, proved convincingly that to describe 1830 as the end of history – as was done by some patriotically inspired historians shortly after the Belgian revolution – was an illusion. At the same time this antagonism also affected the credibility of the type of Belgian scientific synthesis created by Pirenne. At that period, the activities of the professional historians in academia can be characterized as rather uncommitted in their research of 'national' themes. They were not openly involved in political debates on the Belgian national idea. Journalists and politicians, however, borrowed heavily from academic literature, transforming the historians' views into intellectual weapons for their own visions of the nation. This happened especially on the Francophone side, partly because their position as French-speakers came under incessant pressure from the Flemish Movement.

Many of the Francophones in Flanders, who belonged mostly to the upper class, were unwilling to yield. As a reaction against the spate of language laws in the 1890s, which improved the position of Dutch in the public sphere, a Francophone counter-movement sprang up in the last decade of the nineteenth century. This so-called 'Walloon' Movement aimed to maintain the 'status quo' on the linguistic level, meaning the maintenance of bilingualism in Flanders and French monolingualism in Brussels and Wallonia. It received initial support not so much from Wallonia but from the French-speaking upper class in Flanders and Brussels. In fact, it was more of a 'Francophone' than a 'Walloon' Movement. Regarding the principle of freedom of language, it refused to countenance the Flemish people's demand for linguistic homogeneity within their territory. It wanted official bilingual status for Flanders to be maintained, i.e., it wanted every citizen to be able to use French always, at all official levels, in Flanders as elsewhere in Belgium. But now – unlike decades earlier when they had accepted bilingualism – the Flemings saw this position as protecting the privileges of an élite.[21] They rejected it, not only on the cultural grounds of Flemish sub-nationality, but also – and even more – on the social grounds that it would mean discrimination against the non-Francophone lower classes.

After the turn of the century the centre of gravity of the Walloon Movement shifted towards Wallonia proper. It then included in its programme (alongside the political/linguistic goals) the defence and appreciation of the Walloon heritage, and Walloon interests in general. As had happened earlier in Flanders, at the eve of the first world war Walloon activists chose an emblem (a red cock on a yellow field), a motto ('*Wallonie toujours*') and a Walloon national day (the last Sunday of September, in commemoration of the Belgian revolution of 1830). This shift from a defence of the interests of the French-speaking minority in Flanders to a defence of Walloon interests was not complete. Its ultimate aim in fact remained the defence of both the regional development of Wallonia and personal linguistic freedom for Francophones to speak their language everywhere in Belgium, irrespective of regional boundaries.[22]

In 1897, the lawyer and socialist politician Edmond Picard coined the term '*âme belge*' (Belgian soul). Picard believed that Belgium, despite its two ethnic groups and two languages, had one national soul, characterized by a mixture of elements from the two ethnic and linguistic groups, which had merged through history to produce something specifically Belgian. He accepted bilingualism, including in Flanders, and opposed the establishment of monolingual territories which, in his view, would inevitably lead to secession. This theory was immediately used and abused by a militant Belgian nationalism in Francophone clothing which, at the eve of the first world war, gained major support among the intellectuals, and particularly lawyers, around the weekly *Journal des Tribunaux*, in Brussels. It became a second force opposing the Flemish Movement. As it was used as an argument against the Flemish demand for monolingualism, it was rejected by the Flemish Movement.

The idea of an *âme belge* was in fact a return to one of the solutions developed by the first generation of historians after Belgian independence. For Belgian nationalists at the turn of the century, however, it was less an ordering principle for the interpretation of the past than a weapon with which to defend Belgian unity against all that was regarded as inimical to it. As such it was a blow to the vision of Pirenne, whose ideas and position were reduced to a caricature, not only by the defenders of Belgian unity grouped around the *Journal des Tribunaux*, but also by the militants of the Flemish Movement who, in addition, regarded him as a mere Belgian nationalist and no longer respected him as the honest and great historian he actually was.[23]

There was also a more moderate type of defence of Belgian unity, represented by the official Belgian establishment. This view of the nation referred mainly to two themes in national history: on the one hand, the medieval 'Belgian liberties' as a core element of the 'Belgian character', and on the other, the oppression of those liberties for centuries by neighbouring imperialist powers. When Germany attacked Belgium in August 1914, King Albert I referred to a number of historical events, which were adapted to the obvious duality of the two sub-nations existing at the time. The King asked the Flemings to remember the battle of the Golden Spurs (in 14th-century Flanders) against French domination. At the same time, he asked Walloons to bear in mind the 600 inhabitants of the municipality of Franchimont in Liège, who had attempted to stop the invading troops of the Duke of Burgundy (15th century).[24] There was a new wave of Belgian nationalism during the first weeks of the War. The thesis of a national unity based on the historical and cultural diversity of the Belgians – sometimes referred to with the saying ''Fleming' and 'Walloon' are merely first names, our family name is 'Belgian' – was not, however, to last very long.

Belgium versus Flanders

Everything changed with the Great War.[25] Nationalism lost its previous innocence. A radical minority of Flemish activists had been growing impatient with the lack of significant progress in transforming Flanders into a monolingual Dutch-speaking area, the so-called 'Dutchification' of Flanders. Now the war was offering them new political opportunities, as the Germans were actively seeking allies among the Flemish population. Activists living in occupied territory were enticed by the German call and agreed to reform and even split the occupied Belgian State with 'German help'. Fuelled to a large extend by the 'Flamenpolitik' of the German occupier, the radical activists developed a Flemish nationalism which was blatantly anti-Belgian. Of course their reforms were reversed after the war. They themselves were put on trial and condemned as 'traitors' by the Belgian courts. But their anti-Belgian Flemish ideology was kept alive by many of them who fled the country, to the Netherlands or Germany, from were they prepared the 'revenge' that was to come during the second world war, in 1940-1945.

Throughout the war years, and especially in the 1920s, Belgian nationalism became more radical, and outspokenly anti-Flemish. Under the influence of the concept of integral nationalism as developed by the French nationalist Charles Maurras, according to which the benefit of the nation was the first and only touchstone for human behaviour, Belgian nationalism became a fully-fledged, overtly right-wing ideology. It constituted a platform against those who were regarded as a threat to the strength of the Belgian nation. Threats were seen in a Flemish Movement demanding language rights, in Catholics and socialists dividing the Belgian community ideologically and along class lines, in Jews and foreigners, who should be mistrusted, and in the neighbouring states that were allegedly cherishing imperialistic dreams to the detriment of Belgium.

On the other hand, for the more radical members of the Flemish Movement, 'anti-Belgianism' was the touchstone of real Flemish nationalism. They wanted to dissolve the Belgian political framework, if necessary by overthrowing the parliamentary system, and in the 1930s linked their nationalism to fascism. Their blueprint for a new order was based on the idea of pure ethnic origin. Language was not a sufficient criterion for membership of the national community. This type of Flemish nationalism was exclusive and ethnocentric. It emphasized the differences between 'our own people' and 'outsiders', and as a result turned against both French-speakers and Jews on Flemish territory. It provided a breeding-ground for National Socialism and for collaboration with the Nazi occupiers in the second world war.[26]

The radicalization of many Flemish activists during the first world war resulted in a split in the Flemish National Movement which was never to be fully healed. The Movement was divided into two factions: one remaining loyal to Belgium, the other taking an anti-Belgian stance. The first position attracted the majority of the Flemish Movement, who hoped that their loyalty would be rewarded with monolingual status for Flanders. A minority of the Flemish Movement chose to support Germany, in the hope that the occupiers would immediately address all pre-war Flemish grievances. This faction ended up taking an anti-Belgian position, as its choice was, naturally, condemned by the Belgian government, which was now in exile in France but from there continued the struggle against Germany. Among Flemish soldiers fighting in the trenches of Flanders fields – such as Hendrik Borginon, Adiel Debeuckelaere, Joris Van Severen and Frans Daels – Flemish nationalism was strengthened by the humiliation of Dutch-speaking privates by their Francophone officers. They were not yet anti-Belgian, however, and risked their lives for the fatherland every day;

some of them became more radicalized during the war, partly owing to the disciplinary repression against Flemish study-groups, which the authorities viewed as a breeding-ground for insubordination. In the diaries they wrote at the front, some of them demanded home rule for Flanders once the war was over.

After the first world war, it was not the radical activists – who were condemned for treason and collaboration with the enemy – but the loyal faction of the Flemish Movement that became the leading one. It focused on cultural and linguistic issues. The majority of its members developed a kind of dual national consciousness. They were supporters of the Flemish national cause, and also loyal Belgians. They wanted to stick to the language laws as an instrument for complete 'Dutchification' of Flanders. That could be achieved, they thought, within the confines of the existing Belgian state and with full respect for the democratic institutions. Eventually, after two decades of political struggle, they succeeded in establishing a monolingual Dutch public life in Flanders. This process of 'Dutchification' was almost completed by the eve of the second world war.

Officially, Belgian nationalism in the inter-war period tried to be impartial as far as language was concerned, in order to be accepted everywhere in the country. It used both French and Dutch as a means of expression, and the many patriotic celebrations commemorating the heroes and victims of the war were held in both languages. But for the members of the Flemish Movement, both moderate and radical, Belgium had lost its soul. Flemish culture was emancipating itself. An increasing number of Flemish intellectuals exclusively used the Flemish language. Publications, songs, festivals, meetings and celebrations by non-official organizations referred only to Flanders, the Flemish people and the Flemish soul. Catholic student and youth movements idealized Flanders and Flemish culture in a romantic way. All kinds of group activities, such as theatre festivals, were organized by Catholic student associations, who tried to mould the personality and character of their members in a Flemish and Christian atmosphere. They also strove to bring their message of a renaissance of the Flemish culture home to the local population. This mission was supported by Catholic mass organizations in the 1920s and 1930s. One could say that cultural nationalism, entwined with a concern for the preservation of Catholicism, affected a large part of the Catholic population in Flanders.

New perspectives on history corresponded to these shifts in national identity. Gradually, a vision of the past without Belgium – which could be labelled *a*-Belgianism – emerged, including among the more moderate members of the Flemish Movement. The type of historical approach put forward by Henri Pirenne was rejected as being 'Belgian nationalist'. It was then substituted by Flemish or Great-Netherlandic interpretations of the national history. The first step in this direction was made in the 1920s by moderate Flemish nationalists such as Lodewijk Dosfel, who did not consider themselves to be anti-Belgian. Shortly afterwards, this view was also adopted by radical Flemish nationalists. In 1924, one of them published a handbook on Flemish national history with the propagandistic purpose of educating students in the 'correct anti-Belgian line'.[27] 1930 was the year of the Belgian centennial, which was presented by historians such as Hendrik Elias as a commemoration of a century of Flemish oppression by Belgium. That same year he published a book entitled 'Onze wording tot natie' ('Our Development into a Nation').[28] In it, he stated that there existed only a Dutch national identity, and that there had never been a Southern-Netherlandic or Belgian one. Belgium had to be fought against in order to establish an independent Flanders. In 1932 Elias became a member of parliament for the Flemish nationalist party 'Het Vlaamsche Front', which was transformed in 1933 into a fascist Flemish nationalist party (VNV, Vlaamsch Nationaal Verbond, or Flemish National Union). In World War II, the party opted for collaboration with the Nazis and in 1942 Elias became its 'Leader'. This would cost him ten years of imprisonment after the war, a time he used for writing a four-volume book on the history of Flemish nationalism.[29]

By the inter-war period Elias and many other Flemish intellectuals had already been deeply influenced by the publications of the Dutch historian Pieter Geyl. Geyl was at that time professor of Dutch history at University College London, and, as a Dutch civil servant, official consultant of the Dutch Government on matters concerning Britain. In the 1920s and 1930s he became one of the most important figures of the Great-Netherlandic Movement, a group of Dutch and Flemish nationalists who dreamed of the unification of the Netherlands and Belgium in one Great-Netherlandic state. His writings on the history of the Low Countries exerted a deep influence on Flemish intellectuals. Geyl tried to prove that Belgium was not a real nation, and that it had only emerged as a result of international power-politics. In his eyes, a real Southern-Netherlandic or Belgian identity had never existed. Their 'regional peculiarities' were to be regarded as the result of the splitting of the Low Countries in the 16th century, and of the (united) Kingdom of the Netherlands in 1830. Both events were to be seen as unfortunate historical accidents, whereas the touchstone of national identity in the Low Countries was language. The Dutch-speakers were the core of the national community. From his first historical publication on this issue in 1925 until the final volume of his history of the Netherlandic nation in 1959 – and in fact also in other essays published up until his death in 1966 – Geyl claimed to offer a less partisan and more scientifically valuable synthesis than Pirenne.[30] In the inter-war period he was deeply involved in the radical Great-Netherlandic and Flemish nationalist movement, and this commitment only ended with his appointment in 1937 as professor of history at the State University of Utrecht in the Netherlands. Geyl's publications had major political significance. They provided a scientific basis for the anti-Belgianism of the radical

Flemish nationalists who – as historians in the previous century had done to defend Belgian nationalism – were adopting the framework of foreign rule, in order to defend their anti-Belgian stance. The Flemish nation had been under the yoke of the Romans, the Spanish, the Austrians and the French, but not of the Dutch. It was now time for Flanders to liberate itself from the Belgian yoke and to unify with the Netherlands.

In the 1930s, the young historian Robrecht van Roosbroeck started editing a history of Flanders.[31] The first of six volumes appeared in 1936, the year in which Pirenne died, and the last volume would only be published in 1949. Van Roosbroeck was a convinced anti-Belgianist and a member of the Flemish nationalist party. During the second world war he was – as a reliable collaborator – appointed professor of history at the State University of Ghent by the German occupiers. Nevertheless, throughout the whole period of his editorial work, he was able to find collaborators in broad circles, and both anti-Belgian and pro-Belgian historians wrote chapters in the book, which proved that it was possible to combine different views and interpretations of national history within the one book. Its most important political effect, however, was the fact that now Flanders too, after Belgium, finally had an 'official' history of its own.[32]

In 1938, several famous professors from all the Belgian universities joined Pieter Geyl on the editorial board of a new scientific journal that was devoted to the history of the Low Countries as a whole, the 'Nederlandsche Historiebladen'.[33] This new journal was of course a scientific endeavour, but at the same time it also had a political flavour as it seemed to favour Geyl's Great-Netherlandic vision. This, however, was more appearance than reality. Since 1937, Geyl no longer emphasized a linguistic community as the starting-point for defining the nation. He had silently shifted to the 17 provinces of the Burgundian era. This was to a large extent the same position as that adopted earlier by Pirenne. Geyl was able to make this silent shift easily and almost unnoticed because, at the same time, his Flemish colleagues from Leuven and Ghent, the professors Leo Van der Essen and Hans Van Werveke also slightly adapted Pirenne's vision. They based their concept of Belgian history on Pirenne, but at the same time declared that they embraced a pan-Netherlandic approach. What they left out was language as the core element in the history of the Low Countries – the view hitherto propagated by Geyl. As Geyl was no longer insisting on language as a criterion, it looked as if both Flemish historians were now adopting Geyl's former Great-Netherlandic paradigm, which in fact they were not. All three now agreed upon a new 'pan-Netherlandic' approach that was actually based upon Pirenne's vision.[34]

Between the two world wars, Flemish identity underwent a transformation from being a kind of by-product of Belgian identity to a more a genuine and independent national identity. It ceased to be a sub-nationalism and became a sub-state nationalism. The creation of a monolingual Flemish territory played a key role in this transformation. A shift in national consciousness also took place in the Walloon Movement which, at the end of the thirties, started to focus exclusively on the defence of Walloon territorial interests, leaving aside the defence of bilingualism in Belgium. Its influence remained rather limited, compared to the impact of the Flemish Movement.

Before the second world war, Belgium defended a foreign policy of neutrality and non-alignment, which was strongly supported by King Leopold III. This led to a reinterpretation of the Belgian national idea. In a speech on American radio in October 1939, King Leopold III emphasized 'the distinguished place that Belgium has held throughout the history of the Western world' as 'a fountain-head of Christian civilization' and as 'the very incarnation of individual liberty'.[35] In the same month the Belgian Prime Minister, Pierlot, asked several well-known historians and journalists to write articles of an historical nature to explain and defend the policy of neutrality. Historians such as Charles Terlinden from Leuven University and Louis de Lichtervelde replied favourably, contributing to a reconstruction of the Belgian past in which the core elements were the constitution of 1830 and political liberties.[36]

During the second world war there was a left-wing-inspired revival of Walloon consciousness, which set itself against possible fascist and Catholic Flemish domination in Belgium.[37] But on the whole the Walloon Movement tended to align itself with the Belgian resistance. In the underground press the idea of a 'Walloon people' seems to have been widely accepted. During the war, the fascist leader Léon Degrelle first legitimized the collaboration of its Walloon Rex movement as an attempt to recreate the Burgundian Netherlands – with German help – as a sort of Greater Belgium. Later he dropped this fantasy and aimed directly at the incorporation of the territory of Belgium into the German Reich. At the same time, anti-Belgian Flemish nationalists collaborated with Germany, in an attempt to destroy Belgium and take over political power in Flanders. The policy followed by the occupying German authorities certainly nurtured a Flemish nationalist striving for power. But this had strong Great-Netherlandic overtones, and its anti-Belgianism was counterproductive to the political and economic goals of the German authorities. In its efforts to achieve legitimacy, the German military command in Brussels gradually adopted more and more elements of traditional Belgian rhetoric, in which – once again – Belgium was depicted as the meeting-place of the Romance and Germanic cultures. This led to the paradoxical situation where, for strategic reasons, the German authorities were protecting Belgian national identity against the anti-Belgian and Flemish nationalist forces which they had themselves lured into collaboration.[38]

Among the majority of the Flemish people, who would have nothing to do with collaboration, there was renewed respect for the Belgian nation. In the world of Belgian academic history, little changed. The majority of professional historians continued their research as if there were no occupation or fascist regime at all. Marnix Beyen describes the atmosphere in the period 1938-1947 as 'the historiography of common sense'. Belgian historians simply did not commit themselves to any great national cause. For most of them, their professional code was more important than political considerations. Even outspoken 'Belgian' historians did not refuse to write articles for books that tended to favour 'Flemish' history.[39]

Linguistic Borders and Federalization

The situation on the academic level hardly changed in the first few years after the second world war. A politically uncommitted scientific approach remained the normal attitude of Belgian historians – this despite the fact that one of the major scientific enterprises was the writing of a 'General History of the Low Countries', which was first drafted in 1942 and was published, in 12 volumes, between 1949 and 1958. To a certain extent this enterprise seemed to represent the triumph of the Great-Netherlandic approach as it had been introduced by Geyl in the 1920s, but this was only partly the case. Many collaborators disagreed with the Great-Netherlandic idea. In several parts of the book, in fact, there was more of a juxtaposition of chapters, dealing with the North and the South respectively, than an integrated narrative in which developments in the two countries where presented in a cohesive way. It remained a patchwork of contributions, in which not only the different historical traditions of Belgium and the Netherlands led to different approaches, but where – apart from a few exceptions – the two national histories were presented as if they were almost completely different stories. And above all: as we explained earlier, the Great-Netherlandic concept had itself changed dramatically, mainly on the initiative of Van der Essen, but with the de facto consent of Geyl. Instead of a model in which the language as such was the determining factor, it had become a paradigm in which the historical reality of the 17 Burgundian provinces formed the core element. As Beyen has pointed out, the period immediately after the second world war was characterized by a situation in which the Belgian national framework was not regarded as an untouchable dogma by Belgian historians – Flemings or Francophones. The Flemings zoomed in to take a Flemish position, or out in order to gain an overall Dutch perspective. The Francophones moved from a Belgian to a Walloon position, remaining, however, more loyal to the Belgian blueprint. The long-term effect of this phenomenon was that two strands, Flemish and Francophone, gradually developed within Belgian historiography.[40]

This development on the academic level only partly matched the evolution in Belgian public opinion. Opposition to the collaboration by the anti-Belgian Flemish nationalists prompted a new Belgian nationalism during and immediately after the war. At the same time, the majority in the Flemish Movement remained loyal to Belgium. It developed a Belgian-Flemish stance, in favour of protecting the Dutch language in Belgium, but not aimed at the dismantling of the Belgian State. For a time it even abandoned the concept of Flemish political autonomy, because striving for this would have reminded Belgian public opinion too much of the policy of the pre-war fascist VNV. Such an association might have jeopardized its ultimate goal of a flourishing Flemish culture in the Flemish-Belgian sub-nation. This abandonment implied a return to the programme put forward by the Flemish Movement in the years prior to World War I.

However, this pro-Belgian stance was not to last. It was undermined by a widespread Flemish perception that the repression of Flemish collaborators after the war had been unfair. A large section of public opinion in Flanders was convinced that the motives of these Flemish intellectuals had been purely idealistic and this, in their view, diminished their guilt. There were also differences in the attitudes of public opinion of Flanders and Wallonia to the role of King Leopold III during the second world war. The King had refused to join the Belgian government in exile and had decided to remain in occupied Belgium. A majority of public opinion in Flanders and Wallonia condemned this attitude, but this criticism was far stronger in Wallonia. A referendum was held and it showed a different majority in Flanders, which voted in favour of the King, from that in Wallonia, which opposed him. Most of the votes nation-wide supported the King, but he preferred to resign in favour of his son, Baudhuin. This referendum was particularly important in the history of Belgium, as it indicated for the first time that Flanders and Wallonia could take opposing political positions.

For younger generations of Flemish intellectuals the credibility of the Belgian nation was further undermined by what they perceived as a wave of 'Frenchification' engulfing the country. Catholic youth movements especially were developing an exclusive loyalty to Flanders. From the 1950s onwards, an indifference to the Belgian national idea, or even anti-Belgian feelings, developed, even among Flemish supporters who years earlier had seen themselves as loyal Belgians. The Flemish political front underwent a certain amount of radicalization in the 1960s. The *Volksunie*, a new Flemish national party, then enjoyed electoral success. This party propagated the idea of a federal state with greater autonomy for Flanders. It was also an 'anti-repression' party, campaigning for amnesty for the condemned collaborators. It drew much of its support from among the younger generation that had been brought up in the Flemish cultural nationalism of youth movements.

In the meantime, a Walloon identity was developed south of the language border, based on the concept of its 'own territory'.[41] Unlike in the period after the first world war, when the Walloon Movement was still Belgium-oriented and linked with the Francophone communities in Brussels and Flanders, since the end of the 1930s it had progressively affirmed a more pronounced territorial character. A distinctive pattern of social economic development — notably the decline of the coal and steel industries — further encouraged this stronger focus on the Walloon region. Economic and social issues, rather than cultural ones, thus helped to create a new sense of Walloon identity. It gained momentum in the winter of 1960-61, when a general strike, which was led by the socialist trade unions and affected the whole country, was supported particularly strongly in Wallonia. This strike marked the beginning of a popular Walloon Movement, which drew up a programme of anti-capitalist structural reform, in which socialist and Walloon forces merged.

The government, alarmed by the revival of both Flemish nationalism and Walloon regionalism, wanted to bring about linguistic pacification. Its aim was to create single-language areas as far as possible, and so to push the language question into the background. Language borders were drawn in the early 1960s. Brussels became officially bilingual, and in some municipalities in Flanders and Wallonia close to Brussels, or adjacent to the language border, special arrangements were introduced for the other language group. But the government failed to push the language question into the background. The new language laws only served to highlight the differences between the two language communities. They encouraged the Flemish to strive harder to make their country completely monolingual, at the same time paving the way for the breakthrough of fully-fledged political Flemish nationalism among the Flemish people. The discussion about the Catholic University of Leuven in the 1960s served as a catalyst for this. The university was divided into two different sections, where Dutch and French were spoken, respectively, but it was situated in the Flemish area, just beyond the language border. The Flemish Movement — and particularly Flemish student organizations — saw the presence of such a large French-speaking group as a threat to the monolingual character of the Flemish territory, and demanded the expulsion of the Francophones under the motto 'Walen buiten!' (Walloons go home!). Flemish student revolts in 1966 and 1968 led to the fall of the government and finally to the splitting of the university. The French-speaking part (the Université Catholique de Louvain) was transferred to Wallonia (in Louvain-la-Neuve), with the Flemish university (Katholieke Universiteit Leuven) remaining in Leuven.

The forced expulsion of the French-language section from Leuven increased anti-Flemish feelings in Wallonia and had the same impact on the Walloon Catholics as the 1960-61 strike had had on the Walloon socialists. Both events provided the Walloon Movement with a basis for mass appeal. It also increased the attractiveness of the regional and language parties. These changes of attitude in Flanders and Wallonia led to the splitting, along linguistic lines, of all the political parties that were still operating on a Belgian scale (christian democrats, liberals and socialists). In addition to the nationalist parties, these newly formed monolingual parties in turn became the mouthpieces of their own linguistic communities and regions. The state structures were also to change in response to the changing perceptions of national identity. The reform of the Constitution in 1970 transformed Belgium into a federal state, with three Communities (French-, Dutch- and German-speaking), and three Regions (Flanders, Wallonia and Brussels). Responsibility for cultural affairs was transferred from the federal level to the newly established community councils, while regional economic development came under the jurisdiction of newly created regional bodies. Further constitutional reforms, however, also had to be implemented. This made it necessary to include the language parties in government, including the Flemish nationalist party, *Volksunie.* Its willingness to compromise caused a major internal party crisis and led to a split. In 1977 the extreme-right and strongly anti-Belgian current broke with the *Volksunie* and formed a new party, the *Vlaams Blok*. This party has enjoyed uninterrupted electoral success since 1978, particularly because of its anti-migrant position, which it shares with the extreme right-wing political parties elsewhere in Europe. In 1980, 1988 and 1993 further constitutional reforms led to greater autonomy for the regions and communities. Today Belgium comprises – apart from the federal institutions – five councils or parliaments and as many governments, but in an asymmetric form: on the Flemish side there is only one government and parliament for both Region and Community. The German and French Communities have their own bodies, as do the Walloon and Brussels Regions.[42]

Historiography in a Federalized Institutional Setting

The increasing importance of the regional and linguistic aspects of the nation- and state-building process went hand in hand with a reorganization of scientific activities. This also affected the teaching of the past. In the textbooks for secondary schools and in the teaching materials for universities, traditional national Belgian history – the History of the Fatherland – disappeared, after being under fire from two directions, above and below. The 12-volume *General History of the Netherlands* which was published after the war was followed by the launching of scientific reviews with a mixed Belgian-Dutch editorial board, and by the organization of Belgian-Dutch historical conferences.[43] This co-operation gradually evolved into a monolingual Flemish-Dutch connection, from which Francophone

Belgian historians were excluded. Since the 1970s, most of the Flemish universities have replaced the course entitled 'History of Belgium' by a 'History of the Low Countries', while the Francophone universities have continued to teach the 'History of Belgium'. The tradition of writing 'national histories' in the narrow sense did not disappear, however.[44]

A new edition of the *General History of the Netherlands* was published between 1978 and 1985 in 15 volumes,[45] and was far more than simply a re-edition of the previous one. Again, the majority of contributors were Dutch-speakers, and although it appeared to sanction the 'Great-Netherlandic' approach, it only did so in relation to the geographical boundaries of its subject matter. Where perspective was concerned, there was no underlying common concept that could be described as 'Great-Netherlandic', or any other 'national' character, to be found in it. Even then, the new 'standard work' received a good deal of criticism for its complicated structure, its lack of coherence, and its ambivalence about whether it was aimed at a general educated public or a specialist one. One critic even labelled the book an 'ornamental tomb' for historiography in Dutch on the Low Countries, instead of its 'monumental highlight'.[46]

The ideal of a general history of the Low Countries was gradually replaced by the concept of a comparative approach to the parallel and different developments in Belgium and the Netherlands. In 1976, Ernst H. Kossmann of the University of Groningen published a comparison between the histories of Belgium and the Netherlands since 1780.[47] It was a purely scientific endeavour, without any political or ideological purpose, and at some points it even 'deconstructed' the 'national past'. In 1993 a small team of professors from Belgian and Dutch universities wrote a single-volume history of the Low Countries in Dutch. J.C.H. Blom and Emiel Lamberts edited this publication.[48] It became a widely used textbook for university students of history, in both Flanders and the Netherlands.[49] Such a comparative approach has become more and more fashionable, in particular in research projects begun during the last few decades.[50]

The 'Belgian' historical approach was not only undermined by the top-down 'general Netherlandic' or 'comparative' approach – it also found itself sidelined by the greater degree of interest shown in the history of the communities and regions – so from a bottom-up direction. Since the 1970s there has been a growing scientific historiography dealing specifically with the linguistic communities. The history of the Flemish Movement was the first to acquire academic recognition. This happened as early as the 1950s. In the early 1970s, research on the Flemish Movement began to be organized at the Flemish universities on a regular basis. This coincided with the restructuring of the Belgian State along federal lines. An Encyclopaedia of the Flemish Movement was published in two volumes in 1973-75[51] – this contained some scientific articles without a strong political bias, but also many contributions of a rather propagandistic nature. In the 1970s and 1980s several histories of Flanders and Wallonia were also published. There was obviously a need for a historical legitimization of the now officially recognized communities and regions.

In the 1990s, Flemish intellectuals distanced themselves somewhat from the process of nation-building in Flanders. The new encyclopaedia on the Flemish Movement, which was published in three volumes in 1998,[52] was more critical of the Movement than its predecessor in the 1970s. The majority of the contributions were no longer written by Flemish political activists, but by professional historians. All the contributions were very carefully reviewed by an editorial board, which comprised academics from all the Flemish universities. The publication of this new encyclopaedia may indicate that partisan history for propagandistic purposes is a thing of the past. A further sign of increased professionalism in the historiography of the Flemish Movement has been the publication, since 1980, of a scientific journal which is exclusively devoted to its history and has become the forum for discussion on that subject among historians.[53]

Walloon historiography in the 1990s is in some respects comparable to the Flemish publications of the 1970s. Books on Walloon identity and history more often have an overtly partisan bias than is at present the case in Flanders. This may reflect the fact that Wallonia is still in search of its own identity. It is grappling with questions such as the exact relationship between the Walloon region and the Belgian Francophone community as a whole.[54] One can expect, though, that here too the less partisan historiography will gradually become the dominant one.[55]

While professionalism in the historiography of the national past – in all meanings of the word – is apparently increasing, a new phenomenon is coming to the fore. Research and publication projects are receiving more financial support from the different governmental authorities on the federal, regional and community levels. This may be interpreted as a growing attempt at an official appropriation of the past.

In Flanders, both processes – the increasing professionalism of historiography and the official appropriation of the past – are leading to a certain alienation of the Flemish Movement from its historical memory. The historiography on the Flemish Movement, which is less anti-Belgian, less indignant about past oppression, and less moralistic, is also less committed to 'the cause'. Its usefulness for mobilization is decreasing. The radical militants do not like it any more.

Changes in the social basis and political character of the Flemish Movement have taken place in parallel with federal reforms. Since the end of the 1970s, Flemish nationalism has ceased to be a grassroots movement. It is no longer fuelled by teachers and youth movements, but has become, just like Belgian nationalism in the 19th century, an 'official' reality. The Flemish national Movement has attained a degree of fulfilment with the creation of Flemish institutions that are conceived as a manifestation of the Flemish national identity. Like 'Belgian' nationalism, 'Flemish' nationalism has become 'banal nationalism', to use the term coined by Michael Billig – an almost unnoticed official reiteration in everyday life, not recognized as nationalism but at the same time constantly flagged in the media through routine symbols and habits of language.[56] Besides this 'banal nationalism', its other face, the militant voluntary, intentional nationalism of the movement and their activists, is of course also still very much alive.

Very few young intellectuals feel attracted to Flemish nationalism. They have never experienced any form of 'oppression' by French-speakers and have never felt like second-class citizens in their own state. Moreover during their time at school they were never steered towards a commitment to the Flemish national cause, as was the case for previous generations. The new generation of Flemings often has the impression that their so-called Flemish identity is something invented and imposed upon them by the Flemish authorities and politicians. Some of them again embrace a Belgian national identity, because they think it has less ethnic content and carries more guarantees for the building of a democratic and open society. This shift must also be interpreted against a broader cultural background. A non-ideological postmodernism has become the predominant fashion in intellectual life, affecting approaches to history. Flemish historians are more eager to deconstruct the national identity than to make a contribution to it. Some go so far as to deny that the 'invented' concept of national identity and community refers to anything real.[57]

Conclusion

Despite the waning of ideology in these 'post-modern' times, and despite the fact that historiography is now abandoning an overtly partisan nationalistic approach, there is still an official use of the national past by authorities. The 'banal nationalism' they produce on the level of regions and language communities, in order to legitimize their political identity, is reminiscent of the closeness of the Belgian authorities to writers, artists and historians in the decades following Belgian independence.

The legitimacy of the new Flemish and Walloon authorities cannot be based on the concept of a Belgian nation as defended by Belgian patriots after 1830. For these new authorities, the 'Belgian revolution' of 1830 was merely 'a new historical regime' in a long succession of regimes which has led to the present form of federalization. Both Flemings and Walloons still voice their historical grievances against each other. The Flemings refer to the lack of respect Francophones have shown in the past for the Dutch language. The Walloons refer to an intolerant ethnic Flemish nationalism that showed its undemocratic face during World

War II. They also blame the oppressive Belgian state, as it is dominated by a Flemish majority (*l'Etat belgo-flamand*), and consequently discriminates deliberately against the Walloon region.

The way in which the practice of historiography reflects the process of nation- and state-building has, however, also undergone profound changes during the transformation of Belgium from a unitary state, as established in 1830, into the present federal framework. Flemish and Walloon identities emerged as sub-nationalisms in a unitary state, but then transformed themselves into sub-state nationalisms, which were to be integrated into a federal framework. These transformations have led to corresponding changes in how the Belgian identity has been conceived. All of these modifications were accompanied by a radical rethinking in historiography, even though such reinterpretations were not merely a reflection of changing attitudes on the part of political élites or public opinion. Individual historians have often defended their own political views on the future of Belgium. The history profession has protected itself against political intrusion through the use of its own professional standards. The institutional setting in which historiography has been put into practice in Belgium has been radically transformed since the time when all Belgian universities used French exclusively. Since the transformation of Ghent into a Dutch-speaking university in 1930, the 'Dutchification' of scientific life in Flanders has been followed by the federalization of scientific institutions. This reform of scientific policy has led to a mutual estrangement of Flemish and Francophone historians. Flemish historians are more intensively involved in co-operation projects with their Dutch than with their Francophone colleagues. Further reforms in the Belgian state and further shifts in national identities may be expected. Among the possible alternatives in a reform of the state, full secession cannot be ruled out. But any of the changes that come may be expected to find expression in new reconstructions of the Belgian past.

Discussions among Belgian historians are currently focusing on the correct method for linking collective memory to historical representation, and on how national identity should be fitted into historical narrative. Such debates are taking place on both the public and academic levels. As has been demonstrated above, historians in Belgium have now become far more cautious than their predecessors when it comes to legitimizing any kind of nationalism.

Notes

1 For a better understanding of this whole situation it may be useful to clarify some terms and facts. The term 'Flanders' refers to the Dutch-speaking area north of the linguistic border which runs from east to west, 'Wallonia' refers to the French-speaking area south of that line,

and 'Brussels' to the 19 municipalities forming the Brussels region: a bilingual island surrounded by Flemish territory. Today there are 5.5 million inhabitants in Flanders, 3.1 million in Wallonia and 1 million in Brussels. In Flanders the language is Dutch, like in the Netherlands; in Wallonia it is French, like in France. 'Flemish' refers to the region and the community, not to the language. The small German-speaking community in the eastern part of Belgium (now a part of the Walloon Region) is the result of territorial war gains made after World War I, and comprises less than 1% of the Belgian population, with approx. 70,000 people.

[2] For more historical background see Louis Vos, 'Shifting Nationalism: Belgians, Flemings and Walloons', in Mikulas Teich and Roy Porter (eds), *The National Question in Europe in Historical Context*, Cambridge, Cambridge University Press, 1993, pp. 128-147, with a critical bibliography on the subject, and also Kas Deprez and Louis Vos (eds), *Nationalism in Belgium. Shifting Identities 1780-1995*, London, Macmillan, 1998. An edition of important original texts (cornerstones of the Flemish movement), translated into English, is Theo Hermans (ed.), Louis Vos & Lode Wils (co-eds), *The Flemish Movement. A Documentary History. 1780-1990*, London, Athlone Press, 1992, with a bibliography of studies in English. See also: Lode Wils, *Van Clovis tot Happart. De lange weg van de naties in de lage landen*, Leuven, Garant, 1992, and Lode Wils, *Vlaanderen, België, Groot-Nederland. Mythe en geschiedenis*, Leuven, Davidsfonds, 1994.

[3] In this and the following paragraphs we have closely followed the important article (in English) by our colleague at the KU Leuven, Professor Jo Tollebeek, 'Historical Representation and the Nation-State in Romantic Belgium (1830-1850)', *Journal of the History of Ideas*, Vol. 59, 1998, pp. 329-353. Quotation p. 330.

[4] *Ibid.*, pp. 334-335, referring to an article by Lode Wils, 'Het beroep op "de oude Belgische vrijheden" in het midden van de 19de eeuw', *Standen en Landen*, Vol. 32, 1964, pp. 113-22.

[5] For what follows also: Jo Tollebeek, 'Historical Representation and the Nation-State in Romantic Belgium (1830-1850)', *op. cit.*, pp. 338-345, and also Jean Stengers, 'Belgian National Sentiments', in : Arend Lijphart (ed.), *Conflict and Coexistence in Belgium. The Dynamics of a Culturally Divided Society*, Berkeley, Institute of International Studies, 1981, pp. 46-60.

[6] Tollebeek, 'Historical Representation and the Nation-State in Romantic Belgium (1830-1850)', *op. cit.*, p. 348.

[7] Jo Tollebeek, *De ijkmeesters*, Amsterdam, Bakker, 1994, p. 61.

[8] Tom Verschaffel, *Beeld en geschiedenis. Het Belgische en Vlaamse verleden in de romantische boekillustraties*, Turnhout, Brepols, 1987.

[9] Lut Pil, 'Painting at the Service of the New Nation-State', in Deprez and Vos, *op. cit.*, pp. 42-50.

[10] Piet Couttenier, 'National Imagery in 19th-Century Flemish Literature', in Deprez and Vos, *op. cit.*, pp. 51-60.

[11] Philippe Raxhon, 'Henri Conscience and the French Revolution', in Deprez and Vos, *op. cit.*, pp. 72-80.

[12] Christian Berg, 'The Symbolic Deficit. French Literature in Belgium and 19th-Century National Sentiment', in Deprez and Vos, *op. cit.*, pp. 61-71.

[13] *Ibid.*, p 65, referring to Jean-Marie Klinkenberg, *Style et archaïsme dans la légende d'Ulenspiegel*, Brussels, 1973; Marnix Beyen, *Held voor alle werk. De vele gedaanten van Tijl Uilenspiegel*, Antwerp, Houtekiet, 1998.

[14] Lieve Gevers, *Bewogen jeugd. Ontstaan en ontwikkeling van de katholieke Vlaamse studentenbeweging. 1830-1894*, Leuven, Davidsfonds, 1987. Lode Wils, *Honderd jaar Vlaamse beweging, geschiedenis van het Davidsfonds*, 3 vols, Leuven, Davidsfonds, 1977-1985-1989.

[15] Henri Pirenne, *Histoire de Belgique*, Bruxelles, 7 vols, 1900-1932. See also: Bryce Lyon, *Henri Pirenne. A Biographical and Intellectual Study*, Ghent, Story-Scientia, 1974, with a complete bibliography of Pirenne's work, and Lode Wils, 'De Grootnederlandse geschiedschrijving', *Revue Belge de Philologie et d'Histoire*, Vol. 61, 1983, pp. 322-366.

[16] Jo Tollebeek, 'Historical Representation and the Nation-State in Romantic Belgium (1830-1850)', *op. cit.*, and *idem*, *De ijkmeesters, op. cit.* pp. 70-74.

[17] Aristide R. Zolberg, 'The Making of the Flemings and Walloons: Belgium, 1830-1914', *Journal of Interdisciplinary History*, Vol. 5, No. 2, 1974, pp .179-235.

[18] Miroslav Hroch, *Social Conditions of National Revival in Europe. A Comparative Analysis of the Social Composition of Patriotic Groups among Smaller European Nations*, Cambridge, Cambridge University Press, 1985.

[19] Although in his book Hroch also deals with the Flemish Movement, he mainly confines himself to a description of the social background of the supporters of that Movement. The application of his 'phases' model to the Belgian situation has been worked out mainly by Lode Wils and the author of this article.

[20] Emmanuel Gerard, 'The Christian Workers' Movement as a Mass Foundation of the Flemish Movement', in Deprez and Vos, *op. cit.*, pp. 127-138.

[21] Chantal Kesteloot, 'Mouvement Wallon et identité nationale', *Courrier Hebdomadaire du CRISP*, No. 1392, 1993.

[22] Chantal Kesteloot, 'The Growth of the Walloon Movement', in Deprez and Vos, *op. cit.*, pp. 139-161.

[23] Lode Wils, 'De Grootnederlandse geschiedschrijving', *Revue Belge de Philologie et d'Histoire*, Vol. 61, No. 2, 1983, pp. 322-366; Louis Vos, 'Een kritische analyse van de Grootnederlandse geschiedschrijving', *Wetenschappelijke Tijdingen*, Vol. 42, No. 3, 1983, pp. 176-192.

[24] Anne Morelli (ed.), *De grote mythen uit de geschiedenis van België, Vlaanderen en Wallonië*, Antwerpen, EPO, 1996. In this book see especially: Jo Tollebeek, 'De guldensporenslag. De cultus van 1302 en de Vlaamse strijd', pp. 191-202; and Sophie Rottiers, 'De eer van de zeshonderd Franchimontezen', *op. cit.*, pp. 65-75.

[25] Lode Wils, *Flamenpolitik en aktivisme*, Leuven, Davidsfonds, 1974.

[26] Bruno De Wever, *Staf de Clercq*, Brussel, Grammens, 1989; Bruno De Wever, *De greep naar de macht. Vlaams-nationalisme en nieuwe orde. Het VNV 1933-1945*, Tielt-Gent, Lannoo, 1994. Louis Vos, *Bloei en ondergang van het AKVS. Geschiedenis van de katholieke Vlaamse studentenbeweging. 1914-1935*, Leuven, Davidsfonds, 1982.

[27] L. Deman (= Leo Dumoulin). *Handboek der Vlaamsch-nationale Geschiedenis*, Tielt, Lannoo, undated (probably published in 1924).

[28] Hendrik J. Elias, *Onze wording tot natie*, Kortrijk, Steenlandt, 1932.

[29] Hendrik J. Elias, *Geschiedenis van de Vlaamse Gedachte*, Antwerpen, Nederlandsche Boekhandel, 1963-1965.

[30] Pieter Geyl, *De Grootnederlandsche Gedachte*, 2 vols, Haarlem, Tjeenk Willink, 1925-1930; Pieter Geyl, *Geschiedenis van de Nederlandsche Stam*, 4 vols, Amsterdam, Wereldbibliotheek, 1930-1959.

[31] Robrecht van Roosbroeck (ed.), *Geschiedenis van Vlaanderen*, 6 vols, Brussel/Antwerpen, Standaard, 1936-1949.

[32] Marnix Beyen, *Een bewoonbare geschiedenis. De omgang met het nationale verleden in België en Nederland, 1938-1947*, unpublished PhD thesis, Department of History, KU Leuven 1999, pp. 592-595.

[33] Lode Wils, *Vlaanderen, België, Grootnederland. Mythe en geschiedenis*, Leuven, 1994, p. 385.

[34] Marnix Beyen, *op. cit.*, pp. 595-597.

35 *Ibid.*, p. 39

36 *Ibid.*, pp. 38-45.

37 Wils, *Van Clovis tot Happart. De lange weg van de naties in de lage landen, op. cit.*, especially important for the postwar developments.

38 Beyen, *Een bewoonbare geschiedenis, op. cit.*, pp. 352-354.

39 This was the case for example with the publication of a book entitled *100 Great Flemings*: see Marnix Beyen, 'Een werk waarop ieder Vlaming fier kan zijn. Het boek *100 Groote Vlamingen* (1941) als praalfaçade van het Vlaams-nationale geschiedenisbouwwerk', in Jo Tollebeek, Georgi Verbeeck en Tom Verschaffel, *De lectuur van het Verleden. Opstellen over de geschiedenis van de geschiedschrijving aangeboden aan Reginald de Schryver*, Leuven, Universitaire Pers, 1998, pp. 411-440.

40 Beyen, *Een bewoonbare geschiedenis, op. cit.*, p. 612.

41 Kesteloot, 'Mouvement Wallon et identité nationale', *op. cit.* and *idem*, 'The growth of the Walloon Movement', in Deprez and Vos, *op. cit.*, pp. 127-138.

42 Jos Bouveroux, *Het Sint-Michielsakkoord. Naar een federaal België*, Antwerpen, Standaard Uitgeverij, 1993. Rolf Falter, *Tweedracht maakt macht. Wegwijs in het federale België*, Tielt, Lannoo, 1994.

43 The two most important and leading reviews are: *Bijdragen en Mededelingen betreffende de Geschiedenis der Nederlanden* and *Tijdschrift voor Geschiedenis*. For the history of the Belgian-Dutch (now Flemish-Dutch) historical conferences see: F.W.N. Hugenholtz, 'De Nederlands-Belgische historische congressen sinds 1939', *Theoretische Geschiedenis*, Vol. 19, No. 2, 1992, pp. 186-203. They are still organized every year: twice in the Netherlands, the third year in Flanders.

44 Lode Wils' *Histoire des nations belges* is subtitled (in the French edition of 1996): '*Belgique, Flandre, Wallonie: quinze siècles de passé commun*'. Political histories of the period since the end of the 18th century, dealing with Belgium alone, have always existed. Classics among them are: the book by Theo Luykx, *Politieke geschiedenis van België van 1789 tot heden*, Brussel, Elsevier, 1964, and the one by Jan Craeybeckx and Els Witte, *Politieke geschiedenis van België*, Brussel, VUB-uitgaven, 1978, both many times amended, expanded and reprinted.

45 *Algemene geschiedenis der Nederlanden*, 15 vols, Haarlem, Fibula-Van Dishoeck, 1977-1983.

46 Wim Verrelst, 'Een praalgraf voor de nederlandstalige geschiedschrijving' *Digo*, Vol. 5, No. 3, 1982, p. 180.

47 Ernst Heinrich Kossmann, *De Lage landen. Anderhalve eeuw België en Nederland. 1780-1940*, Amsterdam/Brussel, Elsevier, 1976. Also published in English as *The Low Countries. 1780-1940*, Oxford, Oxford University Press, 1978. Later expanded to: *De Lage Landen 1780/1980. Twee eeuwen België en Nederland*, Amsterdam/Brussel, Elsevier, 1986.

48 Recently this book was also published in English: J.C.H. Blom and Emiel Lamberts (eds), *History of the Low Countries*, Oxford, Berghahn, 1999.

49 The Dutch students, however, unlike the Flemish ones, do not have to read the chapters dealing with the Southern Netherlands – or Belgium – from the sixteenth century on.

50 A recent example is the book by the Flemish historian Raoul Bauer, *De Lage Landen, een geschiedenis in de spiegel van Europa*. Tielt, Lannoo, 1994. Some years ago, the Dutch and Flemish governments set up a framework for comparative research in the Netherlands and Flanders providing money for projects carried out by a team of two researchers, one Fleming and one Dutch, and normally lasting for four years.

51 *Encyclopedie van de Vlaamse Beweging*, 2 vols, Tielt, Lannoo, 1973-1975.

52 *Nieuwe Encyclopedie van de Vlaamse Beweging*, 3 vols, Tielt, Lannoo, 1998.

53 *Wetenschappelijke Tijdingen op het gebied van de geschiedenis van de Vlaamse beweging*, 4 issues a year.

54 See, for example, Philippe Destatte 'Present-day Wallonia. The Search for an Identity without Nationalist Mania', and José Fontaine 'Four Definitions of Culture in Francophone Belgium', both in Deprez and Vos, *op. cit.*, pp. 219-228 and pp. 153-161 respectively.

55 So, inter alia, the publications by Chantal Kesteloot, a bilingual researcher at the Ceges (Centre d'Etudes et de Documentation Guerre et Sociétés contemporaines) in Brussels, who is preparing a PhD on the Walloon Movement at the Université Libre de Bruxelles. See for example Chantal Kesteloot, *The Growth of the Walloon Movement, op. cit.*

56 Michael Billig, *Banal Nationalism*, London, Sage, 1995.

57 See for example the underlying tone in many of the contributions to the book by Raymond Detrez and Jan Blommaert, *Nationalisme. Kritische opstellen*, Antwerpen/Berchem, EPO, 1994.

Michel Huysseune

8. Imagined Geographies:
Political and Scientific Discourses
on Italy's North-South Divide

As a secessionist movement, the Lega Nord, which promotes the formation of an independent northern Italian state named 'Padania', distinguishes itself by its professed anti-intellectualism. Its clearly populist discourse – Umberto Bossi, the Lega's leader, describes it as *popolano*, folksy – is scorned by the Italian intellectual community, which is generally hostile to the Lega. But together with its populist rhetoric the Lega has developed a framework for argument based on research in the social sciences. The highbrow version of the Lega's discourse focuses on several issues that are considered relevant within the mainstream Italian intellectual debate, such as the crisis of the Italian state, the process of European integration, and Italy's place in this process. The Lega legitimizes the secession of northern Italy by referring on the one hand to the inadequacy of the Italian state and the weakness of Italian national identity, and on the other to the territorial dimension of this weakness, namely, the sharp divide between the rich North and poor South, which it interprets as an ethnic divide between 'Padanians' and 'Italians'.[1]

Social scientists are generally strongly opposed to secession, but they share many of the Lega's critiques of the Italian state. Although they dismiss the Lega's Padanian identity, many scholars interpret Italy's North-South divide as a normative dichotomy between a modern, civic North and a backward, less civic South – an opinion contested only by a minority. The political opposition between the Lega and the Italian intellectual community is thus contrasted by their often shared views on Italy's problems. In the first part of this chapter, we will discuss these parallels in the different interpretations of the role of the Italian state, and in particular in debates on the territorial dimension of its policies. In the second part, we will describe the Lega's Padanian identity, compare it with scholarly representations of North-South differences as a deeply-rooted cultural divide, and present the scientific critiques voiced in opposition to such representations. In the third part, we will analyse how these diverging interpretations of Italy's North-South divide fit into a more general evaluation of the Italian process of nation-building. These debates shed light on the ideological outlook that produces affinities between social scientists and the Lega Nord, and they reveal the methodological problems involved in comparing societies and interpreting their differences.

Rejecting/Reforming the Italian State

From its origins, the Lega has presented itself as an anti-state and anti-establishment movement, and its secessionism is emblematic of the cleavage between it and mainstream public opinion. Even when the Lega tones down its secessionism, and proclaims its willingness to accept a federal or confederal reform of the Italian state, such proposals conceive of the state as being based on a freely established contract, whose parties maintain the right to dissolve it at any time.[2] This vision of the state clearly divides the Lega from mainstream intellectuals, since the latter (even if they are sometimes willing to accept a federal constitutional reform) refuse to question the unity and indivisibility of the Italian state. The right to secession is considered very definitely off-limits – the public debate on the Lega has hardly ever touched on this issue, since it is almost always assumed that secessionist proposals are illegal,[3] and within the Italian intellectual community the pro-secessionist stance of the political scientist Gianfranco Miglio, for a time the Lega's ideologist, has remained exceptional. This anti-secessionism is taken for granted rather than argued about: apart from the occasional comment about the loss of international economic and political visibility and power that would accompany the formation of an independent Padanian state, references to Italian identity are apparently considered sufficient to counter secessionism.

The radical nature of this opposition, however, is mitigated by a shared critical attitude towards the Italian state. The Lega's policies in fact derive their legitimacy from the credibility of many of its critiques of the Italian state, especially as these were voiced at a time (particularly the early 1990s) when the state was undergoing a serious crisis, with the disclosure of major corruption scandals (commonly known as *tangentopoli*, 'kickbacktown') in which the political élite was deeply involved. The Lega claims that the Italian state is inefficient and too centralized. It overtaxes its citizens, its Byzantine bureaucracy inhibits private initiative, and it is dominated by political parties, a phenomenon called *partitocrazia* ('partitocracy'). Although this dominance is mainly associated with the christian democrats (*Democrazia Cristiana*, DC), who held power continuously from 1945 to 1992, in the Lega's view the recent crisis of *partitocrazia* and the dissolution of the DC has not put an end to a Rome-based system of power.

For the Lega, the Italian state is not only overcentralized, it also implements territorially differentiated policies. The Lega emphasizes the complicity between the state and the South, claiming that the former is essentially a machine that taxes the North only to squander money in the South. The Italian state thus inhibits the autonomous development of the North, and is also inadequate in supporting the northern economy: it has not done enough to provide infrastructure for the North, nor is it helpful in supporting northern economic penetration of foreign markets. The Lega sees the northern regions as colonies of the Italian state. It actually uses the rhetoric of internal colonialism, characteristic of some European regionalist movements of the 1970s, which were generally leftist and Marxist-inspired. In his seminal book on internal colonialism, Michael Hechter has argued that the British state has consistently followed policies advantageous to England, and more particularly London and the Home Counties, and disadvantageous to the Celtic fringe (Scotland, Wales and Ireland). As a result of these policies – which he has defined as internal colonialism – the fringe regions are poorer and economically less developed, they remain economically dependent on the English core, and they are under-represented in the nation's ruling élite.[4] The Lega uses the same phraseology in the reverse situation, as it claims that the colonial Italian state is inhibiting the development of the richer North.[5] When condemning economic and cultural colonization by the Italian state, it often refers – as well as to the alleged discrimination against Padanian culture(s) and the over-representation of southerners in the Italian state apparatus – to the Italian welfare state, which has imposed a universal system of education and social security instead of leaving the North the opportunity to develop self-organized, private social and educational services.[6]

In the academic world, the Lega's critique of the Italian state has received a differentiated response. Its assertions of state inefficiency are considered well founded by friend and foe alike. Similar critiques have frequently been voiced by Italian and foreign scholars.[7] Already in 1977 the American political scientist Sidney Tarrow analysed the relation between centre and periphery in the Italian state (as compared with France), reaching a conclusion similar to the one the Lega was to voice more than ten years later. He described Italy as a state where the innumerable, uncoordinated ways in which the central government intervenes in the periphery enforce inefficiency, so that the clientelistic networks typical of Italy function as unofficial substitutes for inadequate administrative structures. The political parties were heavily involved in these networks, and even the opposition parties like the PCI, the Italian Communist Party (*Partito Comunista Italiana*, now the DS, *Democratici di Sinistra*, Democrats of the Left) made use of them. Political parties thus acted as unofficial mediators between the centre and the periphery, between citizens and the state.[8]

The emergence of the Lega has again drawn the attention of public opinion and social scientists to the importance of sub-national government in Italy. Books on the issue, such as the one published in 1993 by the American political scientist Robert D. Putnam, *Making Democracy Work* (based on research that predates the Lega), have attracted vast media coverage.[9] Putnam's research has shown clearly that local and regional governments have greater legitimacy and are considered more trustworthy than central government, particularly in northern Italy. Within Italy, both the *tangentopoli* crisis and the Lega's successes have in fact prompted a myriad of generally federalist proposals for institutional reform of the state, but their intention to counter the Lega's secessionist stance has prevented a calm debate on the issue. Although most proposals for federalism refer to the inefficiency of the Italian state on the one hand, and a concern for a regional government at once more efficient and closer to its citizens on the other, the Lega's presence has left its mark on the debate on federalism and has steered discussions on the issue towards Italy's North-South divide and the territorial dimension of the policies of the Italian state.[10]

In arguing that the Italian state's policies have a territorially differentiated impact, favouring the South, the Lega refers in the first place to the way money in southern Italy has been invested. Until recently, it claims, control of state spending in the South was exercised by politicians more interested in maintaining clientelist networks than in stimulating the development of their region, and in fact their clientelist logic led to a wilful neglect of public services – since the generalized availability of such services would undermine their own position as gatekeepers offering access to them. This judgement on (past) spending in the South is almost unanimously accepted, and has lent credibility to the Lega's representation of northern Italy as a cow perpetually milked by the Italian state in order to subsidize southern parasitism. The Lega in fact assimilates parasitism to the welfare state – an amalgamation facilitated by the parasitic characteristics the Italian welfare system has effectively developed (the most notorious instance being fake disability pensions)[11] – and it argues that the productive and dynamic North has no need of a universal system of social protection. Privatized social protection should be based first and foremost on inclusion in the labour force – 'workfare' instead of welfare.[12]

As an alternative to the Italian state, the Lega proposes self-government for regional entities relying on their own territorial economic resources, and it believes that the conditions for such self-government are present in northern Italy.[13] This being so, the modern, productive North is ready for inclusion in the competitive environment of the European Union, in a Europe of the regions, while the Italian state and the South, both allegedly parasitic, lack this modernity. In its more radical statements, the Lega proposes the exclusion of southern Italy from the European Union, an exclusion rhetorically emphasized by regarding the Italian state and the South as African. In its more moderate moments, and particularly when addressing an intellectual audience, it confines itself to prescribing a drastic neo-liberal economic cure for the South, to redeem it from its parasitic past.[14]

Many social scientists would agree with the Lega's opposition between a modern northern society and a South and an Italian state characterized by their backwardness.[15] Particularly in the years before Italy was accepted into the European Monetary Union in 1998, anxieties about Italy's backwardness being an impediment to its integration into Europe were frequently voiced in similar terms to – and with the same arguments as – the Lega's. This convergence between mainstream concerns and the Lega's representation of the policies of the Italian state comes to light in discussions on the latter's distributive policies. The image of a modern northern Italy, financially exploited by the state to subsidize the South, has become a commonplace reproduced by social scientists both in Italy and abroad.[16]

The veracity of such an interpretation is hardly ever checked. A closer examination of the redistributive policies of the Italian state, however, even on the basis of the data given by the Lega, already makes it possible to draw a much more nuanced picture. Four northern regions certainly receive the lowest per capita spending: Lombardy, Piedmont, the Veneto and Emilia-Romagna. But those that receive the largest amount of money per capita, even according to the Lega's data, are the special-status regions, with the northern Valle d'Aosta and Trentino-Alto Adige heading the list.[17] The southern mainland regions admittedly receive more than the four northern regions mentioned above, but the amount is substantially the same as that received by several central regions included in the would-be Padanian state, and less than northern Liguria. While the Lega may have a *prima facie* justification for claiming that several northern regions contribute more than they receive, its representation of the redistributive policies of the Italian state as being marked by a North-South divide can only be regarded as misleading.

Social scientists who have analysed the territorial dimension of the redistributive policies of the Italian state confirm this more nuanced picture. The *intervento straordinario* ('extraordinary intervention') for the development of the *Mezzogiorno* (southern Italy), often used as an argument to demonstrate the profits the South has derived from the state – was, overall, a substitute for normal contributions, rather than a supplement to them. Including other aspects of redistributive policies, namely welfare allocations, does not fundamentally alter this result. The higher amount received for disability and subsistence pensions in the South is counterbalanced by the proportionally larger number of labour pensions in the North. In general, it is difficult to establish with certainty which part of the country benefits most from redistributive policies.[18]

Notwithstanding the nuanced results of research on the redistributive policies of the Italian state, and even of the data produced by the Lega, the Lega's view of the North as being fiscally exploited by the Italian state in order to subsidize the South has become a commonplace, used without much thought even by many social scientists and intellectuals. This viewpoint also marks proposals for full fiscal autonomy (or *federalismo fiscale,* 'fiscal federalism', the term currently used in Italy), i.e. the possibility for each region to keep its income entirely for itself, since they almost always intend to free the North from contributing to the South.[19] Such rejections of the principle of inter-regional redistributive policies are generally informed by a neo-liberal rejection of welfare policies, but the more widespread assumption that the North is a victim of national fiscal policies has enhanced the intellectual and political credibility of such proposals.

The debate on the redistributive policies of the Italian state reveals the viewpoints shared by the Lega and mainstream intellectuals and scholars. The Lega's appearance on the scene has in fact led to an overall paradigm shift, from a traditional scholarly interest in the Southern Question to a contemporary focus on the Northern Question. Even though the Lega's secessionism is rejected, the Lega itself is nevertheless regarded as representing the dismay of northern Italians at the inefficient state and southern vices. The ideological predominance of neo-liberalism has undoubtedly helped to give legitimacy to the Lega's arguments against the welfare state and redistributive policies that favour the South.[20] The Lega has thus benefited from the intellectual disengagement of the 1980s, and the dismissal of the Gramsci-inspired leftist tradition, which was much more attentive to the Southern Question. But its arguments derive additional legitimacy from the past, and particularly from (widely-held) assumptions about the devious ways in which state money has been wasted in the South, which gives them credibility outside neo-liberal circles. In this way, the emergence of the Lega has reinforced the collective tendency to belittle the problems confronting these regions, which is reflected in the shift in interest towards the Northern Question.[21] Although it can easily be argued that southern Italy continues to face much more serious problems than the North, there is nowadays relatively speaking a neglect of the Southern Question. Notwithstanding this northern focus, however, discussions and analyses of Italy's problems are still conceived within a national framework, like the solutions that are proposed – an approach the Lega rejects.

A Padanian Identity and Italy's North-South divide

Unlike mainstream Italian intellectuals, the Lega sees the flaws of the Italian state as a symptom of the non-existence of an Italian nation. As a legitimization for secession, the Lega argues that northern Italians have a distinct Padanian identity. In the Lega's representation of a Padanian nation, three different elements can be discerned: a definition of the Padanian people which underlines ethnic differences between Padanians and Italians, a civic definition which focuses on the historical and cultural differences between northern and southern Italians, and finally, a definition of northern Italy as an aggregate of peoples who share a history of struggle against the all-invading power of central governments.

Although these three definitions are partly compatible, the difference between them is symbolized in the approximate territorial delimitation of the would-be Padanian nation-state. In its geographically most extended version, as expressed in the declaration of independence of 15 September 1996, Padania includes all the Italian regions north of Rome – an economic and political demarcation of the territory characterized by what the Lega regards as the northern culture of economic efficiency and civic virtues – and excludes all the regions with an allegedly southern culture (for the Lega, this includes Lazio, the region around Rome). Such a division, however, poses severe problems for the Lega when it comes to constructing a homogeneous identity, since the central regions included are culturally (and especially in their dialects) closer to the rest of Italy than to the northern regions, while their border with the South also appears to be an artificial construct. The Lega also, therefore, presents a smaller version of Padania corresponding to a geographical entity: Italy north of the Apennines (traditionally a natural border), centred around the plain of the river Po (to which the name Padania refers), which includes the most competitive regions of northern Italy (Lombardy, Piedmont, Emilia-Romagna and the Veneto), and which is also culturally more homogeneous, with its dialects in particular differentiating it from the rest of Italy.[22]

In proposing a Padanian identity, the Lega also accepts the existence of regional sub-identities. In its proclamation of independence, it defines Padania as an aggregate of regional nations, each of which corresponds to a currently existing Italian region. Such an affirmation of regional sub-identities has enabled the Lega to include its original components, regionalist leagues. Notwithstanding its acknowledgement of these sub-identities, however, regionalist particularism is a threat to the Lega's organizational homogeneity and to its all-inclusive northern focus. Regionalism is strong, particularly in the Veneto, whose dialect and references to the glorious past of the Venetian republic allow a Venetian identity and the construction of a regional tradition to be affirmed with a certain credibility.[23]

To affirm the existence of a commonly shared northern identity, the Lega therefore attempts to construct a common history of northern Italy. For example, it has presented the history of the Lombard or Padanian people as an exemplary tradition of struggle against a centralized, predatory state – a narrative that enables it to include historical personalities like Saint Ambrose (archbishop of Milan in the fourth century), and events like the struggle of the twelfth-century Lombard League against the emperor Frederick Barbarossa. In this re-deployment – in a regional and anti-centralist vein – of themes borrowed from national history, Umberto Bossi and the Lega can easily represent themselves as the heirs to a heroic civic tradition.[24] The Lega has nevertheless considerable difficulty in putting forward a generic northern history, and its frequent references to the Lombard League can do little to hide the fact that such moments of northern political unity have been extremely rare, if not unique. The alternative – presenting regionalized versions, often centred around a particular city-state like Milan or Venice – is historically more plausible, but entails the risk of introducing divisive issues, particularly in a region where local identities are still strong.[25]

While historical constructions of Padanian identity attempt as far as possible to incorporate the whole of northern Italy, ethnic constructions of the Padanian community focus on its smaller version, Italy north of the Apennines. According to this version, these regions are inhabited by a homogeneous community, marked by its pre-Roman Celtic inheritance, which has throughout its history maintained a common culture and a sense of community.[26] Such an interpretation reflects wishful thinking rather than a scientific reconstruction of the history of northern Italy. Cultural and, in particular, political divisions characterized the history of these regions until the unification of Italy in 1860. To the extent that a common identity existed before independence – an identity confined to the social élite and the intelligentsia – it is clear that this identity was Italian. Other references to a common, Padanian culture are likewise inconclusive: decorative styles and culinary habits are local or regional, not 'Padanian',[27] and Catholicism does not distinguish Padania from the rest of Italy. At best, it can be claimed that the regions north of the Apennines form a geographical unit and have related dialects, distinct from those in the rest of Italy.[28]

The Lega's affirmation of a Padanian identity is certainly the issue that creates the sharpest divide between it and a large majority of the intellectual community. Intellectuals and scholars generally have not even bothered to refute what they regard as nonsense, and confine themselves to sarcastic dismissals. The Lega's reconstruction of regional identities is likewise deemed artificial. Although scholars agree that local and (sub-regional) provincial identities have always been strong, they argue that regional identities – except in the special-status regions – have weak historical roots, with the partial exception of the Veneto.[29]

While the Padanian ethnic and historical identity are summarily rejected, the Lega is much more successful in presenting a northern civic identity, focused on the image of the virtuous *popolo produttore* (the 'producing people'). The Lega describes northern Italians as economically enterprising people who are competitive on the global market but who nevertheless remain rooted in their communities. They possess a Calvinist work ethic on the one hand, and Catholic moral and family values on the other. Their attachment to tradition and local identity is combined with openness to the outside world, and this finds its expression in their common Padanian identity and their integration into the European Union.

This description of the Padanian people echoes the contemporary interest of social scientists from Italy and abroad in what is called the Third Italy, the regions of northern Italy outside the Milan-Turin-Genoa industrial triangle. In recent decades, these regions have undergone a rapid process of industrialization characterized by the preponderance of small and medium-sized enterprises with local roots. Throughout the Third Italy, highly specialized industrial districts have become strongly competitive on the national and international markets. Social scientists tend to underline the endogenous and auto-propulsive dynamics that sustain these local systems (and thus their independence of the Italian state), and to highlight their roots in local culture. They focus on the economic successes of these industrial districts, and neglect the negative social side-effects of such a development model. Their idealized descriptions, by now rife in academic literature, are deployed by the Lega to offer a positive image of northern Italians as *il popolo produttore*.[30]

While social scientists generally consider the Lega's claim for a national Padanian identity a bluff, they often accept its contrast between a virtuous, productive and economically thriving northern Italy, with its hard-working inhabitants, and the South, marked by the influence of organized crime, economic backwardness and parasitism. The differences between northern and southern Italy on which the Lega bases its discourse can be traced back, at least in part, to hard facts – the southern economy *is* undoubtedly less competitive than its northern counterpart, unemployment *is* much higher in almost all southern regions, and organized crime does have mainly southern origins, even if it cannot be assimilated to the South as a whole. Since the North-South divide has proved to be persistent, Italian – and to a lesser extent foreign – intellectuals and scholars have attempted to offer an explanation for this divide.

By emphasizing the North-South contrast, the Lega has in fact drawn fresh attention to a debate as old as, if not older than, the Italian state: even before unification, eminent politicians had expressed reservations about incorporating southern Italy (until 1860, the Kingdom of the Two Sicilies) into a unified state, and throughout the history of the Italian state the North-South divide has remained a crucial element in its political geography. The Lega explains the contrast between a 'productive' North and a 'parasitic' South by the cultural characteristics of northern and southern Italians, and particularly the strong work-centred culture of the former and the absence of such a culture in the South. The Lega stops short of biological racism, and acknowledges the possibility that southerners may redeem themselves from their defects by adopting northern virtues. At times, when addressing itself to an intellectual audience, or when attempting (particularly in 1993) to attract a following in central and southern Italy, the Lega has even (up to a point, but never completely) de-territorialized the opposition between productive and parasitic Italians.[31]

Overall, the Lega's imaginary geography, in which northern Italy is conceived as a more modern and morally superior society, corresponds to the predominant mode of interpretation of Italy within the intellectual community. Scholarly representations of Italy that follow this pattern, however, reveal the methodological risks inherent in this approach. They have a tendency to exaggerate systematically differences between northern and southern Italy, and thus to idealize northern Italy, as is demonstrated by mainstream representations of the industrial districts of the Third Italy. Pride in northern Italy's past, its medieval communal traditions and its crucial contribution to the Renaissance is certainly justified, but there is a clear tendency to downplay the less positive aspects of the North's past and present. Characteristically, the northern origin of Italian fascism is seldom discussed, and Putnam for example, in his reconstruction of the civic traditions of the North, neglects this issue.[32]

Descriptions of the South, on the contrary, readily focus on its negative qualities. This process was enhanced by the emergence of the Lega, which started a vogue for trashing the South in the Italian media.[33] A characteristic example is the journalist Giorgio Bocca, a prominent member of Italy's cultural establishment, who in 1990 published a book entitled *La disunità d'Italia* (Italy's Disunity) which describes southern Italy as a country devoid of civilization, dominated by organized crime. This corruption, he claims, threatens to contaminate the North, since the state has already degenerated thanks to southern mores, but fortunately the Lega represents the sane forces of resistance.[34] Viewing the North-South contrast as a moral divide is in fact a traditional way of interpreting Italy. Back in 1962, the historian Luciano Cafagna referred to the long-standing tradition of *antimeridionalismo* (anti-southern points of view), the tendency of northerners to regard the South as corrupt and the state itself as infected by this corruption.[35]

The hegemony of the 'northern' approach is revealed in its use by foreigners, assumed to be unprejudiced. Robert D. Putnam's *Making Democracy Work* purports to explain the differential in efficiency between regional governments (much more efficient in the North), and does this by referring to cultural differences. He contrasts the co-operative and civic culture of the northern Italians with the 'amoral familism' of southern Italians, i.e. their exclusive defence of the interests of the nuclear family.[36] Like several other contemporary scholars in Italy and abroad, he holds the defects of southern culture responsible for its backwardness. Assumptions about the flaws of southern culture also appear in recent research on the entrepreneurial capacities of northern Italians, which often takes it for granted that such capacities are much weaker or non-existent in the South.[37] These authors admittedly refuse to interpret differences between the North and the South as an ethnic divide. Putnam, for example, explains the gap in efficiency between the North and the South by path dependence: a virtuous circle has created a modern, civic and economically successful North, a vicious circle a backward South. But by rooting this path dependence in a long historical tradition, in Putnam's case by interpreting northern virtues as deriving from the medieval Italian city-states and southern vices from the feudal realm of the authoritarian emperor Frederick II, such explanations reify the North-South opposition, and thus in turn lend legitimacy to a political discourse that in fact redefines such differences in ethnic terms.

The opposition between a virtuous North and a South lacking in these virtues is by no means accepted by all social scientists. Scholars from southern Italy, or those who focus their research on southern Italy, have continually voiced their criticism of stereotyped negative representations of the South and the unilateral vision behind them. In a methodological critique of such representations, Carmine Donzelli, a prominent student of southern Italy,[38] has given an overview of the empirical and methodological errors social scientists commit in representing the South. Their errors tend to be predetermined by their dichotomous vision of Italy, and they therefore underline the negative qualities of the South, which mark its Otherness. Positive aspects of the South are neglected, while any continuity between the North and the South is too quickly overlooked. They describe the South as an eternally backward society, and generally downplay the monumental changes that have taken place there, particularly since the second world war. The South is too readily portrayed as a society beyond salvation, an inferno – an image Donzelli contests in the title of his article, in which he compares the South with purgatory, thereby offering it the possibility of redemption, and thus improvement.[39]

In this context, it is not surprising that scholars studying southern Italy have been the ones most involved in discussing the meaning and interpretation of Italy's North-South-divide. Their reflections are of particular interest, since they highlight the political significance of interpretations of this divide. In his introduction to his *Breve storia dell'Italia meridionale* (A Short History of Southern Italy), published in 1993, at the pinnacle of the Lega's success, the historian Piero Bevilacqua affirms the importance of avoiding distorted and stereotyped representations of southern Italy. He deplores the fact that the media still use traditional, generally negative representations of the *Mezzogiorno*, and neglect the important contribution of a new generation of historians and social scientists to an understanding of the South. Those who systematically put forward stereotyped representations of the South bear a moral and political responsibility for northern secessionism, since their contributions have given legitimacy to the Lega's unilateral vision of Italy.[40]

Bevilacqua contrasts the subjectivity of the media with the objectivity of scientists. The historian Gabriella Gribaudi highlights instead the role of social scientists in reproducing negative stereotypes of the South, which southerners themselves have often accepted. Mainstream social scientists perceive the South as backward, and they adapt, reinterpret or ignore empirical data that cannot be fitted into this framework.[41] Referring to the ethnic conflicts in Eastern Europe, she notes that interaction does not automatically lead to understanding, and the intellectual debates on Italy's North-South divide confirm this opinion. There is no institutional or language barrier to divide scholars from northern and southern Italy, and scientific publications criticizing stereotyped representations of the South are easily accessible. Scholars nevertheless continue to reproduce such stereotyped visions, even though the methodological errors behind them have repeatedly been denounced, and the emergence of the Lega has shown that they are in danger of being politically manipulated. The facility with which northern Italian intellectuals and outsiders reduce the South to a homogeneous and inferior Other can in fact, as the anthropologist Jane Schneider argues, be regarded as an Italian version of Orientalism – the construction of a stereotyped and homogenizing discourse on the Other in order to affirm one's own cultural superiority.[42]

Diverging Visions of the Italian State and its History

While the mainstream interpretation of Italy's North-South divide can be seen as grounded in a stereotyped opposition, it derives its relevance from being the hegemonic discourse on Italy. Its attachment to the Italian state separates this 'northern' discourse from the Lega's secessionism, but they both interpret Italy's North-South divide as a moral hierarchy. Their view is contested only by a minority of scholars, who criticize their stereotyped representations of southern Italy and their reified opposition between a civic and modern North and the South as the negative Other. These three points of view – the Lega's 'Padanian' outlook, the mainstream 'northern' one, and the minority 'southern' one – can be considered ideological perspectives on the Italian state and its North-South divide, all rooted in different interpretations of the history of Italy as a unified nation-state and of the Italian process of nation-building.

To deconstruct Italian national identity, the Lega argues that the Italian state has been unable to create an Italian nation. On unification, in 1860, national sentiments were weak, and present only within a small élite. The famous statement made at the time by the prominent politician Massimo d'Azeglio, 'now that Italy is made, we need to make Italians' (incidentally often quoted by the Lega), testifies to the sense of mission felt by the post-unification élite, but also its isolation. Historians for example have emphasized the élitist nature of the unification process, and the inability or unwillingness of the post-unification élite to integrate the popular classes into the new state, or to take their aspirations into consideration. Recently, some historians have also argued against the traditional historiography of the *Risorgimento* (the process of national unification), which described the Italian state as its inevitable outcome. They deny the centrality of the process of nation-building, which in their view was only one of the possible outcomes of the political struggles of Restoration Italy. The emergence of the Lega has, moreover, again drawn attention to the strong regional diversity within Italy during the *Risorgimento*.[43]

The Lega combines an affirmation of the artificiality of the *Risorgimento* with the removal of the sacred aura surrounding its heroes, King Victor Emmanuel II, Cavour, Garibaldi and Mazzini. Although public opinion does not readily accept this denigration of national symbols, the Lega's polemics against the process of unification coincide with a more general preoccupation with what went wrong with the *Risorgimento*, and particularly with the process of forming the Italian state.[44] Many of the latter's defects have their roots in unification. According to Tarrow, its peculiarities are a consequence of how it was organized after 1860: a centralized system of prefects to control the population was weakened by limiting the scope of their responsibilities (mainly political and social control), with, as a consequence, overlapping intervention by a multiplicity of government bodies, and overall inefficiency.[45] The British historian Denis Mack Smith has argued that the unclear division of power between the king and the parliament was instrumental in limiting political responsibility and increasing corruption.[46]

Although academic debates on the *Risorgimento* have revised the Italian nationalist hagiography, they have rarely questioned the existence of the Italian nation as such. Generally speaking, the present-day existence of an Italian identity is taken for granted, and the undeniable attachment to Italy expressed up to now even by the more Lega-minded regions gives this assumption credibility.[47] The linguistic unification of Italy, the spreading of the use of standard Italian side by side with or instead of regional dialects, is perhaps the most visible sign of the roots the Italian nation has put down.[48]

Italian intellectuals share this loyalty to Italy, and the Lega's anti-Italian rhetoric has in fact led to a renewed interest in Italian national identity. The historian Mario Isnenghi has pointed out that, with the emergence of the Lega, scholars have consciously re-oriented their research programmes towards rediscovering the content of such an identity. Hence their interest in periods that marked the formation of the Italian nation, such as the *Risorgimento*, the first world war, the Resistance movement of 1943-1945 and the post-war foundation of the Italian republic.[49] But more often than not these debates bring out the controversial character of such events. Analogously, partisans of a positive, civic identity for Italy quite often have a defensive attitude to such an identity, and tend to despair of its feasibility. This defensiveness demonstrates the weakness of Italian national identity: its exaltation takes the form of a passionate masochist nationalism, the proclamation – at once proud and shame-faced – of the defects of Italians.[50] The attachment to national identity is thus combined with uncertainty about its content.

The core of the weakness of Italian national identity lies in its relation to the Italian state. As the American political scientists Sidney Almond and Gabriel Verba already noted almost forty years ago, the content given to this identity is seldom political. Italians appreciate their country's culture, art and literature, and voluntarily praise its beauty. But they seldom extend such a positive appreciation of their country to its political institutions, towards which most of them react negatively.[51] Although it has been in existence now for more than a century, the Italian state has been unable to create an active sense of common togetherness based on civic values. When the historian Ruggiero Romano traces an Italian identity back to the late medieval period, this identity includes the unpunished arrogance of the leading classes, the delicate nature of public relations, and consolidated forms of corruption.[52]

Within Italy, there is a strong tendency to interpret problems such as the defects of the state or the lack of civic virtues as signs of the country's backwardness. Italy is perceived as being insufficiently modern, despite empirical evidence to the contrary, such as its economic strength and the high figures for consumption and life expectancy. The need for modernization is a central issue in the political and intellectual debate in Italy, and its predominant interpretation identifies modernity with the United States and Western Europe.[53] Intellectuals readily interpret Italy's deviations from this model as a lack of modernity and, in a revealing parallel with the North-South dichotomy within Italy, they contrast Italy's real or alleged vices with a stereotyped and sociologically unrealistic ideal model, which is assumed to exist outside Italy.[54] Following a long-standing tradition, mainstream scholars often explain Italy's backwardness by the corrupting influence of an allegedly deviant or barbarian South. Anxieties about Italy's international status certainly explain the tenacity of such interpretations, since by locating backwardness in the South they redeem northern Italy as a modern, European region.

This outlook is vehemently opposed by scholars who reject the stereotyped identification of the South with backwardness. These have produced an alternative interpretation of the role of the Italian state. Without denying the part played by endogenous cultural factors, they argue that the state was crucial in reproducing the oft-denounced flaws of southern Italy and the North-South divide. The so-called barbarian revolts of southern Italians after unification can in their view be explained by the harshness with which the new state imposed itself. Likewise, corruption in the South has always occurred in connivance with northern interests, and with the active collaboration of the state. Since the second world war, the state has played an important role in modernizing and developing the South, but its intervention has reproduced (albeit in a different form) many of the old problems that used to beset southern Italy. If southern Italy today has a social structure that is less responsive to civic culture and economic development, this is mainly the result of the efforts of the state apparatus – and particularly the christian democrats, who dominated until 1992 – to maintain a structure that was advantageous for their own interests.[55]

To counter images of southern backwardness, students of southern Italy affirm its integration into Europe, its modernity and its normality.[56] The problems of the South are not caused by its backwardness – rather they reveal the risks inherent in the processes of economic development and modernization.[57] Even when these scholars discuss the particular features of the history of the South, including its negative aspects, they point out that its problems are those of Italy as a whole, resulting from the particular nature of the Italian state.[58]

Mainstream social scientists, however, tend to view the state as favouring the South (as the unverified allegations regarding its distributive policies showed), they minimize its role in reproducing the South's problems, and analogously ignore its support of the economic development of the North.[59] In a study of state subsidies to small-scale industrialists, Linda Weiss has pointed out how the growth of small industry in northern Italy has been encouraged by policies that promote it strongly while offering little support to small-scale entrepreneurs in the South.[60] This fact, however, is generally not acknowledged in scientific literature, where the development of local systems is usually described as an auto-propulsive, endogenous movement. Many researchers appear to take it for granted that positive developments in Italy are caused by the autonomous mechanisms of the market, while negative developments are due to intervention by the state. Such a view can easily be given a territorial projection, associating the North with the former, the South with the latter, and thus lending scientific legitimacy to the Lega's North-South divide. Like the Lega, these researchers combine (often justified) critiques of the Italian state with a misinterpretation of its policies, an ideologically-coloured denial of the actual territorial dynamics of these policies.

Conclusion

Overall, scholars in Italy reject the Lega's secessionism and two of the main arguments that sustain it – the existence of a Padanian nation, and its view of the state as based on a freely established contract whose parties maintain the right to dissolve it. But they generally share its negative vision of the Italian state, and concur with its interpretation of Italy's North-South divide. The weaknesses of the Italian state have certainly facilitated the Lega's task, since they enable it to place its secessionist proposals within a framework of critiques of the state's dysfunctioning, which even its most ardent opponents consider credible. To give such critiques a secessionist dynamic, the Lega has embedded them in a discourse that combines an affirmation of Padanian ethnic identity with economic ideas close to neo-liberalism. By presenting northern Italy as a community ready for integration into the global economy, and contrasting it to the archaic Italian state, the Lega offers a theme to which public opinion and mainstream scholars are sensitive. Both make use of a stereotyped interpretation of Italy which reconstructs the virtues of the North as culturally given, and the action of the state as an external fact, linked with southern vices. The case of Italy demonstrates how such a hierarchy can be converted into a nationalist ethnic discourse, in which the presence of an inferior Other can legitimize secession and the breaking of the bonds of national solidarity.

Mainstream social scientists share with the Lega Nord an outlook in which differences between the two parts of Italy are interpreted as a polarity, an opposition which is given a normative value. This outlook is grounded in strongly-felt concern about the country's alleged lack of modernity and anxiety over its international status, reinforced by the view of many foreign scholars who regard Italy's modernity as borderline. Relegating backwardness to the South, emphasizing the positive characteristics of northern Italy (particularly the ones that have attracted laudatory comments abroad, such as the industrial districts of the Third Italy) then becomes for Italians, and particularly northern Italians, a strategy for asserting more firmly their country's favourable position among modern states and for legitimizing its inclusion in the European Union.

The parallels between the thinking of the Lega and that of mainstream social scientists and intellectuals result from a shared imaginary geography, whereby countries and regions are classified according to their degree of modernity. This classification predetermines the observations made by scientists, and biases their judgement in favour of the more modern North – or, at an international level, the United States and Western Europe. It enables them to downplay the complexity of the processes that have produced, and continue to reproduce, regional differences. The Italian debate thus reveals the importance of avoiding a stereotyped and biased representation of regions and nations, and the need for self-conscious reflection on the terms and methods used in inter-regional comparisons. It also shows, however, how an imaginary geography and the ideological value attributed to it can shield social scientists from embarking on such a reflection.

Notes

1 Throughout the text, I refer to the 'South' and the 'North' as symbolic categories corresponding to the Italian categories 'Il Sud' and 'Il Nord'. They may be understood as the equivalents of nations, and they are hence given a capital S and N respectively. The terms 'northern Italy', 'southern Italy', 'northern Italians' and 'southern Italians' simply refer to regional distinctions, and are therefore in lower-case.

'South' and 'North' also refer to geographical entities, although the 'South' is the better defined unit (it includes the regions of Sicily, Sardinia, Calabria, Campania, Puglia, Basilicata, Abruzzi and Molise). Besides the northern regions (Valle d'Aosta, Piedmont, Liguria, Lombardy, Trentino-Alto Adige, Veneto, Friuli-Venezia Giulia and Emilia-Romagna) the 'North' may include some central regions (Tuscany, Umbria, Marche), although one central region, Lazio (where Italy's capital, Rome, is located), is systematically not included in the North.

2   Gaspare Nevola, 'La politica della secessione', *Rivista italiana di scienza politica*, Vol. 28, No. 1, 1998, pp. 119-156, and especially p. 145. The Lega's programme is set out in Umberto Bossi and Daniele Vimercati, *Vento dal Nord*, Milano, Sperling & Kupfer, 1992; Umberto Bossi and Daniele Vimercati, *La Rivoluzione*, Milano, Sperling & Kupfer, 1993; Umberto Bossi, *Tutta la verità. Perché ho partecipato al governo Berlusconi. Perché l'ho fatto cadere. Dove voglio arrivare*, Milano, Sperling & Kupfer, 1995; and Umberto Bossi and Daniele Vimercati, *Processo alla Lega*, Milano, Sperling & Kupfer, 1998. For an overview of the Lega's history, its political view-points and its programmatic changes, see Ilvo Diamanti, *La Lega. Geografia, storia e sociologia di un soggetto politico*, Roma, Donzelli, 1995; and Roberto Biorcio, *La Padania promessa*, Milano, Il Saggiatore, 1997.

3   Nevola, *op. cit.*, p. 127.

4   Michael Hechter, *Internal Colonialism. The Celtic Fringe in British National Development, 1536-1966*, London, Routledge & Kegan Paul, 1975.

5   The Lega's use of the rhetoric of internal colonialism appears to be a legacy from its origins, when it was sponsored by the autonomists from the Valle d'Aosta. Bossi occasionally refers to authors who have theorized on internal colonialism, such as Robert Blauner (Max Ottomani, *Brigate rozze. A Sud e al Nord del senatore Bossi*, Napoli, Tullio Pironte Ed., 1992, p. 108), without discussing their theories.

6   Pier Paolo Poggio, 'Il naturalismo sociale e l'ideologia della Lega', in Giovanni De Luna (ed.), *Figli di un benessere minore. La Lega, 1979-1993*, Scandicci, La Nuova Italia, 1994, pp. 137-196.

7   E.g. Sabino Cassese, *Lo stato introvabile. Modernità e arretratezza delle istituzioni italiane*, Roma, Donzelli, 1998; and Paul Ginsborg, *A History of Contemporary Italy*, Harmondsworth, Penguin, 1990.

8   Sidney Tarrow, *Between Center and Periphery. Grassroots Politicians in Italy and France*, New Haven Conn./London, Yale University Press, 1977.

9   Robert D. Putnam, *Making Democracy Work. Civic Tradition in Modern Italy*, Princeton, N.J., Princeton University Press, 1993.

10 Proposals for a reform along federal lines certainly do not always share the Lega's focus, and several proposals for federalism, particularly from the centre-left, actually emphasize regional collaboration, and particularly co-operation between Southern and Northern regions. See e.g. Vannino Chiti, 'L'Italia fra federalismo vecchio e nuovo', *Nuova Antologia*, Vol. 132, No. 2204, 1997, pp. 39-63. The current debate, however, remains marked by the Lega's stance, as is shown by the emphasis on the issue of fiscal federalism (see below).

11 For a discussion on the Italian welfare state, and particularly the circumstances that caused its parasitic excrescence, see Giulio Scaramellini, Elena dell'Agnese and Guido Lucarno, 'I processi redistributivi', in Pasquale Coppola (ed.) *Geografia politica delle regioni italiane*, Torino, Einaudi, 1997, pp. 337-400.

12 Poggio, *op. cit.*

13 Alessandro Casiccia, 'Illusioni antistataliste e realtà neostataliste', *Nuvole*, No. 12, 1996, pp. 57-60.

14 Bossi and Vimercati, *La Rivoluzione, op. cit.*, pp. 194-196; Giancarlo Pagliarini, 'Le ragioni della Lega', *Nuvole*, No. 12, 1996, pp. 35-48, especially pp. 44-48.

15 E.g. Piero Bassetti, *L'Italia si è rotta? Un federalismo per l'Europa*, Roma/Bari, Laterza, 1996; Roberto Mainardi, *L'Italia delle regioni. Il Nord e la Padania*, Milano, Bruno Mondadori, 1998.

16 E.g. Allen Buchanan, *Secession. The Morality of Political Divorce from Fort Sumter to Lithuania and Quebec*, Boulder/San Francisco/Oxford, Westview Press, 1991, p. 115; Milica Zarkovic Bookman, *The Economics of Secession*, New York, St Martin's Press, 1992, pp. 106-107.

17 Pagliarini, *op. cit.*, p. 41. The author of the article, Giancarlo Pagliarini, was budget minister for the Lega in the Berlusconi government in 1994 and can thus be considered well informed. The five special-status regions – Valle d'Aosta, Trentino-Alto Adige, Friuli-Venezia Giulia, Sardinia and Sicily, inhabited by ethnic minorities or characterized by secessionist tendencies – were granted autonomy after the second world war (Friuli only later, in 1964), and have a larger measure of autonomy than the other regions (which obtained regional self-government later, in 1970). The position of the four Northern regions – Lombardy, Piedmont, the Veneto and Emilia-Romagna – on the giving side of fiscal redistribution is confirmed by Scaramellini *et al.*, *op. cit.*, pp. 349-351. These four regions clearly pay more in taxes per capita than they receive, while the other regions either receive more or break even.

18 A good overview of these redistributive policies is given by Scaramellini et al., *op. cit.*

19 It should be noted, however, that the proposals for the practical application of fiscal federalism considerably diminish the radicalism of this principle, since they generally include the continuation of some forms of regional distributive policies. See e.g. Giuseppe Valditara, 'La Bicamerale e il federalismo', *Federalismo & Libertà*, Vol. 5, No. 1, 1998, pp. 35-44. Such caution is informed by an awareness of the centrifugal dynamics its implementation would cause. Cf. Giorgio Ragazzi, 'Federalismo fiscale e questione meridionale', *Federalismo & Società*, Vol. 2, No. 1, 1995, pp. 29-57.

20 E.g. Bassetti, *op. cit.*; Mainardi, *op. cit.* It should be noted, however, that although the Lega is clearly influenced by neo-liberal economic theories, its vision of society with an emphasis on the Padanian community and its networks of solidarity is in many ways very different from neo-liberal doctrines.

21 Scaramellini *et al.*, *op. cit.*, pp. 343-344; Biorcio, *op. cit.*, pp. 133-134.

22 The borders of even this smaller version of Padania are shifting. Sometimes it corresponds to the regions belonging to the 'North-West' and 'North-East' entities used in official statistics. On other occasions, when the cultural unity of Padania is emphasized, the right to self-determination of the linguistic minorities within these regions (particularly the German-speaking South-Tyrolians and the French-speaking inhabitants of the Valle d'Aosta) is asserted.

23 Percy Allum and Ilvo Diamanti, 'The Autonomous League in the Veneto', in Carl Levy (ed.), *Italian Regionalism. History, Identity and Politics*, Oxford/Washington D.C., Berg, 1996, pp. 151-169.

24 Guido C. Bolla and Luigi F. Imperatore, *Da Ambrosio a Bossi. Lotte per la libertà nella Padania*, Milano, Edi. B.I., 1992; Gilberto Oneto, *L'invenzione della Padania. La rinascita della comunità più antica d'Europa*, Bergamo, Foedus Editore, 1997.

25 Stefano Cavazza, 'L'invenzione della tradizione e la Lega Lombarda. Note introduttive', in Aldo Bonomi and Pier Paolo Poggio (eds). *Ethnos e demos. Dal leghismo al neopopulismo* (Iter, No. 8), Milano, Mimesis, 1995, pp. 195-213, especially pp. 207-208.

26 Oneto, *op. cit.*, pp. 79-93.

27 According to Oneto (*ibid.*, p. 109), this demonstrates the unity in diversity of Padanian culture, but this argument seems specious, since it could be applied to any context.

28 *Ibid.*, pp. 63-75.

29 E.g. Adrian Lyttelton, 'Shifting Identities: Nation, Region and City', in Levy (ed.), *op. cit.*, pp. 33-52; Allum and Diamanti, *op. cit.*

[30] E.g Sandro Fontana, *La riscossa dei lombardi. Le origini del miracolo economico nella regiona più laboriosa d'Europa. 1929-1959*, Milano, Mondadori, 1998; Mainardi, *op. cit.* For critiques of these representations see Aldo Bonomi, *Il capitalismo molecolare. La società al lavoro nel Nord Italia*, Torino, Einaudi, 1997.

[31] Bossi and Vimercati, *La Rivoluzione*, *op. cit.*

[32] Gianfranco Bettin, 'Le radici della cultura civica nell'Italia divisa', *Quaderni di Sociologia*, Vol. 37, No. 5, 1993, pp. 161-171, especially p. 165.

[33] Sidney Tarrow, 'Making Social Science Work Across Space and Time: A Critical Reflection on Robert Putnam's "Making Democracy Work"', *American Political Science Review*, Vol. 90, No. 2, 1996, pp. 389-397.

[34] Giorgio Bocca, *La disunità d'Italia*, Milano, Garzanti, 1990.

[35] Luciano Cafagna, *Il Nord nella storia d'Italia. Antologia politica dell'Italia industriale*, Bari, Laterza, 1962, p. 332.

[36] The concept of 'amoral familism' was coined by the American political scientist Edward Banfield, who explained the backwardness of the Southern village he studied in 1955 by what he called the ethos of amoral familism, encapsulated in the adage 'Maximize the material, short-run advantage of the nuclear family; assume that all others will do likewise' (Edward C. Banfield, *The Moral Basis of a Backward Society*, New York, The Free Press, 1967 (1958), p. 83). In his view, this ethos inhibited the development of modernity. Both the concept itself and its generalized application to Southern Italy have been the object of heated polemics, and most commentators agree that it should be applied with caution, and certainly not unduly generalized to the entire South (see e.g. Paola Filippucci, 'Anthropological Perspectives on Culture in Italy', in David Forgacs and Robert Lumley, *Italian Cultural Studies. An Introduction*, Oxford, Oxford University Press, 1996, pp. 52-71, especially pp. 54-55; and Gabriella Gribaudi, 'Images of the South', in *Ibid*, pp. 72-87, especially pp. 83-84 and 86).

[37] Anna Cento Bull and Paul Corner, *From Peasant to Entrepreneur. The Survival of the Family Economy in Italy*, Oxford/Providence, Berg, 1993, p. 127.

[38] Carmine Donzelli is director of the IMES (*Istituto meridionale di storia e scienze sociali*, the Southern Institute of History and Social Sciences), the most prominent research institute on Southern Italy, which publishes the interdisciplinary review *Meridiana*.

[39] Carmine Donzelli, 'Mezzogiorno tra "questione" e purgatorio. Opinione comune, immagine scientifica, strategie di ricerca', *Meridiana*, No. 9, 1990, pp. 13-53.

[40] Piero Bevilaqua, *Breve storia dell'Italia meridionale dall'Ottocento ad oggi*, Roma, Donzelli, 1993, pp. 10-11.

[41] Gabriella Gribaudi, *op. cit.*, p. 84.

[42] Jane Schneider, 'The Dynamics of Neo-orientalism in Italy (1848-1995)', in Jane Schneider (ed.), *Italy's 'Southern Question'. Orientalism in One Country*, Oxford/New York, Berg, 1998, pp. 1-23.

[43] For a critical overview, see Lucy Riall, *The Italian Risorgimento. State, Society and National Unification*, London, Routledge, 1994.

[44] Such preoccupations are shared by many historians of different political views (excluding perhaps the most overtly nationalist currents). One of the major influences in this debate is in fact Gramsci's interpretation of the *Risorgimento* as a passive revolution, almost without popular participation.

[45] Tarrow, *Between Center and Periphery*, op. cit., pp. 60-65.

[46] Denis Mack Smith, *Italy and its Monarchy*, New Haven, Conn., Yale University Press, 1989.

[47] Two polls, held in 1996 in the regions where the Lega is strongest – Piedmont, Lombardy, the Veneto and Friuli-Venezia Giulia – have shown that in these regions only a minority of around

20-25% approves of secession. More than half of the respondents rejected secession as disastrous and morally unacceptable, while a quarter considered it advantageous, but morally unacceptable (Ilvo Diamanti, 'Il Nord senza l'Italia?', *Limes*, No. 1, 1996, pp. 15-30; Ilvo Diamanti, 'Il Nord senza l'Italia? L'independenza diventa "normale"', *Limes*, No. 1, 1997, pp. 297-308). If, to paraphrase Renan, a nation is a daily plebiscite, the Italian nation continues to be the dominant option, although these results certainly show that this choice has lost its self-evident character.

48   Tullio Di Mauro, 'La questione della lingua', in Corrado Staiano (ed.), *La cultura italiana del Novecento*, Bari/Roma, Laterza, 1996, pp. 423-444. A few minorities in border regions have maintained their linguistic diversity, in particular German-speakers in South Tyrol, French-speakers in Valle d'Aosta, Slovenians at the north-eastern border, and pockets of Friulese- and Ladino-speakers in the North-East. However, most of these minorities are not or are only marginally concerned with the Lega's secessionism.

49   Mario Isnenghi, 'La mémoire divisée des Italiens', *Hérodote*, Vol. 89, No. 2, 1998, pp. 39-54.

50   Tim Mason, 'Italy and Modernization: A Montage', *History Workshop*, No. 25, 1988, pp. 127-147, especially p. 131. This defensive attitude also has political consequences, such as the parliament's rejection in 1991 of a bill to introduce new rights for minority languages. Although this bill was not related to the Lega's secessionist proposals, intellectuals involved in re-proposing an Italian national identity, like Gian Enrico Rusconi, nevertheless campaigned for its rejection as a threat to national unity, since such a recognition could also be used to legitimize the 'Padanian' dialects (Anna Laura Lepschy, Giulio Lepschy and Miriam Voghera, 'Linguistic Variety in Italy', in Levy (ed.), *op. cit.*, pp. 69-80; Di Mauro, *op. cit.*).

51   Gabriel Almond and Sidney Verba, *The Civic Culture. Political Attitudes and Democracy in Five Nations*, Princeton, N.J., Princeton University Press, 1963; Lieven De Winter, Donatella Della Porta and Kris Deschouwer, 'Comparing Similar Countries: Italy and Belgium', *Res Publica*, Vol. 38, No. 2, 1996, pp. 215-235, especially pp. 231-232; Loredana Sciolla, *Italiani. Stereotipi di casa nostra*, Bologna, Il Mulino, 1997, p. 52.

52   Ruggiero Romano, *Paese Italia. Venti secoli di identità*, Roma, Donzelli, 1997. See also Gian Enrico Rusconi, *Se cessiamo di essere una nazione*, Bologna, Il Mulino, 1993.

53   Mason, *op. cit.* 1988; John Agnew, 'The Myth of Backward Italy in Modern Europe', in Beverly Allen and Mary Russo (eds), *Revisioning Italy. National Identity and Global Culture*, Minneapolis, University of Minnesota Press, 1997, pp. 23-42. The importance Italian intellectuals attach to the issue of modernity cannot, however, be explained simply by American influence. As Tim Mason (*op. cit.*, 130) makes clear, Italian concerns about modernity are a native product, which has grown out of elements of Italian Marxism and Italian liberalism, and has incorporated elements from Italian and German philosophy and French historiography of the Annales School.

54   Michael Eve, 'Comparing Italy: The Case of Corruption', in David Forgacs and Robert Lumley, *Italian Cultural Studies. An Introduction*, Oxford, Oxford University Press, 1996, pp. 34-51.

55   Ginsborg, *op. cit.*; Tarrow, 'Making Social Science Work Across Space and Time'.

56   Bevilacqua, *op. cit.*

57   Giuliano Minichiello, *Meridionalismo*. Milano, Edizione bibliografica, 1997, p. 91.

58   Donzelli, *op. cit.*; Bevilacqua, *op. cit.*

59   E.g. Putnam, *op. cit.*, Fontana, *op. cit.*

60   Linda Weiss, *Creating Capitalism. The State and Small Business since 1945*, Oxford, Basil Blackwell, 1988.

Xiaokun Song

9. Intellectual Discourses in the Taiwan Independence Movement[1]

Attempts have been made to establish theories of secession for both analytical and normative purposes. Comparative studies of present-day secessionist movements have been conducted in the search for a comprehensive analytical framework. Looking critically at several political theories, Ralph R. Premdas has designed a framework that strives to be both simple and comprehensive at the same time.[2] Summarized briefly, he proposes five dimensions to be examined in an empirical case-study of a secessionist movement: 1) the causes of secession, including the primordial variables (language, religion, race, values or culture and territory), and the secondary factors (neglect, exploitation, domination and internal colonialism, repression and discrimination, and forced annexation); 2) the organization, ideology and leadership of the movement; 3) the governing regime and its institutional framework; 4) modes of conflict management; 5) the international dimension, such as external allies, support or intervention.[3] When discussing these five dimensions, Premdas points to the importance of the role of intellectuals in the movement. In his view, 'the right to secede and determine a group's destiny is asserted in diametrical opposition to another sacred right, that of a state to safeguard its sovereignty and territorial integrity: the latter is also a right sanctioned by the UN. Secession, then, is not an uncontested moral claim made in a vacuum and yielded to without argument and challenge'.[4] In the secessionist and anti-secessionist movements, therefore, what counts is not only the physical power but also the moral discourse of the parties involved.

It is my endeavour in this chapter to analyse the secessionist movement in Taiwan with the focus on the role of pro-secession intellectuals and their discourses. Along with the historical evolution of the movement, several points need to be looked at closely. These include the role of intellectuals in the movement, the major disciplines employed in the pro-independence discourse, the content of the discourse and the implications of this case-study for the discussion on secessionist movements in general. Owing to the limited scope of this chapter, it will not be possible to analyse the anti-secessionist intellectual discourses in the People's Republic of China and in Taiwan, and the debates between pro- and anti-secessionists.

Background

Territory

Today our understanding of Taiwan includes the island of Taiwan itself, the Pescadores (Penghu) Islands (numbering 64 in all), the Offshore Islands (the Jinmen and Mazu groups, also known as the Quemoy and Matsu groups in English) and a handful of islands in the South China Sea. The island of Taiwan is geographically separated from Mainland China by 100 miles of water. There are also several other names for Taiwan: Formosa (a name given by the Portuguese, the first Westerners to set foot on the island – a word meaning 'beautiful' in their language), Nationalist China, the Republic of China (ROC), and more recently 'Island China'. To avoid confusion, throughout the text the terms 'Taiwan Island' and 'Taiwan' will be used when referring to different geographical territories, the former meaning the main island and the latter including all of the islands.

Population and Ethnic Composition

Taiwan has a population of 22 million people, which is divided into three (sub-) ethnic groups: Taiwanese, Mainlanders, and Aborigines. According to the 1990 census, approximately 85 per cent are Taiwanese, 14 per cent Mainlanders, and slightly more than 1 per cent are Aborigines. One important criterion for differentiating between the ethnic groups is the date of their settlement in Taiwan. The Aborigines and their descendants, who are of Malay-Polynesian origin, are the original inhabitants of Taiwan.[5] The Taiwanese and their offspring are those who emigrated from Mainland China before the second world war. This category is further subdivided into two groups, mainly according to linguistic differences: the Hoklos, a people originally from the Fujian and Guangdong provinces who started immigrating to Taiwan from the seventeenth century onwards and who speak a Fujian dialect known as Hoklo; and the Hakkas, who also originated mainly from the same two provinces, from the eighteenth century onwards, and speak another dialect – Hakka.[6] The Mandarin-speaking Mainlanders comprise the troops and followers of the Kuo-ming-tang Party (the Nationalist Party, KMT) who retreated to Taiwan between 1945 and 1949 following the KMT's defeat in the civil war, and their descendants – Mandarin being the official language in China.

Brief History of Taiwan in Relation to the Mainland

From historical records, we know that between 1264 and 1294, during the Yuan dynasty, the Pescadores (Penghu) Islands were incorporated into Fujian province. In 1372, the succeeding Ming dynasty also continued to exercise judicial powers of inspection over these islands. Taiwan Island, however, was not on the map of the Chinese Empire at the time. In 1622, the Dutch occupied the Pescadores (Penghu) Islands, using the place as a base for the transit trade of its East India Company. Following the war between the Chinese Empire and the Netherlands, the Dutch were forced to retreat to Taiwan Island, and for the next 30 years they turned it into a base for Dutch colonial expansion. When the Ming dynasty was destroyed by the Manchus from the North and replaced by the Qing dynasty, Zheng Chenggong (also known as Koxinga) of the Ming Dynasty and his troops defeated the Dutch and, in 1662, drove them from Taiwan Island. Zheng and his followers then used it as their base, in order to fight against the Manchus and to restore the Ming dynasty. The rule of Zheng's family over Taiwan Island was ended in 1683 by the Qing dynasty. From then on, the whole of Taiwan was officially included on the map of the Chinese Empire, as part of Fujian province.

In 1894, the Sino-Japanese (jiawu) war broke out, resulting in the total defeat of China. Taiwan Island and the Pescadores (Penghu) Islands were consequently ceded to Japan under the Sino-Japanese Peace Treaty (also named as the Shimonoseki Treaty), signed the following year. Thus began 50 years of Japanese colonial rule, brought to an end only with the surrender of Japan in World War Two. Under the San Francisco Treaty of September 1951, Japan gave up its claim to Taiwan and the nationalist ROC took over.

As its defeat in the civil war was clearly imminent, between 1945 and 1949 the KMT gradually retreated from the mainland to Taiwan. Since the founding of the People's Republic of China (PRC) in 1949, the confrontation between the Chinese Communist Party (CCP) of the PRC and the KMT of the ROC across the Taiwan Strait has gone through different phases. Between 1949 and the late 1970s, the two sides were openly hostile. The slogan of the Communist PRC was 'liberate Taiwan', while the nationalist ROC swore to 'take over the mainland'. After the Korean War, the confrontation between the two sides had actually become part of the Cold War, with one in the communist bloc and the other siding with the West. The military presence of the US navy, the Seventh Fleet in the Taiwan Strait since 1953 contributed to the stalemate of the confrontation. Although the US had lent Taiwan its protection and made it one of its strategic bases in the Pacific, it did not support the KMT government's plan to take over the mainland by force. That the KMT government failed to get full support from its American 'big brother' was best illustrated by the loss of its seat in both the UN General Assembly and the Security Council to the PRC in 1971, and the normalization of Sino-American relations in 1979.

The hostile confrontation across the Strait began to thaw in the late 1970s. On the mainland side, the PRC proceeded to reform. The Chinese government designed a new strategy for reunifying the mainland and Taiwan, this being the famous 'one country, two systems' policy later applied to the former British colony, Hong Kong. On the other side of the Strait, modernization and democratization have characterized the development of Taiwan over the last two decades. The KMT government dropped its hostile 'three Nos' policy towards the mainland (i.e., no compromise, no contact and no negotiation), and renounced its claims to Mainland China in May 1991. Furthermore, informal exchanges, such as trade, investment and tourism, have taken place across the Strait since the mid 1980s. No official talks on unification have yet been held, as the two sides cannot agree the basis on which such talks should be conducted. There is still no agreement as to the precise objectives, conditions or formal status of these negotiations – they are still at the stage of 'negotiations about negotiations'. The Beijing government would like to negotiate with Taipei in a central-local framework, while Taipei insists this should be a negotiation between two equal governments or political entities. Meanwhile, the development of the Taiwan Independence Movement has further complicated the picture.

The Taiwan Independence Movement

The secessionist movement in Taiwan did not emerge as an organized movement until 1947-48. By Taiwanese academics it is often labelled the 'modern Taiwan Independence Movement' (TIM). A diachronic examination of its evolution would not, however, take 1947-48 as its starting point, since the political development of Taiwan society in two earlier periods is just as important for an understanding of the emergence of the TIM. The first period was from 1895 to 1945, when Taiwan was under Japanese occupation. The anti-Japanese movement and the experience of colonization helped shape a distinct Taiwanese consciousness. The second period, from 1945 to 1947, witnessed the beginning of the KMT's rule over Taiwan and several clashes between the KMT and the local population, which later gave rise to the modern independence movement. A brief review of these two periods will be helpful before we turn to the movement itself.

1895 – 1945

The cession of Taiwan to Japan following the Sino-Japanese war in 1895 initiated the anti-Japanese movement in Taiwan. Feeling betrayed by the Qing court and facing the repressive Japanese colonization, the Taiwanese took up anti-Japanese struggles in various forms. The proclamation of the Democratic Republic of Taiwan in the same year was part of a major mobilization against the occupation. The former governor of Taiwan, T'ang Ching-sung, was elected president by the local nobles. Following the short-lived republic, the Taiwanese engaged intermittently in armed uprisings and guerrilla warfare against the Japanese until 1916.[7]

After 1916, the Japanese changed their ruling policies from the previous military repression to full-scale assimilation coupled with 'bread-and-butter' policies. As the Japanese regarded Taiwan as their 'unsinkable warship' and used it as a base for their military expansion in the Pacific area, the economic development of Taiwan did not follow the general pattern of the colonial economy, namely, that the colony should be deprived of its raw materials and become merely a market for manufactured goods from the colonizing country. Instead, from the 1930s the Japanese helped to develop infrastructure in Taiwan, such as the irrigation system for agriculture. The industrialization of Taiwan, which was subsequently to become the basis for the economic miracle, also began at that time. To assimilate the Taiwanese culturally, the language policy – namely, that all Taiwanese had to learn and speak Japanese – was also enforced. Despite the unjust and forceful nature of this policy, it provided the different ethnic and linguistic groups in Taiwan, for the first time, with a common language for communication. By the 1940s, the standard of living in Taiwan was far higher than that of the mainland.

After the first world war, with the introduction of the Western notion of self-determination, and inspired by the Home Rule movement in other parts of the world, the anti-Japanese activists changed their strategies. From the earlier form of uprisings and guerrilla warfare, the struggle evolved into a non-violent movement. In this period, intellectuals (especially those who had received their education abroad, mostly in Japan) played a leading role. Two strategies were employed at the time. On the one hand, there was the 'Licensed Reform' group whose aim was to extend the autonomy of the Taiwanese people through reforms within the colonial system. The Movement of Petition for the Establishment of a Taiwanese Parliament in 1920 was one such effort to gain self-governance for Taiwan without overthrowing Japanese rule. On the other hand, the more radical type of movement, led by the Taiwanese Communist Party (founded in 1928), promoted the idea of independence for the Taiwanese nation and carried on the anti-colonial revolution. The two forms of the anti-Japanese struggle were reflected not only at the social and political levels but also at the cultural level. The formation of the Taiwan Cultural Association (*Taiwan wen-hua hsieh-hui*) in 1921 aimed to lay a broad cultural foundation for the political movement. It accounted largely for the emergence of Taiwanese New Literature, New Drama and New Art in the 1930s. Today, it is generally agreed among Taiwanese scholars that a certain Taiwanese consciousness began to take shape during this period. However, with the outbreak of the Sino-Japanese War in 1937, the Japanese repressed all these movements in order to stabilize Taiwan as one of its bases for its so-called Holy War. Although most leaders of the movements continued their fight after fleeing to Japan, Hong Kong and the mainland, the movement in Taiwan itself was crippled.

1945 – 47

When the KMT's troops first arrived in Taiwan in 1945, the local population welcomed them warmly. As most of them retained strong links with the mainland and still identified with Chinese culture, the prospect of ending Japanese colonial rule and returning to the motherland raised high social expectations and enthusiasm. However, disappointment and disillusion soon replaced the initial optimism. The expectation that Taiwanese could now share power with their 'mainland brothers' was crushed by the KMT. Assuming the role of victor and occupier, the KMT exercised its rule with repression and corruption. Politically and culturally, Taiwanese were discriminated against. Ch'en-i, the Governor of Taiwan appointed by Chiang Kai-shek, pursued more authoritarian policies than the Japanese colonial governor had. The language policy banned the use of Japanese and enforced Mandarin in all educational and cultural activities. The majority of government posts were allocated to Mainlanders, regardless of their professional capacities. Economically, large quantities of raw materials were transported to the mainland where the KMT and the CCP were still at war. Within a year of the KMT's taking over, inflation disrupted the economy, and famine occurred in Taiwan, which had been previously unheard of. The disillusionment felt by the Taiwanese was best illustrated by a popular saying at the time: 'the dogs (the Japanese) go but the pigs (the KMT) come'. Many Taiwanese considered the KMT's rule to be much worse than that of the Japanese.[8]

Consequently, antagonism grew along an ethnic line separating the Mainlanders and the Taiwanese. The terms '*pen-sheng-jen*', meaning 'local people of this province', and '*wai-sheng-jen*', 'peoples from the outside provinces', were used to label the Taiwanese and the Mainlanders respectively. This ethnic cleavage, reinforced by political, economic and linguistic injustice, cut so deep that it led to the confrontation between the KMT government and various sectors of the population just one-and-a-half years after the KMT took control of Taiwan.

On 28 February 1947, a small incident triggered off the island-wide anti-KMT and pro-home rule movement. As a result, the whole of Taiwan Island was organized into two camps: the right-wing camp, comprising many local-oriented organizations, sought a high degree autonomy for the Taiwanese through institutional reforms, whereas the left-wingers, the 'People's Alliance', led by the Taiwanese Communist Party, favoured an armed uprising and joined the voluntarily organized armed force, the so-called 'February 28 Troops'. Both camps set autonomy, not independence, as their goal, and this is illustrated by the 'Forty-two Demands of the Taiwanese' put forward in March 1947 by the Committee to Resolve the February 28 Incident. The Demands were announced to Taiwan, the KMT's Nanjing government and the international communities in Mandarin, Hoklo, Hakka, English and Japanese. The Committee hoped to negotiate with the KMT's Nanjing government on terms of reform that would grant Taiwan the status of an autonomous region within the ROC. The KMT government, however, had no intention of negotiating. Instead, they opted for military repression. After the crackdown on the February 28th Movement, the KMT imposed martial law, which was to last for 38 years. The élite in the Movement who fled from Taiwan gave up the idea of autonomy and resorted to a struggle for independence for Taiwan.

From 1948 to the Present

In 1949, after the total retreat to Taiwan by the ROC government and the remaining KMT troops, Chiang Kai-shek turned Taiwan into a military base with a view to taking over the mainland. Taipei became the temporary capital of the ROC while the whole of Taiwan remained a province, with Tai-chung city as its provincial capital. The KMT's adherence to the 'one China' policy and its claim to be the only legitimate government of China contradicted the reality that the ROC presided only over Taiwan. Several measures were taken to legitimize the KMT's version of Chinese nationalism and its claim to both the mainland and Taiwan. First, the Mainlanders arriving in Taiwan during and after the second world war were obliged to maintain their original provincial classification when registering officially. Such a measure helped to create the illusion that there were still different constituencies from all parts of China under the KMT government. Second, the constitutional constraints on presidential power were suspended, with the addition of a number of emergency measures, which were justified on the basis of the Chinese nationalist revolution. This allowed Chiang to impose martial law on Taiwan by emergency decree. Under the office of the president, Taiwan was transformed into a police state where the military penetrated civilian life at all levels. The organization of opposition parties was prohibited and there was no freedom of press or speech. Third, as only elections in mainland constituencies could express the will of the Chinese nation, the representatives elected on the other side of the Taiwan Strait in 1947 and 1948 would remain in office until unification could take place.[9] Fourth, the use of Mandarin (the official language in China) was imposed as the language of education and instruction. Mandarin was identified with love for one's country, while the use of dialects within school grounds was prohibited. Fifth, education and academic research were geared towards strengthening the KMT's version of Chinese nationalism. Under such circumstances, the practice of Communism and the propagation of the ideas of Taiwan independence were classified among the most serious crimes. Owing to the tight control in Taiwan, the TIM began as an underground movement and was, most importantly, carried on overseas.

The Alliance for the Re-liberation of Taiwan under the leadership of Thomas Liao was formed in Hong Kong in September 1947.[10] On 1 September 1948, Liao sent a petition to the UN appealing for Taiwan to be put under the temporary trusteeship of the UN, and for the natives of Taiwan to be allowed to decide by referendum either to revert to China or to become independent. In February 1956, a 'provisional government of the Republic of Taiwan' was established in Tokyo, with Liao as provisional president of Taiwan. At the same time, large numbers of Taiwanese students studying abroad engaged actively in the independence movement. The Young Formosan Association, founded in Japan on 28 February 1960, and the Committee for Formosans' Free Formosa, established in the US in January 1956, were examples of such student organizations. They sought to promote the idea of independence for Taiwan on an international platform through various means, such as journals, demonstrations and seminars. In 1970, the majority of these organizations united under the banner of the World United Formosans for Independence (WUFI), with their headquarters in New York.[11] The WUFI had a worldwide range with an underground Taiwan branch in Taipei, an American branch in Los Angeles, a Japanese branch in Tokyo, a European branch in Paris, and a South American branch in São Paulo.

Meanwhile, in Taiwan, although an organized independence movement became impossible thanks to the strict controls, a number of intellectuals continued an individual struggle for independence despite the threat of imprisonment and the death penalty. The strong moral revolt expressed by their resistance was very much in line with what was being done at the same time by dissidents under other authoritarian regimes, for instance, in Eastern Europe. A case in point was in 1964 when, together with two students, Dr P'eng Ming-min, director of the political science department of the National Taiwan University, drafted the 'Declaration of Formosan Self-Salvation'. Before they could distribute the print-outs of the declaration, they were arrested.[12]

In the 1970s, with the loss of the UN seat to the PRC in 1971 and the normalization of Sino-American relations, the ROC became increasingly isolated on the international scene. Moreover, the economic boom in Taiwan, together with the impact of the third, worldwide wave of democratization during this period, awakened the democratic consciousness of the Taiwanese people. The activists for democracy formed an alliance with the secessionists against the

KMT and its authoritarian regime. Setting aside ethnic differences, prominent activists and scholars combined their efforts in the organization *Tang-wai* (meaning 'outside the party'), to promote democratization in Taiwan.

In response to the changing external and internal factors, under Chiang Ching-kuo, son of Chiang Kai-shek, the KMT shifted the focus of its policy from a military take-over of the mainland to domestic economic development. In the government, the process of Taiwanization was initiated.[13] In the increasingly pluralistic Taiwan society, discussion touching on the core of the Taiwan problem – namely, Taiwanese identity and the independence of Taiwan – became increasingly publicized. The KMT progressively evolved into a more tolerant party. In 1986, in defiance of the KMT's ban on opposition parties, members of *Tang-wai* formed the Democratic Progressive Party (DPP). A few months later the KMT government responded to this transformation of public consciousness by lifting the 38-year-old martial law and the ban on opposition parties and a free press. Thus began the transformation of Taiwan from authoritarian rule to a democratic society.

Moving from the underground out into the open, from overseas to Taiwan, from the illegal to the legal, the TIM entered a new phase. In the ensuing decade, independence organizations spread throughout Taiwan.[14] The means used by political parties and populist organizations to promote the idea of independence included all forms of media, such as radio, television, newspapers, journals and the internet, and other legal activities such as mass rallies, demonstrations and election campaigns. In the closing years of the twentieth century, the DPP gained increasing popular support and developed into a genuine opposition party.[15] In March 2000, its candidate Ch'en Shui-pian won the presidential elections. The DPP did not, however, manage to gather majority support in the parliament at that time. Only a minority of the electorate has been convinced by its national programme.

The Role of Intellectuals in the TIM

Throughout the history of the TIM, the intellectuals of Taiwan have always played the key role. They have been the initiators and advocates of the ideas on independence, the explorers of the theories, and organizers, leaders and participants in the actual movement throughout the whole life of the TIM. As we mentioned earlier, the TIM is a political movement that developed alongside the construction of Taiwan nationalism. Nationalism as a political movement has been noted by many students of political science as emerging first in the minds of the intellectual and political élite, and then spread by them to the population at large. It is the élite's drive to create a nation that gives rise to a broader, popular sense of nationhood. A few concrete cases can be cited here to illustrate the important role played by intellectuals throughout the development of the TIM.

One clear example of the active involvement of intellectuals in the TIM is the Association of Taiwan University Professors, founded in 1990 with the promotion of independence for Taiwan as its primary mission, alongside other aims, such as the promotion of Taiwanese culture. Members of the association, i.e., university professors, were ardent supporters of the DPP. And later, when some of them considered that the DPP was putting political gains above the commitment to independence, they withdrew their support and helped to found another political party, the Taiwan Independence Party (*chien-kuo-tang*), in 1996.[16] The intellectuals participating in the TIM are not necessarily of Taiwanese origin, and many have undergone a transformation from having a Chinese identity to a Taiwanese one, as revealed in a case-study conducted by Lee Hsiao-feng.[17] The experience of the historian, Ch'en Fang-ming, is a case in point: he shifted from being a 'Chinese on Taiwan' with a strong Chinese identity to a 'Taiwanese on Taiwan' promoting the idea of independence. In 1999, he was the Minister for Culture and Propaganda in the shadow government of the DPP, and he pursued the study of Taiwan's history in order to strengthen the ideological basis of the TIM.

For a better understanding of the role of intellectuals in the TIM, an examination of their ideas and theories would be illuminating. Hence, in the following section, an analytical synthesis of the pro-independence discourse will be made.

The Pro-Independence Discourse

One feature of the TIM's pro-independence discourse is its extensiveness – it covers a wide range of disciplines and topics. Apart from history, which is a discipline commonly employed in almost all secessionist movements, political science, ethnic studies, anthropology and international law are of special importance in the discourse of the TIM. To a lesser extent, economics is also used to support the idea of independence. A state in the contemporary world comprises several elements: a defined territory, a permanent population, an effective government and the capacity to enter into relations with other states. The choice of the above-mentioned disciplines is an effort to demonstrate that Taiwan has in effect met almost all the criteria for being a state except one, namely, international recognition. In the following section we shall try to group the pro-independence arguments given by the TIM scholars under several disciplines, while bearing in mind that in reality these arguments usually overlap. We will not analyse the truthfulness of these arguments or describe the discussions with scholars who defend the positions of the KMT or the Chinese Communist Party. The aim of the following section is to see how TIM scholars make use of various academic disciplines to advance their political goals.

From the Perspective of History

Both the KMT and the CCP base themselves extensively on historical research when making their claims to sovereignty over Taiwan. Their enquiries into the historical links between the two sides across the Strait – links such as cultural, trade and administrative ones – presuppose 'the truth of the claim that these links somehow become political and binding down the generations'.[18] Hence the argument that 'Taiwan is part of China'. The TIM intellectuals reject the validity of turning historical links into some kind of political principle. As the Taiwanese writer Lee Ao puts it, why should claims to Taiwan based on the historical record be any more valid than the claim of, say, modern Turkey to the lands that once formed the Ottoman Empire?[19]

TIM scholars state that, although historically Taiwan was a part of China during the Qing dynasty, the Qing court was of a different political order, and so at that time China was not a modern nation-state. The Chinese state in the modern sense was not in place until the foundation of the ROC in 1911. In their view, it would consequently not make sense to draw the borderline for the new state on the basis of the historical boundaries of the Chinese Empire. While acknowledging the fact that there are tenuous links between Taiwan and the mainland, TIM scholars are stating that Taiwan has not been 'an inalienable part of China since ancient times'. Citing from historical records, they point to the fact that, before 1684, Taiwan Island had always been regarded by the Qing court as a land of barbarians, and it was only after 1684 that Taiwan was annexed to the Chinese Empire.[20] More importantly, they argue that the Shimonoseki Treaty signed in 1895, according to which Taiwan was to be ceded to Japan in perpetuity, was a legally binding document.

As the TIM scholars see it, the importance of Taiwan in the construction of the KMT's Chinese nationalism changed over time with the changing international environment. Although the cession of Taiwan to Japan in 1895 had served as one of the many sparks that triggered off the quest for Chinese nationalism, Taiwan was not an issue for Chinese nation-building at the time. Between 1911 and 1941, the KMT was virtually silent on the subject of claims to sovereignty over Taiwan. TIM activists have stated that in the draft constitutions of the ROC in 1925, 1934 and 1936, Taiwan did not appear as a province in the new republic. Instead, among the lost territories listed in the Three Principles of the People, it is indicated that, although Taiwan initially played a symbolic role as a 'lost territory' of the Qing order, this did not necessarily imply that the sovereignty of the Chinese nation should be asserted over it.[21]

The claim to Taiwan by the KMT, according to TIM scholars, was only made after the American entry into World War Two when Chiang used his position within the Allied camp to make demands concerning Taiwan. After the war, with the CCP and the KMT each joining different camps in the Cold War, the CCP likewise claimed sovereignty over Taiwan in order to justify its anti-imperialist nationalism. In writing the biography of Hsieh Hsüeh-hung, the leader of the Taiwanese Communist Party, historian Ch'en Fang-ming opposes the claim made by the CCP that the anti-Japanese movement led by the Taiwanese Communist Party in the late 1920s was a movement of its sub-branch. The subordination of the Taiwanese communist movement to the CCP is, in his view, a distortion of historical fact. As he sees it, the advocacy of 'Taiwanese Independence' and the 'principle of self-determination' by the Taiwanese Communist Party had drawn a clear line separating the anti-Japanese movement in Taiwan from that on the mainland.[22] The TIM scholars generally agree that the incorporation of Taiwan into either the nationalist or the communist version of Chinese nationalism is the result of the Cold War. Taiwan, they argue, has been a victim of the interplay of the super-powers in the Cold War.

Apart from the above-mentioned arguments, historians and educators supporting the TIM have, since the 1980s, called for a reorientation in both research and education on history. They strongly criticize the ignorance of Taiwan's history in both scientific research and the educational system arising from the KMT's assimilation policy. With the democratization of Taiwan, historical research institutes, organized on a popular basis, have mushroomed in the last two decades.[23] The educational curriculum is also undergoing adjustments. These changes, in the view of educators and historians who support the TIM, are indispensable for the formation of a Taiwanese nation.

From the Perspective of International Law

Both the PRC and the ROC argue that they legally recovered their rightful territory from Japan at the end of the second world war. Several documents are put forward as evidence to support these claims. First, the Cairo Declaration of 1 December 1943 demanded that Japan should return Taiwan and the Pescadores (Penghu) Islands to the ROC. Second, the Potsdam Proclamation of July 1945 reiterated the demand set forth in the Cairo Declaration. Third, on 2 September 1945 Japan signed the document of surrender, stating its acceptance of the Potsdam Proclamation. Fourth, according to the highest command from the Allied headquarters on 15 October 1945, the Japanese army was to surrender and to relinquish sovereignty over Taiwan and return it to China.[24] In response to these above-mentioned arguments from the other parties, TIM scholars have questioned their validity by making extensive use of the discipline of international law. Their arguments have three focal points.[25]

First, it is argued that neither the Cairo Declaration nor the Potsdam Proclamation is an international treaty. According to some TIM scholars, they are nothing more than a non-self-executing statement of intention. As the 'third party', Japan was not present at the signing of either. Since Taiwan was then legally Japanese territory, no legal document concerning a change of sovereignty over Taiwan could be legally valid without the consent of Japan. Hence, neither declaration had – in the view of those international lawyers who support the TIM – any legally binding force as far as the settlement of the dispute over Taiwan was concerned. They could not serve as a justification for the claim to sovereignty by the ROC or the PRC. In their view, the only legally valid document concerning the status of Taiwan is the San Francisco Peace Treaty, signed later, in September 1951, between 48 Allied countries and Japan. The second article of this treaty states that Japan gave up all its sovereignty and territorial claims with regard to Taiwan – it does not specifically provide that sovereignty over Taiwan should be restored to China. This article, they say, therefore cannot be interpreted as lending support to either the PRC or the ROC's claim over Taiwan. When signing the Sino-Japan peace treaties with the ROC and the PRC, in 1952 and 1978 respectively, Japan merely reiterated its disclaimer of sovereignty over Taiwan. Regarding the PRC's claim to sovereignty over Taiwan, the Japanese official position is that it 'understands and respects' such a claim.[26] The word 'recognize' is not used. TIM scholars interpret this as meaning that the Japanese government does not recognize the PRC's sovereignty claim over Taiwan.

According to TIM scholars, it therefore follows that no international treaty has ever granted either the ROC or the PRC sovereignty over Taiwan. Taiwan at the end of the second world war, consequently, should be regarded as 'undetermined territory', and the dispute over sovereignty should be left to be settled by the local population, in accordance with the principle of self-determination. It was very much thanks to this understanding that, in the 1950s, the idea of placing Taiwan under the UN's temporary trusteeship was quite popular in the TIM.

Secondly, at the same time as these authors oppose the legal claim to sovereignty of Taiwan by the KMT, they nevertheless acknowledge that the ROC government has in fact been exercising its jurisdiction over Taiwan for more than 50 years. According to the principle of *uti possidetis* (as you possess, you shall continue to possess) in international law, the ROC government has in their view acquired de facto sovereignty over Taiwan. But these pro-TIM scholars go on to argue that, despite this, the KMT government has been exercising oppressive authoritarian rule in Taiwan, which de-legitimizes its rule. Furthermore, the KMT's adherence to the 'one China' policy up to the early 1990s, and to the name 'Republic of China', have resulted in the isolation of Taiwan on the international scene. As the PRC has been internationally recognized as the only China, the ROC has lost its entitlement to claim sovereignty over the whole of China.

Thirdly, some Taiwanese scholars from the discipline of international law use the distinction between 'government succession' and 'state succession' in international law in an attempt to refute the PRC's claim to sovereignty over Taiwan.[27] By 'government succession' is meant that, when a new government replaces the old one by means of constitutional change or through revolution, the integrity and continuity of the sovereignty and jurisdiction of the state remain unchanged. In principle, the new government succeeds to all the rights and responsibilities of the previous government. State succession arises when there is a definitive replacement of one state by another over a given territory. It is important to note that the phrase 'state succession' does not connote any principle of presumption that after the change of sovereignty, a transmission or succession of legal rights and duties occurs. The rights and responsibilities of the new state should coincide with its present jurisdiction. Having made such a distinction, the authors observe that, as it withdrew to Taiwan, the KMT government has never been fully overthrown by the new Beijing government. In their view, the Beijing government has emphasized time and again that the PRC is a new state with regard to its international relations and has taken on the international obligations and engagement of the KMT government on a selective basis. Consequently, the TIM scholars argue that the Beijing government – as a new government of a new state, the PRC, and not a new government of the ROC – cannot claim to be the successor of the KMT government. Thus, the exercise of its sovereignty should coincide with its present-day jurisdiction. TIM scholars have argued that – since the Beijing government of the new state, the PRC, has never ruled Taiwan – the claim of the PRC to exercise sovereignty over Taiwan is not in accordance with international law (even though the world community of states defends the PRC's 'one China' position on this matter).[28]

From the Perspective of Anthropological and Ethnic Studies

The pro-independence discourse focuses a good deal on the notion of Taiwan nationalism. The use of 'Taiwan nationalism' in place of 'Taiwanese nationalism' in this text is deliberate. As in the (sub-) ethnic differentiation in Taiwan, 'Taiwanese' is used as a label for the first group of immigrants from the mainland in the sixteenth and seventeenth centuries, in contrast to the 'Mainlanders', which refers to the second group, who arrived between 1945 and 1949. The discussion on Taiwan nationalism has gone through a radical transformation concerning the understanding by Taiwan nationalists of what constitutes a Taiwan nation. Prior to the 1960s, the discussion of Taiwan nationalism ran mainly along the lines of ethnic/racial division. Thus, only the Taiwanese (those who immigrated to Taiwan before the second world war) constituted the Taiwan nation, whereas the Mainlanders (those who immigrated to Taiwan from 1945 to 1949) were excluded. Since the 1960s, there has been a major breakthrough in the discussion of Taiwan nationalism within academic circles. By discarding nationalism on an ethnic/racial basis, the Taiwan nation as a political and civic community became the bearer of Taiwan nationalism. In the process of transforming the content of Taiwan nationalism, political theory played a decisive role. The renewed version of Taiwan nationalism will be discussed in the next section. In this section, we shall try to look at the earlier notion.

One possible explanation as to why the earlier TIM scholars defined Taiwan nationalism on an ethnic/racial basis lies in the semantic confusion caused by terms such as 'ethnic group', 'nation', 'nationalism' and 'minority group' in Chinese.[29] Nation and nationalism were both relatively new notions from the West. When introduced into China at the beginning of this century, 'nation' was translated as '*minzu*', exactly the same word as for 'ethnic group', and 'nationalism' was '*minzu zhuyi*'.[30]

Using some of the findings of anthropological and archaeological studies on Taiwan, TIM scholars state that, before the arrival of the Dutch in 1624, Taiwan was an aboriginal society. The original inhabitants of Taiwan were of Malay-Polynesian origin. From the angle of ethnolinguistics and physical anthropology, TIM scholars argue that the original inhabitants of Taiwan could not have originated from South China, as stated by the PRC.[31] However, simply trying to prove the non-Chineseness of the original inhabitants of Taiwan is not enough, since the majority of the Taiwan population have been immigrants arriving from Mainland China over the centuries. To demonstrate that the modern Taiwanese are different from the Han Chinese, some TIM scholars have gone one step further, arguing from an evolutionary perspective. As the earlier pioneering immigrants from the mainland were largely male, they argued that the multiplication of the population in Taiwan was largely due to intermarriage between the male pioneers and the female aborigines. Thus emerged a new ethnic group of mixed blood. Given their frontier origin and their common experience, the members of this ethnic group – so the theory goes – developed their own social consciousness as Taiwanese. In his work *Taiwan Nationalism* (*Taiwan minben zhuyi*), Liao, the early leader of post-war TIM, maintained that 'today's Taiwanese have their inheritance from the Indonesian, Portuguese, Spaniards, Dutch, Fujianese, Cantonese and Japanese; in other words, Taiwanese blood is a mixture of the Aboriginal, Han Chinese, Japanese, Latin and Teutonic races'.[32]

Another prominent TIM scholar and political leader, Shih Ming, also insisted on the mixed ethnic origin of the Taiwan nation. In his early publication in 1968, *Taiwan Nation – Its Formation and Evolution*, he stated: 'The main members of our Taiwanese society are the descendants of the Han pioneers who first coexisted with the aborigines and later assimilated them. Throughout the four-hundred-year historical experience (...) a single and inherent community, the Taiwan nation, has come into being on the basis of its distinct natural environment and common destiny (...) a nation completely different from the Chinese.'[33] However, neither Liao's 'mixed-blood Taiwan nation' nor Shih Ming's ethnic theory found much popular support in Taiwan society. Other TIM scholars further challenged their views. Then the discussion of Taiwan nationalism took a new turn with the involvement of political scientists.

From the Perspective of Political Science

Not convinced by the attempts to base Taiwan nationalism on race or ethnic differentiation, some TIM scholars started to clarify the concept of nationalism in the 1960s. Among them, P'eng Ming-min's contribution is significant. Much influenced by Ernest Renan's *Qu'est-ce qu'une Nation,* he enquires what elements constitute the foundations of the modern nation-state. He comes to the conclusion that its most vital component is not an objective element such as biological origin, culture, religion, or language, but 'a sense of common destiny and belief in shared interests'. 'These subjective feelings', he argues, 'which rise out of a common history, are not necessarily related to the objective criteria of biology, religion, and language'.[34] The modern nation-state is first and foremost a political community. Thus national identity, or nationalism, is a political identity based on freedom of political association, rather than on the objective criteria of an ethnic community.

The implications of P'eng's idea about nationhood are far-reaching. In essence, the discussion of Taiwan nationalism changes from its previous focus on ethnicity to a more civic version. That is to say, a nation in the modern sense is a free political association based not merely on objective criteria such as ethnic distinctiveness, language and cultural heritage, but more on the subjective affiliation of a certain group or groups of people. TIM scholars argue that it is because a nation is a political association, not an ethnic group, that some modern states have been able to come into being, despite their ethnic heterogeneity, or that several states can grow out of one homogeneous ethnic group.[35] This argument rejects the use of historical links by the KMT and the CCP as a justification for their claims on Taiwan. It further affirms the right to self-determination and to free political association as the justification for Taiwan independence. Some TIM activists draw a parallel between the TIM and American independence. They argue that the fight for Taiwan independence is for the pursuit of liberty, which, they say, is inherently democratic in nature. Moreover, criticizing the authoritarian nature of the KMT and CCP regimes, they perceive the TIM as making a major contribution to the promotion of democracy and humanitarian values in the world.

The academic discussion and reflection on the Taiwan nation helped lead to a shift in the perception of their nation by the Taiwan political movement. In the mid 1970s, the TIM began to promote a new notion of the Taiwan nation according to which 'no matter where you were born, or when you arrived in Taiwan, as long as you identify yourself with Taiwan, you are a member of the Taiwan nation'.[36] This understanding is labelled 'non-differential identity' (*wucabie rentonglun*). The importance of 'non-differential identity' is that it is no longer exclusive, that it aims to overcome the sub-ethnic divisions in Taiwan society by rallying both Taiwanese and Mainlanders.

Conclusions and Avenues for Further Research

Reconsidering the history of Taiwan, one cannot help but be struck by the complexity of the historical, social and political environment in which the TIM has evolved. In striving for an independent State of Taiwan, the independence-seekers have to justify their position against the claims to sovereignty over Taiwan made by both the ROC and the PRC. Like other nationalist movements in the world, intellectuals with nationalist aspirations are involved in the process of nation-building and state-building. The pro-independence intellectuals, as shown in this chapter, are involved in the TIM not only through their actual political participation but, more importantly, through their reflection on notions such as 'the Taiwan nation' and 'Taiwan nationalism'. Various disciplines in social science have been present in the nationalist discourse, namely, history, ethnic studies, international law and political science. The present chapter has shown the arguments put forward from different academic perspectives in support of the course of independence. It should be pointed out here that this analysis aims merely to present the arguments in the nationalist discourse – in order to facilitate their comparison with other secessionist movements in the conclusions to this volume – rather than to discuss their truthfulness. No normative assessment has been made, nor have the scientific counter-arguments from the PRC side been examined.

One particularity in the evolving nationalist discourse is the changing concept of the Taiwan nation. Among intellectuals, a shift in their understanding of their nation has occurred. The Taiwan nation, which was previously defined as primarily an ethnically (racially) based community, is now increasingly perceived by most TIM intellectuals to be first and foremost a political community based on voluntary self-identification by the individual. Recent studies on Taiwan nationalism also point to such a shift in the national identity and suggest the emergence of a civic nationalism in Taiwan.[37] Notwithstanding the more inclusive understanding of nationalism, TIM intellectuals and activists largely disagree about whether or not the Taiwan nation is already in place. As shown by opinion polls on national identity, the percentage of the population identifying themselves as Chinese still exceeds that of those who identify themselves as Taiwanese.[38] Political developments in Taiwan in recent years have demonstrated that the KMT has also been receptive to the changing content of the idea of a Taiwan nation as promoted by the TIM. Notions such as 'living community on Taiwan' and 'new Taiwanese' appear frequently in its discourse and were even part of the political thinking of the previous President, Lee Teng-hui.

The redefined Taiwan nationalism in the minds of intellectuals and politicians does not necessarily mean, however, that a similar shift has taken place in the national identity of the population at large. As Eric Hobsbawm states in *Nations and Nationalism since 1780*, 'national identification and what it is believed to imply, can change and shift in time, even in the course of quite short periods. In my judgement this is the area of national studies in which thinking and research are most urgently needed today'.[39] The case of Taiwan, where such a shift in national identity is currently taking place, thus offers scholars an opportunity to study such a transition. Further studies of this new national identity in Taiwan should address a number of issues. On the one hand, for political development on Taiwan itself, one should ask whether the newly forged civic national identity will help consolidate democratization on Taiwan, and whether it will reduce the ongoing friction between the sub-ethnic groups. On the other hand, for cross-strait relations, one should ask what the implications of this development in Taiwan nationalism are likely to be.

Notes

1   Note on romanization: Throughout the text, pinyin is used for names, places and organizations in the PRC, and the titles in all Chinese references. However, Wade-Giles romanization is used for the names of individuals and organizations in Taiwan, for example with Chiang Kaishek, Kuo-ming-tang, which should be Jiang Jieshi and Guomingdang in pinyin.

2   Ralph R. Premdas, 'Secessionist Movements in Comparative Perspective', in Ralph R. Premdas, S. W. R. de Samarasinghe and Alan B. Anderson (eds), *Secessionist Movements in Comparative Perspective*, London, Pinter Publishers Ltd, 1990, pp. 12-29.

3   *Ibid.* pp. 21-25.

4   *Ibid.* p. 13.

5   A vast amount of research has been carried out in recent years to discover the origin of the Aborigines of Taiwan. From the linguistic point of view, the Aboriginal language in Taiwan is closely related to Malay and Bahasa. From an anthropological viewpoint, the Aborigines of Taiwan have many affinities with the islanders in the South Pacific Ocean in terms of culture, physical make-up and the organizational form of society. In the latest contribution to research on the origin of the Aborigines of Taiwan, the results of DNA tests suggest that Maoris (natives of New Zealand) may have come from Taiwan or may be related to the Aborigines of Taiwan in some way (Source: *South China Morning Post*, August 11, 1998). I am grateful to John F. Copper for providing this information.

6 The common use of 'dialect' is adopted here. However, as in the minds of many people the term tends to denote a subordinate form of a dominant language with only some variations in pronunciation and vocabulary, we would like to point out that here 'dialect' can be used as an equivalent of 'language'. In fact, the question whether a dialect is a limited deviation of a dominant language or should be considered a language in itself is the subject of heated debate even among linguists. Furthermore, in Taiwan some socio-linguists argue that Hoklo, Hakka and Mandarin are 'three branches off the main trunk of the Chinese language'. (For a more detailed study on the relationship between the ethnic groups and their dialects in Taiwan, see Shih Cheng-feng, 'Ethnic Differentiation in Taiwan', *Journal of Law and Political Science (Taiwan)*, No. 3, 1995, pp. 141-166).

7 The republic actually existed for only 10 days, while the resistance movement which attempted to revive it lasted for more than four months. The proclamation of the Democratic Republic of Taiwan – which was a very important event in democratization in Asia, as this was the first republic to be established there – basically sought to fend off Japanese occupation. The desire to remain Chinese – Qing – is clearly discernible from the title of the reign – *yongqing*, meaning Qing forever.

8 See Ch'en Yung-hsing (ed.), *228 xueshu yiantaohui lunwenji, 1991 (Proceedings of the 1991 Conference on the February 28 Incident)*, Taipei, Tsu-li Evening Post Press, 1992.

9 In accordance with this measure, those representatives elected to the National Assembly and the Legislative Yuan (Congress) in 1947 and 1948 who had retreated to Taiwan with the KMT government were given life-long service. Strict rules were later introduced on filling the vacant seats when some of the representatives died. In 1949, the overall representation of the Taiwanese population in the National Assembly was a mere three per cent. The National Assembly and the Legislative Yuan were called ironically by the Taiwanese the 'Thousand-year-long Parliament'. It was not until 1992 that some representatives were forced into retirement and new elections to the Legislative Yuan became possible.

10 Liao was a doctor of engineering, obtaining his PhD from Ohio University in the US.

11 These organizations include the Young Formosans' Free Formosa (Japan, 1950s), the United Formosans in America for Independence (the US, 1966), the United Free Formosa (Taiwan, 1964), the United Formosans for Independence in Europe (Europe, 1967) and the Canadian Committee Supporting Formosan Human Rights (Canada, 1964).

12 In Canada, P'eng obtained his PhD in international aviation law. Because he was internationally known in his field, the KMT sentenced him to eight years' imprisonment, which was quite light under the circumstances. Later, in response to mounting international pressure, his sentence was changed to house arrest. P'eng managed to flee abroad and sought political asylum in the US, continuing his opposition activities as the senior supervisor of the WUFI.

13 Taiwanization means the appointment to government of people from sub-ethnic groups other than the Mainlanders. As a result, by the late 1980s, 70% of the KMT membership of 2.4 million was Taiwanese, and by 1993 the very highest posts in the government were filled by Taiwanese, including that of president (Lee Teng-hui), premier (Lien Tsan), and president of the Judicial Yuan (Congress) (Lin Yang-kung).

14 Besides the DPP, another political party, the Taiwan Independence Party (Chien-kuo-tang), which made the establishment of an independent Taiwan State its political priority, came into being in 1996. Civil-society groups promoting independence abound. Apart from the WUFI, the more recent influential pro-independence organizations include the Taiwan Association of University Professors (founded in December 1990) and the Mainlanders' Association for Taiwan Independence (founded in August 1995).

[15] In early 1993, the DPP claimed more than 35,000 members. In the 1992 election to the national Legislative Yuan, the DPP won one-third of the seats. In the 1994 election for the mayoralty of Taipei, the DPP candidate, Ch'en Shui-pian, defeated his KMT rival and became mayor. The landslide victory of the DPP in the 1997 elections for mayor and magistrates (with DPP candidates winning 12 seats out of the total of 20) was a landmark confirming its popularity.

[16] The DPP was divided between those in the *Hsin-ch'ao-liu* (New Trend), who were eager to promote Taiwan's independence, and those in the *Mei-li-tao* (Formosa) faction, for whom democratization was a more urgent objective. And in the 1996 presidential election campaign the Formosa faction gained the upper hand in the party, leading to the DPP's 'grand reconciliation' strategy in the campaign. The pro-independence faction consequently broke apart to form the Taiwan Independence Party (*chien-kuo-tang*). Since then, the DPP's relationship with the KMT has gradually evolved from the stage of 'loyal opposition' into a phase of 'both competition and co-operation'.

[17] Lee Hsiao-feng (1994), 'guojia rentong de zhuanxiang – yi zanhao Taiwan fanduirenshi de shige gean wei li' (the Change in National Identity – Case-Studies on Ten Opposition Persons in Post-war Taiwan), in *Retong yu guojia: jindai zhongxi lishi bijiao (Identities and National Formation: Chinese and Western Experiences in the Modern World)* , Institute of Modern History (ed.), Sinica, Taipei, Jiuyu Printing Ltd, 1994, pp. 323-362.

[18] Christopher Hughes, *Taiwan and Chinese Nationalism: National Identity and Status in International Society*, New York/London, Routledge, 1997, p. 1.

[19] *Ibid.* pp. 1-2.

[20] For example, in one of the many on-line publications by TIM supporters, Yung-Cheng, Emperor of the Qing dynasty, was quoted as saying 'Taiwan, from time immemorial, was not a part of China. My mighty father reached beyond, conquered and annexed it to Ding's territory.' http://www.wufi.org.forum.

[21] The other lost territories listed in the Three Principles of the People include Korea, Vietnam, Burma, the Ili basin, Bhutan and Nepal (Hughes, *op. cit.*, p. 5).

[22] Ch'en Fang-ming, *Tansuo Taiwan shiguan (Exploring the History of Taiwan)*, Taipei, Tsu-li Evening Post Press, 1992, pp. 26-43 and pp. 241-260.

[23] One example is the non-governmental Research Group on the 2-28 Event (2-28 minjian yanjiu xiaozhu). Together with other civil societies, this research group has effectively organized different social and academic activities to uncover the causes, effects and future implications of the event.

[24] State Council Taiwan Affairs Office, *Zhongguo Taiwan wenti (The Taiwan Problem in China)*, Beijing, Jiuzou Publishing House, 1998, pp. 52-57.

[25] Hsü Ch'ing-hsiong, *Taiwan de guojia dingwei (Defining the Status of Taiwan)*, Taipei, Ts-ying Culture Publishing House, 1995; Chiu Hung-dah, 'The International Legal Status of Taiwan' in Jean-Marie Henckaerts (ed.), *The International Status of Taiwan in the New World Order*, London, Kluwer Law International Ltd, 1996; and Chiu Hung-dah, 'Comments on the White Paper on "The Principle of One China" (pingshu yige zhongguo baipishu)', *Journal Europe* (Paris), 24 February 2000.

[26] Hsü Ch'ing-hsiong, *Taiwan de guojia dingwei (Defining the Status of Taiwan)*, *op. cit.*, p. 42.

[27] Hsü Ch'ing-hsiong, 'Taiwan guojifa diwei zi tantao' (Exploring Taiwan's International legal Status*)*, paper presented to the conference *New Prospects for the Legal System in Taiwan (Taiwan fazhi xinzanwang)*, Taipei, 1996, http://www.wufi.org.tw.

[28] For a discussion on the international status of Taiwan, see also Henckaerts (ed.), *op. cit.*

29 The equivalent Chinese words for these terms are ethnic group – *minzu*, or *zuqun*; nation – *minzu*; nationalism – *minzu zhuyi*; minority group or national minority – *shaoshu minzu*. The term '*minzu*' in Chinese has a connotation of 'pertaining to race'.

30 To resolve this confusion, some TIM scholars have suggested using a phonetic translation for both 'nation' and 'nationalism', as is being done in Japanese.

31 On the basis of two anthropological discoveries in Tso-nan County, Taiwan, in 1971 and 1974, the mainland anthropological society generally holds the opinion that the origin of the Taiwanese Aborigines is closely associated with that of pre-historic humans on the mainland (State Council Taiwan Affairs Office, *op. cit.*, pp. 4-5).

32 Huang Shao-t'ang, 'Zanhou Taiwan duliyundong yu Taiwan minzuzhuyi de fazan' (The Postwar TIM and the Evolution of Taiwan Nationalism) in Shih Cheng-feng (ed.), *Taiwan minzuzhuyi (Taiwan Nationalism)*, Taipei, Avant-garde Publishing House, 1995, pp. 195-227. Quotation, p. 200. Author's translation.

33 *Ibid.* p. 209.

34 P'eng Ming-min, *A Taste Of Freedom: Memoirs of a Formosan Independence Leader*, New York, Holt, Rinehart & Winston Ltd, 1972, pp. 93-94.

35 P'eng Ming-min cited Belgium and Switzerland as examples of where peoples of different origin and background constitute a single state based on feelings of common interest. And the US, Canada, Australia and New Zealand are instances where they mainly share the Anglo-Saxon tradition of common blood, language and religion and, in large part, of laws, yet each exhibits a separate political constitution and forms a separate nation. (P'eng, *op. cit.*, pp. 93-94)

36 See the World United Formosans for Independence (WUFI) home page: http://www.wufi.org and Huang Shao-t'ang, *op. cit.*, pp. 214 -217.

37 See Gunter Schubert, 'A New Rising Nation? The Discourse on National Identity in Contemporary Taiwan', paper presented at the international conference on the 'Development of Contemporary Taiwan and its Implications for Cross-Strait Relations, the Asia-Pacific Region and Europe', Taipei, 1998 and Lin Chia-lung, 'Taiwan's Emerging Civic Nationalism: Origin and Implications', paper presented at the Fifth North America Taiwan Studies Conference, University of Wisconsin – Madison, June 1999.

38 According to an opinion poll in 1995, 35% of the population identify themselves as Chinese, 29% as Taiwanese and 27% as both Chinese and Taiwanese, while 6% are undecided (Dai Bao-chun, 5 June 1995, *Independence Morning Post*).

39 Eric J. Hobsbawm, *Nations and Nationalism Since 1780*, Cambridge, Cambridge University Press, 1990, p. 11.

Raphael Chijioke Njoku

10. An Endless Cycle of Secessionism. Intellectuals and Separatist Movements in Nigeria

'Man has dominated man to his injury.' – King Solomon.

In conceiving modern Nigeria, the British imperial enterprise underestimated the likely problems of merging peoples of diverse cultures into a common political unit.[1] With political independence, which became a reality on 1 October 1960, differences soon emerged as a serious obstacle to nation-building. In Nigeria, as in other African states, the first decade after independence saw the collapse of democracies, civil unrest, military coups and civil wars that left the blundering African élite helpless.

Secession has remained a source of serious concern in Nigeria's politics throughout its four decades of independence. From using threats of secession as an instrument in political negotiation, through several minority protest movements, to outright war, the inclination to construct national identities has remained pronounced throughout the country. This contribution aims to: (1) define the institutional setting for scientific research on issues linked to secession in Nigeria, which will help to clarify the conditions under which intellectuals are studying secession and the influence of these conditions on the overall issues linked to the subject; (2) examine the role of intellectuals and the social sciences within secessionist movements in the country; (3) identify the scientific subjects involved in secessionist polemics and review their exact contents.

Beforehand, an overview of the separatist incidents that have occurred in Nigeria since 1953 will be presented, as a background to understanding the evolutionary processes of nationalist consciousness among the country's estimated 250 ethnic groups. This chapter will concentrate mainly on issues connected with Biafra's secession (1967-70) and that of the Ogoni minority movement, which started in 1990 under the Movement for the Survival of the Ogoni People (MOSOP). The views of both Nigerian and foreign commentators on the national question will be analysed. Except where otherwise indicated, the views under discussion are those of Nigerian scholars.

Separatist Movements in Nigeria: An Overview

From independence onwards, Nigeria operated a three-region structure, as instituted by the colonial government. The regions (northern, western and eastern) guaranteed autonomy only for the three largest ethnic groups: the Hausa-Fulani in the north, the Yoruba in the west, and the Igbo in the east. While the Hausa-Fulani exerted substantial political control as the overall majority, the political and economic life of the nation revolved around the whims and caprices of the big three. This order soon saw the various regional minorities agitating for individual autonomy – a demand to which the three major groups were reluctant to accede. Towards the end of 1963, however, the minorities in western Nigeria were granted a separate (mid-western) region, which increased the number of regions to four.[2] This small concession was obviously not enough to quell increasing protests by minorities against majority domination. To make the situation worse, the large ethnic groups fought among themselves for control of the centre.

The challenge of Biafra (1967-70) marked the zenith of post-independence political brinkmanship in Nigeria. The horrifying passion that attended its thirty months of existence has today made the name 'Biafra' an anathema in the Nigerian geopolitical lexicon. Yet similar movements – albeit of lesser consequence – had preceded the Biafran one. In 1953, the northern region had threatened to secede, following a motion passed by delegates from the south proposing that Nigeria's independence should be granted in 1956. The problem was that the north was not yet ready to compete politically and economically with the south in an independent union. The proposal was then temporarily dropped so that the union could remain intact.[3] From this time onwards, secessionist threat as an instrument of political bargaining was a feature of Nigeria's political evolution.

In 1965, eastern Nigeria witnessed the first violent secessionist movement. Vexed by what was perceived as the federal government's unfair redistribution of oil resources, Isaac Boro declared the secession of his oil-rich Ijaw tribal group in the southeast. The rebellion, which failed to recruit mass support,[4] was suppressed by military action. Nevertheless, group protests continued without receiving due attention by the government until the eve of the civil war in 1967, when more autonomous entities, in the form of federating states, were constituted as a guard against multiple rebellions from aggrieved minority elements.[5]

The next serious threat to political stability came from the Yoruba tribal group, in the west. This conflict was sparked off by an attempt made by the ruling party, the Northern People's Congress (NPC) to break the strength of the opposition party, the Action Group (AG). The NPC was a predominantly northern party, while the AG belonged to the western region. The NPC showed little tolerance for its opponents in the 1964-65 elections. As a result, the western region became a battleground for power struggles. There were widespread riots characterized by the destruction of lives and property as the various parties engaged one another in bloody feuds. The situation was so serious that a state of emergency was declared in the region. Later, prominent Action Group leaders were arrested, tried and imprisoned on charges of treasonable felony. A couple of weeks later, on 15 January 1966, came the first military putsch to arrest 'this obvious break-down of law and order'[6] in the country.

Between one problem and another, in its manner of execution the January coup left the dangerous impression that its leaders – mainly from the Igbo ethnic group – were out to destroy the Republic's first government, led by the Hausa-Fulani, in order to pave the way for Igbo political ascendancy. This suspicion arose from the fact that while prominent politicians in the first Republic and top military officers of northern origin were killed during the coup, those from the east escaped unhurt.[7] Hausa-Fulani and Igbo differences worsened when the subsequent Igbo-led military government hurriedly adopted a unitary system of government, as opposed to the pre-existing federal structure. Soon, violent protests broke out in the north. For northerners, the facts pointed in one direction – Igbo-dominated government, economy, civil service, education, pro-government institutions and all the rest of it.[8]

As a step towards northern secession, a counter *coup d'état* was carried out by northern officers in July 1966. For a couple of months, mutinies against Igbo officers continued across the country. Some 30,000 civilian casualties were recorded.[9] The north designed a separate flag and composed a national anthem in a move to proclaim 'The Republic of the North'. Meanwhile, hostilities in the north were extended as well to other ethnic groups of eastern origin. An estimated one million refugees were driven back into the eastern region, bringing tales of their experiences in the north. Colonel Ojukwu, the eastern region's military governor, had to ask all non-easterners to leave since their safety could no longer be guaranteed following reported cases of revenge in that region.[10]

Later, taking account of two major economic considerations, northerners dropped their bid for secession. One, pursuing this goal would amount to denying themselves access to the strategic southern seas. Two, the region would be cut off from the promising new oil wealth in the southeast.[11] At this point, the new federal military government was confronted with the problem of restoring peace in the country. Usually, war starts in the hearts of men and ends there too. If this is accepted, it was evident that to avert the impending war would be a difficult task. Last-minute efforts to restore peace included an Ad Hoc Constitutional Review Conference in September 1966, during which the east insisted on the inclusion in the constitution of the right to secede. Then came the Aburi talks in January 1967 at the behest of Ghana's military leader, General Ankrah. While the Ad Hoc Committee failed to find a way forward, during the Aburi talks

Ojukwu brought others to accept the logic that all the regions first had to draw apart in a confederate framework in order to stay together.[12] This major but highly controversial agreement offered a brief ray of hope that the country might be saved from the impending disaster. Back in Lagos, the Aburi agreement was critically reviewed. Its full implementation would in effect have meant a sovereign Biafra and the end of the federation. However, the eastern region's leadership refused to accept any compromise. On 27 May 1967, the Nigerian government took a bold step in partitioning the country's four regions into 12 sub-states, in order to destabilize Biafra by fragmenting its cohesion.[13] The east was carved up into three sub-states. While the eastern minorities were granted their long-sought autonomy, Port Harcourt, a predominantly Igbo city, was left outside the Igbo state. To the Igbo, this act was tantamount to an open challenge to secede.[14]

At 2 a.m. on 30 May 1967, the birth of Biafra[15] was proclaimed with the following words:

> The territory and region known as Eastern Nigeria, together with her continental shelves and territorial waters, shall henceforth be an independent sovereign state, of the name and title, the Republic of Biafra.[16]

On 6 July 1967, federal troops began a campaign – initially termed 'a police action' by Lagos – to discourage the Biafran challenge. The rebellion, which later attracted the support of four African states,[17] eventually took the armed forces thirty months to overcome, leaving in its wake more doubts over Nigeria's oneness.

Post-civil-war Nigeria has seen efforts aimed at strengthening the basis of unity in the federal system. Southerners have asked for the power-base to be shifted from the north to the south as a condition for continued co-operation. Although there have been attempts to co-opt rival parties by forming coalition governments, as was witnessed in the first and second republics, since Nigeria's independence the north has dominated central control. In the 1993 presidential election, it looked as if it was finally going to heed the demand it had so long resisted, with the electoral victory of Chief Moshood Abiola, a Yoruba business tycoon. Unfortunately, the then military junta annulled the election without offering any plausible reason,[18] an action that provoked condemnation from the international community. In Nigeria, civil unrest paralysed all aspects of life in the western region, including in Lagos.[19] For months, the country teetered on the brink of another civil war, and citizens of different groups residing outside their own regions fled to the safety of their various ethnic enclaves.

While the impasse lasted, the Ogoni minority movement in the southeast (which could be seen as a resurgence of the previous Isaac Boro-led movement), was gathering momentum. The Ogoni, a community of about 500,000 inhabitants living in an area rich in oil, had been protesting against what they perceived as an unfair share of the oil wealth originating in their area. Under the umbrella of the Movement for the Survival of the Ogoni People (MOSOP), they boycotted the 1993 presidential election, insisting on being paid generous compensation by the federal government and Shell BP, the major oil company in the area. In response to the Ogoni initiatives of producing a national flag and anthem, coupled with periodic violent attacks on oil installations in the area, the Nigerian government under Abacha, the dictator, turned viciously on the Ogonis.[20] As the imprisonment of the winner of the 12 June 1993 presidential election had done before, the eventual execution of MOSOP's leader, Mr Kenule Saro-Wiwa, on 10 November 1995,[21] brought both crises to a stalemate.

So far, an attempt has been made to highlight the evolutionary course of secessionist agitation in Nigeria and the government's responses to the problem. Repressive measures against separatism in Nigeria have not been able to prevent its periodic recurrence. The worrying feeling persists that the federation may eventually break up.[22] With the ghost of Biafran secession still haunting the nation, and the Yoruba ethnic group not bothering to hide their grudges over the 1993 electoral injustices, together with the volcanic[23] nature of separatist movements in the oil-rich Niger Delta, a big question-mark hangs over the basis for national unity. For those communities on whose territories oil revenue is extracted, it seems there can be no happiness under the present federal system unless a fair share of this oil wealth is channelled back to their region. For most Yorubas, and other groups who are opposed to northern domination, the basis for national unity lies in righting the wrong of the annulled 1993 presidential election, won by the late Moshood Abiola, a Yoruba. The election in February 1999 of Olusegun Obasanjo, a Yoruba, as the new Executive President of the federation is scarcely considered by Yoruba intellectuals as sufficient appeasement for the injustice of 1993. For the former Biafrans, especially the Igbos, until they are properly reintegrated into national affairs – and more importantly, are adequately compensated for the loss of those individually-owned lands confiscated by the Nigerian government during the civil war[24] – the struggle is not yet over. And for southerners as a whole, until the seat of power shifts from the north, the future of a united Nigeria appears uncertain. Listening to the strident calls for a sovereign national conference with the fate of the federal structure at the top of its agenda, one is left with the conclusion that the problem of secession in Nigeria is one of fanaticism – a stubborn refusal to change either the topic of discussion or its content.[25]

The Institutional Setting for Scientific Research on Secession

In Nigeria, studies on separatism may be pursued under different headings that contain no direct mention of the word 'secession'. The scare of the thirty-month Biafran challenge remains so potent in the national psyche that governments over the years have resisted all attempts to be drawn into subjects dealing directly with secession. Although universities and individuals do pursue private scholarly research on secession, the bulk of this is actually centred instead on issues to do with nation-building. Social scientists in Nigeria are often engaged in discourses related to secession as members of pressure groups, cultural associations, social movements, pro-democracy organizations, political parties and labour unions such as the Academic Staff Union of Universities (ASUU).[26] For instance, a cultural association might organize a workshop to deliberate on 'the problems of federalism in Nigeria' or 'power domination by the majority'. Political science associations in universities, cultural movements, pro-democracy organizations (such as Action for Democracy (AD), the Civil Liberties Organisation (CLO) and the National Coalition for Democracy (NADECO), which Adonis Hoffman rightly identified as Nigeria's principal opposition group)[27] have in the past constituted forums where scholars have expressed their views on the national question. Issues to do with 'the problems of nation-building in Nigeria', 'problems of democracy', 'human rights' and other such subtle topics are usually explored. In such kinds of academic forums, politically engaged intellectuals present their views on some of these common national interests. Privately owned dailies and weekly tabloids generally cover these occasions.

Recently, some cultural institutions have been involved in the national debate on secessionism. One of these is the 'Oduduwa Cultural Association', a pan-Yoruba tribal movement, consisting of Yoruba intellectuals and politicians. In 1998 the group asked for the federation to be restructured in such a way that 'the people of Yorubaland will be governed like civilized and free people'.[28] Among other issues, this association also demanded that the army and police should be regionalized, since, it said, these forces 'under the control of the northern oligarchy, [have] become veritable instruments of oppression of our people'.[29] Another cultural group is the 'Oha-na-eze Ndi-Igbo', a pan-Igbo movement which, like that of the Yoruba, came into being at the height of Abacha's dictatorship government (1994-98). In a similar call, this association requested that the presidency should be reserved for southerners, in the interest of national peace. Recently Ojukwu, the former Biafran leader and an active member of the 'Oha-na-eze Ndi-Igbo', tried to find a justification for Biafra's war of secession in the rationale that, more than three decades after the end of hostilities, clamouring for the division of Nigeria still continues.[30] His statement has led to speculation on whether another Igbo republic could emerge.

The method of dealing with issues linked to national unity usually favoured by Nigerian governments has been to invite scholars from different ethnic backgrounds and of different ideological persuasions to participate in the constitutional talks that often precede the review of an existing constitution. Such talks address issues that threaten national unity. Past examples include the Ad Hoc Constitutional Conference of 1966, instituted to deliberate on the crisis opposing the federal government and the eastern region; and the 1979 and 1987 constitutional talks which, like the others, involved a variety of élite groups.[31] The 1994-95 Constitutional Conference was held in the wake of civil unrest following the annulment of the 1993 presidential election.[32]

Intellectuals in Nigeria

Before proceeding to examine the role of intellectuals in secessionist movements in Nigeria, it would be useful to clarify who may be regarded as an intellectual in that country. This need arises from the peculiar circumstances surrounding the emergence of the intellectual class in Africa – a recent phenomenon that came with the introduction of Western education to the continent by European missionaries in the latter part of the nineteenth century. The distinctive feature of the African intelligentsia is that it is often difficult to differentiate between an individual who has merely received a Western education and one whose mental activities merit the respect reserved for those who assume the position of 'leader of thought' in their society. In an African society where the majority of the masses are illiterate, the common assumption is that all who have achieved a certain level of literacy are intellectuals. This problem is compounded by the fact that the political élite in the new African states formed the bulk of the first generation of individuals to come into contact with Western education. They therefore jostle for the position of 'leader of thought' with those who are professionally devoted to the pursuit of the fruits of knowledge.

As stated by Tam David-West, the moral commitment of an intellectual may be situated in the broadening of existing horizons of knowledge. He is expected to 'interest himself in a critical analysis of the political, social and economic morality of his society, with a view to suggesting better alternatives whenever he finds the status quo not good enough'.[33] Such an expectation of a critical intelligentsia corresponds to the self-image of Nigerian intellectuals. They have generally been influenced by a concern for social justice and for the protection of individual and group interests. Politically engaged intellectuals employ the tools of the social sciences in moving across their divergent positions during and after periods of national crisis.

Yusuf Bangura, who studied intellectuals, economic reforms and social change in Nigeria, arrived at the conclusion that the intellectual class that emerged in the post-independence African states is under pressure to cultivate its roots in order to remain socially relevant.[34] More often than not, the Nigerian intelligentsia, whom Ayandele has characterized as being alienated from the rest of the society and torn between the forces of tradition and modernity,[35] collaborate and compete with other dominant groups for influence, power and resources. For the state, they can be called upon to provide intellectual input when the occasion demands, through their involvement in peace arbitration, diplomacy, public policy, constitutional talks and their provision of legal advice. As emergent leaders of opinion, they constitute a formidable part of civil society capable of exerting strong pressure that the state cannot ignore. On rare occasions, they may fight with arms, alongside the army. In normal situations, they are looked upon as a source of enlightenment, indispensable for modernization.

A Generation Shift

With regard to incidents of secessionism, the role of intellectuals is undergoing a dynamic process of reconstruction. Changes among the intelligentsia also affect normative positions. This is highlighted by the recent emergence of a crop of so-called revisionist scholars who wish to differentiate themselves from the former generation of scholars. In the past, the efforts of Nigerian intellectuals were directed towards either the achievement of secession or its suppression. They were generally engaged in defending the interests of individuals or particular groups. The revisionists, who emerged in the late 1980s and the 1990s, attempt instead to address the national question from a perspective that transcends ethnic, religious and group prejudices. Thus, in relation to forces trying to pull the Nigerian state apart, revisionist scholars have examined social justice, corruption, ethnicity, human rights and minority rights, military dictatorship and legitimacy, autonomy and inter-group relations, and leadership, as well as other issues related to the imbalances observed in Nigeria's federal system. They focus their discussions on how to achieve a more stable Nigerian state, concentrating on developmental ills and seeking ways of modernizing the socio-economic and political systems. This objective is what dictates the inclination to 'system analysis' and normative evaluations of the Nigerian state observed in their writings.

Four or more reasons may account for this change in attitude on the part of Nigerian intellectuals. One is the fact that, as a younger generation of scholars, they are able to take a more distanced approach to the civil war of 1967-70 and other events of the past which have shaped the views of older scholars. Second, it has been realized that common problems afflict all sections of the citizenry, irrespective of group or ethnic identity. Third, it has become obvious to most intellectuals that secession is not the best solution to the problems facing the country at present. The fourth point is that, with a higher level of education, the Nigerian intelligentsia is acquiring other characteristics. It is now easier to differentiate between a scholar and a guest writer.

Self-Determination

With regard to the Biafran civil war (1967-70), the older historiography, as represented by some intellectuals of that era, focused a good deal of attention on either defending or condemning the activities of the army and the political élite who led the struggle. The bulk of this literature appeared in the period between the civil crisis itself and fifteen years after the end of hostilities. Some of these writers were engaged in Biafra's secessionist struggle, through the organization of public enlightenment programmes,[36] the articulation of principles and goals for the Biafran Revolution,[37] logistics, administration, weaponry, intelligence gathering and even participation in battle, as was the case of literary giant Christopher Okigbo, co-manager of the secessionists' Directorate for Propaganda.[38]

Given the unusual roles in which these scholars found themselves, passions for their own personal cause and that of the group they were defending remained higher than the idea of a national interest. Consequently, the older historiography in Nigeria very openly expressed partisanship in its discourse. This fact explains why the common feature of most discussions during this era was that writers either laboriously put forward justifications for the actions of some individuals or groups during the war, or levelled accusations against targeted individuals for their roles in the national crisis. Attempts to recover lost credibility were made by those who had played inglorious roles in the past. Among these were the 'right-wingers', who were opposed to territorial claims such as those involving Biafra or the Ogoni, and to any similar kind of militant agitation. This group tried to give the impression that they believed national unity was paramount and that the peaceful resolution of a crisis was more rewarding than the violent option. Yet in reality, as the revisionist scholar Chinua Achebe observed, these individuals tended to pursue such national ideals only when furthering their personal interests.[39] On the opposing side were the 'leftists', who regarded secession and war as justifiable under certain political circumstances.

Within the two different camps, however, were some scholars who had swapped from one position to the other. Nelson Otta, for instance, was among those at the forefront of the Biafran secessionist movement. During the course of the war, he dramatically turned against secession. He was the former chairman of the Features Committee of the Propaganda Directorate and editor-in-chief of 'The Biafran Times', and his book, *The Trial of Biafran Leaders*, published in 1980, reveals much about the inconsistent character and low level of credibility of scholars like himself. When he changed sides, in 1968, he suddenly saw Biafranism as being devoid of genuine and honest leadership, alleging that Ojukwu's main aim was to carve out a personal empire for himself.[40] Consequently, his later involvement in the crisis was designed to defeat Ojukwu-led secession. As that of an insider in the ill-fated republic, however, his opinion supported that of Nnamdi Azikiwe who, after defecting in 1968, also concluded that the war had been 'precipitated not necessarily for the survival of easterners but for a more sinister purpose'.[41] In 1960 Azikiwe – an Igbo, who had actually composed the Biafran national anthem – had been co-opted under the First Republic's parliamentary system as the first indigenous president, with Sir Tafawa-Belewa, a Hausa-Fulani, as Prime Minister. Azikiwe later distributed pamphlets describing secession and the war as the result of Ojukwu's tyranny and desire to subject the eastern minorities to oppression.[42] Similarly, in his book *Rebirth of a Nation* Kingsley Mbadiwe, a former Biafran ambassador, recounted how his opposition to secession led to his house arrest and other harsh treatment meted out to him by the governor of Biafra.[43] Although Mbadiwe stated his belief that the Igbos had been wronged, he expressed his regret that Nigeria was then being allowed to disintegrate by hardliners among the rank and file of the ruling hierarchies in both Lagos and Enugu, the former capital of eastern Nigeria.[44] Considering their conspicuous roles at the outbreak of the Biafran secession attempt and their dramatic change of views during the course of the crisis, it is hard not to suspect that Mbadiwe, Azikiwe and Otta were informed by their desire for self-rehabilitation in a united Nigeria.

Other Nigerian scholars opposed to secession – Horatio Agedah, among others – turned to journalism and diplomatic duties, in an attempt to counter Biafra's secessionist propaganda. They defended the Nigerian government's prosecution of the war and its terms for peace. In one publication, Agedah argued that, like United States President Abraham Lincoln who had fought against secession in 1861, General Gowon, the war-time Nigerian head of state, was fighting to preserve the national integrity of Nigeria and to save more than five million people in non-Igbo minority groups in the east, who had been forced under Ojukwu's rebel regime.[45]

In defence of Ojukwu the British scholar Frederick Forsyth, a 'leftist' in the context of this chapter, disagreed with those who condemned Biafran secession. He argued that the east had been driven out of the federation by persecution.[46] In his view, the ex-Biafran leader was the last person to want a division of the country. The decision to secede, he said, had to be regarded as the result of a popular choice made by the 335-strong Consultative Assembly – a high-level body of eastern Nigerian leaders who had been elected by their various communities to advise Ojukwu on Biafran secession.[47] N. U. Akpan, an opponent of secession, admits that after 1966 hatred of the Igbos ran so deep that civil war would have been hard to avoid, with or without secession.[48] Akpan, like Forsyth, seems to over-stress the argument that a peaceful solution to the crisis at this time would have been impossible.

When self-determination for endangered people calls for self-defence, or protection against a lethal attack by an aggressor, it can – according to Allen Buchanan, in a study of secession which also covers Biafra – offer compelling grounds for secession, provided that the victims have not provoked this attack.[49] A similar argument has been used in the discussion on the civil war. As demonstrated in the document entitled 'The Principles of the Revolution', Biafran scholars, defending the legal basis for secession, maintained that Biafra was justified on the ground that the federal government (then) failed to check acts of genocide against easterners in the north. At that point, it was said, 'Nigeria had become a jungle with no safety, no justice and no hope for our people. We decided then to find a new place ... that was the origin of our revolution'.[50]

The American scholar Donald Horowitz, who has studied ethnic conflicts in Nigeria, has asked why Igbos were the only group frequently singled out for attack in all the riots in the north.[51] Concerning the violence against Igbos in the period before the civil war, some analysts see the victims themselves as *agents provocateurs* and blame them for the fate that befell them.[52] Foreign scholar Walter Schwarz, in his account of the crisis, mentioned reports that the Igbos had taunted the aggrieved Hausa-Fulani over the death of their former leaders at the hands of Igbo military officers during the January 1966 military putsch that ended the first republic.[53] In addition, several scholars of the older generation, including the prominent Nigerian political scientist Billy Dudley, rationalized periodic violent actions against Igbos in the north as a product of the victims' public misconduct. In his view, 'the Igbos were attacked not because they were Igbo, but because the name "Igbo" had become more or less synonymous with exploitation and humiliation'.[54] Dudley therefore tried to isolate attacks against Igbos in the north from Ojukwu's politics of separatism, maintaining that there were no premeditated plans to commit acts of genocide against Igbos or other easterners. In other words, secession by Biafra lacked a *locus standi,* as the accusations of genocide – on the basis of which Biafra pushed for secession – referred in fact to spontaneous actions provoked by the victims' unchecked public exuberance.

Kenule Saro-Wiwa, a scholar of the older generation who in 1967 had strongly opposed Biafra's secession, later became one of the most prominent members of the Movement for the Survival of Ogoni People (MOSOP), which started out in 1990 as a social movement.[55] In a similar vein to the Biafran scholars, but this time with reference to the Ogoni struggle, he accused the Nigerian government of promoting social injustice, which he said was robbing Ogoni citizens of their rights in the federation. Saro-Wiwa also indicted the government on charges of genocide, citing threats of cultural extinction in the face of environmental degradation. In his book, *Genocide in Nigeria, the Ogoni Tragedy*, Saro-Wiwa demanded autonomy for the Ogoni as a way of checking the actions of an unjust government. In an appeal to the international community to intervene to promote Ogoni self-determination, he stressed that 'if nothing is done to stop the federal government of Nigeria, the Ogoni people will be extinct within the next ten years'.[56] The Ogoni announced to the world their aspiration to greater autonomy (both political and economic) within the existing federal structure. Reconciling these demands with the acquisition of an Ogoni national flag, anthem and other insignias of distinct statehood probably amounts to what Muyiwa Adeleke described as double-speak, in contradiction to the declared goals of the struggle.[57] According to foreign scholar Claude E. Welch Jr, who has conducted a study on the Ogoni struggle, the intellectual style and sophistication witnessed in the attempt to legitimize the movement indicate an interesting approach to the construction of ethnic identity.[58] From civil litigation at home against the federal government and Shell BP, the struggle assumed international status with the indictment of the Nigerian government at the United Nations General Assembly in 1994.[59] In effect, the Ogoni struggle became a cause that enjoyed popular support abroad but was resented at home. With international outcry followed by sanctions against Nigeria, Saro-Wiwa, at the cost of his own life, fulfilled his promise to bring shame on the Nigerian government over their treatment of the Ogoni.[60] Ben Naamen, who has reviewed Saro-Wiwa's account of the Ogoni struggle, sees most of his claims as propaganda, born mainly out of frustration and an undisguised desperation to put across the case of his beleaguered people. Naamen agrees, however, that the Nigerian government's indifference to the Ogoni was clearly unfair.[61]

A historical issue often raised in secessionist debates in Nigeria is whether a group has a right to secede on the basis of unjust annexation. The introduction of the subject of history into Nigeria's secessionist discourses challenges the change of ownership of the country from the British to the federal government. While Biafra's secessionist movement was not strongly rooted in historical rights of rectification, the issue of the historical right to territory did form a part of the struggle of the Ogonis, whose right was challenged by Yusuf Bala Usman. This historian argued that the territory today held by the Ogoni is first and foremost under the trusteeship of the federal government of Nigeria. In a seminar on 'The National Question', Usman, a Marxist scholar, contended that 'the Ogoni had ceased to own their land when they were conquered by the British in the nineteenth century, and the right to this land was transferred to Nigeria on independence.'[62] In a reply, Saro-Wiwa appealed to history, arguing that his people had the first claim to the territory since they were the first settlers there, and there existed no historical evidence of settlement by conquest.[63]

Some revisionist scholars who have considered aspects of the Biafran and Ogoni struggles in Nigeria assert that each of these groups of secessionists was involved in a fight for self-determination and human rights, as enshrined in the United Nations charter. The charter establishing the Organisation of African Unity (OAU), like that of the UN, condemns any interference in the internal affairs of member states.[64] While the clause on non-interference in the internal affairs of member states provided the Nigerian government with a legal ground for resisting separatism without outside intervention, the clauses defending human rights and the principle of self-determination were used by the aggrieved groups as a legal ground for nationalist agitation.

An elder statesman from a minority ethnic group in the western region, Anthony Enahoro, drew the debate further away from the territorial claims of the Igbos, arguing that 'if Nigeria is dissolved, there are no legal bonds to tie together the Igbos and other tribes of eastern Nigeria who would be [just as] entitled to self-determination as the Igbos.'[65] In other words, the Igbo-led eastern secession was unconstitutional because its leaders had no legal right to the entire territory they were aspiring to pull out of the federation.

Enahoro had also criticized the appeal for international solidarity made by those striving for the self-determination of Biafra, with the argument that the application of this principle in Africa would lead to a senseless multiplication of micro-states. Biafra, while aspiring to be a separate nation-state, realized the benefits inherent in making an appeal to 'pan-Africanism', a concept the secessionists tried to use as an instrument to legitimize their objective. In this call, all peoples of the Black race were summoned to join the revolution, which was later christened a Negro Renaissance. Ojukwu had declared at the time that the struggle was 'not just a movement of the Igbos (…) it is a movement of true and patriotic Africans.'[66] Biafra also highlighted the inflammatory potential of ideological differences between Christian and Moslem OAU countries. Biafranism had insinuated that the struggle was against an Arab attempt to overrun the Negro world as well as a fight against European colonialism.[67] Faced with the dangers of wavering opinions at the OAU, Enahoro, in an address to this organization in 1969, replied that if the wishes of Biafra were to be granted there existed a probability that Nigeria, which harboured over 200 different nationalities, would end up with at least 200 countries. And if Biafranization overran the continent, he added, the OAU would be contending with 2,000 member countries.[68]

From their discussions, it may be ascertained that scholars in Nigeria are of the view that the dangers of ethnic consciousness could increase in a situation where the government neglects the importance of social justice and merit in policies relating to national affairs. The stakes are further raised in a situation where the government takes a partial position during an inter-group conflict. Such acts of partiality might be demonstrated in an instance where it fails in its duty to protect the victims of such a conflict, as was the case in Biafra during the riots in the north in 1966-67; or again where the government chooses the option of brutality and repression against a particular group, who might be protesting against a perceived injustice perpetrated by the state, as was the case with the Ogoni under the regime of Abacha (1993-98). Nevertheless, some scholars caution that such a cause could result in an inter-group conflict, and that the desire for secession is better approached with less violence by the aggrieved parties.

Social Justice and Good Governance

One of the recurring issues connected with the problem of political instability in Nigeria is identified as the absence of social justice in the country. Nigerian philosopher David-West, in his definition of 'social justice', concludes that the term denotes egalitarianism, impartiality and non-prejudice, reward and punishment impartially dispensed.[69] Achebe has tried to explain how the denial of merit as a result of tribal, political, religious or sexual discrimination or other forms of partisanship constitutes 'a form of social injustice, which can hurt not only the individuals concerned, but also ultimately the entire society'.[70] In this analysis, Achebe explained that social injustice promotes the cult of mediocrity, defines the pattern of rewards and victimizes individual citizens and groups, as well as the nation itself. When people are victimized there will be no peace, he reasoned. Without peace, he said, 'no meaningful social programme can be undertaken. Without social justice, order is constantly threatened'.[71] Usually, it is expected that all citizens in a country will be treated as equals before the law and given unhindered access to available opportunities, and that the government will try to distribute social amenities fairly to all parts of the country. Furthermore, the state's security institutions are expected to provide adequate protection for the lives and property of its citizens. Consequently, when the state security apparatus is used to support or aid the oppression of a section of the country, questions are raised as to the legal right of this government to have a claim on the people.

As stated by Achebe, social injustice is a matter not just of morality but also of sheer efficiency and effectiveness.[72] With regard to the Ogoni situation, there is substantial evidence that the government has neither shown good morality nor responded effectively to the issues raised by the Ogoni protests. Dele Omotunde *et al.,* commenting on the paradox of oil exploration and the treatment of oil-producing areas in Nigeria, expressed incredulity at the extent of the federal government's neglect of these communities.[73] And Sam Olukoya, who investigated the deaths related to environmental pollution in the oil-producing areas, arrived at the conclusion that to the communities living in these areas oil exploration has become a curse instead of a blessing.[74] In the view of these authors, a morally responsible government would have made some effort to make available basic social infrastructures such as, for example, safe drinking water, electricity, access roads, hospitals and schools. The government could also have staved off mass revolts if an effective programme of environmental protection had been pursued.

In this light, one may question what ends the government expected to achieve by taking repressive measures against its citizens when they were asking for their basic entitlements. In his examination of the legal basis for the Ogoni revolt, Maduabuchi Dukor, a Nigerian legal practitioner and revisionist scholar, likened the African state to a devouring monster in a mechanized and brutal order of things. Dukor referred directly to the dictatorship regime of the late Gen. Abacha, under whom all opposition met with an unprecedented level of brutality and reprisals. Within such an order, he said, 'there is a compulsive need to protest in order to salvage the innate goodness, relevance, integrity and sense of justice of man'.[75] Protestation, he added, is necessary 'to bring man back to the centre of the stage and to make him more congruous with his environment and with the purpose of his efforts'.[76]

While making the observation that there is a link between at least some of the emerging arguments, some other scholars, such as Achebe and Odunsi Bennett, a fellow revisionist, have presented an all-embracing perspective on the problem, with a special focus on leadership. From this standpoint, Achebe has argued that there is nothing 'basically wrong with the Nigerian character, its land, climate or water. The trouble with Nigeria is simply and squarely a failure of leadership'.[77] In a painstaking analysis of the leadership problem in Nigeria, he stated that the country has not had the good fortune to be blessed with a visionary leader competent enough to unite, manage, remodel, discipline and restructure the society through an exemplary display of fairness, trust, honesty, sense of purpose, patriotism and accountability. These qualities, he said, are lacking in the array of pretenders who have paraded themselves as leaders since Nigerian independence. Different forms of social ills may obstruct the course of nation-building but, he argues, it takes a competent leadership model to bring about lasting change in society – change that other, lesser mortals could benefit from and that sets a standard for national consolidation.[78]

Economic Discrimination and Mismanagement

Economic discrimination, a problem synonymous with Nigeria's unstable political history, forms part of a broader set of issues connected with social injustice which, as stated above, remains one of the major topics of discussion – and reasons for political involvement – of Nigerian intellectuals. Biafra[79] and the Ogoni[80] crisis arose mainly out of attempts to escape economic injustice. These territories, while contributing the greater part of Nigeria's oil-based economic wealth, appear to have received less in the federal government's redistribution policies than other areas. While the facts indicate clearly enough that the redistribution of national resources to all parts of the country has not been carried out according to a fair system, some students of Nigerian politics have looked at the question from the point of view of the economic implications of corruption in national government.

According to foreign scholars Evelyn Rich and Immanuel Wallerstein in their studies of separatist movements in Africa (including Nigeria), a close link exists between corrupt practices in African states and the tendency towards secession.[81] This view has been buttressed by Ojukwu's assertion that the rationale for Biafra's secession was based on the need to eliminate widespread corruption, which he saw as the source of the general inefficiency and social decay in the country.[82] In the same vein, Saro-Wiwa contends that one of the central tenets of the Ogoni Bill of Rights is the quest for social justice for the Ogonis,[83] thereby using a broader definition of social injustice, which includes acts of corruption.[84]

According to Achebe, knowledgeable observers estimate that as much as 60 per cent of Nigeria's national income is regularly consumed by corruption, especially since the second republic, 1979-83.[85] In a study carried out in the Post and Telegram (P&T) Department of the federal ministry of communications in 1983, it was discovered that the government was losing a sum of approximately $50 million a month in salaries to 'ghost workers'. Translating this into a yearly figure, this means that about $600 million are lost to P&T in this particular racket. To illustrate the lessons of his findings, Achebe stated that the amount siphoned off into private pockets at P&T could build two more international airports, or buy three more refineries, or build a dual carriageway from Lagos to Kaduna, or pay the salaries of 10,000 workers on a minimum wage for forty years.[86] Foreign scholar Jeffrey Herbst, who has also analysed Nigeria's problem from the same perspective, came to the conclusion that 'Nigeria's problems actually stem from the peculiarly corrupt political economy, combined with an unfortunately generous oil reserve'.[87] In his study of the brief period between 1990 and 1991, when the Gulf crisis brought about a sharp rise in the price of oil, he discovered that the $14 billion estimated by the World Bank to have accrued to Nigeria in 1990 alone had been misappropriated by the Babangida (1985-93) administration.[88] While the minor insights offered above remain a mere peep into the consequences of corruption for political stability, this line of analysis offers a convincing explanation for the reasons behind the obvious problem of discrimination in the sharing of the national revenue and in the allocation of social infrastructures. Understanding that unchecked corruption may cause the government to fail to satisfy the fundamental needs of the people, Ogoh Alubo, a revisionist, maintains that the unfolding events linked with the Ogoni struggle provide an opportunity to engage in a struggle against the economic and political imperialism imposed on the masses by the ruling group.[89]

Over the past twenty-five years in Nigeria, the evidence of an unfair distribution of the national revenue has been so glaring that scholars unanimously agree on this fact, their position on national unity notwithstanding. Omotunde, an opponent of secession, agreed after an extensive tour of 'oil areas' in 1985 that oil-producing villages, the geese that lay the golden eggs, are among the most wretched and poverty-stricken in the country – a situation he described as the most 'paradoxical phenomenon of modern Nigeria'.[90] It would appear that both the government and the oil concerns involved are interested only in drilling oil from these areas, and care little about the basic needs of the citizens. When Moffat Ekoriko took up the question, both the government and its oil partners agreed that indeed the communities had not been fairly treated.[91] As Paul Ogboman pointed out, until the government meets its moral obligation, there will be continued conflict.[92] Achebe has warned that, for social discontent to be minimized, there is an urgent need to control widespread corruption. Until then, he believes, individual and group resentment will persist.[93]

Minority Rights and Autonomy

Issues in political science discourse in Nigerian secessionist movements centre on the familiar problems of regional domination, xenophobia, minority rights, autonomy for all groups and military authoritarianism, among others. Careful observation reveals that fear of domination in Nigerian politics has changed in content from the fear of foreign subordination to that of inter-group domination. The scope has also changed, from a suspicion of southern domination of the north to a suspicion of majority domination of the minority.[94] It has equally shifted from Igbo – and later Hausa-Fulani – domination of other ethnic groups[95] to the northern domination of the south, with the military as the tangible instrument of this domination.

Scientists have given these movements different interpretations in the context of political instability and the trend to construct ethnic identities in Nigeria. In his critique of the structures in the Nigerian federal system, Okwudiba Nnoli views the problem from the angle of the human factor in ethnic politics. In his study of political trends from independence in 1960 to the collapse of the second republic in 1983, he illustrates how socio-economic advantages, which are secured for individuals and groups through political power, have brought about the politicization of ethnicity in the country and, in so doing, have fostered separatist tendencies. He blames the political élite for translating inter-class and inter-individual socio-economic competition into competition

among communal unions – within which party politics were found to be causing acrimony.[96]

The available evidence shows that, more often than not, political leaders who
fail to secure expected electoral victories resort to making appeals to ethnic or
ideological sentiments, which in turn arouse separatist feelings. Achebe lends
credit to Nnoli's view with the observation that tribalism in Nigeria's political
history denies it national integration. He cites an instance when a popular Yoruba
politician called the country 'a mere geographical expression', with an appeal to
the Yorubas not to vote for his opponents – who were non-Yorubas – during the
1956 western region premiership election.[97] On this evidence, Achebe concludes
that the tendency to retreat into one's ethnic community in order to check rival
opponents from other parts of the country continues to frustrate national unity.

Some revisionist scholars make a case for human rights and minority rights.
According to Eghosa Osaghae, who has made a case-study of human rights and
ethnic-conflict management in Nigeria, the balancing of individual rights and
group rights is paramount for socio-political harmony.[98] As he noted, although
ethnic conflicts are seen in terms of conflicts among ethnic groups, they rarely
occur in purely ethnic forms. Rather, they involve conflicts on the individual and
intra-group levels – with reinforcement coming through the mobilization of
cleavages based on class, religion, race and regionalism.[99] In Nigeria, the human-
rights approach to conflict management (as analysed by Osaghae) gained prominence when the bill of rights was enshrined in the independent constitution of
1960, and subsequent ones. This bill covered civil and political rights – the right
to life, personal liberty, a fair hearing, freedom of thought and religion, freedom
of expression, peaceful assembly and association, among others – mainly on the
individual level. As a flaw, Osaghae notes that there were no clear constitutional
provisions aimed at protecting the weaker and disadvantaged groups in Nigeria.[100] As he sums up with regard to the Ogoni struggle, [group] 'grievances can
not be resolved by individual rights alone. Specific group rights, by whatever
name they might be called – privileges, special treatment, minority protection,
etc. – are called for'[101] in order to achieve stability in an ethnically divided society like Nigeria.

In agreement with Osaghae's individual/group rights solution for managing
inter-group conflicts, Dukor, in a broad definition of the term, has remarked
that these rights include those of the smaller ethnic groups in the federation and
also of confessional minorities in both the northern and southern parts of the
country. In an analysis of the majority/minority relationship as it affected the
Ogoni struggle, he underlines the importance of fostering national cohesion
through positive, concrete measures that should be implemented to remove the
feeling of marginalization among smaller groups in the country.[102] Making a
case for the institution of a genuinely democratic polity in Nigeria, he stresses

that by sharing political power with minorities – especially in Nigeria, where the aggregate number of minorities will form a majority – a framework for peace can be created through democratic integration and pluralism. He argues that the binary system of majority and minority groups would tend to disappear in such a polity.[103] As Osaghae further elaborates, while civil and political rights are sought to protect an individual's liberties and to preserve their human dignity in their relations with others and the state, groups' rights are sought to enhance human well-being on the basis of equality and justice.

In addition, group rights are necessary to protect and further the collective interests of members of the group.[104] Both kinds of rights, in his opinion, are therefore equally important for sustaining national unity in Nigeria. This view hinges on the fact that when latent individual-based conflicts – defined by Osaghae as 'hidden ethnic conflicts', which generally manifest themselves in the usual competition for public-service appointments, admission to educational institutions, trade, etc., among people from different ethnic groups – are not properly managed, they erupt into major conflicts.[105]

Nobel Laureate – and consistent revisionist – Wole Soyinka, in a scholarly analysis of 'the national question in Africa', has considered the debate on separatism from the perspective of the dictatorial regimes and their attendant crisis of legitimacy.[106] An unwavering opponent of military dictatorships in Africa, Soyinka, in a case-study of Nigeria, comes to the conclusion that 'repression strengthens ethnic identity and encourages separatism'.[107] Citing the Ogoni case, he argues that the tragic genocidal onslaught perpetrated by the vicious military dictatorship of Gen. Abacha provoked resentment (even from unexpected quarters) which 'increasingly [tested] the assumptions of nation-being – whether as an ideal, a national bonding, a provider, a haven of security and order, or as an enterprise of productive co-existence.'[108] As he underlines, a nation should share a perception of a community whose fundamental existence is rooted in ideas shared by all human beings. Under a dictatorship, says Soyinka, there is no nation. All that remains is 'a fiefdom, a planet of slaves, regimented by aliens. This marks the period of retreat into cultural identities' – a process he sees as logical, because then 'the essence of nationhood has gone underground'.[109] In this context, he argues that the longer the dictatorship lasts, the more tenacious the hold of that cultural nationalism becomes, attracting to itself all the allegiances, social relevance and visceral identification that should belong to the larger nation.[110] He concludes that a society can talk in terms of nationhood only when the cause of democracy and legitimacy has been espoused, alongside the eradication of military governments. The introduction of a provision allowing for freedom of thought, association and belief, and prohibiting discrimination in social rights, would then foster legitimacy and national unity.[111]

Exploring the ethnic minority question and pushing the quest for autonomy further, Marxist scholar Eddie Madunagu, in a revisionist's critique of existing explanations, has offered a socialist perspective on the national question. In this critique, attention is called to the irreversible historical transformations that have undermined micro-autonomies, not only in Nigeria, but also globally. On this premise, therefore, Madunagu maintains that any formulation of the minority question that ignores its historical character, or merely cites the past autonomy of an ethnic group or community as sufficient grounds for demanding an autonomous state within the Nigerian federation, is unacceptable.[112] Criticizing the policy of state creation in Nigeria – a policy that aims to enhance the federal system through the creation of autonomous units – he argues that, by making available more political, administrative and bureaucratic posts, the polity is only separating the poor from the rich. In this way, he says, a new section of the national bourgeoisie is constituted and given a new home base. The common people remain powerless. By implication, he argues that Nigeria is premised on the false assumption that the most significant divisions between people are ethnic and religious. In reality, as he perceives it, the key problem lies in socio-economic divisions – which divide social classes into rich and poor, in both majority and minority ethnic groups – which means that the root of the social instability in the country is in fact inequality. In his opinion, therefore, side by side with ethnic differences there should be recognition of the existence of rich-poor, exploiter-exploited, oppressor-oppressed dichotomies – a situation he sees as the main source of individual and group discontent. In his view, those who dominate the economic, social and political life of the country – a tiny minority drawn from all the ethnic groups – hold the key to broadening understanding of the ethnic minority question.[113] Summing up, Madunagu asserts that the problem cannot be tackled properly until the principle is laid down that all Nigerians – and not just all the leaders or ethnic groups – are equally entitled to the opportunities available in their country. This, he reasons, will put an end to the autonomy question and its threat to the unity and stability of Nigeria, which will then enter its true historical state in which 'the free development of the individual is the condition for the free development of the country'.[114]

Conclusion

In the course of this chapter, the trends in discourses on secession and alternatives to it were contextually presented as a spectre of endless debates among students of Nigerian politics. The various institutional settings for these discourses have been identified as seminars and symposiums, as well as forums constituted on the initiative of cultural associations, pro-democracy activists and other kinds of civil-society networks. Aside from the debates taking place within these settings, scholarly publications by intellectuals both inside and outside Nigeria provide the most comprehensive body of study materials.

Nigerian discourse on secession has been undergoing a rapid revision as it passes from an older generation, engaged in issues dividing the different interest groups in the country, into the hands of a more professional generation of intellectuals who are trying to offer an explanation of the national question (and who are also politically engaged, although in a different way). In general, incidents of separatism in Africa illustrate the problems inherent in nation-building in modern African states. Regarding Nigeria, scholars have considered social injustice, economic redistribution and the political economy of corruption, they have examined ethnicity, assessed individual and group rights infringements, questioned military dictatorships and illegitimate governments, focused on regime failures and reviewed the agonies of democracy. They have also investigated class inequalities, historical antecedents and leadership.[115] Judged by its content and the manner in which issues are presented, the debate reveals the anxieties felt by a state in search of a common identity, which continues to elude it. For most scholars of the revisionist order, the problem with Nigeria is a product of internal factors to do with social injustice brought about by the domination of one group or part of the country by another.[116] Whether the actual cause of ethnic nationalism in Africa is the internal factor of sectional domination or the external factor of colonialism, the truth is indeed, as King Solomon said, that 'man has dominated [his fellow] man to his injury'.[117]

Notes

1 J. F. Ade Ajayi, 'National History in the Context of Decolonization. The Nigerian Example', in Erik Lonnroth, Karl Molin and Ragnar Bjork (eds), *Conceptions of National History*, New York, Walter de Gruyter, 1994, pp. 64-78. The northern and southern parts of Nigeria were joined together by the British in 1914 for administrative convenience, as at that time the north was unable to generate enough funds to cover the overhead costs of separate colonial administration.

2 Okwudiba Nnoli, in his book *Ethnic Politics in Nigeria*, Enugu-Nigeria, Fourth Dimension Publishers, 1978, pp. 170-171, comments that political gains (electoral advantages), rather than principle, lay behind majority support for minority demands.

3 The North took advantage of its majority in the Federal House of Representatives to defeat the motion, and asked for the reference to 1956 – in the request for Nigerian independence – to be replaced with the phrase 'as soon as possible'. See Walter Schwarz, *Nigeria*, London, Pall Mall, 1968, p. 106.

4 Ken Saro-Wiwa, in an interview entitled 'Secession – will the Ogonis go?', *The News*, Lagos, 17 May 1993, p. 24, described the rebellion led by Isaac Boro as irrational and without a clear objective.

5   Schwarz, *op. cit.*, p. 229; Frederick Forsyth, *Emeka*, Ibadan-Nigeria, Spectrum Books Ltd, 1982, pp. 90-91.

6   G. I. C. Eluwa, M. O. Ukagwu, J. U. N. Nwachukwu, and A. C. N. Nwaubani, *A History of Nigeria*, Onitsha, Nigeria, Africana-Fep Publishers, 1988, p. 261.

7   Claude S. Phillips, 'Nigeria and Biafra', in Frederick L. Shiels (ed.), *Ethnic Separatism and World Politics*, Lanham, Md., University Press of America, 1984, p. 166. This writer remarks that with the Igbo predominance in the coup and the biased nature of the killings, ethnic factors immediately came to the fore.

8   Northerners' fears were understandable. The country had just emerged from colonial rule, and having another form of colonialism would not have been acceptable to them. See Schwarz, *op. cit.*, pp. 205-206.

9   The targets of the second round of killings were not only the Igbos, but also other groups from the east, including the Ijaw, Efik, Ibibio, Ogoja and so on. In the beginning, this fact was to help rally easterners to the secessionist movement that led to the birth of Biafra. See Schwarz, *op. cit.*, p. 218.

10 Eluwa *et al.*, *op. cit.*, pp. 263-267, indicate that when the non-easterners were asked to leave the eastern region, there was increasing hostility in the region in response to the northern massacres. See also Schwarz, *op. cit.*, pp. 191-231.

11 *Ibid.*, p. 210.

12 Forsyth, *op. cit.*, pp. 85-93.

13 Elechi Amadi and Opubo E. Dominabo, 'The Nigerian Civil War', in E. J. Alagoa and Tellena N. Tamuno (eds), *Law and People of Nigeria*, Port Harcourt, Riverside Communication, 1989, p. 154. See also Eluwa *et al.*, *op. cit.*, pp. 266-267.

14 Schwarz, *op. cit.*, p. 230.

15 Often, the question is asked why the secessionists adopted the name Biafra. What may be said for sure is that the name came from the 'Bights of Benin and Biafra', a geographical location around the offshore waters southeast of the Nigerian border with the Republic of Cameroon. This strategic outlet from the east held great importance for Biafra's communication with the outside world. When the channel was closed following a deal between Nigeria and Cameroon, the collapse of the seceding territory became only a matter of time, as arms and relief materials were refused entry into the Republic of Biafra by water. There is also speculation that there once existed a kingdom called Biafra, in the seventeenth century, around present-day Cameroon.

16 Schwarz, *op. cit.*, pp. 229-230.

17 The African countries that recognized Biafra as an independent sovereign state were Tanzania, Ivory Coast, Gabon and Zambia.

18 Peter Lewis, 'Endgame in Nigeria? The Politics of a Failed Democratic Transition', *African Affairs*, Vol. 93, 1994, pp. 323-346. See also Gilbert Khadiagala, 'The Military in Africa's Transitions: Regional Dimensions', *Africa Today*, Vol. 42, 1995, pp. 61-74; and Claude E. Welch Jr, 'Civil Military Agonies in Nigeria, Pains of an Unaccomplished Transition', *Armed Forces and Society*, summer 1995, pp. 593-614.

19 See Mahmud Sakah, 'The Failed Transition to Civil Rule in Nigeria: Its Implication for Democracy and Human Rights', *Africa Today*, Vol. 40, 4th Quarterly, 1993, p. 88.

20 Ima Niboro, 'Abacha's Revenge', *Tell*, No. 46, 13 Nov. 1995, pp. 10-16.

21 Steve Crayford, 'The Ogoni Uprising: Oil, Human Rights, and a Democratic Alternative in Nigeria', *Africa Today*, Vol. 43, No. 2, 1996, pp. 183-189.

22 Wole Soyinka, 'The National Question in Africa: Internal Imperatives', *Development and Change*, Vol. 27, 1996, pp. 279-300.

[23] I have used the word 'volcanic' to qualify the incidents of violence in the Niger Delta because of the off-and-on cases of riots and protests, by youths and different interest groups, against both the Nigerian government and the oil companies in the various oil-producing communities in the delta region.

[24] The federal government confiscated all Igbo-owned landed property located outside Igbo territory, as a kind of punishment for supporting secession. Millions of Igbos living in different regions were forced to return home following the ethnic killings in the north and west, which also affected other easterners.

[25] In a metaphorical speech by the Nigerian delegation to the United Nations General Assembly in 1960, in a reference to Africa's anti-colonial protests, it was said, 'once nationalism is born, you cannot defeat it'. Ironically, this statement is now crucially relevant to ethnic conflicts and secessionist attempts in Nigeria itself. See *General Assembly Official Records*, 10 October 1961, Eighteenth Session, 1031st Plenary Meeting, A/PV, 1031.

[26] The ASUU was established primarily as a labour movement for the protection of the interests of Nigerian academics from various universities. On many occasions, the ASUU has come in direct collision with military dictators in Nigeria, prompting frequent clampdowns by government.

[27] Adonis Hoffman, 'Nigeria: The Policy Conundrum', *Foreign Policy*, 1995, p. 148.

[28] Victor Ogene and Suleiman Anyalewechi, 'Nigeria: The Oduduwa Invocation', *The Source*, Vol. 3, No. 20, 24 August 1998, p. 9.

[29] *Ibid.*, p. 9.

[30] Okey Nwachukwu, 'Sunset Biafra. Can Another Igbo Republic Stand?', *The Source*, Vol. 3, No. 20, 24 August 1998, p. 15.

[31] Reno Williams, 'Old Brigades, Money Bags, New Breeds, and the Ironies of Reform in Nigeria', *Canadian Journal of African Studies*, Vol. 27, 1993, pp. 78-79.

[32] In many such moves, social scientists, working with the army and politicians, produced Nigeria's first independent constitution, subsequent ones such as those of 1979 and 1987, and the 1995 constitution on which the fourth republic was to be founded.

[33] Tam David-West, 'The Intellectuals', in *ibid.*, *Philosophical Essays*, Ibadan, Nigeria, Ibadan University Press, 1980, p. 98.

[34] Yusuf Bangura, 'Intellectuals, Economic Reforms and Social Change: Constraints and Opportunities in the Formation of a Nigerian Technocracy', *Development and Change*, Vol. 25, 1994, pp. 266-267.

[35] E.A. Ayandele, *The Educated Élite in Nigerian Society*, Ibadan, Nigeria, Ibadan University Press, 1974.

[36] Dennis Osadebe, *Building a Nation*, Lagos, Macmillan Publishers Limited, 1978, pp. 187-201.

[37] Emeka Ojukwu, *The Ahiara Declaration. The Principles of the Biafran Revolution*, Markpress, Geneva, 1969. In this document, the reasons for the struggle, its philosophy, scope and overall aims were articulated in order to demonstrate that it was justified.

[38] Ali Marui, *The Trial of Christopher Okigbo*, London, Heinemann, 1975. Christopher Okigbo was a university don and an accomplished poet, widely tipped to be the first African Nobel Laureate for literature. During the civil war, he took to the battlefield out of frustration that Biafra was losing. Unfortunately, he did not survive the struggle.

[39] Chinua Achebe, *The Trouble with Nigeria*, Enugu, Nigeria, Fourth Dimension Publishers, 1983, pp. 5-7 and 11-17.

[40] Nelson Otta, *The Trial of Biafra's Leaders*, Enugu, Nigeria, Fourth Dimension Publishers, 1980, p. vii.

41 Nnamdi B. Azikiwe, cited in Anthony H. M. Kirk-Green, *Crisis and Conflict in Nigeria: a Documentary Source Book 1966-1969*, London, Oxford University Press, 1971, p. 421.

42 Nnamdi B. Azikiwe, *Origins of the Nigerian Civil War*, Apapa, Nigeria, The Nigerian National Press, 1969, p. 16.

43 Kingsley O. Mbadiwe, *Rebirth of a Nation*, Enugu, Nigeria, Fourth Dimension Publishing Company, 1991, p. 203.

44 *Ibid.*, p. 203.

45 Horatio Agedah, 'Why the Federal Forces Will Win the War Against the Rebels', in *Towards One Nigeria*, No. 4, Lagos, Federal Ministry of Information, 1968, p. 15.

46 Forsyth, *op. cit.*, p. 91

47 *Ibid.*, pp. 91-92.

48 N. U. Akpan, *The Struggle for Secession*, 1966-1970, London, Frank Cass, 1971, p. xiii.

49 Allen Buchanan, *The Morality of Political Divorce: From Fort Sumter to Lithuania and Quebec*, Boulder, Westview Press, 1991, p. 65.

50 Ojukwu, *op. cit.*, p. 22

51 Donald Horowitz, at a presentation for doctoral students at the Vrije Universiteit Brussel, 28 January 1998. See also his *Ethnic Groups in Conflict*, Berkeley, California University Press, 1985.

52 John De St. Jorre, *The Nigerian Civil War*, London, Hodder and Stoughton, 1972; Rex Niven, *The War of Nigerian Unity 1967-1970*, London, Evans, 1960; and Schwarz, *op. cit.*, p. 215. All three authors point out the provocative character of the Igbos residing in the Northern region in the period before the civil crisis, which must have added extra bitterness to northerners' grievances.

53 Schwarz, *op. cit.*, p. 215.

54 Billy J. Dudley, *Instability and Political Order: Politics and Crisis in Nigeria*, Ibadan, Nigeria, University of Ibadan Press, 1973, p. 132.

55 It is important to note that Kenule Saro-Wiwa was not originally the architect of the Ogoni movement. He only took over the leadership around 1991-92 and gave it a confrontational flavour.

56 Ken Saro-Wiwa, *Genocide in Nigeria: The Ogoni Tragedy*, Port Harcourt, Saros International Publishers, 1992, p. 103.

57 Adeleke, *op. cit.*, pp. 18-19.

58 Claude Welch Jr, 'The Ogoni and Self-Determination: Increasing Violence in Nigeria', *The Journal of Modern African Studies*, Vol. 33, No. 4, 1995, pp. 635-639.

59 Crayford, *op. cit.*, pp.183-189; Welch Jr, 'The Ogoni and Self-determination: Increasing Violence in Nigeria', 1995, pp. 635-649.

60 See Saro-Wiwa's interview with *The News*: 'Secession. Will the Ogonis go?' p. 24.

61 Ben Naamen, 'Genocide in Nigeria: The Ogoni Tragedy by Ken Saro-Wiwa', Review Article in *Journal of Modern African Studies*, Vol. 32, 1994, pp. 538-539.

62 Yusuf Bala Usman, quoted in Muyiwa Adeleke, 'The Shooting Field: Soldiers Shoot Eleven Ogoni Marchers Protesting Ecological Ravage', *The News*, 17 May 1993, p. 21.

63 Saro-Wiwa, *Newswatch, op. cit.*, pp. 16-21.

64 Cervenke Zdernek, *The Unfinished Quest for Unity. Africa and the OAU*, New York, African Publishing Company, 1977, p. 229.

65 Anthony Enahoro, cited by Claude S. Philips, 'Nigeria and Biafra', in Shiels (ed.), *op. cit.*, pp. 147-148.

66 Ojukwu, *op. cit.*, pp. 19-20.

67   These were dangerous ideas which almost damaged the support enjoyed by Nigeria at the OAU. See *ibid.*, pp. 19-20. The federal government's management of the changing content of the crisis was commendable.

68   Anthony Enahoro, as a federal government delegate, in a statement at the OAU conference held in Addis Ababa (Ethiopia) in 1969. See Evelyn Jones Rich and Immanuel Wallerstein, *Africa, Tradition and Change*, New York, Random House, 1972, p. 375.

69   Tam David-West, 'Social Justice: Its Meaning and Implication?' in *ibid, Philosophical Essays*, Ibadan, Nigeria, Ibadan University Press, 1980, pp. 170-176.

70   Achebe, *op. cit.*, pp. 21-22.

71   *Ibid.*, p. 24.

72   *Ibid.*, p. 19.

73   Dele Omotunde *et al.*, 'Paradox of Oil Areas', *Newswatch*, 13 Dec. 1985, p. 13.

74   Sam Olukoya, 'Why they Seethe', *Newswatch*, 3 Dec. 1995, pp. 10-14.

75   Maduabuchi Dukor, 'The Sovereign and the Minority', *Champion*, 16 April 1996, p. 4.

76   *Ibid.*, p. 4.

77   Achebe, *op. cit.*, p. 1.

78   *Ibid.*, pp. 1-63. Benneth Ade Odunsi, who carried out a study on the impact of leadership instability and democratic process in Nigeria in the period from 1960 to 1995, shares Achebe's views. According to the findings of this study, the pervasive political wrangling, civil strife, economic disorder and social malaise endemic in Nigeria today flow in part from ineffective leadership – a common problem among African states. The dilemma, he concluded, is how to find a unifier – a patriotic, enlightened and visionary leader. Benneth Ade Odunsi, 'The Impact of Leadership Instability on Democratic Process in Nigeria', *Journal of Asian and African Studies*, Vol. 31, Nos 1-2, 1996, pp. 66-81.

79   Buchanan noted that, before the civil war, Biafra constituted 22% of the Nigerian population. In terms of national revenue, the region contributed 38% of the total, and received 14% from the government. At this period, oil exporting was still more or less at the prospective stage. Buchanan, *op. cit.*, p. 41.

80   Ekumopere Richard Asanebi, in a letter to *Newswatch*, 18 December 1995, p. 4, stated that by 1992 the Ogoni represented 0.56% of the total population, and contributed approximately 4% of federal government earnings.

81   Evelyn Jones Rich and Immanuel Wallerstein, *op. cit.*, pp. 373-374.

82   Ojukwu, *op. cit.*, pp. 20-22.

83   Saro-Wiwa, *Newswatch*, *op. cit.*, p. 25.

84   Saro-Wiwa, 'They are Killing my People', *The News*, Lagos, 17 May 1993, pp. 23-27.

85   Achebe, *op. cit.*, pp. 40-41.

86   *Ibid.*, p. 39.

87   Jeffrey Herbst, 'Is Nigeria a Viable State?', *The Washington Quarterly*, Vol. 19, No. 2, 1996, pp. 151-172. Quotation p. 156.

88   *Ibid.*, pp. 160-161.

89   Ogoh Alubo, 'The Besieged Country', *Newswatch*, 18 December 1995, Vol. 22, No. 25, p. 6.

90   Omotunde, *op. cit.*, p. 13.

91   Moffat Ekoriko, 'Whose Duty is it?', *Newswatch*, 23 December 1985, pp. 12-14.

92   Paul Ogboman, cited in Moffat Ekoriko, *op. cit.*, p. 14.

93   Achebe, *op. cit.*, pp. 42-43.

94   In 'A Historical Analysis of Voter Behaviour in Nigeria, 1960-97', a paper delivered at the *Political Science Seminar*, A.I.C.E. Owerri-Nigeria, Summer 1998, pp. 1-13, Innocent Uzoechi

reports on his discovery that regional minorities often vote for parties other than the one dominated by their respective regional majorities.

95 Saro-Wiwa, commenting on why he failed to support Biafra, stated that the Igbo-led rebellion did not guarantee independence for eastern minorities. He said that [Ojukwu] 'was trying to steal a country – to take the rest of us'. Ken Saro Wiwa, 'They are Killing my People', *op. cit.* In other words, the minorities were suspicious of Igbo political designs during eastern secession. Consequently, they denounced secession as soon as the eastern region was split into three sub-states.

96 Nnoli, *op. cit.*

97 Achebe, *op. cit.*, p. 5.

98 Eghosa E. Osaghae, 'Human Rights and Ethnic Conflict Management: The Case of Nigeria', *Journal of Peace Research*, Vol. 33, No. 2, 1966, pp. 171-188.

99 Osaghae, *op. cit.*, pp. 172-173.

100 *Ibid.*, pp. 181-182.

101 *Ibid.*, p. 186.

102 Dukor, *op. cit.*, p. 1.

103 *Ibid.*, p. 1.

104 Osaghae, *op. cit.*, p. 174.

105 *Ibid.*, p. 172.

106 Soyinka, *op. cit.*, pp. 279-300.

107 *Ibid.*, p. 279.

108 *Ibid.*, p. 280.

109 *Ibid.*, p. 280.

110 *Ibid.*, pp. 297-298.

111 *Ibid.*, pp. 298-299.

112 Eddie Madunagu, *Problems of Socialism: The Nigerian Challenge*, London, Zed Press, 1982, p. 42.

113 *Ibid.*, p. 48.

114 *Ibid.*, p. 49.

115 Uzoechi, *op. cit.*, p. 1.

116 Achebe, *op. cit.*, 1983, pp. 1-22. Suberu, 'The Travail of Federalism in Nigeria', in Larry Diamond and Marc Plattner (eds), *Nationalism, Ethnic Conflict and Democracy*, Baltimore, The John Hopkins University Press, 1994, pp. 56-70.

117 Ecclesiastes, 8:9.

Michel Huysseune and Bruno Coppieters

Conclusion

The introduction to this volume outlined three fields of enquiry. First, the contributors were interested in the type of institutional setting in which history and the social sciences are practised. It was important to address the question of whether this setting favoured a close – or even an instrumental – relationship between political leaders and scholars during a secessionist process. The second field of enquiry entailed identifying the kinds of scientific disciplines that were involved in the public debates on secession, and the types of normative arguments that seemed to be in strong need of scientific support. The third field represented analysis of the particular criteria for scientific objectivity and truthfulness used in discourses for, against and about secession. How do scholars involved in such debates reflect on these criteria – on both the epistemological and deontological levels? The authors have adapted all these questions in relation to their subject matter. In addition, they adopt a selective approach to them depending on their own interests and scientific specialization. These three fields of enquiry guide our comparisons between the cases analysed in this volume. It should further be noted that some issues – such as the consequences of particular institutional settings for scientific research on methodological choices, or a particular conception of objectivity – need to be analysed from different angles, with the result that these types of questions are addressed more than once in the following overview.

Ten Cases Compared: an Overview

The contributions to this book analyse a wide variety of secessionist crises. Of the cases described, the largest group is located in Eastern Europe (Yugoslavia, Ukraine, Tatarstan, Chechnya and Abkhazia), a focus that corresponds to the close attention paid by scholars since the end of the 1980s to the intra-state conflicts in the post-communist world. The other secessionist movements and processes described are to be found in Western Europe (Northern Italy, Flanders), Africa (Nigeria), Asia (Taiwan) and North America (Quebec). Each of the countries or regions displays a particular political and institutional configuration in which academics are currently debating the future of their nation. The Eastern European forms of interaction between scientific knowledge and politics during secessionist crises, for instance, reveal many differences as regards their development and outcome, even though a common communist past has largely predetermined the post-communist pattern of conflicts. Nevertheless, these cases also have a number of common characteristics – insofar as the political role of scientific knowledge is concerned – which they share with those in Asia, Africa and the Western world.

In the case of Ukraine, for more than a century intellectuals have played a central role in creating a national identity. 'Ukrainian studies' provided a framework for their long-term involvement in developing knowledge of Ukrainian society and history. This national intellectual affirmation took place largely in exile. The affirmation of a Ukrainian identity was countered first by the tsarist government and, after a brief revolutionary interlude, by the Soviet one, which imposed a 'Soviet' vision of Ukrainian history and society in which every Ukraino-centric perspective was gradually replaced by a Russo-centric view of past history. Post-independence scholarship now heralds a return to the tradition of 'Ukrainian studies', but it remains marked by the methodological heritage of Soviet scholarship. An even older tradition – of community-oriented scholarship in the populist tradition, and of other forms of involvement in political affairs by intellectuals – is also present in the Ukrainian case.

The discussion of the Chechen case shows the close connection between the rewriting of national history and political mobilization for sovereignty and independence. The overriding concern with the survival of a people who have undergone the most brutal forms of colonization and deportation explains the propagation of a culture of remembrance and the active retrieval of those aspects of the past that had been consigned to oblivion by tsarist and Soviet governments. Heroic resistance in the past legitimizes armed struggle in the present, while the virtues of eighteenth- and nineteenth-century heroes are projected onto today's Chechen warlords.

Tatar intellectuals have always faced particular problems in their efforts at nation-building. Rarely have political circumstances favoured nationalist mobilization, with the exception of brief periods of democratization in the wake of the dissolution of the tsarist and, later, the Soviet empires. The Tatar question is conditioned, moreover, by the complex geopolitical situation of a dispersed nation. In the present political framework, which was constructed in Soviet times, ethnic Tatars form only half of the population of the Republic of Tatarstan, and the majority of Tatars in the Russian Federation live outside the republic's boundaries. The Tatar regime and many nationally-minded intellectuals address this problematic situation using a gradualist and inclusive strategy – in which federalism and the defence of the interests of all components of the multinational people play a prominent role. Secession is viewed only as a last resort, to be pursued if Moscow opts for a repressive policy towards the Tatars. This strategy is echoed in the Tatar historical narrative, which highlights the past existence of a distinct, oppressed Tatar nationality and the legitimacy of the Tatar Republic as a sovereign state and a distinct subject of international law, but at the same time accepts the need for peaceful coexistence between Tatars and Russians and for the inclusion of Tatarstan in the Russian Federation.

The institutional context and scholarly traditions of the former Soviet Union have left a strong imprint on the competing affirmations of national identity by Georgians and Abkhazians. The persisting conflict between the two national communities is rooted in a situation of unequal power, institutionalized during the Soviet period. According to the Soviet constitutional framework, Georgia was a Union republic, whereas Abkhazia had the lower status of an autonomous republic, and was thus greatly dependent on both the Soviet and the Georgian authorities. The unequal privileges granted to the Georgian and Abkhazian 'titular' nations led to a conflict of legitimacy. Both Georgian and Abkhazian intellectuals sought political legitimation of the leading role of their own ethnic community in the republic which bore their name. Unequal privileges institutionalized a structural conflict at the academic level: during Soviet times, academic circles in Abkhazia defended the right either to upgrade Abkhazia's political status or to join the Russian Federation. In each case, this amounted to claiming the right to secede from Georgia.

The particular federal features of the institutional framework for research in Yugoslavia were largely responsible for the dissolution of the Yugoslav intellectual community. The growing powers of the constituent republics of Yugoslavia stimulated the production of nationalistic scholarship. A significant shift took place for instance with the internationally renowned 'Praxis group'. This group of philosophers and social scientists had at first striven for a socialist reform based on the universalist values of the Yugoslav regime. In the 1980s, during the crisis of the Yugoslav federal arrangement, many members of this group increasingly turned to a defence of national republican interests. At the same time, economic historians in Serbia and Croatia protested against discriminatory forms of economic redistribution, for which they held the Yugoslav federal state responsible.

Historiography in Quebec is tackled in the paradox of the increasing political affirmation of Quebec's distinct identity over the last three decades, which has coincided with a decline in historians' interest in Quebec as a distinct society. While previous generations of historians highlighted Quebec's status as an endangered nation, a victim of discrimination, contemporary scholars highlight its normalcy. This is done from an ostensibly value-free viewpoint, without recourse to nationalist rhetoric. This very discourse on 'normalcy', however, helps reinforce the new nationalism, which uses affirmations of Quebec's modernity in its striving towards sovereignty.

Belgian historiography has traditionally been a core element in the intellectual process of nation-building. This was already the case when the country gained independence in 1830. Since then, however, the images it has produced of Belgium and its constituent nations have changed dramatically. From the late nineteenth century onwards, in the wake of the emergence of new forms of national mobilization in both Flanders and Wallonia, historians have been either devising alternative national identities for the Flemish- and French-language communities, or attempting to enforce the view of an overarching Belgian national identity. The various narratives thus constructed have coexisted without really establishing a dialogue. This situation of mutual estrangement has been consolidated by the recent federalization of the country. Federalism has tempered the nationalist fervours of historical scholarship, but at the same time it has institutionalized the separation between Dutch- and French-speaking scholars.

The debate in Italy between secessionists and their adversaries is focused on the issue of institutional modernity and economic competitiveness. The northern Italian secessionist movement, Lega Nord, deploys the image of a modern, 'European' North contrasting with a backward, 'African' South in order to argue for the independence of the North and the creation of a 'Padanian' state. This discourse derives its credibility from mainstream scholarship in history and the social sciences, which frequently interprets the country as having an imagined geography which, likewise, contrasts northern Italy's modernity with southern Italy's backwardness. Notwithstanding the almost unanimous opposition to secession by the intellectual community, scholarly and secessionist discourses reveal converging interpretations of Italy's problems.

The secessionist discourse of the Taiwanese pro-independence intellectuals has been determined by the highly specific context in which they have had to operate. In the aftermath of the civil war in China, Taiwan became the stronghold of the Chinese nationalists of the Kuomintang (KMT), who regarded themselves as the legitimate rulers of China, while at the same time the People's Republic of China claimed sovereignty over Taiwan. The so-called native Taiwanese (who had been living in Taiwan before 1949) were discriminated against and their political representatives repressed by the KMT. The intellectuals of the Taiwan Independence Movement (TIM) developed their nationalizing discourse clandestinely. The ethnic identity originally proposed by the TIM at first highlighted their opposition to the dominance of the KMT and the Mainlander élites. They underlined those characteristics of the Taiwanese that distanced them from the Chinese. While still emphasizing Taiwan's historical specificity and the legitimacy of its independence, the TIM then abandoned its previous insistence on ethnic differentiation. This favoured an inclusive view of nation-building, based on the concept of a New Taiwanese community. This shift towards a civic identity parallels the process of political democratization and rapprochement between the KMT and the TIM.

The strong attachment of many intellectuals in Nigeria to the idea of national unity is partly a consequence of the trauma of the Biafran war. Nowadays, reflections on this secessionist war go beyond a simple legitimization of the political claims of either the central state or the secessionists (as was generally the case during and immediately after the war). In recent years, Nigerian intellectuals have combined a deep concern with national unity with a sharply critical attitude towards the Nigerian state. They have analysed its deficiencies – corruption, and political and economic discrimination – and formulated reform proposals with an emphasis on social justice and good governance.

The cases discussed in this volume are conspicuous by their diversity, and thus validate the broad definition of secessionist processes and movements proposed in the introduction. Secessionist movements deploy a wide range of activities, stretching from the striving for greater autonomy within a federal framework at one end of the spectrum to an aspiration to full independence at the other, and including a wilful ambivalence between the two poles ('sovereignty' in Quebec, or the oscillations between secession and federalism by the Lega Nord in Italy). Secessionist groups claim to speak on behalf of a nation – and where national identity is weak, they attempt to reinforce it. Secession clearly entails a programme of nation-building. The specific weight of nationalism can vary, however, and nationalism is not necessarily the main motive behind secession: in the cases of Croatia, Serbia, Ukraine and Tatarstan, some members of the communist leadership reinvented themselves as nationalists, without entirely abandoning the specific mind-set that had been typical of the nomenklatura under the previous regime. In cases where political aspirations are directed towards greater autonomy within a federal framework, as in Flanders, such a move is supported by nationalist, social-democratic and christian-democratic tendencies.

Science as a Social Institution and a Political Tool

The cases studied in this book reveal various forms of the politicization of scholarship in history and the social sciences, but at the same time they highlight the variety and complexity of the relation between the scholarly and political realms. The most drastic forms of instrumentalization appear not only in extreme situations, like civil wars, but also in the case of state-imposed visions of the nation in authoritarian regimes. The contributions on Ukraine, Georgia and Abkhazia,

Chechnya and Tatarstan analyse the multiple ties that linked scientific research to the decrees of the Communist Party during the Soviet period. They all show how the writing of history at the various levels of the Soviet federal framework was constrained by an officially imposed 'Soviet' and strongly Russo-centric historical narrative, which severely curtailed research on other nationalities. In the case of Georgian-Abkhazian relations, a Georgio-centric view of the history of Abkhazia overlayed the Russo-centric one, which was common to all history-writing in the Soviet Union.

Politically dependent scholarship in the social sciences had difficulty in claiming to be scientific, when much of it was turned into propaganda or produced only low-calibre scholarship. Soviet scholarship failed to standardize cognition in a way that ensured coherence and congruence with reality.[1] This lowering of scientific standards in the social sciences, through their politicization, had dangerous repercussions for the Soviet Union, as was dramatically illustrated during perestroika. The reforms came too late to reorganize scientific research. The institutional setting for this research collapsed with the dissolution of the communist state structures. The lack of funds for education and research in newly independent republics such as Georgia and Ukraine then led to a brain drain from scientific institutions to more profitable branches of the economy or to the state administration. The consequences of this process were just as decisive in determining the general level of scientific research and scholars' dependence on the political authorities as the previous political restrictions imposed on academic freedom by state authorities had been. The post-Soviet period, despite the greater opportunities for scientific debate and links with the outside world, can therefore be regarded in many respects as being in continuity with Soviet scholarly traditions. This concerns the general level of scientific production, the continuous dependence of scholarly research on political support, and the general mind-set that produces normative statements in a scientific discourse. Despite the national or democratic ideals they may stand for, from many points of view intellectuals in the post-Soviet period must be analysed as Soviet intellectuals.

Notwithstanding the common communist tradition, the Yugoslav case differs markedly from the Soviet Union in its far weaker tradition of instrumentalization of the social sciences, due to a higher degree of intellectual freedom since the second half of the 1960s. Both nationalist-minded intellectuals and the Praxis group of critical intellectuals had (admittedly precarious) opportunities for voicing dissenting viewpoints. The federal structure of scientific research favoured centrifugal tendencies, with the research institutes of each republic developing a nationalist approach. That the authorities did not necessarily appreciate the nationalist stance of intellectuals is borne out by the reception they gave the Memorandum of the Serbian Academy of Sciences, published in 1986. The authorities were in fact initially reluctant to support the demands formulated in the Memorandum, which was only adopted two years later, in 1988, by the Serb communist leader Slobodan Milošević.

The political dependence of scientific research in the former communist countries is analysed in this volume by the contributions on Ukraine, Georgia, Abkhazia, Chechnya, Tatarstan, Serbia and Croatia, which were all parts of a federal arrangement. Here, political intervention took place at both federal and republic levels. In the case of the Western federations analysed in this volume (Belgium and Canada), the regional governments of Flanders and Quebec have far-reaching powers when it comes to financing education and research, and at the same time they find themselves having to legitimize their political status or defending the right to a greater political autonomy. In the case of Flanders, research programmes in historiography and social science are to a large extent supported by the regional political authorities, and this dependence affects the choices made by academics. This confirms the thesis put forward in the introduction to this volume, that societies that are late in acquiring statehood are characterized by institutional arrangements to ensure that social scientists are closely linked to the public authorities.

Although a 'within-system' bias is quite a probable consequence of a more bureaucratic type of scholarship, as suggested in the introduction, it is not always fruitful to interpret the close relations between political practitioners and academics as necessarily leading to a type of scholarship that merely serves and justifies political interests. Parallels between scientific and political discourses may, for instance, reveal a common outlook and shared viewpoints among the scholarly community and the political élites that go beyond an instrumentalist relationship. Historiography in Flanders and Quebec is a special case when it comes to the type of interaction between the scientific and political worlds. Where Flemish historiography is concerned, substantial state support is given to publications on the Flemish Movement.[2] Many of the Movement's activists, however, do not identify with the more recent academic writings on it. As long as the Flemish Movement contested the unitary Belgian state, its history-writing was strongly politicized, with political activists frequently contributing to it. Since the federalization of Belgium, writing on the history of the Flemish Movement has become more scientific, less militant. A similar shift has taken place in Quebec, where the contemporary generation of historians claims to conduct value-free scientific research, as opposed to the 'engaged' contributions of previous generations.

A comparison between the development of historiography and the social sciences in communist regimes in Eastern Europe on the one hand, and in late nations in Western Europe on the other, thus shows that closeness between scholars and the authorities may affect the quality of scientific research negatively, but that this is not always or necessarily the case. A 'within-system' bias is undoubtedly a logical consequence of research selected on the basis of the needs of the public authorities, but such a political bias does not necessarily lead to a lowering of traditional scientific standards. Far more important than any closeness between the two worlds, or a 'within-system' bias, is the degree of academic freedom enjoyed by scholars and the extent to which they are exposed to criticism from their peers.

And indeed, different types of dependence by scholars on public authorities are possible. In the Eastern European cases described in this volume, academic research was made completely dependent on state support. Scientific policies interpreted efficiency exclusively as a form of political legitimation. Owing to the absence of free scientific debate, discussions on methodology were to a large extent replaced by censorship and political criticism. The dependence on the political authorities, and the need to legitimize political decision-making, directly determined methodological choices, such as the dominance of ethnogenesis in archaeology and ancient history. The scientific activities of the Yugoslav Praxis group, which was able to achieve a certain amount of autonomy vis-à-vis the state authorities and had developed a dense co-operative network with left-wing scholars in other parts of the world, may count in this respect as a notable exception in Eastern Europe. The quality of their research confirms the view that a certain degree of academic freedom should be regarded as the first pre-requisite for high-quality scientific production.

In the Western world, the links between policy and research are based on particular traditions. In Flanders and Quebec, universities and research centres – even when they are entirely dependent on public finances – are able to organize education and research according to the traditional principle of academic freedom. Methodological pluralism is not at stake when scholars are involved in policy-oriented studies. Even in those cases where state authorities define the contents of policy-oriented projects, formal procedures protecting the traditional principle of academic freedom are increasingly being applied in the identification of the recipients and in the development of the projects. Low-calibre scholarship is largely useless to the public authorities themselves, either for identifying policy objectives or for legitimizing particular policies. If policy-oriented scholarship claims to be scientific, it will have to withstand additional scholarly critique. A comparison between all the case-studies presented in this volume would tend to confirm that a highly differentiated approach should be adopted regarding the link between the degrees of political and academic freedom prevailing in a country.

In many of the cases discussed, intellectuals have played a key role in nationalist mobilizations. Following Hroch's scheme of the stages of nationalist mobilization, referred to in the introduction to this volume, where the first stage consisted of the emergence of scholarly interest in nationalism, several of the secessionist crises discussed can in fact be seen as a transition from the second stage of patriotic agitation, in which students and the intelligentsia try to convince 'the people' of the importance of their own national identity, to a third stage, in which the movement gains mass support. This has effectively been the case in Taiwan, Tatarstan, Georgia, Abkhazia and Yugoslavia. In Italy, on the contrary, the vast majority of the intellectual community strenuously opposes northern secessionism. Since the Biafran war, intellectuals in Nigeria have likewise been opposed to secessionism. Both in Flanders and in Quebec, the role of intellectuals was important in the past, but has now diminished. In Flanders, the Flemish Movement has become institutionalized, and the younger generation of intellectuals is less prone to be attracted by its programme. In Ukraine, achieving independence preceded the involvement of intellectuals in nation-building.

The cases studied differ not only in the degree of involvement of intellectuals, but also in the effects of this involvement. Several of the contributions analyse how and to what extent intellectuals have had a radicalizing role in processes of secession. They have often been involved in antagonistic and confrontational identity-building, with little regard for accommodation between nations. On the contrary, their discourses have exacerbated divisions, since they have focused on the history of one particular ethnic group and have ignored or vilified other groups within the same nation. Georgian dissident intellectuals of the late Soviet era combined their criticism of Soviet imperialism and Russification policies with an exaltation of things Georgian and a disparaging attitude towards the cultures of the minorities in their country. They competed with the 'orthodox nationalism' of the Georgian Communist Party leadership. This led to a mutual radicalization, and to growing fears and increasing forms of political radicalization among the Abkhazian polity. Also among the Abkhazian community, radical intellectuals came to the forefront of the debate on secession. In Georgia and Abkhazia, they were more concerned with rebuilding their national communities than with creating a culture of tolerance and extending democratic rights. Similar dynamics of ethnic self-celebration have also characterized the contributions of intellectuals in the republics of Yugoslavia, both before and since its dissolution.

The case of Belgium shows in another way how definitions of the nation are framed within broader political and ideological discourses. The right-wing Belgicism that emerged during and after the first world war portrayed Belgian identity as threatened by political parties dividing the Belgian community, by the Flemish Movement, Jews and foreigners, and by neighbouring states. Its ideology was paralleled in the strictly ethnic definition of the Flemish nation given by the most radical right-wing faction of Flemish nationalism in the interwar period, which excluded Walloons, Jews and other 'foreigners' from the Flemish nation. Since then, however, such racial Belgicism has been marginalized, while most tendencies within the Flemish movement, and intellectuals supporting it, have likewise rejected racially exclusive concepts of Flemish identity.

The radicalization of a secessionist movement is not of course a necessary consequence of involvement by intellectuals. Definitions of the nation imply a political vision of its constitution, and hence reflect varying attitudes towards values like democracy and social justice, as well as varying assessments of political realities. New national identities may be based on pluralistic views of the nation. Tatar nationalist intellectuals were extremely active in nationalist mobilization in Tatarstan, but they were generally careful to avoid antagonizing other ethnic groups, especially the Russians. By using the concept of 'parity nationalism', which purports to give Tatars and Russians an equal role in the Tatar polity, they attempted to propose a nation-building model that took its ethnic diversity into account. The presence of intellectuals was conspicuous in the leadership of the Taiwanese independence movement too. They were concerned both with the construction of a national identity and with an extension of democratic freedoms. Their relationship with the Mainlanders in Taiwan evolved from antagonism to accommodation: the creation of the notion of 'New Taiwanese' is the result of an intellectual and political revision of the concept of the nation. It expresses a shift from an exclusive to an inclusive political identity. Similar attempts are to be found in the secessionist movement of Quebec, where the political discourses of some 'sovereigntists' reflect a definite shift from the previous exclusive focus on the French-speaking community in Canada towards a territorial perspective from which all inhabitants of the state of Quebec are viewed as Quebecers, regardless of their ethnic background. In the very different context of post-colonial Nigeria, many intellectuals combine a concern for democracy and social justice with a strong attachment to national unity, and hence a disapproval of any strong affirmation of minority identities that would endanger federal stability. Thus, while pro-federalist commentators expressed a certain amount of sympathy for the Ogoni movement – which was able to count on far more sympathy abroad – and showed some understanding of their grievances, this was overridden by hostility towards a movement they perceived as secessionist, and therefore dangerous.

The political effectiveness of a pluralistic historical approach is, of course, context-determined. The political failure of early Belgian attempts to construct a national identity (as proposed by figures like Henri Pirenne) which portrayed a Belgian nation based on the peaceful coexistence and cohabitation of Flemings and Walloons in one national, cultural space, was a consequence of the limited willingness of the political establishment to translate this vision of the nation into policies that accommodated the grievances of the Flemish. A similar phenomenon can be observed in Georgia and Abkhazia. Attempts by Georgian historians to construct a view of national history in which the Abkhazian nationality was part of the Georgian state 'from time immemorial' have likewise failed to convince Abkhazian political élites. This is due not only to the position defended by Abkhazian historiography – that their own statehood was established separately from that of Georgia – but also to their perception that the Georgian leadership is unable and unwilling to accommodate the claims of non-Georgian nationalities.

An analysis of the relationship between scientific and political discourses reveals common interests, convergences and mutual influences between scholars and practitioners. Only in some cases can this relationship be described in terms of instrumentalization. Scholars do not stand outside the body politic, and their contributions reflect the political concerns of the nation in which they work. The interests of the state on the one hand, and the political impact of secessionist mobilization against the state on the other, influence but by no means necessarily determine discourses in historiography and the social sciences. Several of the cases discussed show how intellectuals have also played an important role in criticizing biased viewpoints and partisan uses of the social sciences. Each of the cases reveals the complexities of the relation between intellectuals, the institutional context in which scholarship is produced and the production of nation-building discourses. Intellectuals may concern themselves with things national, disseminate their knowledge as a mobilizing tool, contribute to the construction of national identities, or even reproduce officially imposed discourses. The political pluralism of the intellectual community and the presence of universalist ideals and standards of scholarship offer powerful counterweights to nationalist intolerance and exclusiveness. The cases of Taiwan, Nigeria and Tatarstan demonstrate that this is so not only in countries with a well-rooted democratic tradition.

The Choice of Scientific Disciplines and Arguments

In the contributions to this book, history takes pride of place. The construction of a shared past remains the most obvious means of demonstrating the specificity of a community. Almost all secessionist movements deploy historical narratives to affirm their own identity. Even in cases where contemporary concerns dominate the debate, as in Italy, secessionists and their adversaries nevertheless tend to introduce the issue of a national past into the debate. Questions like 'What does the nation stand for?' and 'Who belongs to the nation?' tend to be answered in historical terms, in a narrative that gives national identity a meaning rooted in the past.

In some of the cases discussed here, avoiding the politicization of historical issues or controversies may be an explicit choice. In Nigeria, the reluctance of many intellectuals to use historical arguments may be connected with the use of history by ethnic minorities to claim national continuity and territorial rights based on pre-colonial realms, and with the risk of facing divisive interpretations of previous conflicts. Nigeria as a polity is in need of a legitimacy that history cannot offer (yet), because of the artificiality of its colonial borders, and because of its turbulent post-independence period. In the republics of the former Soviet Union, on the contrary, historical arguments have been particularly prominent among all the participants in debates on secession. The scholarly practice of ethnogenesis, the study of the formation of peoples, has connected contemporary national identities with the existence of an age-old homogeneous settlement of ancestors on the same territory. This denial of the considerable changes that an ethnic group would have experienced over time has been closely linked to the legitimation of a territorial conception of an ethno-federation. Proof of the presence of a nation on a particular territory from time immemorial has been used to support political claims to exclusive rights over that territory. Such debates have been actively pursued in Georgia, Abkhazia, Ukraine and Chechnya. The essentialist methodology of ethnogenesis is a great incentive to study a nation's remote past. It confirms Anthony Smith's argument that archaeology is particularly suited to lending scientific legitimacy to nation-building, since it combines scientific accuracy (and the material nature of artefacts) with historical imagination, producing a picture of the ancient past sustained by those artefacts.[3] The political importance of archaeology in the former Soviet Union derives from a primordialist definition of the nation, which is, however, less relevant in most of the other cases studied in this book.

The post-Soviet constructions of new historical narratives also have to be understood in a context in which previously marginalized groups attempt to rediscover their identity, and for that purpose try to restore what they consider to be the historical truth. Thus the Tatars attempt to counter the negative stereotypes of the Tatar Golden Horde and to give their nation back its dignity. Contemporary Tatar historical narratives offer a discourse on both ethnic affirmation (the rediscovery of the Tatar past) and ethnic accommodation (inserting this past into a broader Russian framework). Ukrainian historians during the Soviet era attempted to break away from dominant ideological schemes, and particularly the Russo-centric historical narratives, by directing scholarly interest towards the publication of archival material and memoirs, which would 'let the facts speak for themselves' and would give visibility to Ukrainian specificity.

The dramatic nature of historical narratives emerges most clearly in the case of Chechnya, which shows how the construction of such narratives combines memory and oblivion: the rediscovery of the Chechen past, despite attempts to domesticate and/or annihilate the Chechen identity, is combined with an obliviousness of those aspects of the past that show the collaboration and accommodation between Chechens and the Russian and Soviet authorities. Here the restoration of national pride is translated into a discourse that highlights military resistance. Military history is also central to Serb nationalist myth-making, as in the evocation of the battle of Kosovo Polje in 1389. The debates between Serbian and Croatian scholars in the 1980s show, however, how history has also been concerned with more contemporary issues, such as the economic policies of the Yugoslav federation.

National history as proposed by historians from Quebec offers an undramatic counterpart to the Chechen and Yugoslav examples. The contemporary version of Quebec's history presents a narrative of national self-affirmation, and one that confirms especially a tradition of entrepreneurship, in which the issue of discrimination is of very minor importance compared with the historical narratives of previous generations. The evolution of scholarship in Flanders has followed a similar pattern to that in Quebec, and nowadays highlights economic modernity rather than past oppressions. The Western cases discussed in this volume are characterized by their limited interest in the more remote past. Even the Lega Nord, despite some attempts to give the so-called Padanian identity historical roots in a national myth of Celtic ancestry, highlights contemporary grievances in its nation-building discourse, rather than a historical narrative of national community.

The interest in things past – when useful in the construction of a national identity – does not only give historiography a predominant place among the scientific disciplines involved in discourses for or against secession. The historical approach to other disciplines, such as economics or international law, is also greatly favoured by those who defend secessionist arguments. In Taiwan, history is used in combination with international law in an attempt to prove the invalidity of the claims to the island made by the People's Republic of China. Of the social sciences, economics is the subject most frequently present in secessionist discourses and in related scholarly debates. Economic arguments may come in the form of affirmations of national economic excellence or of economic discrimination against a certain people throughout history. They may further be used to prove a nation's capacity for state-building. Arguments drawn from economics may also be useful to adversaries of secession, in order to prove the lack of viability of a newly independent unit. Arguments drawn from economic history are politically most confrontational in debates on discriminatory redistribution. Such arguments are generally combined with critiques of government policies. This was the case, for instance, in the polemics between Serbian and Croatian economists on the policies implemented by the Yugoslav government, and in the Lega Nord's critique of the post-war Italian state.

Shifts in the way nations are imagined are accompanied by shifts in the selection of scientific disciplines and arguments. The abandonment of a strictly ethnic definition of what it was to be Taiwanese was paralleled by a diminishing interest in scholarly investigations of the historical roots of ethnic groups on the island and in anthropological studies that highlighted the ethnic differences between mainlanders and Taiwanese. Political-science literature on the definition of a nation contributed to the coining of the term 'New Taiwanese' as a new national community to be created on Taiwan. Political science is no less relevant than economics in raising issues such as the inefficiency of an existing state. Political science can, moreover, be instrumental in proposals for alternatives to secession. In Nigeria, discussions on minority rights and autonomy, and more generally on institutional reform, purport to offer peaceful alternatives to secession. The case of Italy shows how the social sciences can be used by a secessionist movement. In its descriptions of an ideal northern Italy, the Lega Nord relies on recent research in the social sciences – especially by sociologists – which has highlighted the economic development of provincial northern Italy, the so-called Third Italy. The tendency of some social scientists to idealize this development, and to interpret it as the result of a civic culture with deep historical roots, has facilitated the political instrumentalization of these descriptions by the Lega Nord.

A wide range of scientific disciplines may play a role in secessionist crises. The contributions to this volume demonstrate that the use of disciplines depends on the political issues and grievances involved on the one hand, and the identity ascribed to the nation on the other. Secessionist crises may see the collaboration of scholars from different disciplines around a nation-building project. The 1986 Memorandum of the Serbian Academy, for instance, which triggered off the emergence of Serb nationalism, was drafted by writers, economists, philosophers, historians and linguists.[4]

The predominant position of history in this volume confirms its place as an intellectual discipline at the borderline where public and scientific discourses meet, allowing the participation of non-professionals. The narratives in which national identities are embedded give a particular relevance to its continuity, and hence history retains its central place in discourses that frame such identities. The concern in the social sciences with concrete policy issues should not be contrasted too strongly with the sometimes myth-making propensities of historical narratives. By shedding light on the roots of contemporary problems that are to be found in the past, history, whose role in national myth-making is often emphasized, can also help correct some of the myths put forward by the social sciences. Debates in the social sciences– for example on discriminatory redistribution – in fact demonstrate not only that the knowledge produced by these sciences does not go unchallenged, but also that these sciences can themselves be prone to mystification. The contributions here also confirm the difficulty of separating the 'scientific' from the 'myth-making' aspects of each discipline. The social knowledge produced by history and the social sciences gives rise to narrative interpretations of society. Such interpretations can be assessed for their objectivity, but can never be simply equated with an 'objective truth', with 'facts that speak for themselves'.

Objectivity and Moral Responsibility

The contributors to this volume have analysed the context-bound production of scientific knowledge and the ideological involvement of their peers in secessionist crises. It is undoubtedly true that such a critical analysis is itself also context-bound and value-laden. The expression of any choice and sympathy for particular views on the nation has to be understood as a contribution, however small, to the making of nations. The historical context in which this book has been produced was described in the introduction as a particular period after the end of the Cold War. In the 1990s, scholars intensively debated the political consequences of particular methodological choices. Studies in nationalism were then largely self-reflexive. The knowledge produced by historians and social scientists was perceived as one of the main forces responsible for the strengthening of nationalist currents in Eastern Europe and other regions of the world. The moral criticism of nationalism and ethnic warfare largely took the form of scientific self-criticism. The ideal of scientific objectivity was most prominent in the debates among historians and social scientists on competing views on the nation.

Such prominence is also to be found in some contributions to this volume, whose authors express their views on scientific methodology and the professional ethics of scholars. The ideal of scientific objectivity is here both an object of social analysis and a professional standard. This does not mean that the concept of scientific objectivity is necessarily made central to the various studies. It is made explicit only in a few of them (such as the contribution on Quebec by Ronald Rudin). But the idea of objectivity is undoubtedly present in all the contributions to the extent that they all address the issues of methodology and/or myth-making.

The contributions to this volume demonstrate the importance of the myth-making aspect in 'nationalizing' discourses. Myths of ancient origins play an important role in the cases of the former Soviet Union and Yugoslavia, where they are sustained by a scholarly vision of historical and territorial continuity of national identity. In the Western cases, however, myths of historical continuity have lost much of their earlier relevance. In Belgium, for example, the various discourses articulating identity (Belgium, Flanders, Wallonia) have gradually relinquished such claims. Intellectuals in Nigeria have explicitly adopted a constructive perspective, abandoning the previous claims of historical continuity and concentrating instead on building national identity as part of the process of creating a socially cohesive national community. The Lega Nord's construction of a Padanian identity, on the other hand, includes a mythical nation-building narrative highlighting the existence and historical continuity of a Padanian nation. Its adversaries summarily reject this narrative but at the same time acknowledge the existence of a 'northern' identity, presumed to be non-national. This acknowledgement reveals the complex status of identities, which at one and the same time are myths and social constructs and are related to social realities.

The myth-making dimension is also present in articulations of national specificity. Ukrainians and Abkhazians have a populist myth emphasizing the limited social distinctions within their communities. Myths of benign paternalism have played an important part in Soviet discourses on the 'benevolent' role of the Russian nation towards other nations, and of the Georgian nation towards the Abkhazian minority.

Far more important for the cohesion of a national community, however, are narratives of victimization. Such myths are or have been present in all the nationalistic discourses analysed in this book. The relevance and strength of these myths vary from one case to another, and are particularly strong in the case of Chechnya, where the narrative of victimization relies on a long history of brutal oppression. In other cases, such as in northern Italy, myths of victimization come across as specious discourses that give a partisan account of history.

Narratives of victimization are frequently based on a perception of the state as representing or privileging the interests of a different community from one's own. Such a perception was a major motive in the secession of Georgia and Chechnya from the Soviet Union, which was perceived as being Russian-dominated. From the Abkhazian perspective, the right to self-determination included the right to secede from the Georgian Union Republic and to constitute its own sovereign statehood. Tatar intellectuals have opposed all attempts to be fully assimilated into the Russian state. Serbs and Croats accused the Yugoslav leadership of giving exclusive privileges to the other constituent nations of the federation. For the Parti Québécois, the Canadian federation represents the interests of the anglophone majority. In the case of Belgium, Flemish nationalists have regarded the Belgian state as being in the clutches of the francophone bourgeoisie, while francophone nationalists, on the other hand, speak of the '*État belgo-flamand*'. Similar claims have been made by the Lega Nord concerning the Southern grip on the Italian state. In Taiwan, demands for democratic reform came from the Taiwan Independence Movement, opposing the monopoly on the state by the Mainlander élites. The repeated crises in the years following Nigerian independence were caused by the fears of some ethnic groups that they would be dominated by others. The power struggle between the major ethnic groups in Nigeria for domination of the newly independent state sparked off frequent political crises and caused the failure of the Igbos' attempt to create an independent Biafra. In all these cases, the exercise of the right to self-determination was seen as being possible either through independence or through more moderate forms of withdrawal from the central authority, such as the creation of a federated state.

In some cases, myths of victimization have faded into the background. In Quebecois and Flemish historiography, they have been gradually replaced by new myths stressing the strength and modernity of the nation. This shift has paralleled a change in strategy. The nationalist discourse in the Quebec of the 1960s and 1970s replaced the strategy of survival with a strategy of *'épanouissement'* – a claim that access to sovereignty would permit the nation to blossom and expand.[5] A similar change of nationalist strategy (but with a demand for increased powers rather than full sovereignty), and corresponding changes in perspective among historians, have taken place in Flanders with the implementation of federal reforms. Even in the case of Chechnya, the nationalist discourse is, similarly, not confined to the myth of victimization, but also highlights positive national qualities. The Chechens affirm their historical agency through a myth of resistance.

Most of the myths analysed do tend to respect facts up to a point, and thus to confirm the limited usefulness of completely fabricated myths that have no basis in historical reality. The construction of a North-South dichotomy in Italy, for example, is based on real differences between the two parts of the country. The construction of Taiwan's civic identity is at the same time both a myth and part of a conscious strategy to give a large section of the Taiwanese population a secessionist political perspective. When such myths exhaust themselves at the political level, or are shown to be of limited use to the scholarly community, they simply fade away. This has been the case in Belgium, where the Great-Netherlandic approach has quietly been abandoned as an interpretative tool.

Overall, national myths not only affirm the presence of a national identity but also highlight the values this identity should incarnate. These may include military virtues in myths of resistance, or may reflect illiberal values such as authoritarianism or exclusiveness. Several contributions to this book draw further attention to the myth of 'modernity' in the Western scientific and political tradition. Historiography and the social sciences frequently incorporate a liberal-democratic model of modernity that features economic strength, entrepreneurial dynamism, democracy and some civic values. Economic modernity looms large in political and scientific discourse in Flanders, Quebec and Northern Italy. Economic modernity also functions as the standard to which many non-Western countries aspire, as is articulated for example in the strong pro-Western and anti-Russian tendency among the Georgian intellectual élites, or in the present interest among Tatar scholars in modernizing currents in Islam's past, such as Jadidism.

The defence of this myth of modernity does not necessarily, however, include the virtue of tolerance. The myth of modernity may feature in a scientific discourse on 'other' societies, with varying consequences. Italy's North-South dichotomy implies a normative preference for the North based on the stereotyped creation of a backward southern 'Other' and on the location of modernity and backwardness in particular geographical regions. Croatian historians contrast their nation's modernity and Europeanness with Serbian 'backwardness' and 'unEuropeanness'.[6] Such visions reflect an aspiration to belong to the select club of superior nations in a deeply unequal international division of economic and political power. The possible negative side-effects are clearest when such myths attempt to exclude an allegedly inferior Other from modernity.

The contributions to this volume present various scholarly approaches to the scientific ideal of objectivity. They also refer to various forms of methodological debates among historians and social scientists. The possibility of open criticism depends on a number of factors, such as political pluralism or the status of scientific research in the overall social framework. This means that the status of myths within scholarly research is highly context-dependent. The case of Ukraine highlights how the Soviet social sciences were centred on an officially produced truth, with little interest in making these truths match the 'empirical reality' of the real world. Their discourse was based on a perception of social reality as being the result of a binary opposition between 'progressive' and 'reactionary' forces. In the post-Soviet context, the production of new myths about national history was facilitated by the continuation of Soviet scholarly practices, despite the rejection of their ideological premises. In Ukraine, for example, a large proportion of history-writing after independence simply substituted Ukraine for Russia as its central focus. This subversion of the Soviet official discourse has produced a '*discours nationalitaire*' which is no less biased than its predecessor.

Notwithstanding a one-party system common to both countries, the Yugoslav political system was more tolerant of open public debate and dissenting opinions than the Soviet one. The nationalist critique of communism which emerged in the later years of the communist regime was, however, certainly not characterized by a deep concern for objectivity. In the debate between Serbian and Croatian economists on discriminatory redistribution, both parties were adept at pointing out each other's methodological errors, but repeated similar mistakes in their own polemical fervour and seemed utterly unwilling to criticize their own premises. The dissolution of the Yugoslav intellectual community into its national components may be judged as an example of intellectual regression, in which the conversion of many former adherents of the universalist philosophy of the Praxis group to exclusive nationalism may count as one of the most significant signs.

Western scholarship has not had to confront officially imposed rules on scientific research, but it remains generally informed by the political context in which it is produced. The case of Italy shows a different relationship between myth-making and scholarly practices from that in Ukraine and Yugoslavia, as described above. Because its political consequences have been judged unacceptable, the myth of a Padanian nation upheld by the Lega Nord is almost unanimously rejected by the intellectual community, even though some constitutive elements of this myth derive from scholarly sources. The overview of historiography in Belgium shows how the mental map used by historians has closely followed political views on the national question, producing Belgicist, Flemish-nationalist and other historical narratives. The presence of a plurality of historical narratives can be regarded as an expression of intellectual pluralism and as indicating an acceptance that the history of a nation can be interpreted from different viewpoints. It may also, however, be seen as reflecting a lack of dialogue between highly compartmentalized scientific research institutions. Flemish and francophone historians are each developing their own vision of Belgian history, with only limited scholarly debate between the two intellectual communities. Such a lack of dialogue, however, never amounts to a situation of splendid isolation. A lack of communication also prevails in another federal country studied in this volume: when writing about their own society, French and English Canadians too largely ignore the scholarship of their co-nationals.

A lack of open academic debate is characteristic of all the secessionist processes studied in this volume, although to very different degrees. Such a lack of dialogue does not necessarily mean that scholars intentionally relinquished their objectivity. Georgian and Abkhazian archaeologists and historians were convinced that their reconstruction of historical material, designed to prove the presence of proto-Georgian or proto-Abkhazian tribes on a particular territory, was factually accurate. They overlooked the extent to which their efforts at reconstruction were inspired by the essentialist premises of the methods of ethnogenesis. Their conception of historical objectivity did not take into account the need for an open academic debate. The case-study on Quebec reveals a quite different view of objectivity, which is, however, also characterized by a lack of critical reflection on its own value system. A large number of Quebec historians are convinced that they are practising a scientific profession. They assume that their value-free approach has emancipated them from the political prejudices typical of the previous generation of politically engaged history-writers. By claiming objectivity, they are in fact eschewing a discussion on the set of values present in their own writings.

Scholarship on nationalism has highlighted the constructed nature of nations, and emphasized the important role played by intellectuals in this process of construction. If nations are 'imagined communities', they are also, however, political realities, or may become so through a process of nationalist mobilization. This raises particular problems in relation to the ideal of scientific objectivity. The key role of intellectuals both in the construction of national identities and in nationalist mobilization, and the possibly dramatic consequences of such mobilization, raises the further question of which 'national' viewpoints may be considered legitimate and confronts intellectuals with their moral responsibility in this process.

A situation of contested identities may favour political pluralism, freedom of research and scientific debate on the idea of a nation. But the existence of an opposition to mainstream concepts of the nation does not in itself guarantee higher scientific standards. Such an opposition may simply reproduce the types of argument it is actually criticizing. More interesting are critical assessments that go beyond unilateral viewpoints and question the premises that lead to reified identities. These assessments tend to confirm the characterization of objectivity as a set of 'character traits' such as the willingness to revise one's judgements when they appear to be ill-founded, the openness to learn from others and the capacity to dialogue in an even-handed and sincere manner with the people one is studying.[7] Seen from this perspective, the ideal of objectivity is value-laden and relates closely to the question of moral responsibility. Scholarship conducted along these lines counters discourses of national exclusiveness and self-congratulatory discourses of national excellence.

The contributions to this book show that this ideal of objectivity is conditioned by several factors. The rules governing the various disciplines certainly offer a framework for an assessment of scholarship. The effective use of scientific criteria and the attainment of this ideal of scientific objectivity is, however, clearly related to a context of political and intellectual pluralism, as is so dramatically revealed in the countries where interpretative frameworks for scientific research are, on the contrary, imposed from above. But even in a context where democratic institutions and long-standing traditions of academic freedom do exist, scientific research on the national question may become the subject of instrumentalization and mystification. Intellectuals' willingness to challenge existing scientific judgements and to revise their own opinions cannot be taken for granted. It can only result from a constant readiness to question both the intellectual premises on which scholarship rests, and the institutional frameworks within which it is exercised.

Notes

1 George Schöpflin, 'The Functions of Myths and a Taxonomy of Myths', in Geoffrey Hosking and George Schöpflin (eds), *Myths and Nationhood*, London, Hurst & Company, 1997, pp. 19-35, especially p. 23.

2 For example, the recent *Nieuwe Encyclopedie van de Vlaamse Beweging* (Tielt, Lannoo, 1998) has been distributed to all schools in Flanders (*De Morgen*, 20 November 1998, p. 4).

3 Anthony D. Smith, *The Ethnic Origins of Nations*, Oxford, Basil Blackwell, 1986, p. 172.

4 Aleksandar Pavkovic, 'From Yugoslavism to Serbism: the Serb National Idea 1986-1996', *Nations and Nationalism*, Vol. 4, No. 4, 1998, pp. 511-528, and especially p. 513.

5 David Cameron, *Nationalism, Self-Determination and the Quebec Question*, Toronto, Macmillan of Canada, 1974, p. 117.

6 Wendy Bracewell, 'National Histories and National Identities Among the Serbs and Croats', in Mary Fulbrook (ed.), *National Histories and European History*, London, UCL Press, 1993, pp. 141-160.

7 Ted Schatzki, 'Objectivity and Rationality', in Wolfgang Natter, Theodore R. Schatzki and John Paul Jones (eds), *Objectivity and Its Other*, New York, The Guilford Press, 1995, pp. 137-60. See the contribution to this volume by Bruno Coppieters.

Notes on Contributors

Bruno Coppieters is Associate Professor at the Vrije Universiteit Brussel. Publications as an author include *Federalism and Conflict in the Caucasus*, Royal Institute of International Affairs, London, 2001 and as a co-editor *Commonwealth and Independence in Post-Soviet Eurasia* (together with Dmitri Trenin and Alexei Zverev), *Conflicting Loyalties and the State in Post-Soviet Russia and Eurasia* (together with Michael Waller and Alexei Malashenko). Both volumes were published by Frank Cass, London, 1998. Further publications as a co-editor: *Georgians and Abkhazians. The Search for a Peace Settlement*, Cologne, Bundesinstitut für Ostwissenschaftliche und Internationale Studien, 1998 (together with Ghia Nodia and Yuri Anchabadze), and *Federal Practice. Exploring Alternatives for Georgia and Abkhazia*, Brussels, VUB Brussels University Press, 2000 (together with David Darchiashvili and Natella Akaba). The last two publications are also available on the internet: http://poli.vub.ac.be/

Moshe Gammer is Senior Lecturer at the Department of Middle Eastern and African History, Tel Aviv University. His fields of interest include the modern and contemporary history of the Northern Caucasus and the Middle East, and history and contemporary politics in Central Asia. He is the author of *Muslim Resistance to the Tsar: Shamil and the Conquest of Chechnia and Daghestan*, London, Frank Cass, 1994, and has written a great many articles on the above-mentioned topics, such as 'Shamil in Soviet Historiography', *Middle Eastern Studies*, Vol. 28, No. 4, 1992. His article 'Collective Memory and Politics: Remarks on Some Competing Historical Narratives in the Caucasus and Russia and their Use of a "National Hero"' was published in the electronic journal *Caucasian Regional Studies*, Vol. 4, No. 1, 1999, http://poli.vub.ac.be/

Michel Huysseune is a senior researcher at the Centre for Political Science at the Vrije Universiteit Brussel. He has published numerous articles on the political, social and cultural aspects of intellectual discourse, including a book on freemasonry, *La franc-maçonnerie. Mythe et réalité*, Berchem, EPO, 1992. His PhD thesis, which he defended in 2001 at the Vrije Universiteit Brussel, analyses the intellectual and academic debates sparked off by the emergence of the Lega Nord in Italy. On this subject he has also published 'Putnam interpreteren vanuit een Italiaanse context', *Tijdschrift voor Sociologie*, Vol. 20, No. 3-4, 1999, and 'Masculinity and Secessionism in Italy: an Assessment', *Nations and Nationalism*, Vol. 6, No. 4, 2000.

Ivan M. Myhul is Full Professor of Political Science at Bishop's University, Lennoxville, Quebec, Canada. His fields of research include public-policy analysis, social knowledge, ideologies, historiography and Soviet and Ukrainian politics. His recent publications include *Politychni ideolohii; porivnialnyi analiz*, Kyiv, Ukrainska Perspektyva, 1997, and 'Ukrainian Nationalising and Minorities Projects, and Foreign Policy', in Katlijn Malfliet and Ria Laenen (eds), *Minority Policy in Central and Eastern Europe: The Link Between Domestic Policy, Foreign Policy and European Integration*, Leuven, Institute for European Policy, 1998.

Raphael Chijioke Njoku completed a Masters programme in European Politics, Cultures and Society at the Vrije Universiteit Brussel and was a lecturer in the Dept of History/Political Science, Alvan Ikoku College of Education, Owerri, Nigeria. He has obtained a PhD in political science at the Vrije Universiteit Brussel with a thesis on the failures of the process of democratization in Nigeria. His latest publications include 'Deconstructing Abacha: Demilitarization and Democratic Consolidation in Nigeria after the Abacha Era', *Government and Opposition: An International Journal*, Vol. 36, No. 1, 2001; 'Chto takoe konsotsionalizm?' in Bruno Koppiters, David Darchiashvili and Natella Akaba (obschaya redakysiya), *Praktika federalizma. Poiski alternativ dlya Gruziii i Abkhazii*, Moscow, Ves Mir, 1999, and 'Consociationalism: Its Relevance for Nigeria', *Nationalism and Ethnic Politics*, Vol. 5, No. 2, 1999.

Ronald Rudin is Professor of History at Concordia University in Montreal, Quebec, Canada. His fields of research are the history of Quebec, the history of Ireland, the social and political implications of historical writing, and commemoration and historical memory. His recent publications include the book, *Making History in Twentieth-Century Quebec*, Toronto, University of Toronto Press, 1997, translated into French as *Faire de l'histoire au Québec*, Sillery, Septentrion, 1998; 'Contested Terrain: Commemorative Celebrations and National Identity in Ireland and Quebec', in Yvan Lamonde et Gérard Bouchard (eds), *La nation dans tous ses états: le Québec en comparaison*, Montréal, Harmattan, 1997, and 'On Difference and National Identity in Quebec Historical Writing', *Canadian Historical Review*, Vol. 80, 1999.

Xiaokun Song is a researcher at the Centre for Political Science, Vrije Universiteit Brussel. She is preparing a PhD on the formation and transformation of national identity in Taiwan. Her recent publications include 'Confederalism. A Review of Recent Literature', in Bruno Coppieters, David Darchiashvili and Natella Akaba (eds), *Federal Practice. Exploring Alternatives for Georgia and Abkhazia*, Brussels, VUB Brussels University Press, 2000, and 'Thinking Federal: the Relevance of Federalism to China', *Regional and Federal Studies*, Vol. 10, No. 3, 2000.

Robert Stallaerts teaches at the Mercator Hogeschool and is a senior researcher at the University of Ghent. His research interests include the interaction of economics and ethics in economic doctrines and the economics of health management. His main publications include articles on the economics and politics of the former Yugoslavia and the books: *Afscheid van Joegoslavië. Achtergronden van de crisis,* Leuven, Garant, 1992, and *A Historical Dictionary of the Republic of Croatia,* Lanham, Md./London, Scarecrow Press, 1995.

Louis Vos is Professor of Modern History at the University of Leuven (Belgium). He is the author of several books and articles on the history of nationalism, student movements and youth associations in twentieth-century Europe. He is co-editor (with Theo Hermans and Lode Wils) of *The Flemish Movement. A Documentary History, 1780-1990,* London, Athlone Press, 1992, and (with Kas Deprez) of *Nationalism in Belgium. Shifting Identities. 1780-1995,* London, Macmillan, 1998. On nationalism in Belgium, he has published 'Shifting Nationalisms: Belgians, Flemings and Walloons', in Mikulas Teich & Roy Porter (eds), *The National Question in Europe in Historical Context,* Cambridge, Cambridge University Press, 1993; 'Nationalism, Democracy and the Belgian State', in Richard Caplan & John Feffer (eds), *Europe's New Nationalism,* New York/Oxford, Oxford University Press, 1996; and 'The Extreme Right in Postwar Belgium: from Nostalgia to Building for the Future', in Stein Ugelvik Larsen (ed.), *Modern Europe after Fascism. 1943-1980s,* Boulder, Social Science Monographs, 1998, 2 vols.

Alexei Zverev is a graduate of the Moscow Foreign Languages Institute and has completed a Masters programme in European Politics, Cultures and Societies at the Vrije Universiteit Brussel. His recent publications include: 'Qualified Sovereignty: The Tatarstan Model for Resolving Conflicting Loyalties', in Michael Waller, Bruno Coppieters, Alexei Malashenko (eds), *Conflicting Loyalties and the State in Post-Soviet Russia and Eurasia,* London, Frank Cass, 1998, and 'The Value of the Tatarstan Experience for Georgia and Abkhazia' in Bruno Coppieters, David Darchiashvili and Natella Akaba (eds), *Federal Practice. Exploring Alterna-*

tives for Georgia and Abkhazia, Brussels, VUB Brussels University Press, 2000. He co-edited (with Bruno Coppieters and Dmitri Trenin) *Commonwealth and Independence in Post-Soviet Eurasia*, London, Frank Cass, 1998.

Index

Index